GOGOL

It is a
sian
were
write
shou
thea
duci
was
Cou
prec
inati
dran
peer
acte

The
in 1
The
terr
plat
enc

NORRIS HOUGHTON, *formerly co-managing director of the Phoenix Theatre in New York and most recently Professor of Drama at Vassar College, is one of the most respected men in the American Theatre today. Among the highlights of his varied career as producer, director, designer and teacher, Mr. Houghton brought to TV in 1958 a stimulating and much praised series of lectures on the contemporary theatre. He is also the author of several books about the theatre, including* Moscow Rehearsals, *and edited* The Seeds of Modern Drama, The Golden Age, *and* The Romantic Influence *in the Laurel Masterpieces of Continental Drama series. The present volume of plays represents Mr. Houghton's idea of a superb repertoire and grew out of a comment which he made while writing the introduction to the Laurel Edition* GREAT RUSSIAN SHORT STORIES.

GREAT RUSSIAN PLAYS

Selected and introduced

by Norris Houghton

THE LAUREL DRAMA SERIES

Published by
DELL PUBLISHING CO., INC.
750 Third Avenue
New York 17, N.Y.

© *Copyright, 1960, by Norris Houghton*

Laurel ® *TM 674623, Dell Publishing Co., Inc.*

All rights reserved

Typography by Robert Scudellari

ACKNOWLEDGMENTS:

The Inspector General, by Nikolay Gogol, translated by
B. G. Guerney, reprinted by permission of the publisher,
The Vanguard Press, from *A Treasury of Russian Literature,*
edited by Bernard Guilbert Guerney. Copyright, 1943,
by Vanguard Press, Inc. *The Inspector General* by Gogol
translated and copyrighted by Bernard Guilbert Guerney, 1943.
All performance rights reserved by the translator,
who may be addressed c/o Vanguard Press.

A Month in the Country, by Ivan Turgenev, adapted by
Emlyn Williams, reprinted by permission of Samuel French, Inc.

The Power of Darkness, by Leo Tolstoy, from *Great Masterpieces
of Russian Drama* translated by George Rapall Noyes
and George Z. Patrick, reprinted by permission of
Harvard University. © Copyright, 1933, by D. Appleton & Co.

The Lower Depths, by Maxim Gorky, translated by Jenny Covan,
reprinted by permission of Coward-McCann, Inc.
Copyright renewed 1950 by Coward-McCann, Inc.

He Who Gets Slapped, by Leonid Andreyev, adapted by
Judith Guthrie, reprinted by permission of Judith Guthrie.
All rights reserved. Applications for production and publication
should be addressed to The International Copyright Bureau Ltd.,
Dewar House, Haymarket, London, S.W.1, England.

First printing—October, 1960
Second printing—February 1964
Third printing—March, 1966
Fourth printing—May, 1967
Fifth printing—October, 1968
Sixth printing—March, 1970

OCT '72

Printed in U.S.A.

WI

Contents

Introduction

If you love and honor the theatre as an "institution," as I
do, you will never forget (should you have been lucky
enough to get there) the impact of your first week of play-
going in Moscow. There your dreams come true: an audience that you sense feels it "belongs" in the playhouse, that
sits on the edge of its collective seat, that laughs uproar-
iously, that weeps unabashedly, that cheers a good performance, that knows the names and histories of all the players,
that for the few hours' passage of the traffic of the stage
gives itself up completely to illusion. The only comparable
experience you will have had in America was at a Rose
Bowl game or a World Series.

And on the stage? Performances long and lovingly re-
hearsed, ensemble acting of a caliber that finds its only
parallel among our performing arts in a concert by one of
our great orchestras: the Boston, say, or the Philadelphia
or the New York Philharmonic. No expense spared to
provide backgrounds lavish or austere as the play demands
—music, lights, costumes, scenery, sound effects—all carefully and imaginatively prepared and integrated.

Ironically, the weakest thing in the theatre is the play
itself, at least if it is a contemporary Soviet drama you are
witnessing. The forty years of the Soviet regime have not
brought forth a single dramatist who deserves to rank along-
side those titans of the theatre: Stanislavsky, Meierhold,
Vakhtangov, Kachalov, Moskvin, Tairov, Okhlopkov and a
half dozen others who bathed the twentieth-century Russian
stage in glory through their genius as stage directors or actors.

To assemble selections of dramatic literature that may

do justice to this unique Slavic genius for theatre I must therefore turn the clock back—back to the time of twice forty years' duration (but really no longer than that) which marked the flowering of the whole Russian drama to date: 1836 to 1916.

In the nineteenth century, England and France, Germany and Spain, not to mention our own country, were theatrically in decline. The world's stages were warmed only by the memories of past fires—the conflagrations lit by the Elizabethans and Congreve and Wycherley, Molière and Racine, Schiller and Goethe, Lope de Vega and Calderón. Then suddenly there were stirrings in two unlikely and hitherto unheard from quarters, Scandinavia and Russia.

Since this is no general anthology and since, interestingly enough, the two emergent phenomena ran parallel and were all but oblivious of each other, there is no need to devote even a paragraph to the aurora borealis that Ibsen and Strindberg brought into being. Rather let us at once turn our gaze toward the stars in the East.

I have set as a beginning date 1836 because that was the year in which Gogol's *The Inspector General* was first performed. In one leap the Russian theatre came of age. The most industrious scholar of Slavic drama can unearth little that is antecedent. One comedy, Griboyedov's *Woe from Wit*, and Pushkin's historical drama *Boris Godunov* are the only earlier works in which the Slavophile can point with pride.

We would not be able to start even in 1836 were it not for the fact that the Tsar himself, Nicholas I, in his infinite wisdom prevented the play from being censored and banned. Certainly lesser bureaucrats would have closed it after the first preview, for seldom has any play laughed—and made its audience laugh—harder at officialdom than *The Inspector General*.

Nikolay Gogol came into this life on April Fools' Day in the year 1809, in the little market town of Sorochints, where every lover of Moussorgsky's *Fair* would feel at home. When he was nineteen (it was the year Tolstoy was born) he left home to seek his fortune in the big city, St. Petersburg. It cannot be said he ever really found it. But he did start to write, and he picked up a small living by teaching at a young ladies' seminary and he did meet there (in St. Petersburg, not the seminary) Alexander Pushkin, Russia's greatest poet.

It was friend Pushkin, we are told, who gave Gogol the idea for *The Inspector General*, when he told Gogol an anecdote about the time he was staying at an inn in Nizhni-Novgorod and was mistaken by the locals for an important official from the capital. But it was Gogol who took the tale and made it into what Vladimir Nabokov claims is "the greatest play ever written in Russian"—a claim echoing Prince Mirsky, the eminent historian of Russian literature, who refers to it in exactly the same words.

As a theatrical practitioner I am loath to support such an assertion without witnessing a performance on the stage, and this (it is the single exception among the works in this volume) I have never been able to do. I am prepared to believe, however, on reading alone that this play ranks among the great pieces of original and imaginative comedy.

If it is a mystery why the Tsar allowed the play to go on, perhaps we can promise that, surprisingly enough, the monarch recognized the piece for what it is, not really social satire, not the bitter attack on corruption in high places which many people have claimed it to be, but rather a fanciful joke at the expense of humanity—only one-half Dickens, the other half Lewis Carroll. (Bobchinski and Dobchinski have always reminded me of Tweedledum and Tweedledee.) If Gogol were writing today, it would not be for a radical journal but for the columns of *The New Yorker* that he would pour forth his fantastic and hilarious caricatures of contemporary society. His was that kind of gaily satiric view. And what fun Whitney Darrow Jr. or George Price would have with those scenes, with the Mayor and the Postmaster, with Hlestacov and Ossip and Lyapkin-Tyapkin the Judge and all the others that make up the rogues' gallery.

For *The Inspector General* bulges with vividly imagined characters, even as it is semi-vacant of plot. To say that the latter is entirely dependent on that perennially funny comic device, mistaken identity, might lead you to suspect it of being another farce like *Charley's Aunt,* which depends on the same device. A comparison only gives point to the general distinction between farce and comedy: situation is everything in *Charley's Aunt,* character nothing; exactly the opposite is true of Gogol's play. The one thing —and the great thing—they have in common is the power to make you laugh.

Gogol died in 1852 at the age of forty-three. This was his only first-rate play, even as *Dead Souls* was his only great novel and *The Overcoat* his only great short story. When you have read all three, however, you will trebly mourn the early demise—after he had passed through a state of intense melancholy—of this most original genius in the history of Russian letters.

It is quite reasonable to say of Russian drama as of Russian fiction, that its prevailing style is realistic, that the unique gift of Russian writers has been their capacity to observe and record with extraordinary understanding, sympathy and accuracy the spectacle of life as it is lived around them at every level of experience. Having made that generalization, it must immediately be set down that the first two plays in this collection are not precisely realistic at all. Most critics are in agreement with one of their number who averred that "Gogol took scant interest in reality as such but relied for the creation of his characters entirely on his unaided imagination."

Now in turning to the second play, Turgenev's *A Month in the Country,* which I include here in the version by Emlyn Williams that was produced by the Phoenix Theatre in New York, I am struck less by the realistic than by the romantic and lyrical tone that suffuses this delicate comedy. I remarked in my Introduction to Dell's volume of *Great Russian Short Stories* that Turgenev had been called "the

Schumann of Russian literature" and that "in his world there is always 'an aroma of syringa in the air.'" I like those allusions, for they epitomize for me the glow and fragrance of this gently nostalgic play.

You must not, however, be altogether seduced by the romantic and lyrical atmosphere. Underneath it is a hard substratum of keenly observed psychological truth. The tangled skein of amorous complications—Rakitin's love for Natalia colliding with her husband's devotion to her; Natalia's infatuation for the young tutor Beliaev colliding with her ward Vera's adolescent love for him; not to mention neighbor Bolshintsov's somewhat less romantic but still ardent pursuit of Vera and the Doctor's of Elizaveta Bogdanovna—all is as understandingly traced and as gently unwound as though it were being done by Chekhov himself, the master psychological realist of the Russian stage, who was not to be born until six years after this play appeared.

Turgenev's mastery of his material perhaps partly derives in this instance from his own experience. At any rate, in the matriarchal figure of Natalia's mother-in-law—who happily stands peripheral to the unfolding drama—can be seen the author's own mother, a despotic tyrant who made his childhood intolerable. (He had been born in 1818, heir to a vast estate on which we are told were five thousand serfs.) And the Rakitin-Natalia relationship Turgenev drew from his own bitter-sweet experience with the famous singer Pauline Garcia (Mme. Viardot), the love of his life, whom he met during the years he lived in Western Europe, whom he followed about even as Rakitin followed Natalia, and who was to be one of the reasons why he spent so few of his mature years in Russia.

Like Gogol, Turgenev's fame as a dramatist rests on only one play, but it is a masterpiece. Again like Gogol, the play's interest lies less in its unfolding story than in its characters. It is at the same time in them that the difference appears. For Gogol's characters are fantastic creations of a vivid imagination; Turgenev's are, on the other hand, drawn from life, recognizable, warm, palpitating human beings with sentiments and weaknesses and yearnings that draw us to them—and cause us sometimes to laugh at them —just because they are so much like our own. Finally, like Gogol, Turgenev's fame is tripartite. It rests as much, or more, on his great novel *Fathers and Sons* and that extraordinary collection of short stories, *A Sportsman's Sketches*, as on *A Month in the Country*.

This versatility represents a phenomenon in literary history, for Russia's greatest dramatists were also her greatest masters of prose fiction. (Only Dostoevsky did not make a mark on the stage comparable to his contribution in the field of the novel.) And the next play in this collection offers further evidence of this phenomenon, since it comes from the pen of the author of two of the world's greatest novels, *War and Peace* and *Anna Karenina*, Leo Tolstoy.

"I am not an orphan on the earth so long as this man lives on it." Thus wrote Maxim Gorky of Tolstoy in his famous *Reminiscences*. In that simple sentence he gave tongue to the universal response to Tolstoy's all-encompassing genius. But not only did his friends feel this kinship. Everyone who has read the big novels and the short stories has come under the spell of his universal mind and heart.

The chance to have this spell work upon us in the theatre comes more rarely, because his plays are fewer in number and are seldom performed in this country. Since the 1920s when our own John Barrymore and the great German actor, Alexander Moissi, both performed in New York *Redemption* (which bears the alternate title of *The Living Corpse*), there have been no major presentations either of it, of *The Light That Shines in Darkness*, *The Fruits of Enlightenment* (Tolstoy's satiric comedy which Bernard Shaw once referred to as "the first of the Heartbreak Houses and the most blighting") or of the play included in this volume, *The Power of Darkness*.

This last play was written in 1887 when its author was in

his sixtieth year, a decade after he completed *Anna Karenina*, and after he had already passed through the moral and religious crisis that was to result in his "conversion" to mystical Tolstoyan Christianity. And this chronology is important to our appreciation of *The Power of Darkness*.

Perhaps the reason this tragedy is seldom performed today (it was a perennial favorite in the art theatres of Europe in the late nineteenth century) is that its prospect of humanity is so harrowing, its characters so degraded, its naturalism so stark that our theatre-going public, which wants the stage to "entertain" it, shies away from a sordid spectacle that is so black. (One is reminded of the only partial success of an equally black contemporary play, *The Visit*, by Frederick Duerrenmatt, which even the box-office allure of the Lunts could not altogether save.)

Of course, Tolstoy's peasant drama is not meant to be unrelieved darkness. The evil that swirls in noisome eddies through this tragedy is swept up into the dazzling light of that final moment which gives the play its reason for being. I urge you, therefore, not to cast the play aside in revulsion against such horrifying scenes as the smothering of the baby, but to persevere to the end.

Gorky recalls that Tolstoy once turned to him and said, "The flesh should be the obedient dog of the spirit, running to do its bidding; but we—how do we live? The flesh rages and riots, and the spirit follows it helpless and miserable."

You might say that *The Power of Darkness* was written out of that reflection, until you come to the last page. Then you discover that Tolstoy has passed beyond to affirm the possibility of moral regeneration, of consequent expiation and final salvation. The spirit that has been following the flesh "helpless and miserable" suddenly leaps up and asserts itself. "They that dwelt in darkness have seen a great light" appears to be Tolstoy's text, although it is not until the final curtain that the light breaks through.

You cannot approach any play of Anton Chekhov with the idea of discovering a "text," for there is none. There is only life with its trivialities, its crises, its laughter, its tears, its heartbreaks, its exultations.

Of all the dramatists represented in this collection, Chekhov is doubtless the most widely known in this country; his plays are more frequently performed, have certainly had a greater influence on our own contemporary playwrights than those of any other Russian. At the same time he has been less properly understood than any artist I can name.

"The dominant note of Chekhov's plays," writes Mirsky in his authoritative *History of Russian Literature* for example, "is one of gloom, depression and hopelessness." And this was the accepted attitude of most critics during the quarter century following his death, an attitude in which his brilliant interpreters at the Moscow Art Theatre acquiesced even during his lifetime, to the intense disapproval of Chekhov himself. I myself disagree with Mirsky. Certainly there are moments dominated by "gloom, depression and hopelessness." Who among us but the most ardent disciples of the late Dr. Coué has not experienced them? But to pass from this to a generalization about the whole body of Chekhov's dramatic work is to shut one's eyes and ears to the buoyancy, the affirmations, the laughter and the hope that shine out of scene after scene.

In *The Sea Gull*, the first of that great quartet of dramas on which Chekhov's fame in this field rests (the others being *Uncle Vanya*, *The Three Sisters* and *The Cherry Orchard*), the young woman who seems to *be* the sea gull, returns from a career on the stage to the scenes of her childhood at the climactic moment of the play and cries to her former sweetheart, a young poet: "Since I have been here, I keep walking about and thinking, thinking and feeling that my soul is getting stronger every day. Now I know, I understand, Kostya, that in our work—in acting or writing —what matters is not fame, not glory, not what I dreamed of, but knowing how to be patient, to bear one's cross and have faith. I have faith and it all doesn't hurt so much, and when I think of my vocation, I am not afraid of life." Is this an outburst of hopelessness?

Listen to another character in another and greater play, Vershinin in *The Three Sisters*: "In two or three hundred years life on earth will be unimaginably beautiful, marvelous. Man needs such a life and though he hasn't it yet, he must have a presentiment of it, expect it, dream of it, prepare for it." Is this counsel of gloom and depression? The same optimism shines out of *The Cherry Orchard,* and if you read the play with an ear to catch it, especially in the speeches of the young people Trofimov and Anya, you will hear it and will be forced to agree with me—and with its author incidentally, who insisted the play was a comedy.

The art of Chekhov is difficult to analyze; it is elusive, haunting, reveals itself shyly. More than any of the plays in this volume *The Cherry Orchard*, like all Chekhov's plays for that matter, must be seen in a sensitive and understanding performance to be appreciated. To describe the plots of any of his plays is pointless, for none tells a story in the usual sense. None has heroes, heroines or villains in the accepted theatrical manner. All are plays about a group of people living somewhere in the country, individuals whose relationships, quiet but intense, often incapable of being outwardly communicated, form the dramatic texture.

This particular play dramatizes the disintegration of the old order in Russia and the emergence of a new—one oriented toward hardheaded materialism. But the conflict between the two orders, or between reality and illusion, or between Lopahin and the Ranevskys (a very strange conflict this last, for the estate manager who becomes the new owner, and destroyer, of the cherry orchard acquires it only over his own protest, so to speak)—this conflict is presented by Chekhov as dispassionately as only a truly objective observer of life can do. His characters weep copiously, but do not be misled by their tears: their creator is sympathetic but *he* is not weeping.

As you read *The Cherry Orchard* you must be aware of one thing early discovered by the great actors of the Moscow Art Theatre for which Chekhov wrote the last three of his four great plays; namely, that his characters mean much more than they say. You see, Chekhov was aware that people so often utter words and mean something quite different. His genius was to catch the current of life that lies beneath the surface, that is revealed only in pauses, in stifled exclamations, in broken sentences, in apparently random remarks. So listen for what the Russians call the subtext. The heart of the play lies there.

Chekhov was a dying man when he wrote *The Cherry Orchard;* the end came for him only a few months after its first performance in January, 1904. A physician, forty-six years of age, he was unable to save himself from the ravages of tuberculosis. If he contributed to the theatre but a half-dozen full-length plays and a handful of one-acters, he nevertheless made a mark on modern drama, principally through his revelation of psychological truth, that is unmatched by any other playwright save Ibsen.

"I have read your play. It is new and unmistakably fine." Thus wrote Chekhov to Maxim Gorky in a letter dated July 9, 1902. But Chekhov continued, "The tone is gloomy, oppressive; the audience unaccustomed to such subjects will walk out of the theatre." The play was *The Lower Depths* and Chekhov was wrong: at its production by the Moscow Art Theatre the audience did not walk out; neither did they walk out in Berlin in 1903–1904 where it had an uninterrupted run of over five hundred performances; nor have they been walking out during the succeeding half-century that the play has remained in the Moscow Art Theatre's repertoire. Having seen it performed there I can testify that it is one of the most moving theatrical experiences of a lifetime.

Much of the ebb and flow of life in *The Lower Depths* is reminiscent of Chekhov's own plays, but with a difference that lies in the life depicted. All of Chekhov's plays are concerned with middle-class gentry and the doctors, schoolteachers, farmers and servants that frequent their households. *The Lower Depths* (more literally translated "At the Bottom") is, as you will discover, concerned with

the sediment of society—thieves, whores, drunkards, pan-
handlers, down-and-out tradesmen.

Our own Eugene O'Neill, having frequented Jimmy the
Priest's saloon in his youth, knew its habitués from close
observation and could in consequence write *The Iceman
Cometh* with the ring of authority. Likewise Gorky, who had
led a seamy youth, without education, tramping homeless over the face of Russia, doing all sorts of odd jobs,
frequenting such hangouts as the one depicted here and
mingling with the dregs of society, could write with power
born of experience. (There is, incidentally, a more than
superficial resemblance, it seems to me, between O'Neill's
study of reality versus illusion and Gorky's masterful treatment of the same theme, even though the two arrive at opposite conclusions as to the efficacy of the "pipe dream.")

It is no wonder then that Gorky acquired more than
sympathy and understanding for the masses: it was an easy
step to become their champion, himself in the process turning Marxist. When he was elected in 1902 (at the unprece-
dented age of thirty-three) to honorary membership in the
Imperial Academy of Science, it is equally no wonder that
the government stepped in and annulled the election of this
"radical."

After the Revolution, however, with the Russian world
turned upside down, Gorky became the new government's
most honored man of letters. He died in 1936, pondering
perhaps on the ironies of a life that had known all the
sweet and bitter tastes of oblivion, world-wide fame, cal-
umny and vindication.

As a dramatist he never produced a better play than the
one I have included in this collection, although before the
Revolution there had been *Children of the Sun* and one or
two more, and during the post-1917 era *Yegor Bulichev,
Dostigaev and Others*—two-thirds of an unfinished trilogy.

The last play in this collection, *He Who Gets Slapped*,
by Leonid Andreyev, stands as an extraordinarily effective
theatre piece rather than as an abiding creation of dramatic

literature. Gorky's reminiscences of Andreyev prepare us for this work. "To Andreyev," wrote the author of *The Lower Depths,* "man appeared poor in spirit, a creature interwoven of irreconcilable contradictions of instinct and intellect, forever deprived of the possibility of attaining inner harmony. All his works are 'vanity of vanities,' decay and self-deception. And, above all, he is the slave of death and all his life long he walks dragging its chain."

It is less as a philosophical drama, however, than as a play of backstage circus life that *He* attracts me. If you will allow your imagination to conjure up sharp images of Zinaida the female lion-tamer, of Consuela the bareback rider, Bezano the other young bareback rider who loved her, Polly and Tilly and Jackson the clowns, the hangers-on and roustabouts, the offstage roar of the crowd, the shadowy tent, the calliope music, and above all the ambiguous brooding figure of "He" himself, you will see how attractive this play is to a creative director like Tyrone Guthrie, who staged the last revival of it in New York in 1946 (and whose wife is responsible for the rather free adaptation I have included herein, because it seems more successfully to capture this flavor than more literal versions).

Andreyev is regularly described as a symbolist, although the long short story that is for me his masterpiece, *The Seven Who Were Hanged,* is as realistic a bit of writing as a Flaubert or a Faulkner could concoct. *He Who Gets Slapped* combines both genres. Stark Young, the distinguished American drama critic, observed this duality and remarked that the play's "poignancy is profound and elusive and sinister; and the gaiety and bustle of its action is an irony on the foolish stir of our living above its hidden depths and beauty, the life of the soul in the midst of the circus."

He Who Gets Slapped was first produced by the Moscow Art Theatre in 1915. The guns of World War I were already thundering. In 1917 came the greater thunder that was the Bolshevist revolution. Andreyev, an ardent anti-Bolshevik, lived two years into the new regime and died in self-appointed semi-exile at his home in Kuokkala, Finland, in 1919.

When the thunder had rumbled away there was silence in the theatre. No great voices have spoken these forty years. But because the Slavic love of drama is indeed so strong, surely the silence is only a pause.

NORRIS HOUGHTON

The Inspector
General

NIKOLAY GOGOL

Translated by B. G. Guerney

CHARACTERS

ANTON ANTONOVICH SKVOZNIK-DMUHANOVSKI, *The Mayor*

He has already grown gray in serving the public and, in his own way, is very, very far from being a foolish man. Even though he is a taker of bribes, he nevertheless carries himself with very great dignity; he is rather serious—even a moralist, to some extent; he speaks neither too loudly nor too softly, neither too much nor too little. His every word is fraught with significance. His features are coarse and harsh, like those of every man who has started in an exacting service at the bottom of the ladder. His transitions from fear to joy, from abasement to arrogance, are quite rapid—those of a man with but roughly developed spiritual tendencies. He is generally togged out in his uniform frock coat, the buttons and buttonholes being prominent features, and in jack-boots, highly polished and spurred. His hair is grizzled and closely cropped.

LUKA LUKICH HLOPOV, *Superintendent of Schools*

AMOS FEDOROVICH LYAPKIN-TYAPKIN, *The Judge*

A man who has read five or six books and is hence somewhat inclined to freethinking. A great hand for making conjectures, and for that reason lends profundity to his every word. The actor portraying him must always preserve a significant mien. He speaks in a bass, with a rather excessive drawl, hoarsely and strangled, like one of those grandfather clocks that go through a great deal of hissing as a preliminary to striking.

ARTEMII PHILIPOVICH ZEMLYANIKA, *Director of Charities*

A very stout, unwieldy, and clumsy man but, for all that, as foxy as they come and a knave. No end obliging and as active as can be.

IVAN KUZMICH SHPEKIN, *The Postmaster*
So simplehearted that he is naïve.

PETER IVANOVICH BOBCHINSKI and PETER IVANOVICH DOBCHINSKI
Both landowners—but of those who prefer to live in town instead of on their estates. Both are rather squat, rather short, both inquisitive and extraordinarily like each other. Both have neat little bay-windows. Both speak in a patter, helping that patter along with gestures and their hands—excessively so. DOBCHINSKI is a trifle taller and more serious than BOBCHINSKI, but BOBCHINSKI is more free-and-easy and lively than DOBCHINSKI.

IVAN ALEXANDROVICH HLESTACOV, *a government clerk from the capital*
A young man (twenty-three), very slender, very thin—somewhat on the silly side and, as the saying goes, there's nobody home. One of those fellows who, in the Civil Service, are called the lamest of lame-brains. He speaks and acts without any consideration of anything. He is utterly incapable of giving undivided attention to any one idea. His speech is jerky, and his words pop out in an utterly unexpected way. The more ingenuousness and simplicity the actor evinces in this role the more successful he will be. HLESTACOV's dress is the last word in style.

OSSIP, *Hlestacov's Servant*
Like all servants who are getting on in years. He is serious of speech; his eyes are somewhat cast down; he is a moralist and fond of sermonizing to himself moral lectures intended for his master. His voice is almost always even; when he speaks with his master it takes on a stern, abrupt, and even a somewhat rude

tone. He is far more intelligent than his master and therefore catches on to things more quickly, but he doesn't like to talk too much and, as a knave, prefers to keep his mouth shut. He is dressed in a long jacket, either gray or blue, and much worn.

CHRISTIAN IVANOVICH HÜBNER, *District Doctor*

FEODOR ANDREIEVICH LULUCOV
IVAN LAZAREVICH RASTACOVSKI } *Retired Officials*
STEPAN IVANOVICH KOROBKIN
Prominent citizens in the town.

STEPAN ILYICH UHOVERTOV, *Inspector of Police*

SVISTUNOV
PUGOVITZIN } *Policemen*
DERZHIMORDA

Typical bullies—while Derzhimorda is the prototype of all uniformed, small-town bullies.

ABDULIN, *A Shopkeeper*

MISHKA, *The Mayor's Servant*

WAITER *at the inn*

A GENDARME

ANNA ANDREIEVNA, *The Mayor's Wife*
A provincial coquette, not entirely elderly yet, her education about evenly divided between romantic novels and album verse, and cares about the pantry and the maid-servants. Very inquisitive, and evinces vanity and conceit whenever there is a chance. Occasionally gets the upper hand of her husband, merely because he cannot find a ready answer. But this dominance is utilized only for trifles and consists of lectures and sneers. She has four complete changes of costume during the play.

MARIA ANTONOVNA, *The Mayor's Daughter*

WIFE OF THE SUPERINTENDENT OF SCHOOLS

KOROBKIN'S WIFE

THEBRONIA PETROVNA POSHLEPKINA, *The Keysmith's Wife*

CORPORAL'S WIDOW

GUESTS (both sexes); SHOPKEEPERS; TOWNSPEOPLE; PETITIONERS.

The parts not commented upon above do not require any special explanations. Their originals are almost always before our eyes.

The cast should pay particular attention to the last tableau. The concluding speech (the GENDARME'S*) must stun everybody, suddenly and simultaneously, like an electric shock. The entire group must shift its poses in an instant. The exclamation of astonishment must escape all the feminine characters simultaneously, as if from but a single pair of lungs. Failure to carry out this business exactly may ruin the whole effect.*

No use blaming the mirror if it's your own mug that's crooked.   FOLK SAYING

act 1

Scene I

A room in the MAYOR'S *house. Early morning.*

At rise: MISHKA *is dusting hurriedly; straightens out chairs and table, looks over room, exits.*

ANNA *enters, casts housewifely look over room, unnecessarily shifts a vase and adjusts a curtain, and, after another look, exits.*

MARIA *runs on girlishly, looks around her, peeps through windows, and hearing someone approaching, scampers off in girlish fright.*

The MAYOR *stomps on; looks over the room absent-mindedly; he seems worried and takes a few steps through the room.*

Enter two POLICEMEN; *they flank the door. They are followed by the* DIRECTOR OF CHARITIES, *the* SUPERINTENDENT OF SCHOOLS, *the* JUDGE, *and the* DISTRICT DOCTOR.

They gather around the table amid a general atmosphere of expectancy.

MAYOR: I've called you together, gentlemen, to let you in on a most unpleasant bit of news. There's an Inspector General on his way here. And not only that, but he has secret instructions, too.

DIRECTOR OF CHARITIES: What! An Inspector General?

JUDGE: An Inspector General?

MAYOR: An Inspector General, straight from the capital, and traveling incognito.

JUDGE: There's a fix for you.

DIRECTOR OF CHARITIES: Well, there hasn't been much trouble lately, so now we'll have plenty and to spare.

SUPERINTENDENT OF SCHOOLS: Good Lord! And with secret instructions, mind you!

MAYOR: It's just as though I felt this coming. I kept dreaming all last night of a couple of rats—and most unusual they were, somehow. Really, I'd never seen anything like them—all black, and of a most unnatural size! They came, sniffed around, and then ran off. Here, I'll read you a letter I've just received from Chmihov [*turning to* DIRECTOR OF CHARITIES]—you know him. Here's what he writes: "Dear friend and benefactor"—[*mumbles in a low voice to himself, his eyes running quickly through the letter*]—"to inform you . . ." Ah, here it is: "hasten to inform you, among other things, of the arrival of a government official with instructions to inspect the whole province and particularly [*raises his right index finger with great significance*]—our district. I have learned this from most reliable sources, even though he pretends to be a private individual. Since I know that you are no more innocent of certain little transgressions than other people, inasmuch as you are a clever fellow and dislike to let slip anything that may come to hand." [*Pause.*] Oh, well, we're all friends here! [*Resumes reading.*] "I advise you to take certain precautions, for he may arrive at any moment—if he has not arrived already and is not stopping somewhere incognito. Yesterday I—" Well, from there on he deals with family matters: "Sister Anne has come to visit us with her husband; her brother has grown very fat but still plays the fiddle"—and so on. There, that's the situation!

JUDGE: Yes, the situation is an extraordinary one—simply extraordinary! There's something back of all this.

SUPERINTENDENT OF SCHOOLS [*to* MAYOR]: But what's all this for? What brought this on? Why should the Inspector General be coming here?

MAYOR: Why, indeed! It must be fate, evidently! [*Sighs.*] Up to now, glory be, they were getting after the other towns; now they've caught up with us.

JUDGE [*to* MAYOR]: I think there's a deeper motive here, and one of a political nature, rather. This visit means that this country is ... yes ... this country is about to declare war and the Department of State, now—you see?—has sent an official to find out if there is any disloyalty anywhere.

MAYOR: You sure have taken in a lot of territory! And yet you're supposed to be intelligent! Disloyalty—in a county seat! Where do you think our town is, on a foreign border? Why, if you were to gallop at top speed for three years in any direction you wouldn't come to any other country!

JUDGE: No, I must tell you you haven't grasped ... you don't ... the Government ... the Government has some thoroughly considered ends in view; it doesn't matter that we're so far in the sticks—the Government still has something in the back of its mind—

MAYOR: Whether it has or not, at least I've warned you, gentlemen. Look sharp; I've taken certain steps as far as those things under my jurisdiction are concerned; I advise you to do likewise in your departments. [*Turning to* DIRECTOR OF CHARITIES.] You especially! Beyond a doubt the official, as he is passing through, will want to see before anything else the charitable institutions under your supervision—therefore, do everything possible to make things look decent; you might put clean gowns on the patients in the hospital—and the patients themselves ought not to look as if they'd just been through a blacksmith's shop—the way they usually do when no visitors are expected.

DIRECTOR OF CHARITIES: Oh, well, that's a small matter. The clean gowns can be managed, if you like.

MAYOR: Right! Also, the patient's case-history ought to be written out on a card at the head of the bed, in Latin—or even in Greek. [*Turning to* DISTRICT DOCTOR.] That's your department, since you're the District Doctor. Write down who the patient is, what day and month—and year—the patient was admitted. It's a pity your patients smoke such strong tobacco that you sneeze your head off the minute you set foot in the hospital. Also, it mightn't be a bad idea if there weren't so many of them—their number will immediately be put down to poor management or the inefficiency of the Doctor.

DIRECTOR OF CHARITIES: Oh, as far as treatment goes, we [*patting* DISTRICT DOCTOR'S *arm*] don't go in for any fancy medicines—the more chances you give nature the better. Our patients are all simple folk: if any one of 'em is going to pop off, pop off he will anyway; and if he's going to get well, he'll get well just so. And besides, it would be rather difficult for our friend here [*patting* DISTRICT DOCTOR'S *back*] to make himself understood—he doesn't know a damned word in our language.

DISTRICT DOCTOR [*mouths out something that sounds like a cross between*]: *Ja* and *Oui.*

MAYOR [*to* JUDGE]: And I'd advise you also to turn your attention to our administrative buildings. Take your anteroom, now, where the litigants usually come—your court attendants have gotten into keeping their geese there, together with the goslings, and they're forever getting underfoot. It's a praiseworthy thing, of course, for any man to go in for poultry-raising and things like that, and really, why shouldn't a man go in for raising poultry, even if he is a court attendant? Only, don't you know, it sort of doesn't look right to do so in such a place. I meant to remark on this to you even before, but somehow it kept slipping my mind all the time.

JUDGE: Why, I'll issue immediate orders to have every fowl removed to my kitchen this very day. You might drop in for dinner, if you like.

MAYOR: Besides that, it really looks bad to have all sorts of ragged wash hanging out to dry in the courtroom itself. And right over the closet where you keep all the papers you've got your hunting crop hung up. I know you're fond of hunting, but just the same, for the time being, it might be better to remove it and then, when the Inspector General will have gone on his way, you can hang it up again, if you like. Then there's your clerk. [*Sighs.*] Of course, he's a walking, or rather staggering, encyclopedia of the law, but he always smells as if he had just crawled out of a distillery—and that's not so good, either. I meant to tell you about this, too, ages ago, but my mind was taken off by something—I can't recall just what. There are certain palliatives if, as he claims, that is his natural odor; you might suggest that he go in for garlic, or scallions, or some similar vegetable diet. The District Doctor might help out in this case with some preparation.

DISTRICT DOCTOR [*mouths out same cross between*]: *Ja* and *Oui.*

JUDGE: No, this is something beyond all help by now. He claims his nurse injured him when he was a child and that he's been giving off a slight reek of whisky ever since.

MAYOR: Well, I merely remarked on it. As for internal arrangements and what the letter calls "slight transgressions," there's really nothing much I can say. Why, it's an odd thing even to talk about. There isn't a man living that hasn't some . . . irregularities on his conscience. Surely, all that must have been so arranged by the Lord God Himself, and it's all in vain that the freethinkers talk against it.

JUDGE: Well, what do you consider transgressions? There are transgressions—and transgressions. I tell the whole world I take bribes—but what do those bribes consist of? Why, greyhound pups! That's an entirely different matter!

MAYOR: Well, whether you take them in the form of pups or of something else, they're all bribes.

JUDGE: Oh, never! On the other hand, if somebody gets a fur-lined coat worth half a thousand, and his wife gets a shawl—

MAYOR: Well, suppose you do take your bribes in greyhound pups—what of it? But to make up for that you don't believe in God, you never set foot in a church, whereas I, at least, am firm in my faith and go to church every Sunday. But you—oh, I'm on to you! If you just start talking about the creation of the world it's enough to make one's hair stand on end.

JUDGE: Why, I arrived at all that by my own self—through my own intelligence.

MAYOR: All I have to say is that there are some cases where too much intelligence is worse than none at all. However, I merely mentioned the county courthouse in passing, whereas, if the truth were told, hardly anyone will ever look in there. It's such an enviable spot—the Lord God Himself watches over it. On the other hand, you [*turning to the* SUPERINTENDENT OF SCHOOLS], as the Superintendent of Schools, ought to be particularly careful as far as the teachers are concerned. They are, of course, men of learning and received their education in different colleges, and so on, but just the same they have some mighty queer ways about them—things that go hand in hand with their learned calling, naturally. One of them—the fellow with the fat face, for instance, I can't recall his name—well, he simply can't get along without making a face every time he gets up on the platform. Like this. [*Mugging.*] And then he starts in fiddling with his necktie and ironing out his beard. Of course, if he pulls a face like that at a pupil it isn't so bad; perhaps that's even just as it should be—I'm no judge of that. But you just judge for yourself: if he should ever pull anything like that on a visitor, things might go very badly. The Inspector General, or somebody else, might consider that the face was meant for his benefit. And the devil alone knows what the upshot might be.

SUPERINTENDENT OF SCHOOLS: But really, what am I to do with him? I've spoken to him several times already. Why, just the other day, when one of our foremost citizens happened to drop in on his class, this teacher pulled a face that was a masterpiece even for him. His heart was in the right place when he did it, but just the same it meant a bawling-out for me: Why were radical ideas being implanted in the mind of our young people, and so on.

MAYOR: I am compelled to make a similar remark to

you about the professor of history. He has a slew of learning in that head of his—anybody can see that; and he has accumulated no end of information—only why does he have to explain things with such earnestness that he forgets himself? I happened to hear one of his lectures; well, while he was speaking about the Assyrians and the Babylonians things weren't so very bad; but when he came to Alexander of Macedonia—well, I simply couldn't begin telling you what came over him! I thought there was a fire, by God! He dashes off the platform and, with all his might and main, smashes a chair against the floor! Well, now, Alexander the Great is a hero and all that—but why smash chairs? The public funds are bound to suffer thereby—

SUPERINTENDENT: Yes, he's a hotheaded fellow! I've already reprimanded him several times for this trait of his. "Well," he says, "do whatever you like, but I'm willing to lay down my life for scholarship!"

MAYOR: Yes. Such, evidently, is the inexplicable decree of the fates, the man of learning is bound to be either a drunkard or to pull faces that are enough to curdle milk.

SUPERINTENDENT: May God save me from having to teach! You're afraid of everything then; everyone interferes, everyone wants to show that he, too, has scholarship.

MAYOR: Things wouldn't be so bad if it weren't for that damned incognito! Suppose he were to drop in? "Ah, so you're all here, my dear Sirs? And who," he'll say, "who is the Judge?"—"Lyapkin-Tyapkin."—"Well, fetch this Lyapkin-Tyapkin here! And who is the Director of Charities?"—"Zemlyanika."—"Well, fetch this Zemlyanika here!"—There, that's what's bad!

POSTMASTER [*entering*]: Will you please explain to me, gentlemen, just what's what? Who's the official on his way here?

MAYOR: Why, haven't you heard?

POSTMASTER: I did hear something from Bobchinski. He dropped in to see me at the Post Office.

MAYOR: Well, what do you think of all this?

POSTMASTER: What do I think? Why, I think it means we're going to be at war with the Turks.

JUDGE: Just what I said! I was thinking the very same thing.

MAYOR: Both of you are shooting at the moon!

POSTMASTER: No, really—we're going to have a war with the Turks. It's those damned Frenchmen, always messing things up.

MAYOR: What's all this talk of a war with the Turks? It's all very simple; it'll be us that will catch it and not the Turks. That's something we already know—I have a letter.

POSTMASTER: Ah, in that case the war with the Turks is all off.

MAYOR [to POSTMASTER]: Well, now, where do you stand?

POSTMASTER: Well, what about me? Where do *you* stand?

MAYOR: Where do I stand, now? It isn't that I'm afraid, exactly, but still, to a very slight extent . . . I'm uneasy about the businessmen and the gentry. They're saying that they're fed up with me; but, by God, even if I did accept a little something from this one or that one, it really was without any prejudice. I'm even wondering [*taking the* POSTMASTER *by the arm and leading him off to one side*]—I'm even wondering if there weren't some complaints against me. For really, now, why should an Inspector General be heading this way? I say, couldn't you—for all our sakes—take every letter that goes through the Post Office—both the incoming and the outgoing, and sort of . . . unseal each one a little, don't you know, and kind of glance it through, to see if it doesn't contain some complaint or other, or simply an exchange of information? If it doesn't, it can be sealed up again—or it may be delivered just as it is, "opened by mistake," don't you know—

POSTMASTER: Oh, I know, I know. You don't have to teach me. I do it not so much out of precaution but more out of curiosity; I'm no end fond of finding out if there's anything new going on in the world. And it's mighty interesting reading, let me tell you. Now and then there's a letter that's simply delightful to read—what vivid descriptions, what tender passages! And what lofty morality—better than in any metropolitan daily!

MAYOR: Well, now, tell me—haven't you read anything about a certain official coming from the capital?

POSTMASTER: No, there wasn't a word about any official from the capital—but there's a great deal about two other officials from two other cities. What a pity it is, though, that you don't get to look over the mail; there are some dandy items. One, for instance, where a certain Lieutenant describes a ball to a friend of his, in a most playful mood. Very, very good. He described that ball with great feeling —very great feeling. I've purposely kept that letter by me. Would you like to have me read it to you?

MAYOR: Well, this is hardly the time for it. So do me that favor—if you should come across a complaint, or someone informing, just hold the letter back, without the least hesitation.

POSTMASTER: With the greatest of pleasure.

JUDGE: Watch out; you'll get into trouble some day over that.

POSTMASTER: Oh, Lord!

MAYOR [glaring at the JUDGE]: It's nothing, it's nothing! It would be another matter if you were to use such letters publicly—but this is all in the family.

JUDGE: Yes, this is beginning to look like a grand mess! I must own up I was coming to you [turning to MAYOR] to present you with a fine pup. Own sister to the hound, you know. You must have heard about the lawsuit that two of our landowners have started recently—and now I'm in the seventh heaven: I hunt rabbits with dogs on both their lands.

MAYOR: My dear fellow, I have no heart now for your rabbits; I've got that damned incognito stuck in my head. I expect the door to fly open any minute—and bingo!

BOBCHINSKI [piling in with DOBCHINSKI; both are out of breath]: Something extraordinary has happened!

DOBCHINSKI: The news is so utterly unexpected!

ALL: What is it? What is it?

DOBCHINSKI: Whoever would have thought it? We come to the hotel—

BOBCHINSKI [*breaking in on him*]: Peter Ivanovich here and I come to the hotel—

DOBCHINSKI [*breaking in in his turn*]: Oh, now, Peter Ivanovich, if you'll only let me I'll tell everything—

BOBCHINSKI: Oh, no, if you'll only let me, now! Let me, do! You'd hardly be able to tell it, if it comes to that—

DOBCHINSKI: And you'll get all muddled up and won't remember everything.

BOBCHINSKI: Yes, I'll remember—I will, so help me! Don't interrupt, now—let me tell the story. Don't interrupt! Do me a favor, gentlemen—tell Peter Ivanovich not to interrupt—

MAYOR: Come, speak, for the love of God! What's up? My heart is down in my boots. Sit down, gentlemen! Help yourselves to chairs. Here's one for you, Bobchinski, and one for you, Dobchinski. [*All seat themselves around the two* PETER IVANOVICHES.] Well, now, out with it!

BOBCHINSKI: Allow me, allow me—I'll tell everything in order. No sooner did I leave you, after you received the letter that confused you so much, than I immediately dropped in on—now please don't interrupt, Peter Dobchinski! I already know everything—*everything*—EVERYTHING! Well, then, if you please, I dropped in on Korobkin. But, not finding this Korobkin at home, I turned in at Rastacovski's, and not finding Rastacovski in either, I dropped in on Shpekin, the Postmaster, you see, so's to tell him of the news you received, and as I was coming from there, I met Peter Dobchinski—

DOBCHINSKI: Near that place where they sell hot cakes—

BOBCHINSKI: Right—near the place where they sell hot cakes. Very well. Having met Dobchinski, I said to him: "Have you heard the news our Mayor has received by mail, from a most reliable source?" But he'd already heard this [*turning to* MAYOR] from your housekeeper, whom you had sent to Pochechuev's house to fetch something—I don't know just what it was—

DOBCHINSKI: A small brandy keg—

BOBCHINSKI [*pushing* DOBCHINSKI's *hands away*]: A small brandy keg. And so Dobchinski and I started off for Pochechuev's house—come, Dobchinski, don't you interrupt me now! Please don't interrupt! So we started off for Pochechuev's house, but on the way Dobchinski says to me, he says: "You've no idea what a rumpus my stomach is raising! I haven't eaten a thing since morning, and my stomach is simply crying for food"—that's Dobchinski's stomach, mind you. "And," he says, "they've just delivered some fresh salmon at the hotel, so we might just as well have a bite." No sooner had we stepped into the hotel than a young man—

DOBCHINSKI: Not at all of a bad appearance, and in civilian clothes—

BOBCHINSKI: Yes, yes—not at all of a bad appearance, and in civilian clothes. Well, he strolls through the room, don't you know, with such a thoughtful expression—such a serious face. And the way he carried himself! And [*fluttering his fingers near his forehead*] he seems to have a lot up here—oh, a lot! It was just as though I had a hunch, and I said to Dobchinski here, I said: "There's more here than meets the eye!" Yes, sir! By that time Dobchinski had already made a sign to the owner—you know him: his name is Vlass; his wife was confined three weeks ago—a boy, it was, and what a lively one, to be sure—he's going to run a hotel, just like his daddy. So, having called this Vlass over, Dobchinski here ups and asks him, on the quiet: "Who," he asks, "may that young man be?" To which Vlass answers: "This young man," he says—I wish you wouldn't interrupt now, Dobchinski; please don't interrupt! You could never tell the story, so help me—never. You lithp! you have but one tooth in your head, I know, and that one whistles. "This young man," Vlass says, "is a government official"—that's just what he said! "He's come from the capital now, and his name," Vlass says, "is Hlestacov, and he's on his way north, and," he says, "he's behaving mighty queer; he's staying here for the second week now, hardly ever sets foot outside the place, calls for everything on credit, and won't lay out as much as a copper in cash." The minute he said that to me, it was just as though a light broke in on me from up above. "Ah!" I says to Dobchinski—

DOBCHINSKI: No, Bobchinski, it was me that said "Ah!"

BOBCHINSKI: All right, you said "Ah!" first, and then I said "Ah!" too. "Ah!" said Dobchinski and I. "And what reason would he have for staying here if his way lies north?" Yes, sir! Well, now, he and none other is that very official—

MAYOR: What official?

BOBCHINSKI: The official you were notified about, if you please—the Inspector General.

MAYOR [*thoroughly frightened*]: Whatever are you saying—the Lord be with you! It can't be he!

DOBCHINSKI: It is he! He'll neither pay nor go away. Even his transportation pass specifies that he's traveling north.

BOBCHINSKI: It is he, it is he—honest to God it is he! What an observant fellow—he took in everything. He noticed that Dobchinski and I were eating salmon—the main reason we had chosen salmon was on account of Dobchinski's stomach—well, he looked right into our plates, too. Why, I was simply scared stiff!

MAYOR: Lord have mercy on us sinners! What room has he got at the hotel?

DOBCHINSKI: Number Five—under a flight of stairs.

BOBCHINSKI: The same room where those army officers had a fight last year, the day they arrived.

MAYOR: And has he been here long?

DOBCHINSKI: Why, it must be two weeks by now.

MAYOR: Two weeks! [*Aside.*] May the Lord and all His saints deliver us! The Corporal's widow was flogged within these two weeks! No provisions were issued to the convicts! The people are carrying on in the streets—and the streets themselves are downright filthy! It's a disgrace and a shame! [*Clutches his head.*]

DIRECTOR OF CHARITIES [*to* MAYOR]: Well, what do you

say? Shall we start for the hotel and pay him a formal call?

JUDGE: No, no! Let the clergy and the businessmen of the town call on him first. Even according to procedure—

MAYOR: No, no! Let me attend to everything in my own way. Life has had its difficult moments before this—but they passed, and there were even times when I was thanked. Who knows, perhaps God will deliver us this time as well. [*To* BOBCHINSKI.] He's a young man, you say?

BOBCHINSKI: Yes, a young man; twenty-three, or a little over twenty-four.

MAYOR: So much the better; you can get things out of a youngster much quicker. It's hell when you come up against an old devil, but with a young fellow everything is right on the surface. You get everything set in your own bailiwicks, gentlemen, while I'll go by myself—or even with Dobchinski here, if you like—privately, sort of strolling by, don't you know, and just dropping in to find out if our transient visitors are having any unpleasant experiences in our town. Hey, there, Svistunov!

SVISTUNOV [*rushing forward from his post near the door*]: What do you wish, sir?

MAYOR: Go this minute and fetch the Inspector of Police —or no, I'll need you. Tell somebody else to go and bring the Inspector of Police to me here, as soon as possible, and then you come back here.

[SVISTUNOV *bustles out, almost at a run.*]

DIRECTOR OF CHARITIES [*to* JUDGE]: Come, come! There really may be some trouble.

JUDGE: Why, what have you to be afraid of? All you have to do is slap clean gowns on your patients and you've covered up everything.

DIRECTOR OF CHARITIES: Gowns my eye! The patients are supposed to be on a strict diet, but there's such a reek of cabbage in all the corridors that you have to hold your nose.

JUDGE: As for me, I feel quite calm. Really, now, who'd ever think of dropping in at a county courthouse? And if anyone should ever get it into his head to look over any of the papers, he'd curse the day he was ever born. It's fifteen years now that I've been on the bench, yet if I ever as much as glance at a report I just sigh and give it up as a bad job. Solomon himself wouldn't be able to decide what's true in it and what isn't.

[*Exeunt* JUDGE, DIRECTOR OF CHARITIES, SUPERINTEN-DENT OF SCHOOLS, *and* POSTMASTER; *in the doorway they collide with the returning* SVISTUNOV.]

MAYOR: Well, is the carriage ready?

SVISTUNOV: Right at the door.

MAYOR: Go outside and—or, no, hold on! Go and fetch me . . . why, where are all the other police? Didn't I give orders for Prohorov to be here, too? Where is he?

SVISTUNOV: He's at the station house; the only thing is he's out of the running.

MAYOR: What do you mean by that?

SVISTUNOV: Why, just this—he was brought in this morning dead drunk. We've thrown two buckets of water over him so far, but he hasn't come to yet.

MAYOR [*clutching his hair*]: Oh, my God, my God! Go on out, fast as you can—or wait; run up to my room first—do you hear—and bring me my sword and my new hat. [*To* DOBCHINSKI.] Well, let's go.

BOBCHINSKI: Me too, me too! Let me go along too!

MAYOR: No, no, Bobchinski—you can't, you can't! It'd be awkward, and, besides, there'd be no room for you in the carriage.

BOBCHINSKI: That's nothing, that's nothing, I'll manage somehow; I could even trot behind your carriage, if you'll let me hold on. All I want is just one tiny peep through the crack of the door, don't you know, to see how the young man acts—

MAYOR [*to* SVISTUNOV, *as he takes sword from him*]: Run right away, take some of the police, and let each one of them take . . . Just see how nicked and banged up that sword is! That damned little shopkeeper Abdulin sees right well that the boss of the town has an old sword but never thinks of sending him a new one! Oh, what a wise crowd! As it is, I'm thinking they're already drawing up complaints on the sly. [*Turning to* SVISTUNOV *again.*] Let each one of your men take a street in hand—what in hell am I saying? Not a street but a broom—let each man take a broom in hand and sweep the whole street that leads to the hotel, and sweep it clean—the street, I mean—do you hear me? And you watch out—you, you, I mean! I'm on to you; you pretend to be friendly but steal silver spoons and shove them in your bootleg. Watch out! I've got my ear to the ground. What did you pull on that shopkeeper Chernayev —eh? He gave you two yards of broadcloth for a uniform —so what did you do but swipe the whole bolt? Watch out! You're taking bribes 'way above what your rank entitles you to!—On your way now! [*Exit* SVISTUNOV; *enter* INSPEC-TOR OF POLICE, *whom the* MAYOR *addresses.*] Ah, there you are! Tell me, for God's sake—did you get lost in the shuffle? What does it look like for the Inspector of Police to be away at such a time?

INSPECTOR OF POLICE: I was here all the time—right at your gate.

MAYOR: Very well, listen: The official from the capital has arrived. What steps have you taken?

INSPECTOR OF POLICE: Why, I've followed your instructions exactly. I sent Pugovitzin and a few policemen under him to clean up the sidewalks.

MAYOR: And where's Derzhimorda?

INSPECTOR OF POLICE: Derzhimorda has gone off with the fire engine.

MAYOR: And Prohorov is drunk?

INSPECTOR OF POLICE: Drunk as a lord.

MAYOR: How did you ever allow such a thing to happen?

INSPECTOR OF POLICE: Why, the Lord only knows how it all came about. There was a brawl just outside the town yesterday; Prohorov went out there to preserve law and order, but was shipped back fried, somehow.

MAYOR: Tell you what you do: Pugovitzin, now, is a

pretty tall fellow, even for a cop; so, for the looks of things, you station him at the bridge. And then break up the old fence around where the shoemaker lives, as fast as you can, and make it look as if we were planning to build something there. The more demolition there's going on, the greater the inference that the head of the town is active. Oh, my God—why, I forgot that there are about forty cartloads of all sorts of garbage dumped behind that fence. What an atrocious town this is! No sooner is a monument put up on any spot—or even a fence, for that matter—than they'll pile up all sorts of rubbish there! The devil alone knows where it all comes from! [*Sighs.*] And another thing: should this newly arrived official get to asking anybody working for the city if they're satisfied, let 'em say: "Yes, Your Honor"—but if any one of 'em should turn out to be dissatisfied—well, I'll really give him something to be dissatisfied about later on. Ah, me, but I have sinned; I have sinned much! [*Picks up cardboard hatbox instead of his hat.*] May God grant that all this blow over as soon as possible, and after that I'll put up such a candle as no one has ever yet put up; I'll make each son of a bitch of a shopkeeper in this town come across with a hundred pounds of wax for that candle. Oh, my God, my God! Come, let's go, Dobchinski! [*Puts on hatbox instead of hat.*]

INSPECTOR OF POLICE: Sir, that's a hatbox and not a hat.

MAYOR [*hurling hatbox to one side*]: So it is, so it is—and to hell with it! Yes, and if he should ask why the chapel for the hospital hasn't been built yet—for which a certain sum was appropriated five years ago—don't forget to say that construction was begun on it but that it burned down. I even submitted a report to that effect. Otherwise, like as not, somebody may get absent-minded and blab his fool head off and say that it was never as much as started. And you might tell Derzhimorda not to be so free with his fists; that fellow gives shiners to everybody, just on general principles—both to the just and the unjust. Let's go, let's go, Dobchinski! [*Goes out but immediately returns.*] Yes, and

don't let the soldiers out into the street without their full
equipment; they're such a crummy lot they'll put their uniforms on, true enough—but there won't be a thing underneath.

> [*Exeunt all.* ANNA, *wife of the* MAYOR, *and* MARIA, *his
> daughter, dash on.*]

ANNA: Where are they now? Where are they? Oh, Lord!
[*Opening door.*] Where's my husband? Anton! Tony!
[*Speaks fast.*] And it's all your fault! It's all on account of
you! You had to start fussing around. "Just this pin! Just
this collar!" [*Runs up to window, leans out, and calls.*]
Tony, where are you going? Where? What? Did he come?
You mean it's the Inspector General? Has he a mustache?
What kind of a mustache?

MAYOR [*off*]: Later on, later on, my love!

ANNA: Later on? What an idea—he'll tell me later! I
won't have it later! Just one word is all I want—what is he,
a Colonel? Eh? [*Contemptuously, withdrawing from window.*] He went off. Oh, I'll make him pay for this! And
it's all this girl's fault: "Mamma dear, Mamma dear, wait,
I'll just pin up my collar! I'll be ready right away!" There,
that's what you get for your "Right away"! And we didn't
get to find out anything. And it's all her confounded co-
quetry: she heard that the Postmaster was here and right
off started primping before the mirror—now from this side,
now from the other. She imagines he's after her! In reality
he only makes a face at you the minute your back is turned.

MARIA: Well, Mother dear, what can we do about it now?
We'll find out everything in a couple of hours anyway.

ANNA: In a couple of hours? Thanks, no end! I'm ever
so much obliged to you for that answer! How is it you
never thought of saying that in a month we can find out
still better? [*Leans out of window.*] Avdotya! Eh? Well,
Avdotya, have you heard somebody has just come to town?
You haven't? How stupid you are! He shoos you away?
Let him! You just go ahead and get it out of him! You
couldn't? That's the trouble with you—all you have on

your mind is men and all that sort of nonsense. Eh? They
went off too fast? Why, you should have run after the
carriage. Go on, go on with you—this very minute! Do
you hear me? Run and find out where they went. And be
sure to find out everything, to the last detail. Find out who
the stranger is and what he looks like—you hear me? Look
through the keyhole and find out everything—and also
what color his eyes are, whether they're dark or not, and
come back in a minute or so—do you hear? Hurry, hurry,
hurry, hurry!

[*She keeps shouting until the curtain comes down
upon her and* MARIA, *both of them standing at the window*.]

CURTAIN

Scene II

*An attic room at the hotel—little more than a cubbyhole.
A bed, a table, and a chair comprise practically all the
furnishings.*

*A valise, an empty bottle, boots, a clothes brush, and
other such articles are strewn about the room.*

OSSIP [*discovered lounging on his master's bed with his
boots on*]: Oh, hell, but I want to eat! My stomach is raising as much of a racket as a whole regimental band! There,
we'll never manage to reach home—and that's that. Well,
what can you do about it? It's going on two months now
that the great man left the capital. He squandered all his
money on the way, the little darling; now he's stuck here
with his tail betwixt his legs and is lying low. Why, there
was plenty—plenty and to spare—for traveling expenses;
but no, he has to show off in every town we come to, you
see. [*Mimics* HLESTAČOV.] "I say, Ossip, go and look at the
rooms, and pick out the best; and you might order the very

best they have for dinner—I can't dine poorly, I must dine well." It wouldn't matter so much if he really amounted to something—but then he's nothing but a common pen-pusher, at the very bottom of the Civil Service! He'll scrape up an acquaintance with every passing stranger and then sit down to cards with him—and now just see what his cards have brought him to! Eh, I'm fed up with such a life! On the level, it's much better in the country; there may not be so much going on but, on the other hand, there's less to worry you: you get yourself a wench, and loll in bed all day and eat dumplings. Of course, if the truth were told, there's no disputing that life in the capital is best of all. You must have money, naturally, but living there is grand and refined—theayters, and trained dogs dancing for your amusement, and everything else your heart may desire. And then there's housemaids and such, flirting with you now and then—what girls! [*Smirks and shakes his head.*] Hell, everybody treats you fine; you never hear an impolite word. If you get tired of walking, you just jump in a cab and sit there like a lord—and if you don't feel like paying the driver you don't have to, really—there's hardly a house that hasn't got an exit on some other street; all you've got to do is to give him the slip, quick, and then the devil him-self won't ever find you. There's one bad thing, though: one day you eat swell but the next you all but pass away from hunger—like now, f'r instance. And it's him that's to blame for everything. What can one do with a fellow like that? His old man sends him money for living expenses—and that's all he needs: he's off on a spree the minute he gets it. He won't go a step on foot; not a day passes but he sends me out to get theayter tickets for him; but inside of a week, the first thing you know he's sending me out to sell a brand-new suit as a cast off. Sometimes he'll let every-thing go, down to his last shirt, until he's got nothing left but his worn-out uniform. Honest to God! The finest cloth, mind you; he'll spend as much as a hundred and fifty for the coat alone—and then sell it for twenty; as for the pants, there's no need even mentioning them—they're practically given away. And what's the reason for all this? It's all because he won't get down to business; instead of going to his office he traipses around or plays cards. Oh, if your old man was ever to find out! He wouldn't give a damn that you're working for the Government but just let your pants down and let you have it so hot you'd be eating your meals off a mantel for a week. If you've got a job, attend to it. Why, just now the proprietor said he wouldn't send up any more meals till you've settled for what you've had up to now; well, and what'll happen if we don't? [*Sighs.*] Oh, Lord, what wouldn't I do for a bowl of soup! I feel I could eat up the whole world now. I think there's somebody coming; it must be he, for sure. [*Hastily gets off the bed.*]

HLESTACOV [*entering*]: Here, take these. [*Hands cap and cane to* OSSIP.] Ah, loafing on my bed again?

OSSIP: What would I want to be loafing on your bed for? Do you think I never saw a bed before, or what?

HLESTACOV: You're lying; you were so loafing on it—see how you mussed it all up.

OSSIP: Why, what would I be wanting with it? Do you think I don't know what a bed is? I have me own legs and I can stand—what do I need your bed for?

HLESTACOV [*pacing the room*]: Take a look—maybe there's a pinch of tobacco left in the wrapper.

OSSIP: Well, now, how should there be any left there? You smoked the last shred four days ago.

HLESTACOV [*still pacing the room, twists his mouth in all sorts of ways, then in a loud and assured voice*]: Listen, Ossip! I say, now—

OSSIP: What do you want?

HLESTACOV [*in a voice just as loud but no longer as assured*]: You go there—

OSSIP: Where?

HLESTACOV [*in a voice not at all assured nor loud—in fact very near begging*]: Why, go down to the dining room ... tell them ... to send up something for my dinner—

OSSIP: Well, no, I don't feel like going there at all.

HLESTACOV: How dare you, you idiot!

OSSIP: Why, just so; it won't make no difference even if I was to go—nothing will come of it. The proprietor said not to serve you no more dinners.

HLESTACOV: How dare you refuse? What sort of nonsense is this?

OSSIP: And that's not all, neither, "I," he says, "will even go to the Mayor; it's the third week now that I haven't seen the color of your master's money. Why, you and your master," he says, "are both dead beats, and your master is up to all sorts of tricks. We, now," he says, "have seen plenty of such con-men and scoundrels."

HLESTACOV: Well, I can see you're only too happy to be telling me all this, you brute.

OSSIP: "If things go on like this," he says, "every man jack will be coming to this place, make himself to home, run up a bill, and in the end you won't be able to kick him out, even. I got no intentions of fooling around," he says, "I'm going straight off to lodge a complaint, so's to get him out of here—and into jail."

HLESTACOV: There, there, you fool, that'll do! Go on, go on—tell him what I said. What a coarse brute!

OSSIP: Why, I'd better call the proprietor himself to come up to you.

HLESTACOV: Who wants the proprietor, now? You go and tell him yourself.

OSSIP: Oh, now, really—

HLESTACOV: Go ahead, then, and the devil take you! Go on—call the proprietor! [*Exit* OSSIP.] Oh, but I'm famished! Dreadfully famished. I took a little walk, just so, thinking maybe my hunger would pass—but no, it won't, the devil take it! Well, if I hadn't gone off on a bat on the way here, there would have been money enough to take me home. That damned Infantry Captain all but knocked the props from under me—he can deal the most amazing hands to himself at stuss! He sat in at the game for no more than a quarter of an hour or so—and did he trim me! But completely. And yet, for all that, how I'd have liked to have another go at him! Only circumstances were against it. Circumstances are everything. What a vile hick town this is! They won't give you a thing on credit at the food stores. Why, that's downright mean. [*Whistles: at first an aria from* Robert le Diable, *then the* Red Sarafan, *and finally trails off into something that's neither here nor there.*] Well, I guess nobody wants to come up.

WAITER [*entering*]: The proprietor told me to ask what you wanted.

HLESTACOV: Ah, there, my good fellow! And how are you?

WAITER: Well enough, glory be.

HLESTACOV: And how's everything around the place? Everything going nicely, eh?

WAITER: Yes, glory be—quite nicely.

HLESTACOV: Place all filled up?

WAITER: Oh, yes, quite—glory be.

HLESTACOV: I say, my good man, my lunch hasn't been sent up yet; so won't you hurry things up a bit, please; you see, I've something to attend to right after lunch.

WAITER: Well, now, the proprietor said he weren't going to send up nothing more on the cuff. Why, he was all set to go and lodge a complaint with the Mayor today.

HLESTACOV: Why, what's the idea of complaining? Judge for yourself, my dear fellow—what's to be done, now? Why, I *must* eat. If things go on like this I'm liable to waste away to nothing. I'm as hungry as hungry can be—and that's no joke, either.

WAITER: Right, sir. But the boss said: "I ain't giving him no more dinners till he's paid for those he's already et." Them's his very words.

HLESTACOV: Come, now, reason with him—persuade him.

WAITER: Why, what kind of arguments could I give him?

HLESTACOV: You just explain to him, in all seriousness, that I must eat. Money isn't everything! He thinks just because it may do no harm for a coarse lout like himself to go hungry for a day, others can go hungry as well. Who ever heard of such a thing!

WAITER: I'll talk with him, if you like. [*Exit.*]

HLESTACOV [*solo*]: It'll be rotten if he refuses outright to give me anything to eat. Never have I wanted to eat so much as now. Should I put some of my clothes in circulation, perhaps? Sell my trousers, maybe? No; it's better to starve but come home with the latest outfit from the capital. What a pity that I couldn't get a carriage on credit from some first-class livery stable, for it would have been a fine thing, deuce take it, to arrive in the old home town in a fine carriage, to drive up at a devilish speed to the grand entrance of some neighboring squire, with all the carriage lanterns lit and Ossip perched behind, tagged out as a flunky. I can just imagine what a stir that would create! "Who's that? What's up?" And just then a footman enters [*Drawing himself up and impersonating a footman.*] "Ivan Alexandrovich Hlestacov, from Petersburg; are you at home?" Why, the yokels don't even know what "at home" means! If some country bumpkin of a squire does come to see them, he barges right into the drawing room, bear that he is. A fellow can walk up to one of the neighbor's pretty little daughters: "How delighted I am, Madam—" [*Rubs his hands, bowing and scraping.*] Ugh! [*Makes a wry face.*] I'm actually nauseated, that's how badly I want to eat. [*Enter* OSSIP.] Well, how did you make out?

OSSIP: They're bringing up lunch.

HLESTACOV [*clapping his hands and bouncing on a chair*]: Goody, goody, goody!

WAITER [*entering with a loaded tray*]: This is the last time, now, that the boss is giving you anything.

HLESTACOV: Oh, your boss! I don't give a whoop for your boss! What have you there?

WAITER: Soup and a roast.

HLESTACOV: What, only two courses?

WAITER: That's all, sir.

HLESTACOV: How preposterous! I refuse to accept that! You just tell your boss this will never do! What does he think he's doing? This isn't enough—

WAITER: No, the boss says even this is much too much.

HLESTACOV: And why is there no gravy?

WAITER: There just isn't any.

HLESTACOV: And why isn't there? I saw with my own eyes as I was passing through the kitchen that there were a great many things being prepared. And in the dining room this morning I saw two chubby little men putting away salmon and lots of other things.

WAITER: Well, there is gravy—and at the same time there ain't.

HLESTACOV: What do you mean by that?

WAITER: Why, there just ain't.

HLESTACOV: But what about the salmon, and the steaks, and the chops?

WAITER: That's for them as are the real thing—

HLESTACOV: Oh, you fool!

WAITER: Yes, sir.

HLESTACOV: You're something of a swine. How is it they eat those things and I don't? Why can't I have the same, the devil take it? Aren't they just guests, the same as I am?

WAITER: Why, everybody knows they ain't in the same class.

HLESTACOV: What class are they in then?

WAITER: They're real guests. Everybody knows they pay hard cash.

HLESTACOV: I don't want to argue with you, you fool. [*Ladles out some soup and eats.*] You call this soup? You must have put plain dishwater into the tureen; it hasn't the least taste—but plenty of smell! I don't want this soup—bring me a different kind!

WAITER: I'll take it away then. The boss said if you didn't like it, it was all right with him.

HLESTACOV [*protecting the food with his arms*]: There, there, there! Leave it alone, you fool. You must have gotten used to treating others like that—I'm different, fellow! You can't do this to me—and I advise you not to try. [*Eats.*] Oh, Lord, what soup! [*But he continues to eat.*] I don't think anybody in all this world has ever yet tasted a soup like that; there are some feathers floating around in it instead of good, honest fat. [*Fishes out a bit of chicken and cuts it up.*] Oh, oh, oh—what chicken! Let me have the roast. There's a little soup left over it—you may have it, Ossip. [*Tackling the roast.*] What kind of roast is this? This is no roast.

WAITER: Well, what would you call it?

.. HLESTACOV: The devil alone knows what it is, only it's not a roast. It's just a boot sole, well done. [*Eating.*] What cheats, what scoundrels! Look at the food they give you! One mouthful is enough to make your jaw ache for a week. [*Picking his teeth with his fingers.*] What low-down creatures! Just like splinters—can't pull them out, even, no matter how you try; stuff like that will ruin your teeth. What cheats! [*Wipes mouth with napkin.*] Anything else?

WAITER: No.

HLESTACOV: Scoundrels! Cheats! Why, if there were only a little gravy, at least, or a bit of pastry—the good-for-nothings! All they know is to take the stranger in. [WAITER *and* OSSIP *clear off the dishes and carry them out.*] Honestly, it's just as if I hadn't eaten at all; I've simply whetted my appetite. If I had any change at all I'd send out for a loaf.

OSSIP [*entering*]: The Mayor has just arrived for some reason, and is making inquiries about you.

HLESTACOV [*frightened*]: There it is! What a damned beast that proprietor is—he's already managed to start proceedings! What if he should really lug me off to jail? Well, what of it? As long as I'm treated as a gentleman I may as well go. . . . No, no, I don't want to go! The town is chock-full of officers and natives promenading around—and, as if for spite, I've been putting on airs and winking at a certain merchant's daughter. She winked right back at me, if it comes to that. No, I don't want to go. Why, who does the proprietor think he is? When you come to think of it, how dare he do such a thing? Really, what does he take me for, now? A plain businessman or a manual laborer? [*Screwing up courage and drawing himself up.*] I'll walk right up to him and tell him right to his face: "How dare you! How—"

[*A knock on the door, doorknob turns*—HLESTACOV *turns pale and shrinks into himself.* MAYOR *enters, followed by* DOBCHINSKI, *and stops.* HLESTACOV *and the* MAYOR, *both equally frightened, stare at each other for a few moments, their eyes popping.*]

MAYOR [*recovering a little and standing at attention*]: Hope you are well, sir!

HLESTACOV [*bowing*]: My respects, sir!

MAYOR: Pardon my intrusion—

HLESTACOV: Not at all.

MAYOR: It is my duty, as Chief Magistrate of this town, to see that no advantage is taken of transients and people of standing—

HLESTACOV [*stammering a little at first but, toward the end of the speech, quite loudly*]: Well, what can one do. . . . It's hardly my fault. . . . I really intend to pay—I expect money from home— [BOBCHINSKI *peers in at the door.*] He is far more at fault than I am; he serves me beef as tough as shoe leather; as for his soups, the devil knows what he puts in 'em; I just had to throw some out of the window. He starves me for days at a time. And his tea is most peculiar; you could never tell it's tea by its smell—it stinks of fish. Why should I, then . . . I never heard of such a thing!

MAYOR [*taken aback*]: Do forgive me—I'm not to blame, really. The beef I inspect at the markets is always good. It's brought in by reliable dealers, sober and well-behaved people. I really don't know where he gets his. But if anything isn't just so, why, then. . . . May I suggest that you come with me to other quarters—

HLESTACOV: No, I don't want to. I know just what you

mean by other quarters—the jail. Why, what right have you got to say that to me? How dare you? Why, I'll . . . I work for the Government at the capital! [*Putting on a bold front.*] Why, I—I—I—

MAYOR [*aside*]: Oh, good Lord, how angry he is! He has found out everything—those damned shopkeepers have spilled everything.

HLESTACOV [*blustering*]: Why, if you were to come down with all your men I wouldn't go! I'll take the matter directly to the Prime Minister! [*Thumping the table.*] Who do you think you are, you . . . you—

MAYOR [*drawing himself up at attention, with his whole body trembling*]: Have pity on me—don't ruin me! I have a wife and little ones . . . You don't have to ruin a man!

HLESTACOV: I simply won't have it! What's all that got to do with me? Just because you have a wife and little ones I have to sit in prison? That's just dandy! [BOBCHINSKI *peeks in through door and, thoroughly frightened, hides himself.*] No, thanks ever so much, but I won't have it!

MAYOR [*trembling*]: It's all due to my inexperience—by God, it's all my inexperience. And shortage of funds. . . . You may judge for yourself: my official salary wouldn't keep me in tea and what goes with it. And if there have been any bribes, why, they were the merest trifles—something for the table, or enough cloth for a suit. As for that Corporal's widow who runs a shop, and whom I'm supposed to have flogged—why, that's just slander, by God! It was invented by those who would wrong me; they're the sort who are ready to attempt my life—

HLESTACOV: Well, what of it? I have nothing to do with them. [*Thoughtfully.*] However, I don't know why you talk of those who would wrong you and of some Corporal's widow or other. A Corporal's wife is something else entirely; but as for me, you dare not flog me—you've a long way to go before you can do that. What else? Look whom we have here! I'll pay—I'll pay my hotel bill, but I haven't anything just now. That's precisely why I'm stuck here—because I haven't got a copper on me.

MAYOR [*aside*]: Oh, what a fox! Just see what he's aiming at! What a smoke screen he puts up! Let anybody that wants to try to make him out. A fellow doesn't know what side to tackle him from. Oh, well, come what may, let's have a try at him! Can't lose much by making a blind stab. [*Aloud.*] If you are really short of cash, or anything else, why I'm at your service, at a moment's notice. It's my duty to help out transients.

HLESTACOV: Yes, yes, lend me some money. I'll pay off the proprietor. All I'd like to have is a couple of hundred or even less.

MAYOR [*offering him a sheaf of bank notes*]: Exactly two hundred; you don't even have to bother counting them.

HLESTACOV [*accepting the money*]: Thanks ever so much. I'll send this back to you the minute I get to my country estate. I don't put off things like that. You're a noble fellow, I can see that. Things are entirely different now.

MAYOR [*aside*]: Well, glory be to God, he took the money. Looks as if things will go smoothly from here on. Just the same, I shoved four hundred on him instead of two.

HLESTACOV: Hey there, Ossip! [*Enter* OSSIP.] Call that waiter in here! [*Exit* OSSIP. HLESTACOV *turns to the* MAYOR *and* DOBCHINSKI.] But why are you standing? Be good enough to sit down. [*Urging the reluctant* DOBCHINSKI.] Do sit down, I beg of you!

MAYOR: It doesn't matter; we'll just stand.

HLESTACOV: Be good enough to sit down. I can now see perfectly the goodness of your natures and your hospitality; for I must confess that I was already thinking that you had come to— [*To* DOBCHINSKI.] Do sit down!

[MAYOR *and* DOBCHINSKI *take seats*. BOBCHINSKI *peeks in at the door and listens*.]

MAYOR [*aside*]: I should have acted more boldly. He wants to be considered incognito. Very well; we, too, will put up a bluff; we'll act as if we weren't at all aware just who and what he is. [*Aloud.*] As we—Peter Ivanovich Dobchinski here—he's a landowner hereabouts—and I—as we were walking by in the line of duty, we purposely dropped in here, to find out whether the guests were being treated right, because I'm not like some other mayors, who'll have nothing to do with anything; but, outside of any call of duty, out of Christian regard for my fellow men, I want a good reception to be extended to every mortal, and in this instance, as if in reward, chance has afforded me such a pleasant acquaintance!

HLESTACOV: Same here—I'm very happy also. Had it not been for you, I confess I'd have been stuck here for a long time; I had no earthly idea how I was to square the bill.

MAYOR [*aside*]: Tell us another! He didn't know how he was to pay the bill! [*Aloud.*] May I make so bold as to ask you—where, and to what places, you wish to travel?

HLESTACOV: I'm on my way to the Saratov province—to my own country estate.

MAYOR [*aside, his face assuming an ironic expression*]: To the Saratov province, indeed! Why, he doesn't even blush! Oh, you've got to be up on your toes with this fellow! [*Aloud.*] That's a very good idea, traveling. As for reaching there, they're saying that on the one hand there's a lot of bother in getting horses but, on the other hand, there's nothing like a trip for diverting the mind. For I guess it's mostly for your own pleasure that you're going there?

HLESTACOV: No, my father demands that I come; the old gentleman is angry because up to now I haven't worked myself up to anything worth while at the capital. He's under the impression that the minute you get there they start out handing decorations to you. Yes, I'd like to send him there and see how much headway he'd make in some department.

MAYOR [*aside*]: Just listen, if you please, to the line he

hands out—he even dragged in his old man! [*Aloud.*] And are you planning to stay there long?

HLESTACOV: Really, I don't know. For my father is a stubborn old pepper pot and as stupid as a log. I'll let him have it straight from the shoulder: "Do as you like," I'll tell him, "but I can't live out of the capital. For after all, for what earthly reason should I ruin my life among a lot of hayseeds? The demands of the present day aren't what they used to be; my soul longs for civilized ways."

MAYOR [*aside*]: What a masterly liar! He lies and he lies, but there's never a loose end to give him away. And yet he isn't much to look at, and a kind of short little fellow— looks as if you could squash him on your thumbnail. But you just wait—I'll catch you slipping up yet. I'll sure make you tell us more! [*Aloud.*] That was a very just remark you were pleased to make. What can one accomplish out in the sticks? Why, take this very town; you don't sleep of nights, trying to do your best for your country, without sparing anything, but as for any reward, nobody knows when it'll come. [*Looks over the room.*] This room seems sort of damp, doesn't it?

HLESTACOV: It's a rat hole, and I've never seen the like of the bedbugs here—they bite like dogs.

MAYOR: Well, now! Such a distinguished guest—and he has to suffer! And from whom, mind you? From worthless bedbugs, who should never have come into this world! Like as not, this room is dark as well?

HLESTACOV: Oh, yes, pitch-dark. The proprietor has gotten into the habit of not giving me any candles. At times one feels like doing something, or reading; you may get a notion of writing something, but you can't; it's dark in here— so dark!

MAYOR: Dare I request that you. . . . But no, I'm not worthy of it—

HLESTACOV: Why, what is it?

MAYOR: No, no! I'm not worthy of it—I'm not worthy of it!

HLESTACOV: Come, what's it all about?

MAYOR: If I may make so bold—I've a fine room for you in my house, light, and so comfortable. . . . But no; I myself feel that it would be too great an honor. . . . Don't be angry at me! Really, by God, I suggested it to you out of sheer simpleheartedness—

HLESTACOV: On the contrary, I'll accept with pleasure, if you like. It would be far more pleasant for me in a private home than in this pothouse.

MAYOR: Oh, that would make me ever so happy! And it'll make my wife ever so happy, too! For that's just my nature: I've been taught to practice hospitality ever since my childhood—especially if the guest is a civilized person. Don't get the idea that I'm saying this just out of flattery. No, that's one vice I'm free from; I say this with all my soul.

HLESTACOV: Thank you ever so much. I'm the same way myself: I've no great love for two-faced people. I find your frankness and cordiality very much to my liking, and I'll confess I never ask for anything more than loyalty and respect—and respect and loyalty.

[*Enter* WAITER *and* OSSIP. BOBCHINSKI *peeks in at door.*]

WAITER: Did you call, sir?

HLESTACOV: Yes, let's have the bill.

WAITER: I already handed you a second bill just a while back.

HLESTACOV: I no longer remember what your silly bills were. Come, now, what did they amount to?

WAITER: You ordered a full dinner the first day, while on the second you had just a snack of smoked salmon, and after that you began putting everything on the cuff—

HLESTACOV: You fool—are you going to start itemizing everything? How much do I owe altogether?

MAYOR [*to* HLESTACOV]: Don't upset yourself—he can wait. [*To* WAITER.] Go on, git! The money will be sent you.

HLESTACOV: An excellent idea, that!

[*Puts away his money. Exit* WAITER. BOBCHINSKI *peeks in through door*.]

MAYOR: Would you care to inspect some of the institutions in the town, such as the Department of Public Charities, and so on?

HLESTACOV: Why, what would I find there?

MAYOR: Oh, look them over just so; you'll see how the administration carries on ... the general system ... it might be of interest to a visitor—

HLESTACOV: With the greatest of pleasure; I'm at your service.

[BOBCHINSKI *puts his head in through door*.]

MAYOR: Also, you may wish, later on, to go from there to the District School, to see our method of teaching the various subjects.

HLESTACOV: By all means, by all means.

MAYOR: After that, if you like, you can visit the prison and the town hoosegows—I mean jails—to see how we treat our prisoners.

HLESTACOV: But why pick on jails? It would be better if we inspected just the charitable institutions.

MAYOR: Whatever you wish. Do you intend to go in your carriage, or will you share my buggy with me?

HLESTACOV: Why, I'd better go with you in your buggy.

MAYOR [*to* DOBCHINSKI]: Well, there won't be any room for you now.

DOBCHINSKI: It doesn't matter; I'll manage.

MAYOR [*to* DOBCHINSKI, *in a low voice*]: Listen, you run along—but, what I mean, run as fast as your legs will carry you—and deliver two notes for me; one to Zemlyanika, at the Department of Public Charities, and the other to my wife. [*To* HLESTACOV.] I'll make so bold as to ask your permission to dash off just a line to my wife in your presence, so that she may prepare herself to receive our distinguished guest—

HLESTACOV: Oh, but whatever for? However, here's the ink; the only thing is, I don't know about paper ... unless you use this bill—

MAYOR: It won't take me but a minute. [*Writes, at the same time talking to himself.*] There, we'll see how things will go after a good lunch and a nice, potbellied bottle. Yes, we have a provincial Madeira—not much to look at, but it's strong enough to knock an elephant off its feet. If only I could find out just who he is and to what extent I must be on my guard against him!

[*Having finished, the* MAYOR *hands the notes to* DOB-CHINSKI, *who approaches the door, but at that moment it flies open and* BOBCHINSKI, *who had been eavesdropping on the other side tumbles in. General exclamations.* BOBCHINSKI *picks himself up.*]

HLESTACOV: I say, you haven't hurt yourself by any chance?

BOBCHINSKI: Not at all, not at all—nothing out of the way—just a bump on the bridge of my nose. I'll run over to the Doctor's; he's got a certain kind of plaster, and the bump will go away in no time. [*Exit* DOBCHINSKI, *clucking.*]

MAYOR [*makes a gesture of disapproval to* BOBCHINSKI, *then turns to* HLESTACOV]: It's really nothing. This way, please, I beg you! And I'll tell your man to bring your things over. [*To* OSSIP.] You bring everything over to my place—the Mayor's, now; anybody will show you the way. [*To* HLESTACOV.] Right this way! [*Lets* HLESTACOV *precede him, but, before following him, manages to turn around and say reproachfully to* BOBCHINSKI.] What a man you are! You couldn't find any other place to flop! And you had to stretch out at full length—it looked like hell! [*Exits, followed by* BOBCHINSKI.]

CURTAIN

act 2

Setting same as Act 1, Scene I. At rise: ANNA *and* MARIA *are standing near the window, in the same poses as at Curtain of Act 1, Scene I.*

ANNA: There, we've been waiting a whole hour, and it's all your fault, with your stupid primping. You were all dressed, but, no, you had to fuss around. I shouldn't have listened to the girl at all! How provoking! Not a soul in sight; you might think it was on purpose. You'd think the whole town died out.

MARIA: But really, Mamma dear, we'll find out everything in just a minute or two. Why, Avdotya is bound to be back soon. [*Looks attentively through window and emits a little scream.*] Ah, Mamma dear, Mamma dear, somebody's coming! There, at the end of the street!

ANNA: Where do you see anybody coming? You're forever imagining one thing or another. Well, yes, there is somebody coming. But just who can it be? Rather short . . . in a frock coat . . . whoever could it be? Eh? I must say it's provoking! Who in the world could it be?

MARIA: It's Dobchinski, Mamma dear.

ANNA: How could it be Dobchinski? You're always making things up out of thin air. It's not Dobchinski at all. [*Waves her handkerchief.*] I say, walk a little faster! A little faster!

MARIA: Really, Mamma dear, it is Dobchinski.

ANNA: There you go—just to be arguing! I'm telling you it isn't Dobchinski.

MARIA: Well, now? Well, now, Mamma dear? You can see for yourself it's Dobchinski.

ANNA: Well, yes, it's Dobchinski. I can see that now—so what are you arguing about? [*Shouting through window.*] Walk faster! Faster! You walk so slowly! Well, now, where are they? Eh? Oh, you can tell me from there—it doesn't matter. What? Is he very stern? Eh? And what about my husband? My husband, I said! [*Stepping away from window a little, with vexation.*] What a stupid creature—he won't tell me a thing until he's inside! [*Enter* DOBCHINSKI, *all out of breath.*] There, now, tell me please—doesn't your conscience bother you? I depended upon you as the only decent man, but everybody dashed out and you had to go right after them! And up to this minute I can't get a sensible word out of anybody. Aren't you ashamed of yourself? Why, I was godmother to your little boy and girl, and that's how you acted toward me!

DOBCHINSKI: As God is my witness, dear lady, I ran so hard to pay my respects to you that I can't catch my breath. Greetings, Maria Antonovna.

MARIA: How d'you do?

ANNA: Well, what's what? Come, tell me all about it.

DOBCHINSKI: Your husband sent you this little note—

ANNA [*taking note*]: Well, who is he? A General?

DOBCHINSKI: No, he isn't, but he's every bit as good as any General. So well educated, and his every action is so impressive.

ANNA: Ah, then it must be the very same man they wrote my husband about.

DOBCHINSKI: He's the real thing. I was the first one to find this out—together with Bobchinski.

ANNA: Do tell me everything at last! What happened, and how did it happen?

DOBCHINSKI: Well, glory be to God, everything went off auspiciously. At first he received your husband a trifle sternly, true enough; he was huffy and said that nothing about the hotel suited him, for one thing, but he wouldn't come here either, and that he didn't feel like sitting in jail for his sake; but later on, when he found out how innocent your husband was and when he had talked a little more intimately with him, he at once changed his ideas, and, glory be, everything went well. They've gone off now to inspect the charitable institutions. But I really must tell you that your husband was thinking whether a secret complaint hadn't been lodged against him; I myself had a bit of a scare, too.

ANNA: Why, what have you to be afraid of? You aren't in any government service.

DOBCHINSKI: Oh, just on general principles. You know how it is—when a high dignitary speaks you naturally feel scared.

ANNA: Oh, well! However, all this is nonsense—tell me what he looks like? Is he old or young, now?

DOBCHINSKI: He's young—a young man of twenty-three or close to it, yet he talks just as if he were an old man. "I'll come to your house," he says, "if you like," and [*gesturing vaguely*] this and that—it was all done so grandly. "I," he says, "am fond both of reading and writing; but I find it's a nuisance because this room is a trifle dark."

ANNA: But what's he like, you provoking man—dark-haired or light?

DOBCHINSKI: No, he's more on the auburn side, and his eyes dart here and there ever so quickly, like little animals of some sort—it actually makes you feel uneasy.

ANNA: Let's see what Tony writes me. [*Reads.*] "I write you in haste, dearest, to inform you that my situation was a most lamentable one; but, placing my trust in the mercy of God, for two pickles, extra, and a half-portion of caviar, one-twenty-five—" [*Stops reading.*] I can't understand a thing: what have pickles and caviar to do with all this?

DOBCHINSKI: Why, your husband wrote on scrap paper, he was in such a hurry; there must have been some bill written on it.

ANNA: Ah, yes—that's it. [*Resumes reading.*] "...but,

placing my trust in the mercy of God . . . it seems as if everything will come out right. Get a room ready as quickly as you can for a distinguished guest—the one with the yellow wallpaper; as for dinner, don't bother preparing anything extra, because we are going to have a bite at the Department of Public Charities, with its Director. But as for wines, order as much as possible; tell that shopkeeper Abdulin to send his best, for otherwise I will turn his whole wine cellar upside down myself. Kissing your hand, my dearest, I remain yours, Anton Skvoznik-Dmuhanovski—" Oh, my God, this must surely be attended to as soon as possible. Hey, who's there? Mishka!

DOBCHINSKI [*making a dash for the door and shouting*]: Mishka! Mishka! Mishka!

[*Enter* MISHKA.]

ANNA: Look here: Dash over to Abdulin's shop . . . hold on, I'll give you a note. [*Sitting down at a desk and speaking as she writes.*] You give this note to Sidor, the coachman; let him run over to Abdulin's shop and bring the wine back from there. And you yourself get that room [*pointing*] ready for the guest—and do it right! Put a bed in there, and a washbasin, and everything else.

[*Exit* MISHKA.]

DOBCHINSKI: Well, I'll run along now to see how they're doing with their inspection—

ANNA: Go ahead, go ahead—I'm not detaining you. [*Exit* DOBCHINSKI.] Well, daughter, we'll have to get busy dressing. He's from the capital; God forbid he should make fun of us over something or other. Your blue dress with the little pleats would be the most becoming—

MARIA [*with disgust*]: No, Mamma dear; I don't like that blue dress at all. Not only does Lyapkin-Tyapkin's wife dress in blue, but so does Zemlyanika's daughter, too. No, I'd better put on something bright.

ANNA: Something bright, indeed! Really, you're saying that only to be contrary. The blue will look ever so much better on you, because I want to wear straw-yellow. I'm very fond of straw-yellow.

MARIA: Ah, Mamma dear, straw-yellow is so unbecoming to you!

ANNA: Straw-yellow is unbecoming to me?

MARIA: Yes. I'll stake anything you like it won't become you. One must have absolutely dark eyes to wear straw-yellow.

ANNA: That's just dandy! And aren't my eyes dark? As dark as dark can be! What nonsense the girl spouts! How can they be anything but dark when I always take the queen of clubs for myself whenever I tell fortunes by cards?

MARIA: Ah, Mamma dear, you're more like the queen of hearts!

ANNA: Bosh—absolute bosh! I never was a queen of hearts. [*Exit hurriedly with* MARIA, *but is still heard, off.*] What things pop into your head! Queen of hearts, indeed! God knows what nonsense you talk!

[*As they exit, the door of the room* ANNA *had indicated opens and* MISHKA *sweeps out rubbish,* OSSIP *comes in through main door, lugging a valise on his head.*]

OSSIP: Where do I put this?

MISHKA: This way, Uncle—right this way.

OSSIP: Hold on; give us a chance to rest. What a dog's life! Every load seems heavy on an empty belly.

MISHKA: Tell me, Uncle—will the General be here soon?

OSSIP: What general?

MISHKA: Why, your master.

OSSIP: My master? But what sort of a general is he?

MISHKA: Why, ain't he a general?

OSSIP [*hedging*]: He is—only the other way around.

MISHKA: Well, is he more important than a real general or less?

OSSIP: More!

MISHKA: So that's it! No wonder they're raising such a fuss in our house!

OSSIP: Look here, young fellow—I can see you're a bright lad; suppose you fix up a bite of something for me.

MISHKA: Why, Uncle, there's nothing ready yet that

would be to your liking. You wouldn't want to eat anything plain; but when your master sits down at table you'll get some of the same food.

OSSIP: Well, now, what have you got in the way of plain fare?

MISHKA: Cabbage soup, buckwheat groats, and meat pies.

OSSIP: Bring on your soup, your groats and meat pies! It don't matter—we'll eat anything. Come on, let's lug this in. Is there another way out from there?

MISHKA: There is.

[*Exit both, carrying the large suitcase into the adjoining room. Both halves of main door are flung open by two* POLICEMEN, *who flank the entrance. Enter* HLESTACOV, *followed by* MAYOR, *then the* DIRECTOR OF CHARITIES, *the* SUPERINTENDENT OF SCHOOLS, *and* DOBCHINSKI *and* BOBCHINSKI, *the latter with a plaster on the bridge of his nose.* MAYOR *makes a Jovelike gesture at a scrap of paper on the floor; the* POLICEMEN *rush helter-skelter to pick it up, colliding with each other.*]

HLESTACOV: Fine institutions you've got here. What I like is that you let your visitors see everything; in other towns they wouldn't show me a thing.

MAYOR: In other towns, if I may make so bold as to inform you, the town administrators and officials are more concerned with their own welfare, as it were; but here, if one may say so, we have no other thought save to earn the recognition of our superiors by good order and vigilance.

HLESTACOV: That was a very fine lunch; I ate entirely too much. Why, do you have lunches like that every day?

MAYOR: It was especially arranged for so pleasant a guest.

HLESTACOV: I love a good meal. For that's what one lives for—to pluck the blossoms of pleasure. What do they call that fish we had?

DIRECTOR OF CHARITIES [*trotting up to* HLESTACOV]: Salted scrod, sir.

HLESTACOV: Very tasty. Where was it we lunched? At the hospital, wasn't it?

DIRECTOR: Right, sir! Just one of our eleemosynary institutions.

HLESTACOV: I remember, I remember. There were a lot of cots standing empty there. And have all the patients recovered? There didn't seem to be many of them around.

DIRECTOR: There's half a score or so of them left; all the others have recovered. That's the way it goes—it's the way things are arranged. Ever since I've assumed the post—perhaps this may seem actually incredible to you—all the patients recover like . . . like flies. No sooner does a patient set foot in the infirmary than he gets well—and not so much through the aid of any medicines as through sheer honesty and efficient organization.

MAYOR: And, if I may make so bold as to inform you, the responsibility of being Mayor is ever so harrowing! There are so many problems—take sanitation alone, and repairs, and rectifications. . . . In short, the most intelligent of men might find himself in difficulties; yet, God be thanked, everything runs smoothly. Another Mayor, of course, might strive for his own benefit; but, believe me, that even when one lies down to sleep one keeps thinking—Lord God, how can I arrange things so that my superiors may perceive my zeal? I ask for nothing more. Whether they reward me or not, at least I shan't be perturbed at heart. When good order is maintained throughout the town, when all the streets are swept, the prisoners well kept, and there are only a few drunkards—what more could I desire? I swear I want no honors. Of course, that sort of thing is enticing, but before virtue all else is but dross and vanity.

DIRECTOR [aside]: Listen to that scalawag laying it on! It's a gift from Heaven!

HLESTACOV: Very, very true. I confess I myself am occasionally fond of intellectual pursuits—at times in prose, and at others tossing off some slight verse.

BOBCHINSKI [to DOBCHINSKI]: Quite right, Peter Ivanovich, quite right! His remarks are so . . . so . . . you know! One can see that he has studied the humanities.

HLESTACOV: Tell me, please, don't you go in for diversions of any sort? Haven't you gatherings where one may, for instance, indulge in a little game of cards?

MAYOR [aside]: Oho, brother, I know what you're driving at! [Aloud.] God save us from anything of the sort! There isn't even a hint at such gatherings here. I never as much as held a card in my hands; I couldn't play cards if my life actually depended on it. I never could bear to look at them with indifference; why, if I should but happen somehow to catch sight of a king of diamonds, let's say, I'm overcome with such disgust that I simply have to spit. One time it so happened that I built a house of cards, just to amuse the children, don't you know—and all that night the accursed things kept plaguing me in my dreams. God be with them that play—how can anyone kill precious time over cards?

SUPERINTENDENT OF SCHOOLS [aside]: And yet that scoundrel took me over for a hundred on points, only three days ago!

MAYOR: I'd rather utilize the time for the good of the State.

HLESTACOV: Oh, really now, you're making a fuss over nothing at all. It all depends on how you look at a thing. If, for instance, you were to start hedging when you've lost three quarters of your stakes, then, naturally. . . . No, it's no use talking, it's intriguing to play a game of cards now and then.

[Enter ANNA and MARIA.]

MAYOR: May I make so bold as to present my family: my wife and my daughter.

HLESTACOV [bowing and scraping]: Delighted, Madam, in having the pleasure, as it were, of meeting you—

ANNA: It's still a greater pleasure for us to meet such a personage.

HLESTACOV [posturing]: Pardon me, but mine is so much greater!

ANNA: How can that be! You're pleased to say so only for the sake of a compliment. Be seated, I beg of you.

HLESTACOV: Merely to stand near you constitutes happiness; however, since you absolutely insist, I'll sit down. How happy I am to be sitting near you at last!

ANNA: Pardon me, but I dare not accept the compliment as being really intended for me . . . . I think you must have found traveling very unpleasant after life in the capital?

HLESTACOV: Extremely unpleasant. Having become used to living in society, *comprenez vous,* and then to find yourself suddenly on the road—the filthy inns, the surrounding gloom of boorishness. I must confess, if it weren't for such good fortune which [*glancing at* ANNA *and showing off before her*] has rewarded me for everything. . . .

ANNA: Really, it must be so unpleasant for you!

HLESTACOV: However, Madam, at this moment I am in a most pleasant mood!

ANNA: But that's out of the question—you do me too much honor. I do not merit it.

HLESTACOV: But why in the world not? You do merit it!

ANNA: I live in the backwoods—

HLESTACOV: Yes, but the backwoods, by the bye, also has its points—knolls, brooks, and rills. Well, naturally, no one would compare it with the capital. Ah, the capital! What life, really! You may think, perhaps, that I'm merely a pen-pusher; but no, the Head of the Department is on a friendly footing with me. He'll slap me on the back, like this: "Come and have dinner with me, dear fellow!" I drop in at the office for only a couple of minutes a day, merely to tell 'em to do this thing that way and that thing this way. And immediately a special clerk—and what an old rat he is!—starts scraping away with his pen. [*Imitates a scratchy pen.*] They even wanted to give me a much higher rank, but, I thought to myself, what's the use? And the doorman runs after me with a brush: "Permit me, sir—I want to shine your shoes!" [*To* MAYOR.] But why are you standing? Please do sit down, gentlemen!

MAYOR: Your rank is such that we
can well keep on standing—
DIRECTOR: We'll stand— ⎱ [*Simultaneously*.]
SUPERINTENDENT: Please don't mind us—⎰

HLESTACOV: Never mind ranks—I'm asking you to sit down. [MAYOR *and the others sit down*.] I'm not fond of ceremonies; on the contrary, I actually try to slip by without attracting attention—so I do. But you simply can't hide yourself—you can't, you can't! All I have to do is to go out somewheres, and they all start saying at once: "There," they say, "goes Hlestacov!" And on one occasion they actually took me for a Commander-in-Chief. The soldiers rushed right out of the guardroom and presented arms. It was only later on that an officer, whom I know very well, explained to me: "Why, brother, we actually took you for the Commander-in-Chief!"

ANNA: Do tell!

HLESTACOV: I know ever so many pretty little actresses. For, after all, I've written all sorts of amusing little pieces for the stage. I mingle with all the writers. Pushkin and I are like that. [*Puts middle finger over index finger*.] Many's the time I've said to him: "Well, how are things going, Pushkin, old thing?"—and he'd come right back at me with, "Why, old thing, things are just so-so, somehow!" Most original fellow!

ANNA: So you write, too? It must be so pleasant to feel oneself a writer. You probably publish in the magazines as well?

HLESTACOV: Oh, yes—in the magazines as well. However, I've done ever so many things: *The Marriage of Figaro, Robert le Diable, Norma*. . . . By now I don't remember even the titles. And it all came about by sheer chance; I didn't want to write, but the theatrical managers kept pestering me, "Please, dear fellow, write something for us!" So I thought to myself: "All right, dear fellows, so I will—just to get rid of you!" And right then and there—I don't think it took me more than a single evening, I dashed off everything—and did I astonish all of them! [*Slight pause.*] I have an exceptional facility of imagination. I am really the backbone of the *Morning Telegraph;* my sea novel, *The Frigate Hope,* is still a best-seller, and everything that came out under the name of Baron Brambeus—

ANNA [*breaking in on him*]: Do tell! So you were that famous colyumist?

HLESTACOV: Why, of course. Why, there isn't a poet whose poems I don't doctor. The biggest publisher in the country pays me a retainer of forty thousand a year for that alone.

ANNA: Then *Uri Miloslavski* must also be your work—

HLESTACOV: Yes, it is.

ANNA: There, I guessed it right off!

MARIA: Ah, Mamma dear, it says right on the title page it was written by some Zagoskin.

ANNA: There you go! I simply knew you'd start an argument even over that—

HLESTACOV [*hardly batting an eye*]: Oh, yes, that's right; that's really by Zagoskin; but there's another novel by the same name—well, that one is mine.

ANNA: Well, it surely must be yours I read. How well written it is!

HLESTACOV: To confess the truth, I live by my pen. My house is the best in the whole capital. Everybody knows it! They call it Hlestacov House—just like that. [*Addressing everybody.*] If you're ever in the capital, gentlemen, do me a favor and drop in on me; I urge you, most heartily. And then, I also give grand affairs.

ANNA: I can imagine how tasteful and magnificent they must be.

HLESTACOV: Well, really, they're past all description. In the center of the table is a watermelon—and that watermelon costs a mere seven hundred. Soup in special cans, just arrived by steamer direct from Paris—open a can, and the steam is like—like nothing on earth. Not a day passes without my having to attend dances. There, in the capital, we

have formed our own circle for whist. The Minister of Foreign Affairs, the French Ambassador, and the British, and
the German, and me. And you get so fagged out playing it's
really a shame. When you run up to the fourth floor all you
have strength to say to the cook is, "Here, old girl, take my
coat"—hold on, though: why, I'm mixing everything up;
I've actually forgotten I live on the first floor. My staircase
alone is—well, simply priceless! And it's ever so curious to
peep in at my reception hall, at an hour when I haven't even
opened my eyes. The counts and dukes are milling about
and buzz like so many bumblebees; all you can hear is their
bzz, bzz, bzz! Occasionally you'll find the Premier there—
just hanging around. . . . [*The* MAYOR *and the others are so
awed that they rise from their chairs.*] Even my letters are
addressed "Your Excellency." Once I had charge of a whole
Department, actually. Most odd, that was. The Director had
gone off—but where to nobody seemed to know. Well, naturally, all sorts of discussions sprang up: How was his
place to be filled, who was going to fill it, what was to be
done. Many of the generals were willing enough and tackled
the job, but when they got right down to it—we-e-ll, no, the
matter was entirely too complicated. It was easy enough, at
first glance, but when you got a closer look at it, it turned
out to be the devil and all. Later on they see that there's
no help for it—so they turn to me. And that very moment
all the streets are simply swarming with dashing messengers,
and messengers and more messengers—no end of messengers, and all of 'em dashing about like mad. You can
just imagine, there were thirty-five thousand messengers
alone! Wasn't that some situation, I ask you? "Ivan
Alexandrovich, come and take charge of that Department!" I was somewhat taken aback, I confess; I had
come out in my dressing gown and was just about to
turn 'em down, but then I thought to myself: Suppose
word of my refusal reaches the Emperor? And then
there's my service record to be considered, too . . . "Very
well, gentlemen," I said, "if you like I'll accept the post; I
accept it," I tell 'em: "The only thing is, watch out! I won't

stand for any guff from anybody. You've got to be up on your toes when you work for me. You know me!" And really, whenever I used to pass through the Department it was simply like an earthquake; there wasn't a soul there that didn't quake and quiver like an aspen leaf. [*The* MAYOR *and the others quake in apprehension;* HLESTACOV *works himself up to a real fever pitch.*] Oh, I don't like to fool around! I hauled all of them over the coals. [*Pause.*] Why, even the Imperial Council is afraid of me. And really, why not? That's the sort of man I am! I don't let anybody stand in my way. I always tell everybody "I, I myself know my own self." I'm all over—all over! I drop in at the Palace every day. They'd make me Field Marshal on the morrow —at a moment's notice from me—

[*Slips, and all but flops on the floor, but is deferentially caught and supported by the* OFFICIALS.]

MAYOR [*approaching him and trying to speak, his whole body quaking*]: B-b-but.... Yo ... yo ... yo....

HLESTACOV [*sharply*]: What is it?

MAYOR: B-b-ut.... Yo ... yo ... yo....

HLESTACOV [*as before*]: I can't make out a word. It doesn't make sense.

MAYOR: Yo ... yo.... Your Lexencency—Your Excellency may wish to rest. Here's your room, and everything you need—

HLESTACOV: Rest? Nonsense! However, if you like, I'm ready to take a rest. Your lunch was eckshellent, gemmen! I'm gratified—I'm gratified. [*Declaiming.*] Scrod, *scrod,* SCROD!

[*Exit, solicitously followed by the* MAYOR, *into the side room.*]

BOBCHINSKI [*to* DOBCHINSKI]: There's a man for you, Peter Ivanovich. There's a man that's a man! Never in my life have I been in the presence of so important a personage —I all but passed out, I was that scared. What do you think, Peter Ivanovich: who is he? What's his rank, I mean?

DOBCHINSKI: I think he's nothing short of a general, Peter Ivanovich.

BOBCHINSKI: Well, in my opinion no general is fit to lace the shoes of this fellow! But if he is a general, then he must be a generalissimo at the very least. You heard him: he's got the whole Imperial Council backed up against the wall. Let's go and tell everything to the Judge and to Korobkin. Good-by, Anna Andreievna!

DOBCHINSKI: Good-by, dearest lady!

[*Exeunt* DOBCHINSKI *and* BOBCHINSKI.]

DIRECTOR OF CHARITIES [*to* SUPERINTENDENT OF SCHOOLS]: It's simply frightening! But just why, a body can't tell. Why, we aren't even wearing our uniforms! Well, now, suppose he gets up after a good night's sleep and then dashes off a confidential report to the capital? [*Walks thoughtfully to door with* SUPERINTENDENT OF SCHOOLS, *then turns to* ANNA.] Good-by, ma'am!

SUPERINTENDENT OF SCHOOLS: Good-by!

[*Exeunt both.*]

ANNA: Ah, what an agreeable fellow!

MARIA: Ah! The darling!

ANNA: But mind you, what fine deportment! One can perceive a man from the capital right off. His ways, and all that sort of thing. . . . Ah, but that's fine! I'm awfully fond of young men like that. I've simply lost my head over him. However, I proved very much to his liking; I noticed he was eyeing me all the time—

MARIA: Ah, Mamma dear—it was me he was looking at!

ANNA: Oh, get away from me with your impertinence! That remark is entirely out of place in this instance.

MARIA: No, Mamma dear, he really was.

ANNA: There you go! God forbid that you should ever keep from arguing! It just couldn't be, and that's that. When did he look at you? And what reason did he have to look at you?

MARIA: Really, Mamma dear, he kept looking at me all the time.Why, he glanced at me the moment he began talking about literature, and when he was telling us about how he played whist with the ambassadors he looked at me also.

ANNA: Well, maybe he did, one little time, and even then

he did it just so, just to be nice. "Eh," he must have said to himself, "let's take a look at her—might as well."

MAYOR [*tiptoeing in from* HLESTACOV'S *room*]: Shhhh—sh!

ANNA: What is it?

MAYOR: Really, I'm none too happy now I got him drunk. Well, now, supposing even half of what he said is true? [*Falls into thought.*] But still, how could it be anything but the truth? Once you've got plenty of drink under your belt you come right out with everything. Whatever you've got in your heart is right at the tip of your tongue: Of course, he did touch things up a bit. But then, nobody ever says anything without some added touches. He plays whist with prime ministers and is a regular visitor at Court. So really, now, the more I think of it—the devil knows what's going on in my head, for I'm sure I don't know; it's just as if I were standing up on some belfry, or as if they were about to hang me.

ANNA: But me, now—I wasn't in the least put out; I simply saw him as a well-brought-up man of the world, a man of the highest quality, but as for his rank and position, why, I simply don't take them into consideration, even.

MAYOR: Oh, you women! That one word is enough to settle all argument. All you think of is fuss and feathers. And you'll always pop up with some silly thing or other. You will get off with nothing but a flogging—but your husband's goose will be gone and done for. You, my darling, treated him just as familiarly as if he were some Dobchinski or other.

ANNA: That's something I'd advise you not to worry your head about. There's a little something we know about him. [*Looks at her daughter.*]

MAYOR [*solo*]: Oh, what's the use of talking with you! What a thing to happen, really! I still can't get over my fright. [*Opening door and calling.*] Mishka, call Svistunov and Derzhimorda; their beat is just a little beyond the gates. [*Short pause after closing door.*] Odd how mixed up everything has become in the world; if only people would be impressive to look at, but no, every man is puny and small and as thin as a match—how can a body tell who he is? You take a military man, now—at least his uniform tells you what he is; but even he, when he puts on civilian dress, will look like a fly with its wings snipped off. However, he sure did hold back at that hotel. He sprang such allegories and equivocations on me that it looked as if I'd never get anything sensible out of him. But there, he did give in in the end. And he actually let spill more than he should have. You can see right off he's still a youngster.

[*Enter* OSSIP, *polishing a boot. All make a dash for him, beckoning with their fingers.*]

ANNA: Come here, old fellow!

MAYOR: Shhh! Well? Is he sleeping?

OSSIP: No, not yet; he's still stretching himself every once in a while.

ANNA: Look here ... what's your name?

OSSIP: Ossip, ma'am.

MAYOR [*to his wife and daughter*]: There, that'll do you, that'll do you! [*To* OSSIP.] Now, then, my friend, have they fed you well?

OSSIP: They did that, thanking you most humbly—they fed me right well.

ANNA: Well, now, tell me: there must be ever so many counts and dukes calling on your master?

OSSIP [*aside*]: What's the use of saying anything! If they fed me well now, it means they're going to feed me still better later on. [*Aloud.*] Yes, there's counts calling on him, amongst others.

MARIA: Ossip, darling, your master is such a good-look-ing little fellow!

ANNA: But tell me please, Ossip—is your master—

MAYOR: Now stop that, please! You merely hinder me with such idle talk. Come, what can you tell me, friend?

ANNA: And what might your master's rank be?

OSSIP: His rank? Why, the usual thing—

MAYOR: Oh, my God, how you keep on with your silly

pumping! You won't give me a chance to ask anything that matters. [*To* OSSIP.] Well, my friend, what sort of man is your master? Strict? Is he fond of bawling people out, or isn't he? Eh?

OSSIP: Yes, he's fond of having everything in order. What he's after is having everything regular-like.

MAYOR: Why, I like your face, so I do! You must be a kindhearted fellow, friend. Well, now—

ANNA: See here, how does your master look in his uniform?

MAYOR: Come, that'll do you two chatterboxes. This is a most urgent matter. It concerns life and death! [*To* OSSIP.] As I was saying, I do like you, ever so much. When you're traveling it can't do the least harm to have an extra glass of tea or something; it's cold now. So here's a couple of cart wheels for tea.

OSSIP [*accepting the coins*]: Thank you, ever so humbly. May God grant you all good health for helping a poor man.

MAYOR: Fine, fine; that makes me happy, too. Well, now, friend—

ANNA: I say, Ossip, what sort of eyes does your master prefer, now?

MARIA: Ossip, darling! What a cute little nose your master has!

MAYOR: Hold on, now, give me a chance! [*To* OSSIP.] And now, friend—to what things does your master pay the most attention? What appeals to him most when he's traveling, that is?

OSSIP: It all depends on whatever turns up. He likes best of all to be well received—he likes good entertainment.

MAYOR: Good entertainment?

OSSIP: Yes, good entertainment. There, now, I may be nothing but a serf, yet even so he looks out that I'm treated right, too. By God, whenever we used to stop anywhere, he'd always ask me, "Well, Ossip, were you treated right?" —"Not so well, Your Excellency," I might tell him. "Eh," he'd say, "our host has a mean nature, Ossip. You remind me," he'd say, "when we get back to the capital." But I'd think to myself: "Eh, [*makes a resigned gesture*] God be with that fellow; I'm a simple man."

MAYOR: Fine, fine, and what you're saying is good common sense. I gave you something for tea just now—so here's something else for cookies to go with it.

OSSIP: Why are you so good to me, Your Honor? [*Pocketing the coin.*] In that case I'll drink to Your Honor's health.

ANNA: You come to me, Ossip; you'll get something additional.

MARIA: Ossip, darling, kiss your master for me!

[HLESTACOV *is heard coughing slightly in the adjoining room.*]

MAYOR: Shhh! [*Gets up on tiptoes; rest of scene in* sotto voce.] God save you from making a noise! That'll do you two; go to your rooms.

ANNA: Come along, Maria! I'll tell you exactly what I noticed about our guest; it's something I can tell you only when we're alone. [*Exeunt* ANNA *and* MARIA.]

MAYOR: Oh, they'll have plenty to talk about! I think if you were to listen you'd have to stick your fingers in your ears. [*Turning to* OSSIP.] Well, friend— [DERZHIMORDA *and* SVISTUNOV *clump in.*] Shhh! What clumsy bears, clumping with their boots! Barging in with as much noise as if somebody was dumping a load off a cart! Where in the hell were you?

DERZHIMORDA: I wuz carryin' out orders—

MAYOR: Shhhh! [*Clapping hand over* DERZHIMORDA'S *mouth.*] Listen to him cawing like a crow! [*Mimicking.*] "I wuz carryin' out orders!" Sounds like a foghorn. [*To* OSSIP.] Well, friend, you run along and get whatever your master needs. You can call for anything and everything in the house. [*Exit* OSSIP.] As for you two, you stand on the front steps and don't stir from the spot! And don't let a single stranger into the house—especially the storekeepers! If you'll let even one of 'em in, I'll skin you alive. The min-

ute you see anyone at all coming with a complaint—or
even without a complaint, but maybe the fellow looks like
the kind of a fellow that would want to lodge a complaint
against me—you just let him have it right in the neck! Like
this! Let him have it good and hot! [*Kicks, to demonstrate.*]
You hear me? Shh! Shhhhhhh!

    [*Tiptoes out, after* DERZHIMORDA *and* SVISTUNOV.]

CURTAIN

act 3

Scene I

*Scene same. Next morning. Enter, cautiously and almost
on tiptoes,* JUDGE, DIRECTOR OF CHARITIES, POSTMASTER,
SUPERINTENDENT OF SCHOOLS, *and* DOBCHINSKI *and* BOB-
CHINSKI. *All act as if on dress parade, and the officials are
in their uniforms. The whole scene, until* HLESTACOV'S *entrance, is in* sotto voce.

    JUDGE [*arranging everybody in a semicircle*]: For God's
sake, gentlemen, get in a circle without wasting time, and
try to be as orderly as possible! God be with him—he not
only attends at Court but also bawls out the Imperial Council! Straighten up! A soldierlike bearing, gentlemen—you
mustn't fall down on that soldierlike bearing! You, Peter
Ivanovich—trot over to this side; and you, Peter Ivanovich,
stand right here.

    [DOBCHINSKI *and* BOBCHINSKI *trot over to the places
indicated.*]

DIRECTOR OF CHARITIES: Have it your way, Judge, but we really ought to take some ... action.

JUDGE: And what, precisely?

DIRECTOR OF CHARITIES: Well, you know what.

JUDGE: Palm oil?

DIRECTOR OF CHARITIES: Well, yes—why not palm oil—

JUDGE: A dangerous thing, devil take it; he may raise a hullabaloo, working for the State as he does. Unless, perhaps, we were to do it in the guise of a contribution from the gentry, for some sort of a monument?

POSTMASTER: Or else: "Here, now, some money has come through the mails—and no one knows to whom it belongs!"

DIRECTOR OF CHARITIES: Watch out he doesn't post you somewhere to hell and back again. Look here, that's not the way things are done in a well-regulated State. Why is there a whole squadron of us here? We ought to present ourselves one by one and, when each is eye to eye with him, then ... do whatever has to be done, and there are no ears to overhear. That's how things are done in a well-regulated social order. There, now, Judge—you'll be the first to start the ball rolling.

JUDGE: Why, it would be better if you did; it was in your Department that our important visitor broke bread.

DIRECTOR OF CHARITIES: Well, it might be better, after all, if the Superintendent of Schools took the initiative—as one who enlightens the youth and all that.

SUPERINTENDENT OF SCHOOLS: I can't, gentlemen, I simply can't. To tell you the truth, my upbringing has been such that if anyone, even one step above me in rank, starts talking to me my heart simply sinks into my boots and it's as if the cat has stolen my tongue. No, gentlemen, you must excuse me—you really must.

DIRECTOR OF CHARITIES: Well, Judge, it looks like there's nobody to do it outside of yourself. You never utter a word but it sounds as if Cicero himself were speaking with your tongue.

JUDGE: Come, now! Come, now—Cicero indeed! What will you think of next? Just because once in a while one becomes deeply interested in discussing a pack of house-dogs or a racing bloodhound—

ALL [*badgering him*]: No, dogs aren't all you can talk about—you could have straightened out the trouble at the building of the Tower of Babel! No, Judge, don't leave us in a lurch! Be like a father to us! Really, Judge—

JUDGE: Do let me alone, gentlemen!

[*At this moment* HLESTACOV *is heard clearing his throat and walking about in his room— All try to head off one another in a panic rush to the door—which, naturally, leads to certain casualties. But, for all that, the protests are also in* sotto voce.]

BOBCHINSKI'S VOICE: Ouch! Dobchinski, Dobchinski, you're standing on my foot!

VOICE OF DIRECTOR OF CHARITIES: Gentlemen, let me out of here before I pass away! You've crushed me completely—

[*A few more cries of* "Ouch!"; *finally all push through, leaving stage empty for a few seconds.*]

HLESTACOV [*solo, entering with sleep-laden eyes*]: I must have had some snooze, it looks like. Wherever do they get such soft mattresses and feather beds? I was actually roasting. It looks as if they'd given me something stronger than water; my head is still throbbing. A man can pass his time most pleasantly here, I can see that. I love open-handed hospitality and it pleases me all the more, I must admit, when I'm being entertained from the bottom of the heart and not out of any selfish interest. Then, too, the Mayor's daughter isn't at all hard to look at, and her mother, for that matter, is an old fiddle on which one could still play a tune. . . . Yes, I don't know why, but really this sort of life is to my liking.

JUDGE [*entering and stopping, in an aside*]: Lord God, see me through this safely! My knees are simply caving in. [*Aloud, straightening up and clutching the sword at his side.*]

I have the honor of presenting myself: Lyapkin-Tyapkin, Collegiate Assessor and Judge of the District Court in this town!

HLESTACOV: Be seated, please. So you're the Judge here?

JUDGE: I was chosen for a three-year term by the gentry, ever so long ago, and I've continued on the bench right up to now.

HLESTACOV: I say, though, is there much in being a judge?

JUDGE: During my three-year terms I was proposed for the Order of St. Vladimir, Fourth Class, with the commendation of my superiors. [*Aside.*] I've got the money right in my fist—and my fist feels as if it were on fire.

HLESTACOV: Why, I like the Order of St. Vladimir. The Order of St. Anna, Third Class, isn't so much by comparison.

JUDGE [*aside, thrusting out his fist little by little*]: Lord God, I don't know what I'm sitting on. Just as though I were on pins and needles.

HLESTACOV: What's that you've got in your hand?

JUDGE [*losing his head and dropping the bank notes on the floor*]: Not a thing, sir—

HLESTACOV: What do you mean, not a thing? Isn't that money I see on the floor?

JUDGE [*shivering from head to foot*]: By no means, sir. [*Aside.*] Oh, God, I'm as good as up on charges right now! I can hear the Black Maria rattling up to fetch me away.

HLESTACOV [*picking up the bank notes*]: Yes, it's money, sure enough.

JUDGE [*aside*]: Well, it's all over; I'm lost—lost!

HLESTACOV: Tell you what: suppose you let me have this as a loan—

JUDGE [*hastily*]: Of course, sir, of course—with the greatest of pleasure! [*Aside.*] A little more boldly, now! Get me out of this, Most Holy Mother of God!

HLESTACOV: I've sort of run low on funds on my travels, don't you know, what with one thing and another. However, I'll send this right back to you from my country estate—

JUDGE: Good gracious, don't give it a thought! Why, this is such an honor. . . . Of course, with all my feeble powers . . . my striving and zeal for my superiors . . . I shall try to merit— [*Gets up from chair and stands at attention, his hands at his sides.*] I dare not impose my presence on you any further. Have you any instructions for me perhaps?

HLESTACOV: What instructions?

JUDGE: I mean, aren't you issuing any instructions for the District Court here?

HLESTACOV: Whatever for? For I have absolutely no concern with it at present; no, there are no instructions. Thanks, ever so much.

JUDGE [*aside, bowing and scraping as he makes his getaway*]: Well, the town is all ours now!

HLESTACOV: Fine fellow, the Judge.

POSTMASTER [*drawing himself up as he enters and clutching the sword at his side*]: I have the honor of presenting myself: Court Councilor Shpekin, the Postmaster.

HLESTACOV: Ah, do come in. I'm very fond of pleasant company. Sit down! You've always lived in this town— isn't that right?

POSTMASTER: Just so, sir.

HLESTACOV: Why, I like this little town. Of course, it hasn't got so much of a population—well, what of that? After all, it isn't a capital. Isn't that so—it isn't a capital, after all?

POSTMASTER: Absolutely so, sir.

HLESTACOV: For it's only at the capital that you'll find the *bon ton*—and no provincial geese. What's your opinion —isn't that so?

POSTMASTER: Just so, sir. [*Aside.*] I must say, though, that he isn't at all uppity; he asks about everything.

HLESTACOV: But just the same, you must admit that even in a small town it's possible to live one's life happily.

POSTMASTER: Just so, sir.

HLESTACOV: What, to my way of thinking, does a man need? All one needs is to be respected, to be loved sincerely —isn't that so?

POSTMASTER: That is absolutely correct.

HLESTACOV: To tell you the truth, I'm glad you are of the same opinion as myself. Of course, they'll call me an odd stick, but then that's the sort of nature I have. [*Soliloquizes, even while he is looking right into the* POSTMASTER'S *eyes.*] Guess I might as well make a touch from this Postmaster! [*Aloud.*] What an odd thing to happen to me; I ran absolutely short of funds during my travels. Could you possibly let me have three hundred as a loan?

POSTMASTER: Why not? I would deem it the greatest happiness. There you are, sir. At your service, with all my heart.

HLESTACOV: Very grateful to you. For, I must confess, I have a mortal dislike of denying myself anything while I'm traveling—and, besides, why in the world should I? Isn't that so?

POSTMASTER: Just so, sir. [*Stands up, draws himself erect, and holds on to his sword.*] I dare not impose my presence on you any longer. . . . Perhaps you have some criticism as to the management of the Post Office, sir?

HLESTACOV: No, not at all. [*Exit* POSTMASTER, *bowing and scraping.*] Postmaster, it seems to me that you, too, are a fine fellow. At least you're obliging! I like people like that.

VOICE [*off, quite audibly*]: What are you so scared about?

SUPERINTENDENT OF SCHOOLS [*he doesn't exactly enter, but is practically shoved through the door, right after the above speech; draws himself up, not without trembling, and clutches the sword at his side*]: I have the honor of presenting myself: Titular Councilor Hlopov, Superintendent of Schools—

HLESTACOV: Ah, do come in! Sit down, sit down! Care for a cigar? [*Offering cigar.*]

SUPERINTENDENT OF SCHOOLS [*soliloquizing as he hesi-*

tates]: There's a comeuppance! That's something I'd never foreseen. To take or not to take?

HLESTACOV: Take it, take it! It's a rather decent smoke. Of course not the same thing as at the capital. There, my friend, I'm used to corona-corona-coronas, at twenty-five the hundred; you simply have to blow a kiss after smoking one. Here's a light—get it going. [*Offers light.* SUPERINTENDENT OF SCHOOLS *tries to light cigar, at the same time trembling all over.*] You're lighting it from the wrong end.

SUPERINTENDENT OF SCHOOLS [*soliloquizing, as he drops the cigar from sheer fright and gives up, with a hopeless gesture*]: The devil take it all! My damned timidity has been the ruin of me!

HLESTACOV: You, I can see, are no great lover of cigars. Yet I confess they're a weakness of mine. And also as far as the feminine sex is concerned—I simply can't remain indifferent. What about you? Which do you prefer—blondes or brunettes? [*The* SUPERINTENDENT OF SCHOOLS *is at a total loss as to what to say.*] Now, do be frank with me— is it blondes or brunettes?

SUPERINTENDENT OF SCHOOLS: I dare not venture on an opinion.

HLESTACOV: No, no—don't try to wriggle out of it. I want to find out your taste, without fail.

SUPERINTENDENT OF SCHOOLS: I make so bold as to report. . . . [*Aside.*] Why, I myself don't know what I'm saying!

HLESTACOV: Ah, ah! So you won't tell me. Probably some little brunette has already smitten your heart. Confess— hasn't she? [*The* SUPERINTENDENT OF SCHOOLS *can't utter a word.*] Ah, ah! You've turned red—you see, you see! But why don't you say something?

SUPERINTENDENT OF SCHOOLS: I'm overcome with timidity, Your Hon . . . Excell . . . High. . . . [*Aside.*] My confounded tongue has sold me out! It has sold me out!

HLESTACOV: Overcome by timidity, are you? Well, there really is something about my eyes that inspires timidity. At least I know that there isn't a woman living who can resist them—isn't that so?

SUPERINTENDENT OF SCHOOLS: Just so, sir.

HLESTACOV: However, a deucedly odd thing has happened to me: I've run entirely out of funds on the road. Could you possibly let me have a loan of three hundred?

SUPERINTENDENT OF SCHOOLS [*soliloquizing as he gropes in his pocket*]: What a fix I'll be in if I haven't the money on me! I have it, I have it! [*Takes out bank notes and offers them with fear and trembling.*]

HLESTACOV: Thanks, ever so much.

SUPERINTENDENT OF SCHOOLS [*drawing himself up and clutching his sword*]: I dare not impose my presence on you any longer—

HLESTACOV: Good-by!

SUPERINTENDENT OF SCHOOLS [*aside, as he scuttles out, practically at a run*]: There, glory be to God! Chances are he won't as much as look in at my classes.

DIRECTOR OF CHARITIES [*drawing himself up as he enters and clutching his sword*]: I have the honor of presenting myself: Court Councilor Zemlyanika, Director of Charities!

HLESTACOV: How d'you do! I beg you to be seated.

DIRECTOR OF CHARITIES: I had the honor of accompanying you on your tour of inspection and of receiving you personally in the eleemosynary institutions entrusted to my care.

HLESTACOV: Ah, yes, I remember. You tendered me a most excellent luncheon.

DIRECTOR OF CHARITIES: Only too happy to exert myself in the service of our native land!

HLESTACOV: It's a weakness of mine, I confess, but I do love good food. Tell me, please—it seems to me that you were somewhat shorter yesterday—isn't that so?

DIRECTOR OF CHARITIES: That's very possible. [*After a brief silence.*] I may say that I spare no effort and fulfill my duties zealously. [*Inching forward together with his chair and speaking in a low voice.*] It's the Postmaster here who does absolutely nothing; all his affairs are much neglected; the outgoing mail is always held up . . . you can find out the specific details yourself, if you wish. The Judge, too—he's the one who was here a little while before me—all he knows is to go riding after rabbits; he keeps dogs in the courthouse, and his whole conduct—if I may be frank with you—of course it's for the good of the State that I must do this, even though he's related to me and is a friend of mine —his conduct is most prejudicial. There's a certain land-owner hereabouts; they call him Dobchinski—you've seen him around, I dare say. Well, no sooner does this Dobchinski step out of his house than the Judge is already there, sitting with Dobchinski's wife. I'm ready to take my oath on that. And make a point of looking the little Dobchinskis over; there isn't a one that looks like Dobchinski, but every one of them, even the little girl, is the spit and image of the Judge—

HLESTACOV: You don't say! Why, I'd never even think that.

DIRECTOR OF CHARITIES: And then there's the Superinten-dent of the Schools here. I don't know how the Adminis-tration could ever entrust him with such a post. He's worse than any Red, and he instills the youth with such pernicious doctrines as it would be difficult even to describe. If you care to give me instructions to that effect, I could report on all this ever so much better in black and white—

HLESTACOV: Very well—let it be done in black and white. It'll please me very much. I'm sort of fond, don't you know, of reading something amusing whenever I'm bored. What's your name? I keep forgetting it.

DIRECTOR OF CHARITIES: Zemlyanika.

HLESTACOV: Ah, yes—Zemlyanika. Well, now, tell me, please: have you any little ones?

DIRECTOR OF CHARITIES: Why, naturally, sir: five—two of them are grown up by now.

HLESTACOV: You don't say! Already grown up? And what do you . . . how are they—

DIRECTOR OF CHARITIES: You are pleased to ask, I take it, what they are called?

HLESTACOV: That's it; how are they called?

DIRECTOR OF CHARITIES: Nicolai, Ivan, Elizaveta, Maria, and Perepetuya.

HLESTACOV: Fine, fine!

DIRECTOR OF CHARITIES: I dare not impose my presence upon you any further ... to infringe upon the time dedicated to your consecrated duties— [*Bowing and scraping as a preliminary to leaving.*]

HLESTACOV [*seeing him to the door*]: No, not at all. All that you've told me is most amusing. Please pay me another call sometime. I love that sort of thing, very much. [DIRECTOR OF CHARITIES *steps through door;* HLESTACOV *closes it but immediately goes back and, opening it, calls after him.*] Hey, there! What do they call you? I keep forgetting your full name.

DIRECTOR OF CHARITIES [*in doorway*]: Artemii Philipovich Zemlyanika.

HLESTACOV: If you'll be so kind, Artemii Philipovich: I'm in an odd fix—I've run all out of funds during my travels. Have you four hundred on you by any chance that you could lend me—

DIRECTOR OF CHARITIES [*proffering bank notes*]: I have.

HLESTACOV: It comes in quite handy, I must say. Thanks, ever so much.

[*Exit* DIRECTOR OF CHARITIES. *Enter* BOBCHINSKI *and* DOBCHINSKI.]

BOBCHINSKI: I have the honor of presenting myself: Peter Ivanovich Bobchinski. I'm a landowner, living in this town.

DOBCHINSKI: Peter Ivanovich Dobchinski, a landowner.

HLESTACOV: Ah, I've already seen you around. [*To* BOBCHINSKI.] I believe you fell that time—and how is your nose now?

BOBCHINSKI: Glory be— Please don't worry on that score; there's a scab on it now—a perfect scab.

HLESTACOV: A fortunate thing, that scab. Happy to hear

about it. [*With unexpected abruptness*.] Got any money on you?

BOBCHINSKI: Money? What money?

HLESTACOV: A thousand—to lend me.

BOBCHINSKI: I swear to God I have no such sum on me. But perhaps you have, Peter Ivanovich?

DOBCHINSKI: Not on me, I haven't. All my funds, I must inform you, are placed with the Board of Guardians.

HLESTACOV: Well, if you haven't all of a thousand, have you a hundred or so, perhaps?

BOBCHINSKI [*rummaging through his pockets*]: Have you a hundred on you, Peter Ivanovich? All I have is forty, in bank notes.

DOBCHINSKI [*looking in his wallet*]: All I have is twenty-five.

BOBCHINSKI: Oh, look a little better, Peter Ivanovich! I know you have a hole in your right-hand pocket—surely something must have slipped down the lining of the coat.

DOBCHINSKI: No, really, there's nothing even in the lining.

HLESTACOV: Well, it doesn't really matter. I thought I'd ask. Very well—sixty-five will do. It doesn't matter. [*Accepts money*.]

DOBCHINSKI: I make so bold as to make a request of you, concerning a certain very delicate matter.

HLESTACOV: Just what is it?

DOBCHINSKI: It's of a very delicate nature; my eldest son, may it please you, was born to me before my marriage.

HLESTACOV: Really?

DOBCHINSKI: In a manner of speaking, that is; but he was born to me just as if in wedlock, and I consummated everything properly afterward, through the legal bonds of matrimony, sir. So, may it please you, I would like him to be an entirely legitimate son of mine, as it were, sir, and to have him bear the same name as myself: Dobchinski, sir.

HLESTACOV: Very well, let him be called thus! It can be done.

DOBCHINSKI: I wouldn't trouble you, but I feel sorry for him, on account of his capabilities. He's a lad of great promise; he can recite all sorts of verse and, if a jackknife is handy, he can whittle out a tiny carriage right on the spot, as deftly as any sleight-of-hand artist. There, Peter Ivanovich knows that, too.

BOBCHINSKI: Yes, he's quite a capable lad.

HLESTACOV: Fine, fine—I'll exert myself in this matter; I'll put in a word or two. All this will be managed—I hope. Yes, yes! [To BOBCHINSKI.] Perhaps there's something you wish to say to me?

BOBCHINSKI: Of course—I have a most important request—

HLESTACOV: Well, what is it? What about?

BOBCHINSKI: I beg of you most humbly, when you go to the capital tell all those different high dignitaries, all those senators and admirals, now—tell them that, now, "Your Serenity—or Your Excellency—there's a Peter Ivanovich Bobchinski living in such-and-such a town." Tell 'em just that: "There's a Peter Ivanovich Bobchinski living in such-and-such a town."

HLESTACOV: Very good.

BOBCHINSKI: And should you have occasion to speak to the Sovereign, then tell it to the Sovereign as well; that, now, "Your Imperial Majesty, there's a Peter Ivanovich Bobchinski living in such-and-such a town—"

HLESTACOV: Very good!

DOBCHINSKI: Excuse us for having put you out so with our presence.

BOBCHINSKI: Excuse us for having put you out so with our presence.

HLESTACOV: Not at all, not at all. It has been a great pleasure for me. [Gets rid of them. Solo.] There's certainly a slew of officials here. It seems to me, however, that they must take me for a State dignitary. I must have thrown plenty of dust in their eyes yesterday. What a pack of fools! I guess I'll write about all this to the capital, to Tryapichkin. He dashes off articles and things now and then; let him give them a thorough going-over. Hey, there, Ossip! [OSSIP *pops his head through doorway*.] Fetch me paper and ink.

OSSIP: Right away! [*Disappears*.]

HLESTACOV: And as for Tryapichkin, really, if he ever sinks his teeth into anybody, he's a caution! He wouldn't spare his own father to put a joke over. And he's fond of the coin, too. However, these officials are a kindly lot; that's a good trait of theirs, making me all those loans. Let's see, now, how much money I have exactly. There's three hundred—that's from the Judge. There's another three hundred—that's from the Postmaster. Six hundred, seven hundred, eight hundred—what a filthy bill! Eight hundred, nine hundred . . . Oho, it's over a thousand! Well, now, my Captain of Infantry! Well, you just cross my path now! We'll see who will trim whom at stuss! [*Enter* OSSIP, *with paper and ink*.] Well, you fool, you see how they receive and entertain me? [*Begins writing*.]

OSSIP: Yes, glory be to God! The only thing is . . . You know what?

HLESTACOV: Well, what is it?

OSSIP: Make your getaway. Honest to God, it's time.

HLESTACOV [*writing*]: What bosh! Why should I?

OSSIP: Oh, just so. God be with all of them! You've had a fine time here for a couple of days; well, let that do you. What's the use of getting tangled up with them for long? Give 'em up! Cut it too fine—and somebody else will come along. By God, that's so, Ivan Alexandrovich! And you can hire such dandy horses here—how they'd dash off with you!

HLESTACOV [*writing*]: No. I want to stay on here for a while. We'll go tomorrow, perhaps.

OSSIP: Don't talk of tomorrow! Really, Ivan Alexandrovich, let's get away from here. It's sure a great honor for you, but just the same, you know, it would be better to make tracks as quickly as we can. They must have taken you for somebody else, sure enough—and your father will be ever so angry at you for delaying so long. So really, we ought to dash away in a blaze of glory! And they'd give us fine horses here—

HLESTACOV [*writing*]: Very well, then. Only first of all send off this letter, and you might as well get an order for the post horses at the same time. But watch out that you get good horses. Tell the drivers that I'll give a cart wheel to each one of 'em—so's they'll dash along as if I were an Imperial Courier! And so's they'll sing their songs for me! [*Continuing to write.*] I can just imagine it: Tryapichkin will die laughing—

OSSIP: I'll send it off with one of the men here, sir, whilst I'd better be packing so's not to waste time.

HLESTACOV [*writing*]: Good idea. But bring me a candle.

OSSIP [*going out and speaking off*]: Hey there, brother! You'll bring a letter over to the post office, and tell the Postmaster to frank it, and tell 'em to bring up their best troika for my master—a courier's troika—and they'd best be quick about it; as for the mileage, tell 'em my master rides free; tell 'em the mileage is at government expense. And snap it up, all around, for otherwise, now, my master will be angry. Hold on, the letter isn't ready yet.

HLESTACOV [*still writing*]: I'm curious—where's he living now? On Post Office Street or Gorohovaya? For he, too, likes to change his rooms often—it's cheaper than paying rent. I'll take a chance and address this to Post Office Street.

[*Folds letter, forming it into an envelope, and addresses it.* OSSIP *brings in candle.* HLESTACOV *seals letter.*]

DERZHIMORDA'S VOICE [*off*]: Hey there, you with the beard! The orders is not to let nobody in, I'm telling you!

HLESTACOV [*handing letter to* OSSIP]: There, get that off.

SHOPKEEPERS [*off*]: Let us through, like a good man! You can't keep us out! We're here on business—

DERZHIMORDA'S VOICE: Move on, move on, now! Break it up! He ain't seeing nobody; he's sleeping now.

[*Hubbub increases.*]

HLESTACOV: What's going on there, Ossip? See what that noise is.

OSSIP [*looking through window*]: Some shopkeepers or other; they want to come in but the policeman won't let them through. They're waving papers—probably want to see you.

HLESTACOV [*walking up to window*]: Well, what is it you wish, my dear friends?

SHOPKEEPERS [*off*]: We appeal to Your Worship! Sir, order them to accept our petition!

HLESTACOV: Let 'em in—let 'em in! Let 'em come in. Ossip, tell 'em they can come in [*Exit* OSSIP. HLESTACOV *receives the petitions through the window, unrolls one of them and reads it aloud.*] "To His Nobly Born Serenity, Master of Finance, from Abdulin the Merchant—" what the devil is all this; there isn't any such rank or title, as a matter of fact! [*The* SHOPKEEPERS *troop in.*] Well, what is it you wish, my dear friends?

SHOPKEEPERS [*bowing very low*]: We prostrate ourselves before Your Worship!—We appeal to your mercy!

HLESTACOV: But just what is it you want?

SHOPKEEPERS: Save us from ruin, sir!—We suffer grievous and most unjust oppression!

HLESTACOV: From whom?

ABDULIN: Why, it's all because of the Mayor of this here town. Sir, there has never been such another Mayor as this one. He puts such wrongs upon us as are past all describing. He's been the death of us, entirely, what with his billeting and all—we might as well put our heads in the noose. He don't act rightly, he don't. He grabs you by the beard and calls you a furriner and a vagabond. Honest to God! If it were a matter of our not having paid him proper respects, now, in anything; but no, we always does the right thing; we never kick about comin' across with whatever's owin' to him, cloth for his wife's dresses, say, or his daughter's. But no; all that is too little for him, you see. So help us God—so help us! He'll barge into the store and take whatever comes to his hand; if he lays his eyes on a bolt of cloth, he'll say: "Eh, my dear fellow, that's a fine piece of cloth— bring it over to my house!" Well, naturally, you bring it over—and yet there may be all of fifty yards in that bolt.

HLESTACOV: Really, now? Ah, what a swindler he is!

ABDULIN: Honest to God, there's nobody can recall such another Mayor! You simply gotta hide everything in the shop as soon as you catch sight of him—

ANOTHER SHOPKEEPER: We're not saying anything, even, about delicacies of any sort—but he'll grab at all sorts of trash: prunes that may have been moldering in a barrel for seven years, that no clerk of mine would touch, even—but no, he'll sink his whole paw in that there barrel—

THIRD SHOPKEEPER: When his birthday rolls around, on St. Anthony's day, it sure don't look like we'd overlooked him in any way; there's nary a thing lacking. But no, you gotta to come across with more offerings later—he's got a birthday for every Saint on the calendar! So what can a body do? You give him birthday presents on all the other days as well.

HLESTACOV: Why, he's no better than a highwayman!

ABDULIN: Aye, aye, by God! But you just dare to let a peep out of you, and he'll march a whole regiment up to your house and billet them on you. And, if there's the least objections, he gives orders to put a lock on the shop-door. "I," he says, "ain't goin' to subject you to no corporal punishment, nor to put you to no torture. Them things," he says, "is forbidden by law, but, my dear friend I'll have you livin' off of herring—and that without a drop of water!"

HLESTACOV: Oh, what a swindler! Why, he ought to be sent straight to Siberia for that!

ABDULIN: Why, it don't really matter where Your Worship may pack him off to—so long, that is, as he's as far from us as possible. Don't disdain our marks of hospitality, our Father. We offer you these here heads of sugar, and this hamper of wine.

HLESTACOV: No, you really must not think that of me; I never take any bribes whatsover. On the other hand, if you were to suggest lending me three hundred, for example, it might be an entirely different matter; a loan is something I can accept.

SHOPKEEPERS: If you will favor us, our Father!— [*Dig up bills and coins.*] Better take five hundred, only help us out!

HLESTACOV: I won't have a word to say against a loan. If you like, I'll accept it.

ABDULIN [*offering* HLESTACOV *the money on a silver platter*]: There, if it please you—take the silver platter at the same time.

HLESTACOV: Very well; I can take the little silver platter as well.

SHOPKEEPERS [*bowing*]: Do take the sugar, too, at the same time.

HLESTACOV: Oh, no; I never take any bribes of any sort—

OSSIP: Why don't you take them things, Your Honor? Take 'em! They'll come in handy on the road. Let's have them sugar loaves here, and that hamper! Let's have everything. It'll all come in useful. What you got there—a bit of rope? Let's have that bit of rope too! Even a bit of rope can come in handy; if a cart breaks down, or something like that, it can be spliced together.

ABDULIN: So do us that favor, Your Serenity. For if you don't help us out with our petition, now, then we really don't know what's to become of us; we might as well put our heads in a noose.

HLESTACOV: Absolutely, absolutely! I'll do my best.

[*Exit* SHOPKEEPERS.]

WOMAN'S VOICE [*off*]: No, you dassn't keep me out! I'll complain against you to the great man himself! Don't you push me so hard—it hurts!

HLESTACOV: Who's that? [*Walks up to window.*] And what's the matter with you, mother?

VOICES OF TWO WOMEN: I ask for your mercy, Father! Master, order them to let us in—hear us out!

HLESTACOV [*through window*]: Let 'em come in.

KEYSMITH'S WIFE [*bowing very low before* HLESTACOV *as she rushes on*]: I ask your mercy!

CORPORAL'S WIDOW [*same business*]: I ask your mercy!

HLESTACOV: Why, who might you women be?

CORPORAL'S WIDOW: I'm the widow of Ivanov—a corporal, he was.

KEYSMITH'S WIFE: I'm a keysmith's wife, living in this town—Threbronia Petrovna Poshlepkina; my father was—

HLESTACOV: Hold on; speak one at a time. [*To* KEYSMITH'S WIFE.] What is it you want?

KEYSMITH'S WIFE: I crave your mercy! I am complaining against the Mayor! May God send him every sort of evil, so that neither his children, nor he himself, swindler that he is, nor his uncles, nor his aunts, may have good or gain in anything!

HLESTACOV: Come, what is it?

KEYSMITH'S WIFE: Why, he ordered my husband to be clipped short for a soldier, and yet it weren't our turn yet, swindler that he is! And besides, it's agin the law: my husband's a married man.

HLESTACOV: How could he ever do such a thing?

KEYSMITH'S WIFE: He done it! The swindler, he done it! May God strike him down in this world and the next! And if he's got an aunt, may every nasty thing befall her, and if his father be living, may he croak, the dog, or choke forever and ever, swindler that he is. It was the tailor's son that should have been took, and he's a miserable little drunkard to boot, only his parents come across with an expensive present, so the Mayor he went after the son of Panteleievna, the merchant's wife; well, Panteleievna in her turn sent the Mayor's wife three bolts of linen; so then he tackles me: "What do you want with a husband?" he says. "He's of no use to you any more." But I'm the one that knows whether he's of any use or not; that's my affair, you scalawag, you. "He's a thief," he says, "he mayn't have stolen nothing yet, but that don't make no difference," he says, "he's goin' to steal; and even without that he'll be took for a recruit next year." Why, what will it be like for me without a husband, you scalawag, you? I'm a weak human critter, you low-down thief, you! May all your kin and kindred never see God's own daylight, and if you've got a mother-in-law, may even your mother-in-law—

HLESTACOV [*getting the old woman out of the room*]: Very good, very good! [*Turning to the* CORPORAL'S WIDOW.] Well, and what about you?

KEYSMITH'S WIFE [*leaving*]: So don't forget, our Father! Be merciful to us! [*Exit.*]

CORPORAL'S WIDOW: I've come to complain against the Mayor, Father—

HLESTACOV: Yes, but what is it? For what reason? Tell me in a few words.

CORPORAL'S WIDOW: He flogged me, Father.

HLESTACOV: How did that happen?

CORPORAL'S WIDOW: Through a mistake, my Father. Us women folk, now, got in a free-for-all on the market place, but the police didn't get there in time and they caught me instead. And they let me have it so good and hot that I couldn't sit down for two days.

HLESTACOV: But what can one do about it now?

CORPORAL'S WIDOW: Well, naturally, there's nothing to be done now. But you might order him to pay a fine for that there mistake. There ain't no use of me turning down any bit of good luck, and the money would come in right handy now.

HLESTACOV: Very good, very good. Run along, run along. I'll look into it. [*Shoos her out. Hands, waving petitions, are thrust in through window.*] Who else is out there? [*Walks up to window.*] I don't want 'em, I don't want 'em! Don't need 'em, don't need 'em! [*Leaving window.*] I'm fed up with 'em, the devil take it! Don't let anybody in, Ossip!

OSSIP [*shouting out of the window*]: Get going! Get going! Come around tomorrow. [*Door is pushed open and some sort of woebegone figure in a shoddy overcoat emerges —unshaven, with a swollen lip and his cheek tied up. Several others appear behind him.*] Get out, get out! What's the idea of barging in here? [*Shoves against intruder's belly and squeezes through door together with him, at the same time slamming door to.*]

MARIA [*entering girlishly*]: Ah!

HLESTACOV: What has frightened you so, ma'am?

MARIA: No, I wasn't frightened—

HLESTACOV [*posturing*]: I must say, ma'am, I'm very much pleased at being taken for the sort of man who ... Where did you intend to go, if I may ask?

MARIA: Really, I wasn't going anywhere in particular.

HLESTACOV: But just why weren't you going anywhere in particular?

MARIA: I thought perhaps Mamma dear was here—

HLESTACOV: No, I'd really like to know why you weren't going anywhere in particular—

MARIA: I've intruded on you. You must have been engaged in important matters.

HLESTACOV [*posturing more than ever*]: Why, what are important matters compared with your eyes? ... You couldn't possibly intrude on me; on the contrary, your presence is such a pleasure!

MARIA: You talk just the way they do in the capital—

HLESTACOV: Only to such a bewitching person as yourself. May I offer you a chair—it would make me so happy. But no, you ought to have a throne and not a mere chair—

MARIA: Really, I don't know. ... I really did have to go. [*Sits down.*]

HLESTACOV: What a beautiful kerchief!

MARIA: Oh, now you're making fun of me! Anything to have a laugh at us provincials!

HLESTACOV: Oh, how I wish I were your kerchief, that I might clasp your little lily-white neck!

MARIA: I absolutely can't understand what you're admiring so; it's just an ordinary kerchief. ...What queer weather we're having today—

HLESTACOV: But what does any weather matter, ma'am, compared with your lips?

MARIA: You persist in saying such odd things. ... I'd like to ask you to write some sort of a little poem for my album instead. You probably know a lot of poems.

HLESTACOV: For you, ma'am—anything you desire. Merely demand whatever sort of poem you wish.

MARIA: Something sort of. . . . Something good—new.

HLESTACOV: Oh, what do poems matter! I know no end of them.

MARIA: Yes, but tell me—just what will you write?

HLESTACOV: Oh, what's the use of repeating the lines—I can write them down without that!

MARIA: I'm ever so fond of poems—

HLESTACOV: Yes, I've a great stock of them, of all sorts. Well, if you like, I'll give you this one of mine: "All the world's a stage, and all the men and women merely players." Well, now, I've written others, too. Can't remember 'em all now; however, it doesn't really matter. Instead of that I'd rather symbolize my love which, because of your glance— [*Edges his chair nearer.*]

MARIA: Love! I don't understand love. I've never even known what love is— [*Moves her chair away.*]

HLESTACOV: But why do you move your chair away? It'll be better if we sit closer to each other.

MARIA [*moving her chair away*]: But why closer? It's just as well if there's some distance between us.

HLESTACOV [*edging his chair nearer*]: But why the distance—it's just as well if we're closer.

MARIA [*moving away*]: But what's all this for?

HLESTACOV [*edging nearer*]: Why, it merely seems to you that the chairs are close together, but what you ought to do is imagine that they're at a distance from each other. How happy it would make me, ma'am, if I could clasp you in my embraces—

MARIA [*glancing out of the window*]: What was that? Something seems to have flown past. Is it a magpie? Or some other bird?

HLESTACOV [*kissing her shoulder and glancing through window*]: That's a magpie.

MARIA [*getting up indignantly*]: No, this is too much! What impudence!

HLESTACOV [*detaining her*]: Forgive me, ma'am! I did it out of love, purely out of love.

MARIA: You must consider me some sort of a country girl— [*Makes an effort to leave.*]

HLESTACOV [*still detaining her*]: Yes, out of love—really, it was out of love. Don't be angry at me, Maria Antonovna —I was only joking! I'm ready to get down on my knees to beg your forgiveness. [*Falls on his knees.*] Forgive me— do forgive me! There, you see, I'm on my knees before you!

ANNA [*entering and catching sight of* HLESTACOV *kneeling*]: Ah, what a situation!

HLESTACOV [*scrambling to his feet*]: Eh, the devil take it!

ANNA [*turning on her daughter*]: What is the meaning of this, miss? What sort of behavior is this?

MARIA: Why, Mamma dear, I—

ANNA: Get out of here! Do you hear me—out, out, and don't dare show me your face again! [*Exit* MARIA, *in girlish tears.* ANNA *turns to* HLESTACOV.] Excuse me, please, but I must confess I am so astonished—

HLESTACOV [*aside*]: She, too, is most appealing—very far from bad. [*Throws himself on his knees before* ANNA.] Madam, you can see that I am consumed by love!

ANNA: What, you're on your knees? Ah, get up, get up; the floor is so dusty here!

HLESTACOV: I must learn on my knees—absolutely on my knees!—what my fate is to be: life or death!

ANNA: Really, you must excuse me, but I still can't grasp fully the significance of your words. If I'm not mistaken you're making a request for my daughter's hand—

HLESTACOV: No, it's you I'm in love with! My life hangs on a thread. If you do not crown my undying love, then I am unworthy of earthly existence. With my heart being consumed by flames I supplicate your hand—

ANNA: But, if you will permit me to remark, I am, in a sort of a way . . . married!

HLESTACOV: Oh, that! Love knows no such distinctions, and one of our greatest poets has said: " 'Tis but the laws that condemn." We shall withdraw to some shady stream. Your hand—I crave your hand!

MARIA [*dashing in unexpectedly*]: Mamma dear, Papa

dear said for you to— [*Cries out as she sees* HLESTACOV *kneeling.*] Ah, what a situation!

ANNA: Well, what's got into you? You run in all of a sudden like a cat with conniption fits. There, what do you find so astonishing? What ideas have you gotten into your head? Really, you're like some three-year-old child. It doesn't look in the least as if the girl were eighteen—it doesn't, it doesn't at all! I don't know when you'll become more prudent, when you're going to conduct yourself like a decently brought up young lady, when you will know what the proprieties are, or what decorous demeanor is.

MARIA [*through her tears*]: Really, Mamma dear, I had no idea—

ANNA: There's a draft or something blowing through your head all the time; you are taking Judge Lyapkin-Tyapkin's daughters as your example. Why should you look at them? You shouldn't look at them. You have other examples before you; you have your own mother before your own eyes. There, that's the sort of example you ought to follow.

HLESTACOV [*seizing* MARIA'S *hand but addressing the mother*]: Do not oppose our well-being—bless a constant love!

ANNA [*in astonishment*]: So it's she whom you—

HLESTACOV: Decide: is it life or death?

ANNA [*to* MARIA]: There, you see, you fool? There, you see, it's because of you, because of such an insignificant little baggage, that our guest was pleased to get down on his knees. But no, you have to burst in all of a sudden like a madwoman. There, really, it would serve you right if I were deliberately to refuse him; you aren't worthy of such good fortune.

[HLESTACOV *gets up, brushes his knees.*]

MARIA: I won't act like that in the future, Mamma dear; I won't, honest!

MAYOR [*dashing in, much upset, to* HLESTACOV]: Your Excellency! Do not ruin me! Do not ruin me!

HLESTACOV: What is the matter with you?

MAYOR: Those shopkeepers were complaining to Your

Excellency. I assure you on my honor that not even half of what they're saying is true. They themselves deceive the public and give false weights and measures. The Corporal's widow told you a pack of lies if she claimed I flogged her. She lies! I swear to God she lies. She flogged her own self.

HLESTACOV: The Corporal's widow be damned. I have other things on my mind.

MAYOR: Don't you believe her—don't you believe her! They're all such liars—not even a child that high would believe them. Why, the whole town knows them for liars by now. And as for swindling, I make so bold as to inform you that they're swindlers whose like the world hasn't yet produced.

ANNA: Do you know what honor Ivan Alexandrovich is bestowing upon us? He is asking for the hand of our daughter.

MAYOR: What? What? You're out of your head, Mother! Please restrain your wrath, Your Excellency! She's a little touched—and her mother was the same way.

HLESTACOV: Yes, I really am asking for your daughter's hand. I am in love with her.

MAYOR: I find it impossible to believe, Your Excellency.

ANNA: Not even when you're told so?

HLESTACOV: I'm telling you this in all seriousness. I may go out of my head because of love!

MAYOR: I dare not believe; I am unworthy of such an honor.

HLESTACOV: Yes. If you won't consent to give me Maria Antonovna's hand, I'm ready to do the devil knows what.

MAYOR: I cannot believe it; You are pleased to jest, Your Excellency.

ANNA: Ah, what a blockhead you really are! When he's trying to get the idea into your head!

MAYOR: I cannot believe it.

HLESTACOV: Give her to me—give her to me! I am a desperate man; I am ready for anything; if I shoot myself you'll be hauled up for trial before the court.

MAYOR: Ah, my God! I'm innocent, body and soul—I swear it, I swear it. Please don't be angry! I'll do whatever your mercy may command me to do! To tell you the truth, my head right now is. . . . I don't rightly know myself what's going on in there. I've become such an utter fool now as never before—

ANNA: Well, give them your blessing!

[HLESTACOV *approaches the* MAYOR, *leading* MARIA *by the hand.*]

MAYOR: Ay, may God bless you both—but I'm innocent, I tell you! [HLESTACOV *kisses* MARIA, *while the* MAYOR *stares at them.*] What the devil! It's really true! [*Rubs his eyes.*] They're kissing. Ah, my sainted aunt, they're kissing! He's her bridegroom, sure enough! [*Shouts and hops about in joy.*] Ah, Tony! Ah, Tony! Ah, you Mayor! So that's the way things are going now!

OSSIP [*entering*]: The horses are waiting.

HLESTACOV: Ah . . . very well. I'll be ready right away.

MAYOR: What? Are you leaving us?

HLESTACOV: Yes, I'm leaving.

MAYOR: But just when, may I ask? You yourself were pleased to hint, it seems, at a wedding.

HLESTACOV: Why, it'll be for just a minute, so to say. For a single day, to see an uncle of mine—a rich old codger —and I'll start back no later than tomorrow.

MAYOR: I dare not detain you in any way and hope for your propitious return.

HLESTACOV: Of course, of course, I'll be back in a wink. Good-by, my love . . . no, I simply can't express all I feel. Good-by, dearest! [*Kisses* MARIA'S *hand.*]

MAYOR: Isn't there anything you need for your trip, perhaps? You were pleased to say, I think, that you were short of cash.

HLESTACOV: Oh, no, no need of that at all. [*After a moment's reflection.*] On the other hand, why not, if you feel so inclined—

MAYOR: How much would you like?

HLESTACOV: Well, you gave me two hundred that time—

that is, not two hundred but four—I wouldn't want to take advantage of your error; so, if you like, give me the same amount now, so's to make it an even eight hundred.

MAYOR: In a moment! [*Takes bills out of his wallet.*] And, as if on purpose, it's all in crisp, new bills.

HLESTACOV: Ah, yes, just so. [*Takes bills and examines them.*] A very good thing, that. For they do say it brings new luck to be given new bills.

MAYOR: Precisely, sir.

HLESTACOV: Good-by, Anton Antonovich! I'm very much indebted to you for your hospitality. I confess with all my heart that I've never been so well received anywhere. Good-by, Anna Andreievna! Good-by, Maria Antonovna, my love!

[*Exit, followed by* OSSIP *and all the others.*]

[*Off*]:

HLESTACOV'S VOICE: Good-by, Maria Antonovna, my soul's angel!

MAYOR'S VOICE: But how can you ride in that wretched post carriage?

HLESTACOV'S VOICE: Why, I've gotten used to that. Springs make my head ache.

DRIVER'S VOICE: Whoa, there!

MAYOR'S VOICE: Cover the seat with something, at least— even a mat. Would you care to? I'll order a mat to be brought.

HLESTACOV: No, what in the world for? It's a trifling matter. On the other hand—yes, let 'em bring a mat, if you like.

MAYOR'S VOICE: Hey, there, Avdotya! Go to the store-room and take out a rug. The best one, the Persian one with the blue background! And be quick about it.

DRIVER'S VOICE: Whoa, there!

MAYOR'S VOICE: When may we expect you, then?

HLESTACOV'S VOICE: Tomorrow, or the day after.

OSSIP'S VOICE: Is that the rug? Let's have it here. Put it down—that's it! Now let's have some hay on this side.

DRIVER'S VOICE: Whoa, there!

OSSIP'S VOICE: Here, put some hay on this side. Right here! Some more! That's fine. Now it'll be grand! [*Slaps rug.*] Now you can take your seat, Your Honor!

HLESTACOV'S VOICE: Good-by, Anton Antonovich!

MAYOR'S VOICE: Good-by, Your Excellency!

FEMININE VOICES: Good-by, Ivan Alexandrovich!

HLESTACOV'S VOICE: Good-by, Mamma dear!

[*Sound of a short kiss. Pause. Sound of a prolonged kiss.*]

DRIVER'S VOICE: Giddap, me darlin'!

[*Sound of jingle bells, receding.*]

CURTAIN

[*Slow, coming down completely only as the last sound of the jingle bells dies away.*]

Scene II

Scene: Same evening. At rise: MAYOR, ANNA, *and* MARIA.

MAYOR: Well, now, Anna Andreievna? Eh? Did you ever think of such a thing as this? What a rich prize, devil take it! There, own up—you never even dreamt of it. From an ordinary Mayor's lady and then—holy hell—to become related to such a devil of a fellow!

ANNA: Not at all. I knew it all along. It's such a rarity for you because you're so common; you've never met any decent people.

MAYOR: Mother, I myself am a decent person. But really, now, when one stops to think of it, Anna Andreievna—what fine-feathered birds you and I have now become! Eh, Anna Andreievna? We can fly high now, the devil take it! You just wait—now's the time when I'll make it hot for all those who were so ready to lodge complaints and denunciations against me! [*Opening door a trifle.*] Hey, who's there? [*Enter* PUGOVITZIN.] Ah, it's you, Pugovitzin! Brother, you just summon all the shopkeepers here. I'll fix those dogs! So they're going to complain against me, are they? Why, the damned pack of Judases! You just wait, my darlings! Up to now I've been just going easy with you; you'll find out what real hell is now! Make a list of every man jack who as much as came here to complain against me. And, above all, make a note of those writing fellows— all those writing gents, now, who made up the petitions for the others. And proclaim it to everybody, so that all men may know: that, now, just look at what an honor God has bestowed upon your Mayor; he's going to marry his daughter off not to just any old commoner, but to such a grand man as the world has never yet seen, and who can do everything—everything, everything, everything! Proclaim it to everybody, so that all men may know. Cry it out to all the people; ring all the bells till they crack, the devil take it! If there's going to be a celebration, let it be an all-out one! [PUGOVITZIN *withdraws*.] So that's the way things are going, eh, Anna Andreievna? Well, what are our plans now —where are we going to live? Here or at the capital?

ANNA: At the capital, naturally. How could we ever stay on here?

MAYOR: Well, if it's the capital, the capital it is! But it would be well to stay on right here. Well, now, I guess we'll send mayoring to the devil, eh, Anna Andreievna?

ANNA: Naturally! The idea of being a mere mayor now!

MAYOR: Sure; we can go after a big position in society now. Don't you think, Anna Andreievna? For he's like that [*crosses index and middle fingers of right hand*]—with all the prime ministers and calls at Court; with a pull like that one can work things so's to get in right among the generals. What do you think, Anna Andreievna, can I get in among all those generals, or can't I?

ANNA: I should say so! Of course you can!

MAYOR: Ah, the devil take it, it's swell to be a general! They'll sling a pretty ribbon over my shoulder—and which do you think is better, Anna Andreievna: the red, for the Order of St. Anna, or the blue, for the White Eagle?

ANNA: The blue, of course.

MAYOR: See what the woman has set her heart on! Even a red ribbon would be good enough. Do you know why one wants to be a general? Because, if you have occasion to travel anywhere, you have aides and state couriers galloping ahead of you everywhere you go, demanding horses! And when you get to a post station there won't be anybody getting any horses; every living soul has to bide its turn. All those titled persons, and captains and mayors. But you don't give a good damn, even. You're dining at some governor's—and you simply snub a mayor if you see one standing around! [*Sniggers; sends out peal after peal of laughter; his laughter is simply killing him.*] There, damn it, that's what's so attractive!

ANNA: Anything that is coarse always appeals to you. You must remember that we'll have to change our course of life entirely, that our friends will no longer consist of a hound-loving Judge with whom you go chasing rabbits, or a charity-monger like Zemlyanika; on the contrary, your friends will be of the most ree-fined deportment: counts, and all sorts of society people. The only thing is, I'm really worried about you. At times you'll come out with some such phrase as is never heard in good society.

MAYOR: Damn it, what of it? Words will never hurt you.

ANNA: That sort of thing was well enough when you were Mayor. But life in the capital is altogether different.

MAYOR: Why, they say you can get two particular kinds of fish there so tasty they make your mouth water at the first bite—sea-eels and smelts—

ANNA: All he thinks of is seafood! I absolutely will have things my way. Our house must be the first one at the capital, and my boudoir must be so exquisitely lighted and so scented with ambergris that nobody will be able to set foot in it without puckering up the eyes—like this! [*Blinks her eyes and sniffs daintly.*] Ah, how splendid all this is!

[*Enter* SHOPKEEPERS, *sheepishly.*]

MAYOR: Ah, greetings to you, my fine-feathered friends!

SHOPKEEPERS [*bowing deeply*]: Greetings to you, Father!

MAYOR: Well, my darlings, how are you getting along? How are your goods moving? So, you tea-swilling, yard-stick-swinging swine got a notion of complaining against me, did you? You archknaves, you super-swindlers, you master-cheats and sea-monsters! You're going to complain, eh? Well? Did it get you much? Thought they'd just grab me and clap me into jail! Do you know, may seven devils and a witch take you, that—

ANNA: Ah, my God, what language you're using!

MAYOR [*ruffled*]: Eh, I have more than language to think of right now! [*Goes back to badgering the* SHOPKEEPERS.] Do you know that the very same official to whom you were complaining is now going to marry my daughter? What? Eh? What have you got to say now? Now I'll show you! Ooo-oo-oo-ooh! [*Singles out* ABDULIN.] You cheat the public. You'll get a contract from the Treasury, swindle it to the tune of a hundred thousand by supplying rotten cloth, and then sacrifice twenty yards to me—and you expect a medal for it? Why, if they were to know that, they'd take you and . . . Look at the way he shoves his belly out! He's a businessman; you dassn't touch him; "We won't take no back seat even for no gentry!" Why, a gentleman—damn your ugly-looking puss—a gentleman goes in for learning; even though they may beat him at school it's for a good purpose, so's he'll know whatever is useful. But what about you? You begin with knavish tricks; your boss beats you if you aren't skilled at cheating. While you're still a brat and don't know your paternoster yet, you're already giving short measure, and, soon as your belly fills out and you've got your pockets stuffed, you start in putting on airs! My, my, what a rare fellow! Just because you can drink seventeen samovars dry in a day you think it entitles you to put on airs? Why, I spit in your face, you and your airs!

ABDULIN [*leading the chorus of deeply bowing* SHOP-

KEEPERS]: We're at fault, Anton Antonovich.

MAYOR: Complain, will you? [*Again singling out* ABDU-
LIN.] But who was it helped you to put over that crooked
deal when you were building the bridge, and who entered
twenty thousand for lumber when there wasn't even a hundred's worth? It was me that helped you, you goat-beard!
That's something you forgot. If I'd told on you it would
have been my turn to pack you off to Siberia. What have
you to say to that? Eh?

ABDULIN: We're at fault before God, Anton Antonovich.
The sly Evil One tripped us up. And we'll take our oaths
not to complain from now on. We'll make it up to you in
any way you like, only don't be angry!

MAYOR: Don't be angry, eh? There, you're groveling at
my feet now. Why? Because I've got the upper hand. But
if things were going ever so little your way, why, you dog,
you'd grind me into the very mud—and sink me in with
a piledriver, on top of everything!

SHOPKEEPERS [*bowing to the* MAYOR'S *very feet*]: Don't
ruin us, Anton Antonovich!

MAYOR: "Don't ruin us!" Now it's "Don't ruin us!" But
what were you saying before? [*Ferociously menacing.*] Why,
I ought to take you and— [*With an "I-give-you-up!" gesture.*] Well, let God forgive you! Enough! I'm not the sort
to bear a grudge. Only, mind you, walk the chalk line from
now on! I'm not marrying my daughter off to just any ordinary squire. So let your congratulations be in keeping—
d'you understand? Don't think you can get away with some
measly side of salted sturgeon or a head of sugar! There,
go, and God go with ye!

[SHOPKEEPERS *crawl out. Enter* JUDGE *and* DIRECTOR
OF CHARITIES.]

JUDGE [*in the very doorway*]: Am I to believe the ru-
mors, Anton Antonovich? Fortune has been very good to
you!

DIRECTOR OF CHARITIES: I have the honor of congratulating you on your exceptional good fortune! I was sincerely

glad when I heard of it! [*Approaches* ANNA *and kisses her hand.*] Anna Andreievna! [*Repeats business with* MARIA.] Maria Antonovna!

RASTACOVSKI [*entering*]: I congratulate Anton Antonovich! May God prolong the lives of yourself and the young couple and give you a numerous posterity—grandchildren and great-grandchildren! Anna Andreievna! [*Approaches* ANNA *and kisses her hand.*] Maria Antonovna!

[*Repeats business. Enter* KOROBKIN *and his* WIFE, *and* LULUCOV.]

KOROBKIN: I have the honor of congratulating Anton Antonovich! [*Approaching* ANNA *and kissing her hand.*] Anna Andreievna! [*Repeating business with* MARIA.] Maria Antonovna!

KOROBKIN'S WIFE: I congratulate you with all my heart on your new good fortune, Anna Andreievna!

LULUCOV: I have the honor of congratulating you, Anna Andreievna! [*Kisses her hand; then, turning to spectators, clicks his tongue with a devil-of-a-fellow air.*] Maria Antonovna, I have the honor of congratulating you!

[*Kisses her hand and repeats rest of business. Numerous* GUESTS, *of both sexes, in informal dress, who had been drifting in steadily, crowd around, the men first kissing* ANNA'S *hand, then* MARIA'S, *with exclamations of* "Anna Andreievna!" *and* "Maria Antonovna!" *and the women gushing and kissing* ANNA *and* MARIA. BOBCHINSKI *and* DOBCHINSKI *bustle in, making their way through the thronging guests.*]

BOBCHINSKI: I have the honor of congratulating you, Anton Antonovich!

DOBCHINSKI: Anton Antonovich, I have the honor of congratulating you!

BOBCHINSKI: Congratulations on your good fortune!

DOBCHINSKI: Anna Andreievna!

BOBCHINSKI: Anna Andreievna! [*Both approach at the same time for the hand-kissing ritual and bump their foreheads together.*]

DOBCHINSKI [*kissing* MARIA'S *hand*]: Maria Antonovna, I have the honor of congratulating you! You'll be ever so happy; you'll wear a dress of gold and eat all sorts of exquisite soups; you'll have a most amusing time—

BOBCHINSKI [*breaking in*]: Maria Antonovna! [*Kissing her hand.*] I have the honor of congratulating you! May God grant you all wealth, lots of gold pieces, and a little rascal of a son, so-o big—[*spreading his arms*]—so that you may dandle him on the palm of your hand—yes, ma'am! And the little one will keep on bawling all the time—

[*Imitates a baby crying. A few more guests go through kissing business with* ANNA *and* MARIA.]

SUPERINTENDENT OF SCHOOLS [*entering with his* WIFE]: I have the honor—

HIS WIFE [*running ahead of him*]: I congratulate you, Anna Andreievna! [*She and* ANNA *kiss each other.*] Really, now, I was overjoyed. "Anna Andreievna is marrying off her daughter," they tell me. "Ah, my God!" I think to myself, and I was that overjoyed I say to my husband: "Listen, Luka dear—what good luck has come to Anna Andreievna! There," I think to myself, "glory be to God!" And I say to him, I say: "I'm so delighted I'm simply burning up with impatience to let Anna Andreievna know. . . . Ah, my God," I think to myself, "Anna Andreievna was just waiting for a good match for her daughter, and now fate has been so good to her, things fell out just the way she wanted them," and really, I was so overjoyed that I couldn't utter a word. I cry and cry—there, I simply sobbed. So then Luka Lukich he says to me: "What are you sobbing about, Nastenka?"—"Luka, dear," I say to him, "I don't rightly know myself why"—and my tears keep flowing like a river—

MAYOR: I beg you to be seated, ladies and gentlemen. [*Through door.*] Hey, Mishka! Fetch a lot of chairs in here!

[GUESTS *seat themselves.* MISHKA *brings in more chairs. Enter* INSPECTOR OF POLICE *and three* POLICEMEN.]

INSPECTOR OF POLICE: I have the honor of congratulating you, Your Honor, and of wishing you a long and prosperous life.

MAYOR: Thank you, thank you. Please be seated, ladies and gentlemen.

[*More* GUESTS *seat themselves.*]

JUDGE: Now tell us please, Anton Antonovich, just how all this began—the gradual progress of this matter.

MAYOR: The progress was extraordinary: he was pleased to make a personal proposal—

ANNA [*taking the ball away from him*]: Most respectfully, and in the most refined manner. Everything was extraordinarily well put. "I, Anna Andreievna," he says, "am doing this solely out of respect for your personal qualities." And such a splendid, cultured person, of the noblest principles. "Anna Andreievna," he says, "would you believe it, I don't value my life at a bent pin; I am doing this only because I respect your rare qualities."

MARIA: Ah, Mamma dear, it was to me he said that!

ANNA: Stop that; you don't know anything, and don't mix into what is none of your affair! "Anna Andreievna," he said, "I am astonished. . . ." He was profuse with such flattering things. . . . And when I wanted to tell him that we simply dared not hope for such an honor, he suddenly fell down on his knees, and that in the most genteel manner: "Anna Andreievna! Don't make me the most miserable of men! Consent to respond to my feelings, otherwise I'll put a violent end to my life!"

MARIA: Really, Mamma dear, he was saying that concerning me.

ANNA: Why, of course. It concerned you also; I don't deny that in the least.

MAYOR: And he even scared us no end, actually—said he would shoot himself. "I'll shoot myself, so I will!" he says.

CHORUS OF GUESTS: You don't say!

JUDGE: What an odd thing to happen!

SUPERINTENDENT OF SCHOOLS: Ay, verily, Fate must have guided things so.

DIRECTOR OF CHARITIES: No, not Fate, my Father. Fate is a tough old turkey; it's Anton Antonovich's meritorious services that have brought him this. [*Aside.*] Luck will always pop into the snout of a swine like that.

JUDGE: I'd just as lief sell you that young hound we were dickering about, Anton Antonovich.

MAYOR: No, I've bigger fish to fry now than that hound pup.

JUDGE: Well, if you don't want it, we'll come to terms on some other dog.

KOROBKIN'S WIFE: Ah, Anna Andreievna, how glad I am over your good luck! You simply can't imagine!

KOROBKIN: And where, if I may ask, is your distinguished guest at present? I heard that he has left for some reason.

MAYOR: Yes, he has gone away for a day on a very important matter—

ANNA: To see an uncle of his, and ask his blessing—

MAYOR: And ask his blessing, but no later than tomorrow. [*Sneezes. The* "God bless you's!" *blend and swell into a mighty chorus.*] Thank you all! But no later than on the morrow he's coming back.

[*Sneezes. Again a swelling chorus of* "God bless you's!" *Certain voices are heard above the others.*]

POLICE INSPECTOR'S: I wish you health, Your Honor!

BOBCHINSKI'S: A hundred years and a sackful of gold pieces!

DOBCHINSKI'S: May God prolong your life to forty times forty years!

DIRECTOR OF CHARITIES': Drop dead, you skunk!

KOROBKIN'S WIFE'S: May the devil take you!

MAYOR: I humbly thank you. And I wish you the same.

ANNA: We intend to live in the capital now. For here, I confess, the atmosphere is so . . . far too countryfied! Most uncongenial, I confess. And my husband, now—he'll get a general's rank there.

MAYOR: Yes, ladies and gentlemen, I confess I very much want to be a general, the devil take it!

SUPERINTENDENT OF SCHOOLS: And may God grant that you get to be one!

RASTACOVSKI: What's impossible through human means is possible through the Divine.

JUDGE: A great ship needs deep waters.

DIRECTOR OF CHARITIES: All honor to them that have earned honor.

JUDGE [*aside*]: There, he'll show 'em a thing or two if he ever gets to be a general! There's somebody whom a general's rank fits the way a saddle fits a cow! No, brother, you haven't gotten there yet, not by a long shot. There are folks in this town far better than you, and they aren't generals to this day.

DIRECTOR OF CHARITIES [*aside*]: Look at what's actually trying to worm himself in among the generals, devil take it! For all you know, he may really get to be one. For there are enough high airs about him—may the cunning Evil One take him. [*Turning to* MAYOR.] When the time comes, Anton Antonovich, don't forget all about us.

JUDGE: And if anything should turn up—some opportunity in administrative matters—don't leave us without your favor.

KOROBKIN: Next year I'm bringing my youngster to the capital, so that he may serve the government; so do me a favor, extend your patronage to him, take the place of a father to the poor lonely lad.

MAYOR: I'm quite ready; for my part, I'm quite ready to exert myself.

ANNA: Tony, dear, you're always ready with your promises. In the first place, you won't have time to think of such things. And how can you, and for what reason should you, burden yourself with promises?

MAYOR: But why not, dearest? One can do so, now and then.

ANNA: Of course one can, but then there's no use extending patronage to all the small fry.

KOROBKIN'S WIFE [sotto voce, *to another* LADY GUEST]: Did you hear how she rates us?

LADY GUEST: Why, she was always like that; I know her—you give her an inch and she'll take a yard—

POSTMASTER [*rushing in, all out of breath and waving an open letter*]: An amazing thing, ladies and gentlemen! The official whom we took for the Inspector General wasn't the Inspector General—

ALL: What? He wasn't the Inspector General?

POSTMASTER: Not the Inspector General at all; I found this out through a letter—

MAYOR: What are you saying? What are you saying? From what letter?

POSTMASTER: Why, from a letter which he himself wrote. A letter was brought to me at the Post Office. I look at the address, and I see that it's directed to Post Office Street. I was simply stunned. "Well," I thinks to myself, "he must have come across irregularities in my department and is informing the Administration." So I went and unsealed it.

MAYOR: But how could you ever do it?

POSTMASTER: I don't rightly know myself. Some unnatural force must have impelled me. I had already summoned a special courier in order to send it off posthaste—but such curiosity as I had never before experienced overcame me. I couldn't, I couldn't do it—I felt that I simply couldn't, yet at the same time it was drawing me, simply drawing me to open it. In one ear I hear nothing but: "Hey, there, don't break that seal; your goose is cooked if you do!"—but in the other ear there seems to be some demon sitting: "Break the seal! Break the seal! Break the seal!" And no sooner had I pressed down on the wax than fire seemed to shoot right through my veins, and when I had actually unsealed the letter, by God, I was frozen stiff; my hands were trembling and everything turned black before my eyes.

MAYOR: But how dared you unseal the letter of such an influential personage?

POSTMASTER: Why, that's just where the trick comes in: he's not influential and he's no personage!

MAYOR: What is he then, according to you?

POSTMASTER: Nor fish nor flesh nor good red herring; the devil knows what he is.

MAYOR [*flaring up*]: What do you mean by that? How dare you call him nor fish nor flesh nor good red herring— and the devil knows what, on top of that! I'll place you under arrest—

POSTMASTER: Who? You?

MAYOR: Yes, me!

POSTMASTER: You're not big enough.

MAYOR: Are you aware that he is marrying my daughter, that I myself am going to be a high dignitary—that I'll bottle you up in Siberia, no less?

POSTMASTER: Eh, Anton Antonovich! Why talk of Siberia—Siberia's a long way off. I'd better read the letter to you. Ladies and gentlemen! May I have your permission?

ALL: Read it! Read it!

POSTMASTER [*reading letter*]: "I hasten to inform you, my dearest friend Tryapichkin, of what wonders have befallen me. On my travels I was cleaned out—but thoroughly!— by a certain Captain of Infantry, so that mine host of the local hostelry was all set to put me in the cooler, when out of a clear sky, owing to my physiognomy and dress being those of a citizen of the capital, the whole town took me for a governor-general, or something. And now I am living at the home of the Mayor, having the time of my life, and running after the Mayor's wife and daughter for all I am worth. The only thing is, I haven't made up my mind which one to start up with; I think I'll tackle the mother first, because it looks as if she were ready to grant one any favors right off the bat.—Do you remember what tough times you and I used to have, trying to get our meals without paying for them, and how once, in a pastry shop, the proprietor grabbed me by the collar because I had eaten some tarts and wanted to charge them to the account of His Britannic Majesty? Things are altogether different now. They all lend me money, as much as I wish. And they're all frightfully quaint here. You'd die laughing. I know you write short things of all sorts; find a place for them in your work. First of all, there's the Mayor; he's as stupid as a gray gelding—"

MAYOR: Impossible! There's nothing of the sort in the letter—

POSTMASTER [*showing* MAYOR *the letter*]: Read it yourself!

MAYOR: "—as stupid as a grey gelding—" Impossible! You wrote that yourself.

POSTMASTER: How could I possibly sit down to write a letter like that?

DIRECTOR OF CHARITIES: Read on!

POSTMASTER [*resumes reading*]: "—there's the Mayor; he's as stupid as a gray gelding—"

MAYOR: Oh, to hell with all that! Must you keep on repeating it—just as though it weren't there without all that repetition!

POSTMASTER [*resumes reading*]: Hmm . . . hmm . . . hmm . . . hmm! "—as a gray gelding. The Postmaster, too, is a good-hearted fellow—" [*Cuts short his reading.*] Well, at this point he expresses himself disrespectfully about me as well—

MAYOR: No, you read it!

POSTMASTER: But what for?

MAYOR: No, devil take it, if you're going to read, then read—read everything!

DIRECTOR OF CHARITIES: Allow me, I'll read it. [*Takes letter, puts on spectacles, and reads aloud.*] "The Postmaster is, down to the least detail, just like Mihei, the watchman in our Department; and, just like Mihei, he must be fond of gin-and-bitters, the scoundrel—"

POSTMASTER [*to spectators*]: Well, he's just an atrocious brat who ought to be whipped—that's all!

DIRECTOR OF CHARITIES [*going on with his reading*]: "The Director of Chari . . . i . . . i—" [*Begins stammering.*]

KOROBKIN: Well, what are you stopping for?

DIRECTOR OF CHARITIES: Why, his handwriting is rather hard to make out. However, one can see he's a good-for-nothing!

KOROBKIN: Let me have it. There, I think my eyes are better than yours! [*Tries to take letter.*]

DIRECTOR OF CHARITIES [*holding on to letter*]: No, this place can be skipped—and it's much easier to read further on—

KOROBKIN: Do permit me—I know all about it.

DIRECTOR OF CHARITIES: Well, as for reading it, I'll read it myself—really, it's all easy to read further on.

POSTMASTER: No, you read everything! After all, everything up to now was read out loud.

ALL: Give it up! Give up that letter! [*To* KOROBKIN.] You read it!

DIRECTOR OF CHARITIES: Just a minute! [*Surrenders letter to* KOROBKIN.] Here, permit me— [*Covers part of letter with forefinger.*] —Read from here on.

[*All surround him.*]

POSTMASTER: Read on, read on! Stuff and nonsense! Read the whole thing!

KOROBKIN [*reading*]: "The Director of Charities, Zemlyanika, is a perfect swine—in a skullcap—"

DIRECTOR OF CHARITIES [*to the spectators*]: That's supposed to be witty. A swine—in a skullcap. Why, whoever saw a swine in a skullcap?

KOROBKIN [*going on with his reading*]: "The Superintendent of Schools is saturated—but saturated!—with the fragrance of onions—"

SUPERINTENDENT OF SCHOOLS [*to spectators*]: So help me, I've never so much as tasted onions!

JUDGE [*aside*]: Glory be, at least there isn't anything there about me!

KOROBKIN: "The Judge—"

JUDGE [*aside*]: There it is! [*Aloud.*] Ladies and gentlemen, I think the letter is much too long, and besides, what the devil is there to it—what's the use of reading such rubbish?

SUPERINTENDENT OF SCHOOLS: Don't stop!

POSTMASTER: Don't stop! Keep on reading!

DIRECTOR OF CHARITIES: Yes, you'd better keep on with the reading.

KOROBKIN [*resumes*]: The Judge, Lyapkin-Tyapkin, is *mauvais ton* to the *n*th degree—" [*Pauses.*] That must be French.

JUDGE: Why, the devil knows what it means! Good thing if it means only "swindler"—but maybe it's even worse than that.

KOROBKIN: "But on the whole they're a hospitable and kindhearted lot. Good-by, my dear friend Tryapichkin. I want to go into literature myself, following your example. It's a bore, brother, to lead the life I do; after all, one wants some spiritual food; I perceive that one must really occupy himself with something or other of a lofty nature. Write to me in the Saratov Province—the Village of Podkatilovka." [*Turns letter over and reads address.*] "To the Right Honorable Ivan Vassilievich Tryapichkin, Saint Petersburg, Post Office Street, House Number Ninety-Seven, within the Courtyard, Third Floor, Turn Right."

LADY GUEST: What an unexpected reprimand!

MAYOR: There! When he set out to slit my throat he slit it from ear to ear! I'm killed, killed, killed entirely! I can't see a thing! All I can see before me are some swinish snouts instead of faces, and not another thing! Bring him back—bring him back! [*Waves his arm.*]

POSTMASTER: How can you bring him back? As if on purpose, I ordered the station-master to give him the very best team of three horses, and on top of that the devil himself must have egged me on to give him an order for all the relays of horses ahead.

KOROBKIN'S WIFE: Well, this is an unparalleled mess, sure enough!

JUDGE: But, devil take it, gentlemen! He took three hundred from me as a loan.

DIRECTOR OF CHARITIES: And three hundred from me, too.

POSTMASTER [*with a sigh*]: Oh, and three hundred from me as well.

BOBCHINSKI: He took sixty-five from Peter Ivanovich and me—in bills, sir. Yes, sir!

JUDGE [*spreading his hands in bewilderment*]: But how can this be, gentlemen? Really, now, how was it he took us in like that?

MAYOR [*striking his forehead*]: But what about me? But what about me, now, old fool that I am? I've lost my wits through age, like an old ram! Thirty years of my life have I spent in serving the public; never a businessman, never a contractor could take me in; I hornswoggled swindlers who could show tricks to other swindlers; such cheats and knaves as were wise enough to cheat the whole world did I rope in; three governors have I hoodwinked! But what do governors amount to! [*Deprecating gesture.*] As if governors were even in the running—

ANNA: But this can't be, Tony darling; he's engaged to our Maria—

MAYOR [*really stirred up*]: "Engaged!" He's engaged in a pig's eye! Don't go shoving that engagement at me! [*In a frenzy.*] There, look—let all the world, let all of Christianity look—look, all of you, how the Mayor has been made a fool of! Call him a fool, call him a fool, the old, low-down villain! [*Shakes his fist in his own face.*] Hey, there, you with the thick nose! You took a squirt, a rag like that for a person of importance! There, he's eating up the road now, rolling along to the tinkling of his jingle bells! He'll spread this story through the whole world, nor will it be enough that you'll be a general laughing stock. . . . Some scribbler, some waster of good white paper will turn up, and he'll plunk you into a comedy—that's what hurts! He won't spare your rank, your title, and all the people will bare their teeth, grinning and clapping their hands. [*Turning on the spectators.*] What are you laughing at? You're laughing at your own selves! [*With a* "What's-the-use!" *gesture.*] Eh, you! . . .

[*Stamps his feet in frenzied malice.*] I'd take all these wasters of good white paper and— [*Roars.*] Oo-oo-oooooh! You scribblers, you damned liberals! Seed of the devil! I'd tie all of you in a knot, I'd grind you all into powder and shove you in the devil's hip pocket! And in his hat as well! [*Shakes his fist and grinds his boot-heel into the floor. After a brief silence.*] I can't come to myself to this very minute. There, verily: Him whom God would chastise He first deprives of reason. Well, now, what was there about this snotnose that looked like an Inspector General? Nary a thing! There, not even that much. [*Measures off the very tip of his little finger.*] And suddenly they all set up a chorus: "The Inspector General! The Inspector General!" There, now, who was the first to come out with the rumor that he was the Inspector General? Answer me!

DIRECTOR OF CHARITIES [*spreading his hands*]: If you were to kill me I couldn't explain how all this came about; I'm dazed and in a fog, it seems; the devil must have led me astray—

JUDGE: Why, who do you think was the first to come out with that rumor? They're the ones! [*Pointing to* DOBCHINSKI *and* BOBCHINSKI.] Those two fine fellows!

BOBCHINSKI: So help me, so help me, it wasn't me; I never even thought any such thing—

DOBCHINSKI: I didn't do a thing—not a single thing—

DIRECTOR OF CHARITIES: Of course it was the two of you!

SUPERINTENDENT OF SCHOOLS: Of course. They came running from the hotel as if they were mad: "He's arrived, he's arrived, and he won't lay out any money...." You sure found a fine bird that time.

MAYOR: Naturally, it had to be you two! You two gossips, you damned liars!

JUDGE: May the devil take both of you with your Inspector General and your stories!

MAYOR: All you do is snoop through the town and mix everybody up, you damned chatterboxes; you breed gossip, you bobtailed magpies, you!

JUDGE: You confounded bunglers!

SUPERINTENDENT OF SCHOOLS: Dunce caps!

DIRECTOR OF CHARITIES: You potbellied toadstools!

[*All surround* BOBCHINSKI *and* DOBCHINSKI.]

BOBCHINSKI: Honest to God, it wasn't me—it was Peter Ivanovich—

DOBCHINSKI: Oh, no, Peter Ivanovich, for you were the first to—

BOBCHINSKI: Oh, no—so there! You were the first—

GENDARME [*entering*]: The official sent here in the Emperor's name from Petersburg demands your immediate presence. He is stopping at the hotel.

[*All are thunderstruck by his words. An outcry of astonishment escapes all the ladies simultaneously; all the characters, suddenly shifting their position, become petrified.*]

TABLEAU

The MAYOR *stands in the center, looking like a post, with outspread arms and head thrown back. To his right are his* WIFE *and* DAUGHTER, *each straining toward him with all her body. Behind them is the* POST-MASTER, *who has turned into a living question mark addressed to the spectators. Behind him is the* SUPERINTENDENT OF SCHOOLS, *most guilelessly nonplused. Behind him, near the very side of the proscenium, are three* LADY GUESTS, *leaning together with the most sarcastic expressions on their faces, meant for the* MAYOR *and still more for his* WIFE *and* DAUGHTER. *To the left of the* MAYOR *is the* DIRECTOR OF CHARITIES, *with his head somewhat cocked, as though he were hearkening to something. Behind him is the* JUDGE, *with his arms spread wide, squatting almost to the ground, and with his lips puckered as if to whistle, or to say, "Oh, my sainted aunt! This is it, sure enough!" Behind him is* KOROBKIN, *turning to the spectators with one eye narrowed and putting over a caustic insinuation concerning the* MAYOR. *Behind him, at the very side of the proscenium, are* DOBCHIN-*

SKI *and* BOBCHINSKI, *the arrested motion of their hands directed at each other, their mouth gaping and their eyes goggling at each other. The other* GUESTS *remain where they are, like so many pillars of salt. All the characters, thus pertified, retain their positions for almost a minute and a half.*

SLOW CURTAIN

A Month

in the Country

IVAN TURGENEV

Adapted by Emlyn Williams

CHARACTERS

SHAAF, *Kolia's German tutor*

ANNA SEMYENOVNA YSLAEVA, *Natalia's mother-in-law, Yslaev's mother*

LIZAVETA BOGDANOVNA, *her companion*

NATALIA

RAKITIN, *a friend of the family*

KOLIA, *son of Natalia and Yslaev*

BELIAEV, *his new tutor*

MATVEI, *a manservant*

THE DOCTOR, Ignaty Illyich Shpichelsky

VERA, *Natalia's ward*

YSLAEV, *Natalia's husband, a rich landowner*

KATIA, *a maid*

BOLSHINTSOV, *a neighbour*

The action takes place on Yslaev's estate in the country near Moscow.

The time is in the early forties of the last century.

act 1

Scene I

While the curtain is still down VERA *is heard playing at the pianoforte in the ballroom: a mazurka of Chopin.*

A pause.

The curtain rises slowly.

The drawing room of Yslaev's house on his estate in the country near Moscow, Russia; a summer afternoon. An almost triangular view of the room, with in the left wall ["left" and "right" throughout refer to the audience's left and right] large French window opening on to the garden, and in the right wall [up a step and beyond pillars] folding doors [opening onstage] leading to the ballroom; a smaller window to the left of them; to the right of them, an entrance leading off right, presumably to the hall, the dining room, and the stairs; to the right again, this side of the pillars and nearer the audience, a smaller door leading to the study. The room is beautifully furnished. The native Russian merging into great elegance of detail [markedly French in influence], revealing the taste of a well-bred young hostess. On the left, between the windows and the audience, a desk and desk-chair; a table; in the angle between the French windows and the pillars, a tall ornamented Russian stove; an armchair; a Récamier sofa; a footstool; a long stool; a mirror over desk.

It is a beautiful summer afternoon, in the early forties of the last century.

At the table are seated ANNA SEMYENQVNA YSLAEVA

[*Yslaev's mother*], *a fussy old lady who is used to her own way:* LIZAVETA BOGDANOVNA [*her companion*], *thirty-seven, whose looks have long ago grown shabby through an incessant anxious desire to please her betters: and* SHAAF, *a middle-aged German tutor, ugly, slow and stupid. He has a strong German accent. They are playing preference. At some distance from them are* NATALIA *and* RAKITIN. *She is a beautiful, exquisite creature of twenty-nine, elegantly posed on the sofa; he is a fine-looking, thoughtful man of great breeding, a year or two older. He sits on the footstool almost at her feet, a book open on his knees, looking at her; she has laid down her embroidery and is fanning herself.*

A pause; the music begins again. For a space of time after the curtain rises, the only movement is the fingers of the card-players and the flutter of NATALIA'S *fan, as she listens to the music. The music comes to an end. A pause.*

SHAAF: Har-r-tz.

ANNA: Hearts again? If this goes on, my friend, you'll have the clothes off our backs—

SHAAF [*phlegmatically*]: Eight har-r-tz.

ANNA [*to* LIZAVETA]: Did you ever know such a madcap? I declare, there's no playing with him—

LIZAVETA [*smiling and nodding*]: None at all— [*Sniffing from a box.*] So true—

ANNA: And you stop taking snuff, I've told you how bad it is for you.

LIZAVETA: Just this once—

[*A pause.*]

NATALIA [*to* RAKITIN]: Why have you stopped reading?

RAKITIN [*reading*]: "*Monte-Cristo se redressa haletant*"— [*Looking up at her.*] Are you interested?

NATALIA: No.

RAKITIN: Then why ask me to plow through—

NATALIA: It's perfectly simple why. The other day a woman said to me "Have you read *Monte-Cristo*—my dear, you must, it's captivating!" I didn't say a word at the time, but now I shall be able to tell her I *have* read it, and that it isn't captivating at all. Do go on.

RAKITIN [*looking for his place in the book*]: "Se redressa haletant, et—"

NATALIA: Have you seen Arkady today?

RAKITIN: Yes, ran into him working by the dam.

NATALIA: Was ever a woman blessed with such a pillar of industry for a husband?

RAKITIN: He wanted to explain something to the workmen, and walked into the sand right up to his knees.

NATALIA: How like him— He attacks everything with too much enthusiasm—he tries too hard. And I consider that a fault. Don't you agree?

RAKITIN: Yes, I do.

NATALIA: Oh, how boring of you— You always agree with me. Read me more.

SHAAF [*as* RAKITIN *turns over page*]: Har-r-tz.

ANNA: What, again? Really, Shaaf, this is not to be borne! [*To* NATALIA.] Daughter-in-law, do you know what—daughter-in-law!

NATALIA [*paying attention with difficulty*]: Yes.

ANNA: What do you think, dear, our Prussian friend's beating us with the most monstrous tactics—

SHAAF: Und now aggin zeven har-r-tz.

ANNA [*rising and gathering up the cards*]: We're changing over to whist— [*To* NATALIA.] But where's our little treasure?

NATALIA: Kolia? Gone for a walk with his new tutor.

ANNA: Ah— Now whist— [*Smartly flicking cards.*] Lizaveta Bogdanovna, you're my partner—

LIZAVETA: Oh, do you mean it—an honor—

RAKITIN [*to* NATALIA]: Did you say something about a new tutor?

NATALIA: We acquired one while you were away, for general knowledge.

RAKITIN: Another old fogey?

NATALIA: No— My dear, I tell you what—you know how you love watching people, probing like a dentist into their innermost thoughts—

RAKITIN: Oh come—

NATALIA: I want you to focus your attention on him.

RAKITIN: The new tutor? Why?

NATALIA: Because I like him.

RAKITIN: Describe him to me.

NATALIA: Oh—well. Tall. Fair. Very young—

RAKITIN: Yes?

NATALIA: Very good eyes, that look straight at you, with an expression of great liveliness.

RAKITIN: Yes?

NATALIA: The whole face bears a marked air of vigor—something—

RAKITIN: Go on.

NATALIA: Something—forceful—but you'll see for yourself. There's one thing, though—his manner's a trifle gauche, and that's a grave defect in the eyes of a man of the world like you.

RAKITIN: I'm not in your good books today, I can see that—

NATALIA: Seriously, Rakitin, do have a look at him, it's my opinion he has the makings of a fine man. Though Heavens knows, it's too early to say—

RAKITIN: You have whetted my curiosity.

NATALIA: I'm so glad— Shall we read?

RAKITIN [*reading*]: "*Se redressa haletant, et—*"

NATALIA: But where's Vera? I haven't set eyes on her since this morning— [*As* RAKITIN *shuts his book.*] Ah— Tell me some news.

RAKITIN: What do you wish to hear? About my visit to the Krinitsins?

NATALIA: If you like. How are our newly-weds?

RAKITIN: Time lies heavy on their hands.

NATALIA: Already? *Jamais!* But how did you find out?

RAKITIN: Can one conceal boredom? Everything else, but boredom—no.

NATALIA [*looking at him*]: Can one conceal—everything else?

RAKITIN: I think so.

NATALIA [*a pause. She looks away*]: What did you do there?

RAKITIN: Nothing. I was bored too, and to be bored by one's friends is a calamity. One feels at ease and relaxed, one breathes an air of affection—and one is bored. To extinction. The heart aches stupidly, as if it were hungry.

NATALIA: A clever man like you must often find the world very dull—

RAKITIN [*quietly, with meaning*]: You're talking as if you had no idea what it felt like to live with a creature whom you love and who bores you.

NATALIA: "Love" is a big word— You're a subtle creature, Rakitin, aren't you?

RAKITIN: Am I?

NATALIA: Over-subtle, in fact; it's your Achilles heel. You're as clever as a cartload of old professors. Sometimes, when you and I are talking, I feel we're just—making lace.

RAKITIN: Lace?

NATALIA: Have you ever watched women making lace? They sit in stuffy rooms, and never move an inch to the left or to the right. Lace is a lovely thing, but on a hot day I'd sooner have a drink of icy fresh water.

RAKITIN: Natalia Petrovna, you're annoyed with me.

NATALIA: Am I?

RAKITIN: I don't know quite why, but you are.

NATALIA: When men pride themselves on their subtlety, they have even less insight than when they don't— No, I'm not annoyed with you—

ANNA: At last! He's over-reached himself— [*Rising.*] played right into our hands! The rascal's over-reached himself! My luck's turned, where's my purse— [*She crosses and rummages in the desk.*]

SHAAF [*sulkily*]: It iss de fault von Lizaveta Bogdanovna.

LIZAVETA [*annoyed*]: Oh, I protest! How was I to know that Anna Semyenovna had no hearts?

[*During this,* RAKITIN *rises, walks, then turns and surveys* NATALIA.]

SHAAF: In de future, vid Lizaveta Bogdanovna as my partner, I do not play. [*He counts his winnings and writes figures in a pocket-book.*]

LIZAVETA: That suits me to a T, Herr Shaaf— Well, upon my word!

ANNA [*calling*]: Shuffle the cards, Lizaveta Bogdanovna, and stop airing your views!

RAKITIN [*to* NATALIA]: The more I look at you today, the less I recognize you. You've changed, in some way—

NATALIA: Really? How interesting.

[KOLIA *runs in from the garden, and hurries to* ANNA SEMYENOVNA. *He is an attractive child of ten.*]

KOLIA: Granny! Granny! [*Covering her eyes with one hand.*] Guess what I've got!

ANNA: Now let me think—what can Granny's little treasure have for Granny!— [*As* KOLIA *uncovers her eyes and brings out a bow and arrows from behind his back.*] Oh, what a lovely toy! Now who made this for you?

KOLIA [*pointing to the garden*]: He did!

[RAKITIN *turns,* BELIAEV *appears shyly at the windows. He is a slight, personable youth of twenty-one, carefully but shabbily dressed; at the moment he is particularly coltish and self-conscious, but once he is at ease with people of his own age, all that breaks down and he becomes a high-spirited impressionable student. He carries books.*]

ANNA: Really, it's beautifully put together— [*Rising and going back to the* OTHERS.] —and now to work—

KOLIA: D'you know what, Granny? I shot with it, twice, Granny, twice! I aimed at a tree, Granny, and I hit it! Both times, Granny! Both times—

NATALIA: Show me, Kolia.

KOLIA [*running to her and giving her the bow to examine*]: Oh, Mamma, you should see the way he climbs trees, better than a squirrel—and he wants to teach me the way to, *and* he wants to teach me how to swim on my back— He's going to teach me everything there is, everything in the world, Mamma!

NATALIA [*to* BELIAEV]: It's so very kind of you to take such pains with him. I'm extremely obliged.

[BELIAEV *bows to her.*]

KOLIA [*running to* BELIAEV]: Let's run as far as the stables, Alexei Nikolaich, shall we? And take some bread for Favorite!

BELIAEV: Shall we? That's a good idea—

ANNA [*as* KOLIA *runs out by the windows*]: Come and give Granny a kiss first, darling—

KOLIA [*in the garden*]: Later, Granny, later—

[BELIAEV *smiles sheepishly at* RAKITIN *and* NATALIA *and follows* KOLIA *into the garden.*]

ANNA: What a little pet that child is, what a charmer! [*To* SHAAF *and* LIZAVETA BOGDANOVNA, *insistently.*] Don't you agree?

LIZAVETA: An angel, no more, no less—

SHAAF: Boodiful, boodiful—pass.

NATALIA [*to* RAKITIN]: Well, what did you think of him?

RAKITIN: Think of whom?

NATALIA: Why, the new tutor! You are provoking—

RAKITIN: Let me see, his eyes—yes, it's a good face. He seems very shy, doesn't he?

NATALIA: I tell you what, Rakitin! Let's make a hobby of him!

RAKITIN: How do you mean?

NATALIA: Complete his education! It's a unique chance for sedate, sensible people like us to exercise our virtues. You and I are eminently sensible, are we not?

RAKITIN: You find this boy interesting? He'd be flattered if he knew.

NATALIA: Ah, would he? I'm afraid, my dear, just because you and I study ourselves with the greatest industry, we bask in the belief that we know all about everybody else. But he isn't like us, not the least little bit.

RAKITIN: You're perfectly right. The soul of another man is a dark forest—

NATALIA [*ironically*]: So true, so true—

RAKITIN: Why are you continually mocking me?

NATALIA: If you can't tease one's friends, whom can one tease? And you're my friend. [*Pressing his hand.*] My old friend. As if you didn't know—*ce que vous êtes pour moi.*

RAKITIN: Natalia Petrovna, you play with me like a cat with a mouse!

NATALIA: Oh, do I?

ANNA: That means I've won twenty from you, Herr Shaaf—things are on the mend! .

SHAAF: In de future, vid Lizaveta Bogdanovna as my partner, I do not play.

MATVEI [*enters from the ballroom. He is a manservant, about forty. Announcing*]: Ignaty Illyich Shpichelsky!

[DOCTOR SHPICHELSKY *follows on his heels. He is a big, attractive man, with tremendous personality; behind his social manner (in which breezy exuberance alternates with portentous solemnity, the manner of a born comedian) he hides a sly, watchful and sardonic nature. It is clear from everybody's reaction to him that he is accepted as a great wag.*]

THE DOCTOR: Stuff and nonsense, man, you don't announce a doctor, it'll be the undertaker next! [*As* ANNA *laughs, and* MATVEI *goes back, closing the doors, stifling a smile.*] My undying regards to one and all, and all and one! [*Kissing* ANNA's *hand.*] And how is our charming duenna? Making her fortune?

ANNA: Fortune, the idea—

THE DOCTOR: The season's greeting to Natalia Petrovna, and ditto—[*to* RAKITIN]—to Mihail Alexandrovitch!

NATALIA: How are you, Doctor, are you well?

THE DOCTOR: "How are you, Doctor, are you well"—now what a question, I ask you! What else can a physician do, but burst with health? No doctor worth his salt ever gets ill—he just dies. [*Taking snuff.*]

NATALIA: Do sit down—

THE DOCTOR [*sitting in the armchair*]: And what of *your* health, good lady?

NATALIA: Sound enough, Doctor, but I'm in a bad mood today. And that's a kind of disorder, isn't it?

THE DOCTOR [*rising*]: Ah me, ah me, lackaday— [*With mock seriousness, feeling her pulse.*] Do you know what's the matter with you, Natalia Petrovna?

NATALIA: No, what?

THE DOCTOR: Too serious-minded.

NATALIA [*rapping him with her fan*]: Oh!

THE DOCTOR: There's nothing like a good laugh for bustling up the circulation. [*Sitting again.*] Though a couple of my special pink drops won't do you any harm.

NATALIA: But I'm more than willing to laugh. Now, Doctor, you've a tongue like a rapier—which is what I like and respect you for—tell me something amusing—*vite!*

THE DOCTOR: At your service, peerless lady. Though I wasn't prepared to be held up for jokes at the point of a pistol—blindfolded but unbowed, I walk the plank—

RAKITIN [*sitting on the footstool*]: Ah—

THE DOCTOR: You know Verenitsin Platon-Vassilevitch?

NATALIA: I know whom you mean, yes—

THE DOCTOR: Well, he has a mad sister. 'Smatter o' fact, they're so dead alike that if she's mad he must be too, and if he's sane then she's no lunatic, but that's neither here nor there; all we know is that over every man jack of us there hovers the inscrutable—if rather grubby—finger of Fate; only the other day, with my own fair hands, I poured a basin of cold water over the lady, and when she was dried she was madder than ever—but still— Her brother has a daughter, a greeny-colored wench with pale little eyes, a red little nose and the chance of inheriting three hundred serfs from Auntie, which makes her perfect. Lunatics live forever, so Auntie looks like being with us for quite a time, but one hopes for the best—anyway Papa claps her on the market, and various eligibles bob up: among them a certain Perekusov, thin as a rake and shy as a rabbit, but the highest principles. Papa fancies him, Miss fancies him, slap the young codger on the back, prod him in the belly, and publish the banns— But wait! Scene, the Grand Marshal's Ball, gaiety at its height; hey presto, Jack-in-the-box-out-of-the-blue, Ardalion Protobekassov—[*clicking his heels*]—an officer!

NATALIA: Ahh—

THE DOCTOR: "Mademoiselle, may I have the honor—" [*Clicking his heels.*] One polka. Two more polkas. [*Clicking his heels, smartly, twice.*] Then we sit out, the military eyes start rolling like drums, and mademoiselle's head is turned as neat as a water-tap, swish— Tears, moans, breathe the word "wedding" and she goes into a series of elegant fits. "Bless my soul," thinks Papa, "well, if she wants the officer, I'll prove I'm her great-hearted father, anyway he's got money too." So in the twinkling of a bed-post the officer is invited, does a pinch of courting, offers hand and heart. And then—what?

NATALIA: Happy ever after?

THE DOCTOR: That's what *you* think. Tears and fits again, a terrible rumpus. This time Papa's completely at sea. "Now look here, my girl, which of 'em *do* you want?" And what d'you think her answer is?

RAKITIN: What?

THE DOCTOR: "Papa, I've no idea—and yet my distress is profound. I am a woman who loves two men at the same time." [*An awkward pause. He studies his fingernails. RAKITIN rises slowly.*] And there we are, that's the sort of thing goes on in these parts. [*He takes snuff.*]

NATALIA: I don't find it so staggering. Cannot one love two people at once?

RAKITIN: You think so?

NATALIA [*catching his eye, then rising and walking slowly to the windows*]: I don't know, though—perhaps it proves you don't really love either.

THE DOCTOR [*catching her eye*]: Exactly—hit the nail on the head.

ANNA [*rising*]: My legs have gone to sleep, but I've got my money back— Ah! [*To* SHAAF.] You owe me seventy kopecks, *I*'m going to do the fleecing for a change— [*Walking toward the hall*.] Forty winks before tea, that game's killed me—worth it, though—quick march, Liza, don't dawdle—

LIZAVETA [*rising and scrabbling about on the card table*]: Coming—I'm filling your reticule—

ANNA: My legs, my legs— [*She goes out into the hall.*]

[NATALIA *comes down, sits at the desk, takes up a brush, and makes idle strokes on a watercolor propped on the desk.*]

THE DOCTOR: Lizaveta Bogdanovna, snuff?

LIZAVETA [*simpering*]: I oughtn't to—

THE DOCTOR: Come, give that devil in you a chance—

LIZAVETA: Oh, Doctor—

ANNA'S VOICE [*in the hall, as* LIZAVETA *takes a pinch*]: Liza!

LIZAVETA [*calling*]: Coming!

[*She sneezes, and hurries into the hall.* SHAAF *collects the cards.*]

THE DOCTOR [*to* RAKITIN, *quietly*]: So you've no idea what is the matter with her today?

RAKITIN: Not the faintest.

THE DOCTOR: Well, if you don't know— [RAKITIN *meets his eyes, goes up humming, and plays an idle game of patience;* SHAAF *is still writing in his pocket-book.* THE DOCTOR *clears his throat and crosses to* NATALIA. *With false bonhomie.*] Er—Natalia Petrovna! I have a little matter of business to go into with you!

NATALIA [*painting*]: Business? *Monsieur le Diplomate,* you make me quite nervous!

THE DOCTOR: Actually, it's to do with a third party. A crony of mine.

NATALIA: Do I know him?

THE DOCTOR: You do indeed! He is no less than your neighbor.

NATALIA [*still painting*]: Old Bolshintsov? Yes?

THE DOCTOR: He has asked me to find out what your plans are for your ward.

NATALIA [*turns and stares at him*]: For Vera Alexandrovna?

THE DOCTOR: Not to put too fine a point, this crony of mine—

NATALIA: You don't mean to say he wants to marry her?

THE DOCTOR: The whole thing in a nutshell.

NATALIA: You're being facetious, aren't you?

THE DOCTOR: I'm not, for a change.

NATALIA: But my dear man, she's a child! [*Laughing.*] What a fantastic errand!

THE DOCTOR: Oh, I don't see why—my friend—

NATALIA: Of course one mustn't forget that almost before you're a doctor, you're a businessman—

THE DOCTOR [*jovially*]: You slander me, dear lady—

NATALIA: Who is this *friend* of yours, *Monsieur le Diplomate?*

THE DOCTOR: Excuse me, you haven't given me any indication—

NATALIA: But really, Doctor, I've told you, she's a child—
[VERA *and* KOLIA *run in from the garden, from the left of the windows;* VERA *is a beautiful, immature girl of seventeen, timid and highly strung.*]

KOLIA [*running to* RAKITIN]: Could we have some glue, do you think? Could we have some glue?

RAKITIN [*to* KOLIA]: And what d'you want with glue, suddenly?

[VERA *curtseys breathlessly to* THE DOCTOR, *and sits.*]

KOLIA: Oh, it's necessary, sir, absolutely essential—what d'you think my new tutor's making for me?—a kite!—so we must have some glue, mustn't we—may we?

RAKITIN [*about to ring the bell*]: In a twinkling—

SHAAF: *Erlauben,* sir— Monsieur Kolia has not his Cherman lesson today prepared. [*Taking* KOLIA's *hand.*] *Kommen Sie*—

KOLIA [*imploring*]: Tomorrow—*Morgen, Morgen*—
[*Struggling.*] No, Herr Shaaf—please—

NATALIA: Kolia!

RAKITIN [*to* NATALIA]: It's rather a shame, they're making
a kite, and he's being kidnaped for a German lesson—

SHAAF [*with dignity*]: *Gnädige Frau*—

NATALIA [*severely, to* KOLIA]: Kolia, you've had quite
enough tearing around for one day—

KOLIA: But, *Maman*—

NATALIA: Do you hear me?

KOLIA [*whispering, to* RAKITIN]: Try and get us some
glue, sir, will you, please? Cross my heart, sir? Please?

SHAAF: *Kommen Sie*—yonk vicked man—yonk vicked
man—

[*He pilots* KOLIA *into the ballroom.* RAKITIN *follows
them.* VERA *rises and walks.*]

NATALIA [*seeing her*]: Vera my dear, how flushed you
are! I haven't seen you since this morning. What have you
been doing all this time?

VERA: I've been with the new tutor.

NATALIA [*after a pause, looking at her*]: Really?

VERA: Oh, and Kolia—

NATALIA: Sit down, dear, you must be worn out.

THE DOCTOR [*as* VERA *obeys*]: But running about is good
for one, at that age.

NATALIA: Oh— Ah well, Doctor, you know best—[*To*
VERA.] Tell me what you did in the garden.

[*She crosses and sits in the armchair.* THE DOCTOR
watches them.]

VERA: We played games, then he climbed a tree—

NATALIA: Kolia? Never—

VERA: No no, the—new tutor. He was chasing a squirrel,
and he climbed up and up, till he could shake the top—we
felt quite frightened—then he made a bow and arrow for
Kolia—then he bet me that I couldn't play a mazurka, and
I won, then we ran out again, and then—oh, I don't think
I ought to tell you—

NATALIA: But I insist—

VERA: He crept up to one of your cows, made one leap, and landed on her back. She was so surprised she jumped five feet and spun round like a mad old top, and he laughed so much he fell off, and we laughed till we cried, then he said he'd make a kite, and that's why we came in.

NATALIA [*patting her cheek*]: What a child— Don't you agree, Doctor?

THE DOCTOR: But I don't think it matters. On the contrary.

NATALIA: Don't you?

[VERA *looks at her, puzzled and disconcerted.*]

THE DOCTOR: Bother—I've suddenly remembered—your coachman's on the sick list, and I haven't looked at him yet— [*Going.*] —pray excuse me—

NATALIA: He looks as fit as a fiddle to me, rosy cheeks—

THE DOCTOR: Fever, dear lady, can be very deceptive.

[*He goes out into the hall as* RAKITIN *returns from the ballroom.*]

NATALIA [*rising, to* VERA]: *Mon enfant, vous feriez bien de mettre une autre robe pour dîner.*

VERA [*stammering*]: What— [*Rising.*] —oh—

NATALIA [*suddenly, as* VERA *starts to go to the hall*]: Come here. [VERA *obeys.* NATALIA *kisses her on the brow.*] What a child!

[VERA *smiles awkwardly, kisses her hand, and starts to go.*]

RAKITIN [*whispering to her*]: I've sent the glue.

VERA: Thank you, Mihail Alexandrovitch, so much—

[*She sees* NATALIA *looking at her, and hurries into the hall.* RAKITIN *goes to* NATALIA; *she holds out her hand, which he takes.*]

RAKITIN: Natalia Petrovna, what *is* the matter with you?

NATALIA: The sort of thing that can happen to anybody, surely. Like clouds trailing over the sky— [*After a pause.*] Why are you looking at me like that?

RAKITIN [*simply*]: Because when I look at you like this, I feel happy.

NATALIA [*smiling*]: Ah— [*After a pause.*] Open the study door, Michel, will you? It may make a breeze— [RAKITIN *rises and opens the study door.*] Welcome, O Zephyr-wind! The wild restless creature— [*Looking round.*] Try and drive him out if you can!

RAKITIN: And now you've changed again. Soft and still, like a summer evening after a thunderstorm.

NATALIA: Ah— Has there been a thunderstorm?

RAKITIN: Not quite, but it was gathering.

NATALIA [*after a pause*]: Do you know, Michel, you must be the kindest man in the world?

RAKITIN: But how dull that sounds—

NATALIA: I mean it, you're tolerant, you're affectionate, and you never never change. I owe so much to you; our feeling for each other is so sincere, so innocent— And yet—

RAKITIN: And yet what?

NATALIA: There's something not quite—natural about it, do you know what I mean? Oh, I know we have the right to look not only my husband in the face, but the whole world—and yet— [*Thoughtfully.*] I suppose that's why I have this horrid desire to vent my bad temper, like a child with its nurse—

RAKITIN: With me as the nurse? A flattering comparison indeed—

NATALIA: Sometimes one takes pleasure in tormenting a creature one loves.

RAKITIN [*breathlessly*]: A creature—one loves?

NATALIA: Of course, why should I pretend? I love you.

RAKITIN: Go on.

NATALIA: It comes over me sometimes, like a wave: "I love him," I think to myself; and it's a wonderful peaceful feeling, warming my heart through and through— And yet.

RAKITIN: Another yet?

NATALIA: Well, you've never made me cry, have you? And it seems to me that if it *were* love—

RAKITIN: Natalia Petrovna, no more, do you mind?

NATALIA: No more?

RAKITIN: I'm afraid the happiness I possess may melt into thin air.

NATALIA: Oh, it mustn't do that—

RAKITIN: I'm in your power, you can twist me round your little finger.

[*They look at each other.*]

YSLAEV'S VOICE [*in the ballroom*]: Is the new tutor back from the dam yet?

MATVEI'S VOICE [*in the ballroom*]: I haven't seen him come over, sir—

NATALIA [*rising, quickly*]: Arkady's back—I don't want to see him—

RAKITIN: But my dear—your husband—

NATALIA: I know he's my husband, but I just don't want to see him—

[*She hurries into the study.* RAKITIN *looks after her, puzzled. A pause.* YSLAEV *enters from the ballroom. He is a prosperous landowner, seven years older than his wife; a kind, pleasant man wrapped in his own affairs. He carries building plans.*]

YSLAEV: Ah, Michel—how are you today, my dear fellow?

RAKITIN: But we saw each other this morning!

YSLAEV. So we did, I beg your pardon—I've had a day, I can tell you, up to my neck— [*Crossing and sitting at the desk, comparing his plan with others in the desk.*] D'you know the oddest thing—the Russian peasant isn't at all a brainless fellow, shrewd as they make 'em—but you can tell him something in detail, explain it again, get it crystal clear —and you look at him and realize that not one word has sunk in, not one. The Russian—

RAKITIN: Still worrying about the dam?

YSLAEV: The Russian peasant is no fool, everybody knows that, but he hasn't got that—well, "love of work," is the only way to put it—ah— [*Putting aside the watercolors.*] where's my lady wife, bless her?

RAKITIN: She was in here a minute ago—

YSLAEV: Is it anywhere near tea? I've lost all sense of

time; on my feet since dawn, it's appalling— [*As* RAKITIN *smiles*.] I amuse you, dear boy—but every man has his niche in life; and being a stolid sort of a fellow, I was born to be a farmer, and nothing more. Beliaev han't asked for me, has he?

RAKITIN: Beliaev?

YSLAEV: The new tutor, haven't you seen him? He's no fool, just ran into him in the drive and asked him if he'd see how the workmen are getting on with the new building— [BELIAEV *hurries in from the garden, from the right*.] Well, my boy, how are they? Not doing a stroke, I bet?

BELIAEV: Oh yes, sir, at it hammer and tongs—

YSLAEV: *Are* they? Have they put down the second framework?

BELIAEV: They've started on the third. [*He is more at ease now he is alone with his own sex*.]

YSLAEV: That's something, anyway. Thank you, my boy, very much— [NATALIA *returns from the study, with a large portfolio of paintings*.] Ah, Natalia—how are you, my dear?

RAKITIN: But you're spending the whole day asking the same people about their health!

YSLAEV: I've told you, my dear fellow, it's overwork— snowed under! By the way, have I shown you my new winnowing machine?

NATALIA [*listlessly turning over pages*]: No—

YSLAEV: But my dear, it's the most interesting thing you've ever seen! One flick of the wrist, and the wind whizzes round—a devil of a gale! [*Rising*.] I tell you what— we'll just have time before tea— [*To* RAKITIN.] —Care to see it?

RAKITIN: If you like—

YSLAEV: Coming, Natalia?

NATALIA: I don't understand the first thing about winnowing—

YSLAEV: Back in a trice—

[*He and* RAKITIN *go out into the garden, arm in arm, and disappear to the left.* BELIAEV *hesitates and make to follow them*.]

NATALIA: Are you going out again?

BELIAEV [*turning*]: Me? I was just—going for a walk—

NATALIA: Do you want to?

BELIAEV: No, not—not particularly, I've been walking all day.

NATALIA: That's what I thought. So won't you sit down?

BELIAEV [*bowing awkwardly and sitting*]: That—that's very kind of you, madame.

NATALIA: You're afraid of me, aren't you?

BELIAEV [*overcome with shyness*]: Oh, madame—

NATALIA: But when you get to know me, you won't be afraid of me any more. How old are you?

BELIAEV: Twenty-one.

NATALIA: Are your parents living?

BELIAEV: My father is, madame, yes.

NATALIA [*turning over pages*]: Does he live in Moscow?

BELIAEV: No, madame, in the country.

NATALIA: Have you any brothers and sisters?

BELIAEV: One sister, younger than me.

NATALIA: What's her name?

BELIAEV: Natalia.

NATALIA [*looking up, eagerly*]: Natalia! How very odd—my name's Natalia.

BELIAEV: Really, madame? [*Awkwardly.*] How odd.

NATALIA [*a pause. She places the portfolio on the table*]: And you're very fond of her?

BELIAEV [*rising, politely*]: Yes.

NATALIA: Our Kolia's already very much attached to you.

BELIAEV: I'm so glad. I am naturally anxious to give every satisfaction.

NATALIA: Oh— You see, Alexei Nikolaich, my idea is for him to grow up—free. [*Sitting in the armchair.*] Shall I tell you why?

BELIAEV: Madame?

NATALIA: Because I was brought up in a different atmosphere. [*Motioning him to sit.*] My father was excessively stern; the entire household was frightened of him. Even now I feel the influence of those years of constraint—I know that the first impression I give is often one of—coldness, perhaps— But I'm talking about myself— Were you kept under, as a child?

BELIAEV: I don't really know. Nobody bothered about me, either way.

NATALIA: But your father—?

BELIAEV: Oh, he was always out.

NATALIA: *En voyage,* you mean?

BELIAEV: No, he—he had his visiting.

NATALIA [*puzzled*]: Paying calls?

BELIAEV: In a way, yes; he—[*blurting it out*]—he went round doing odd jobs.

NATALIA: Ah— I beg your pardon— [*Brushing the subject delicately aside.*] Alexei Nikolaich, was that you singing in the garden yesterday?

BELIAEV: Oh— [*Embarrassed.*] The lake is so far from the house, I didn't think—

NATALIA: There's no need to apologize, you have a very pleasant voice— [*Suddenly rising.*] Do you know, Alexei Nikolaich, I feel at ease with you? My chattering away so disgracefully should prove that! We are going to be friends, are we not? [*She holds out her hand. He takes it, hesitatingly, and after a moment of indecision, kisses it. She draws away her hand, confused, as* THE DOCTOR *enters from the hall and sees them.* BELIAEV *crosses with exercise books and collects others from bookcase. Embarrassed.*] Ah, Doctor—

[BELIAEV *drifts behind chair and daybed.*]

THE DOCTOR [*over-hearty*]: Natalia Petrovna, I go into your kitchen for my patient, and there he sits the picture of health, wolfing pancakes and onions! How can a man pursue medicine and the innocent profits deriving therefrom, when that sort of cheating goes on?

NATALIA [*crossing to the mirror over the desk*]: Doctor, *vous êtes impayable*—[*To* BELIAEV, *as he starts to go out.*] Oh, Alexei Nikolaich, I forgot to say—

VERA'S VOICE [*in the hall*]: Alexei Nikolaich!

VERA [*runs in from the hall. Calling*]: Alexei— [*Seeing* NATALIA.] —Oh.

NATALIA: Gracious, child, what a tomboy!

VERA: Kolia wants his new tutor—I mean Kolia asked me about the kite—

NATALIA: I see. *Mais on n'entre pas comme cela dans une chambre*— [*She tidies her hair in the mirror.*]

VERA [*to* BELIAEV]: She did it!

BELIAEV: She didn't! [*They both burst out laughing.* NATALIA *sees them in the mirror, while* THE DOCTOR *watches all three. To* VERA.] You're not making it up?

VERA: Cross my heart—she just fell straight off!

NATALIA [*into the mirror*]: Who fell off?

VERA [*embarrassed*]: Oh— It was our swing—and Kolia's nurse took it into her head to—

[*She catches* BELIAEV's *eye and they both laugh again.*]

NATALIA [*suddenly*]: Doctor!

THE DOCTOR: Madame!

NATALIA: Could I have a word with you?

THE DOCTOR [*hurrying down*]: *A votre service, madame.*

NATALIA [*to* VERA]: She didn't hurt herself, I hope?

VERA: Oh no—[*to* BELIAEV]—but she looked so funny—
[*Both laugh.*]

NATALIA [*turning to them, severely*]: I don't think it was very nice, all the same.

[*Both stand, like scolded children.* MATVEI *enters from the hall.*]

MATVEI [*announcing*]: Tea is served.

NATALIA: And the others?

MATVEI: All in the dining room. [*He goes back into the hall.*]

NATALIA [*pointing to* BELIAEV]: Vera, *allez en avant avec Monsieur.*

[VERA *curtseys demurely to* BELIAEV, *and they both follow* MATVEI.]

THE DOCTOR [*to* NATALIA]: You wanted to tell me something?

NATALIA [*wiping her fingers on a paint-rag*]: Did I? Oh, yes— We haven't yet properly discussed your suggestion have we?

THE DOCTOR: My suggestion? About Vera here and my friend—?

NATALIA: About Vera, and your friend— Well, it was just to say that I'll think it over— Yes, I'll think it over. [*She walks, catches his eye, then goes out into the hall.*]

[*The curtain falls quickly, rising immediately on next scene.*]

Scene II

A corner of the garden; late afternoon of the next day. All we see is a fragment of lofty wall overgrown with creeper, with before it a garden seat facing the audience and a narrow path running from left to right, the whole set very near the audience. The scene is bathed in a soft glow which deepens as the evening advances.

A pause. MATVEI *and* KATIA [*a buxom, pretty servant-girl of twenty*] *stroll slowly from the left; she carries a basket, he a watering-can. He looks worried, she bored. They sit on the seat. A pause.*

MATVEI: Put me out o' me misery, there's a good girl.

KATIA: Matvei Egorych, I don't know *what* to say—it is kind of you—

MATVEI: I'm older than you; it's no good me makin' out I'm not, because I am. But I'm in my prime, and if I may say so, a very good prime too. An' you know yourself what a respectable man I am, an' what more does a woman want than a respectable man?

KATIA: Nothing more at all.

MATVEI: Well?

KATIA: Matvei Egorych, it *is* kind of you—but don't you think we ought to wait—

MATVEI: But, Katerina Vassilevna, excuse me—why? If you're afeared you might not be treated with respect, I can vouch for that—you will have respect from me, Katerina Vassilevna, the like o' which no female ever yet got from a male, so 'elp me God! I've never had anything but good marks from the master and mistress, never a drop passes my lips, an' I'm a respectable man, what more does a woman want?

KATIA: Nothing more at all, it *is* kind of you—

MATVEI: I know it's kind of me, but what's the answer?

KATIA: Oh dear—

MATVEI [*rises, walks, then turns sharply on her*]: It's my 'umble opinion, Katerina Vassilevna, that you didn't always 'um an' 'aw like this.

KATIA [*confused*]: Not always? How do you mean?

MATVEI: It's only lately you've been at it.

KATIA [*blushing*]: I don't know what you're talking about —oh look, here comes that nasty German—

MATVEI: That bilious object, can't stomach 'im—we'll have to thrash it out later—

[*He hurries off, to the right.* KATIA *is about to run off to the left when she runs into* SHAAF, *a fishing rod over one shoulder.*]

SHAAF: Vither, o vither, my fair Katerina, *ja?*

KATIA: The housekeeper sent me to pick some red currants, in a great hurry—

SHAAF: Currant are gut fruit. You are currant fond, *ja?*

KATIA: I quite like them, thank you—

SHAAF: Me currant also fond, he he he! I am fond wid everyting dat you are fond wid. Currant pliss?

KATIA: Oh, I couldn't spare one—I'd catch it from the housekeeper—

SHAAF: I komme catch mit you. [*Pointing to the fishing rod.*] What ist dis you call it? Fishing catch mit fishing-schtick? You underschtand fishing-schtick? You like fishes?

KATIA: I quite like them, thank you—

SHAAF: Also fishes me like, he he he. Do you know what I schpeak mit you now? A leedle sonk, a leedle sonk für Katerina— [*Singing, heavily.*] "*Katerinchen, Katerinchen, wie lieb'ich dich so sehr,"* which means one ting, one leedle ting—loff, loff, loff! [*He tries to put his arm round her.*]

KATIA: Oh no, please—an old gentleman like you, it doesn't look a bit nice—give over!—there's somebody coming— [*She darts off to the right.*]

SHAAF [*muttering, sternly, his skittish manner gone*]: Shaaf, *das ist dumm*—

[*NATALIA enters from the left, arm in arm with RAKITIN; she carries a parasol, he a magazine. She is much more restless than before.*]

NATALIA: Ah, Adam Ivanvich—where's Kolia?

SHAAF: Kolia ist in schkul-room mit Lizaveta Bogdanovna vitch titch him de bianoforte blay.

NATALIA: Good— Have you see the new tutor?

SHAAF: No. He zay dat he choin me. [*He bows and shambles off to the left.*]

NATALIA [*after a pause, calling*]: Adam Ivanvich, we'll come and keep you company while you blay mit your fishing-schtick—what do you say to that?

SHAAF'S VOICE: Boodiful lady, vot an honor, vot an honor—

RAKITIN [*aside, to NATALIA*]: Now why on earth do you want to saddle us—

NATALIA: Come along, handsome stranger. *Beau ténébreux*—

[*They drift out of sight, to the left.* KATIA *appears cautiously from the right.*]

KATIA: That horrible old German, what a blessing, gives me the creeps— [*She sighs, dreamily, then sits on the seat, and hums snatches of a song. Singing.*]

> "Must I love and have no lover
>   While my heart it glows and burns
>   Not with passion, but with Russian
>   Melancholy sighs it yearns—"

Matvei Egorych was right, what he said, about humming and hawing—oh dear— [*Singing.*]

"Not with madness but with sadness
My heart its cruel lesson learns
Not with madness—"

[BELIAEV *and* VERA *enter from the right. He carries a kite.* KATIA *sees them and stops singing.*]

BELIAEV: Katia, why have you stopped? [*Singing.*]
"Not with sadness but with madness
My heart the art of kissing learns."

KATIA [*blushing, and giggling*]: Oh—we don't sing it with *those* words—

BELIAEV: What are you picking, currants? I love currants.

KATIA [*handing him the basket*]: Take them all.

BELIAEV: All? I couldn't do that— Would you like some, Vera Alexandrovna? [*As he and* VERA *take a few.*] Shall we sit here?

VERA: Shall we?

[KATIA *wanders off to the right. They munch for a moment.*]

BELIAEV: Now. [*Showing the kite.*] This fellow's tail's got to be tied on. Will you give me a hand?

VERA: Delighted, sir—

BELIAV [*as he and* VERA *sit on the seat*]: There—[*Arranging kite over her knees.*] Mind you hold it dead straight, or there'll be the devil to pay.

VERA [*laughing*]: I'll be careful. [*He takes tail from her and begins to tie it on the kite.*] But if you sit like that how can I watch you?

BELIAEV [*looking at her*]: Why do you want to watch me?

VERA: To see just how you're tying it on.

BELIAEV: Oh— One minute— [*Moving round so she can see, and calling.*] Katia, where's that lusty treble? Pipe up!

[KATIA *is heard giggling, to the right.*]

VERA: Did you sometimes fly kites in Moscow?

BELIAEV: Good Lord no, I had no time for kites in Moscow! Press with your finger, will you?—No, butterfingers, like this— Do you really think that all we have to do in the great city is to fly kites?

VERA: Well, how *do* you spend your time in the great city?

BELIAEV: Oh— Studying.

VERA: I suppose—[*After a pause.*] you have hundreds of friends in Moscow?

BELIAEV: Oh yes— D'you know, I don't think this string's going to be strong enough—

VERA [*anxiously*]: Are you very attached to them?

BELIAEV: I should think I am! [*Intent on the kite.*] Aren't you fond of your friends?

VERA: I haven't any.

BELIAEV: I mean girl friends.

VERA: Oh.

BELIAEV: Oh what?

[KATIA'S *voice is heard, singing in snatches.*]

VERA: They don't seem to have been very much in my thoughts lately.

BELIAEV: Anyway, how can you say you haven't any men friends? What about me?

VERA [*with a smile*]: Oh, you're different— [*After a pause.*] Alexei Nikolaich, do you write poetry?

BELIAEV: No.

VERA: Oh. [*After a pause.*] At the boarding school I went to, there was one girl who did.

BELIAEV: Wrote poetry? Good Lord— [*Using his teeth to tighten the knot in the string.*] Was it any good?

VERA: I don't really know. She read it out to us, and we all cried.

BELIAEV: Cried? Good Lord, why?

VERA: Because we felt sorry for her.

BELIAEV: For writing such bad poetry?

VERA: Oh, no, because it was so sad.

BELIAEV: Was your school in Moscow?

VERA: Madame Bolusse's. Natalia Petrovna took me away last year.

BELIAEV: Are you fond of Natalia Petrovna?

VERA: Oh, very. She's been so kind to me.

BELIAEV: Are you afraid of her as well?

[*She looks at him; he grins at her.*]

VERA [*smiling*]: A little bit, yes—

BELIAEV [*after a pause*]: And who sent you to the school?

VERA: Her mother, she brought me up. I'm an orphan.

BELIAEV: An orphan? [*Putting down the kite.*] Are you really?

VERA: Yes.

[KATIA *starts to sing again.*]

BELIAEV: My mother died too. So I'm a sort of orphan as well.

VERA: Both orphans—

BELIAEV: It's not our fault, so there's no point in getting depressed about it, is there?

VERA: They say orphans make friends sooner than anybody.

BELIAEV: Do they? [*He looks into her eyes.* KATIA *stops singing. A pause. He goes back to his work.*] How long have I been here? Three, or four—

VERA: Twenty-eight days counting today.

BELIAEV: What a memory! A whole month in the country— There, finished! Look at that tail, there's a swisher for you— [KATIA *returns from the right, goes up to him with her basket. Rising.*] Now to get Kolia—

KATIA: Would you like some more currants, sir?

BELIAEV: No, thank you, Katia.

KATIA [*disappointed*]: Oh— [*She walks slowly back to the right.*]

BELIAEV: Where is Kolia, d'you know?

VERA: Over in the schoolroom with Lizaveta Bogdanovna.

BELIAEV: Keeping a child indoors in this weather—

VERA: Do you know she spoke very nicely about you yesterday?

BELIAEV: Lizaveta Bogdanovna? Did she?

VERA: Don't you like her?

BELIAEV: Never thought about it. [*Finishing off the kite.*]

She can take snuff till she's black in the face, I'm just not interested. [*A pause.* VERA *sighs.*] Why are you sighing?

VERA: I don't know. What a blue sky!

BELIAEV: Is that why you're sighing? Perhaps you're bored?

VERA: Bored? Oh no—

BELIAEV: You're not sickening for something, are you?

VERA: No, but—well— Yesterday I was going up to fetch a book, and suddenly—imagine—I just sat on the stairs and burst into tears.

BELIAEV: Good Lord!

VERA: What could it mean, do you think? Because I'm really quite happy.

BELIAEV [*turning to her*]: Shall I tell you what it is?

VERA: What?

BELIAEV: Growing pains.

VERA: Oh—

BELIAEV [*back to the kite*]: So that's why your eyes looked so swollen last night—

VERA: You noticed?

BELIAEV: Of course I noticed.

[*She looks at him, he is looking at the kite. A pause.* KATIA *is heard singing, very faintly, some way off.* VERA *listens.*]

VERA [*thoughtfully*]: Alexei Nikolaich—

BELIAEV: Hmm?

VERA: Am I like her?

BELIAEV: Not a bit.

VERA [*disappointed*]: Oh.

BELIAEV: For one thing, you're better-looking.

VERA: Am I?

BELIAEV [*he looks at her; an embarrassed pause. Breaking it*]: Well, Vera Alexandrovna, what about young Kolia?

VERA: Why don't you call me Vérochka?

BELIAEV: Shall I? And what about your calling me Alexei?

VERA: Shall I?— [*Starting.*] Oh, bother—

BELIAEV: What is it—

VERA [*in a subdued voice*]: Natalia Petrovna—

BELIAEV [*catching her tone*]: Let's go in to Kolia, shall we? He's bound to have finished his doh-ray-me by now—

VERA: Oh, do you think we ought?

[*They both disappear to the right.* NATALIA *and* RAK-ITIN *re-enter from the left.*]

NATALIA: Surely that was Vérochka scurrying along?

RAKITIN: Was it?

NATALIA: But they looked exactly as if they were running away from us!

RAKITIN: Perhaps they are.

NATALIA: Seriously, I don't think it at all *convenable* for her to be wandering in the garden all by herself with a young man, really I don't.

RAKITIN: I thought you said she was a child.

NATALIA: What? Of course she's a child—but still, it's not quite proper. I shall have to be cross with her.

RAKITIN: How old is she?

NATALIA: Seventeen— [*Sitting.*] Where's the Doctor, he hasn't gone, has he?

RAKITIN [*sitting next to her*]: I rather think he has—

NATALIA: Oh, how provoking, why didn't you get him to stay?—Why a character like that should ever have disguised himself as a provincial apothecary, I can't imagine. He's *so* amusing.

RAKITIN: I had an idea you weren't in a laughing mood today.

NATALIA: Because I've taken against sentimentality? I have, I warn you—nothing, absolutely nothing, could touch me today, I've a heart of stone— But I wanted to see the Doctor, it *is* provoking of you—

RAKITIN: May I ask what about?

NATALIA: You may not, you already know every single thing I do, exactly why I do it—I have an uncontrollable desire to conceal something from you.

RAKITIN: Since I watch you so closely, shall I tell you one thing I have observed?

NATALIA [*a pause. She looks at him, then away*]: I am all ears.

RAKITIN: You won't be annoyed with me?

NATALIA: I should like to be, but I shan't succeed. Go on.

RAKITIN: For some time, Natalia Petrovna, you've been in a state of constant fretfulness.

NATALIA: Go on.

RAKITIN: Not ordinary short temper—but a fretting from within. You appear to be—in conflict with your own self. [*As* NATALIA *traces a pattern in the dust with her parasol.*] I've heard you sigh. Deep long breaths: the sighs of a creature immensely tired, who can never, never come to rest.

[*A pause.* KATIA'S *voice, singing.*]

NATALIA: And what do you conclude from all that, *Monsieur le Microscope?*

RAKITIN: I conclude nothing. But it causes me concern—

NATALIA [*suddenly impatient*]: Oh, for Heaven's sake let's change the subject.

[*A pause.* KATIA'S *voice dies away.*]

RAKITIN: You don't intend going for a drive today—

NATALIA [*suddenly*]: Tell me, what do you think of Bolshintsov?

RAKITIN: Our neighbor, you mean, Afanasy Ivanych?

NATALIA: Yes.

RAKITIN: Well, I never thought to hear you ask tenderly after a beef-witted old jumbo like Bolshintsov. Though I must concede I can't think of anything worse against him.

NATALIA: Oh, he just came into my head.

[*A pause.*]

RAKITIN: Look at the dark green of that oak, against the velvet blue of the sky—the deep glow of those colors—isn't it perfect? What a wealth of life and strength stands embodied in that tree! And then look at this slim young birch;

her tiny leaves shimmer with a sort of liquid radiance, as if they were melting before our eyes— And yet, in her way, the birch is as lovely as the oak.

[*A pause.*]

NATALIA: Rakitin, shall I tell you something?

RAKITIN: Do—

NATALIA: Something about you which I noticed ages ago—[*looking at him*]—I might even say "observed"— You feel the beauties of Nature in a very rarefied way, and expatiate upon them most elegantly; so elegantly, indeed, that in return for the meticulous metaphors you shower upon her, I can imagine Nature saying, "Really, it *is* good of that tall gentleman to say those kind things about me." You court her as a scented marquis in red heels might court a rosy peasant girl. The only fly in the ointment, my dear, is that just as the girl would find every single compliment miles above her head, so Nature doesn't understand a word you say. And shall I tell you why? Because, thank Heaven, she is much coarser than you have any knowledge of; and she's coarse because she's healthy. Birch-trees don't melt or fade away, for the simple reason they're not highly-strung young ladies, they're birch-trees.

RAKITIN: What an onslaught!—I'm a morbid creature: I see.

NATALIA: Oh, you're not the only one. I don't think either of us is spiritually bursting with health.

RAKITIN: That's another thing I've observed.

NATALIA: What?

RAKITIN: Your trick of putting the nastiest things in the most innocent way. Instead of calling somebody an idiot, you turn to him with a smile and say *"Mon cher ami, you and I are fools."*

NATALIA: Well, if the word "morbid" doesn't appeal to you, then I'll just say we're both old. As old as the hills.

RAKITIN: I don't feel particularly ancient.

NATALIA: Do you realize that not ten minutes ago, sharing this same garden seat, two creatures sat together who can truly claim to be young?

[*A pause.*]

RAKITIN: You envy them their artless candor, their innocence—in short, their stupidity?

NATALIA: Do you think they're stupid? Oh, Rakitin, that's so like you! Anyway, what's the point of cleverness if it doesn't amuse? [KATIA *enters from the right, carrying her basket.*] Ah, Katia! Have you been picking fruit, my dear?

KATIA: Yes, madame—

NATALIA: Let me look [*peering into the basket*]: What gorgeous currants, how red they are—

KATIA: Aren't they, madame—

NATALIA: Not as red as your cheeks, though, Katia—

KATIA [*smiling and blushing*]: Oh, madame, do you think so—

NATALIA: I do indeed— [*Suddenly weary.*] You may go, my dear—

[KATIA *curtseys and hurries off to the left.*]

RAKITIN: Another callow creature who appeals to you.

NATALIA: Yes, she's young too. [*Rising, suddenly.*] It's time Vérochka was in. *Au revoir, mon ami.*

[*She opens her parasol and walks slowly away to the right. A pause.*]

RAKITIN: She was right, Mihail Alexandrovich Rakitin— every minute of every day, you spend on the lookout for trivialities, and in the end you've turned into a triviality yourself. [*After a pause.*] And yet— I cannot live without her; to part from Natalia Petrovna would be to leave life itself— What *is* this unrest of hers? Is she tired of me? I know too well the kind of love she bears me—but I had hopes that in time— What am I saying—she's a virtuous woman, and I am not a philanderer—[*smiling wryly*]— worse luck— [*Walking up and down.*] What a beautiful day! [*After a pause.*] Meticulous metaphors, indeed— And why this sudden passion for simplicity? It all seems to go with that new tutor. She couldn't be—no, that's out of the question, she's just in a bad mood; Heaven knows, time will show. [*Sitting again.*]—And it's not the first occasion in your life, my boy, that after a conference with yourself, you've had to throw all your theories overboard, fold your arms meekly and wait for events. [*He opens his magazine.* BELIAEV *comes strolling back from the right.*] Ah, Alexei Nikolaich! Are you after a breath of fresh air too?

BELIAEV: Indeed I am, sir! What a lovely day!

RAKITIN: Won't you sit down?

BELIAEV: Thank you. [*He sits.*]

RAKITIN [*after a pause*]: Did you see Natalia Petrovna?

BELIAEV: Yes, walking over to the schoolroom, with Vera.

RAKITIN: And how do you take to the rustic life?

BELIAEV: Oh, capitally, except for the shooting. That's pretty poor.

RAKITIN: Oh. Are you partial to shooting?

BELIAEV: Very. Are you, sir?

RAKITIN: I'm afraid not. I'm a deplorable shot; much too lazy.

BELIAEV: I'm lazy too, I'm afraid, but not where sport's concerned.

RAKITIN: And entertaining the ladies—are you lazy where that's concerned?

BELIAEV: You're laughing at me, sir— To tell you the honest truth, I'm rather afraid of them.

RAKITIN: The ladies?—Are you? But why should you think I was laughing at you?

BELIAEV: I don't know, I just did. It doesn't matter, sir, really— [*After a pause.*] Could you tell me where I can get some gun-powder?

RAKITIN: Gun-powder? In the town, I should think, but very poor quality—

BELIAEV: That would do—it's not for shooting, it's for fireworks.

RAKITIN: Fireworks? You mean you can make them?

BELIAEV: Oh, yes. I've already picked a spot, on the other side of the lake. As it's little Kolia's birthday tomorrow, I thought it would be just the thing.

RAKITIN: I'm sure Natalia Petrovna will be very touched by your kind thought. [*He has lingered a little over her name.*]

BELIAEV: Oh, do you think so?

RAKITIN: She's taken a liking to you. Did you know?

BELIAEV: Has she really, sir? I'm so glad— Excuse me, sir, isn't that a Moscow magazine?

RAKITIN [*giving it to him*]: Do have it, I've finished—

BELIAEV: Oh, thank you, sir—

RAKITIN: It's a poetry review, I take it because they sometimes publish tolerably good verse.

BELIAEV: Oh. [*Putting down the magazine, disappointed.*] Too bad.

RAKITIN: Why?

BELIAEV: I'm not very struck on poetry.

RAKITIN: Oh. What have you against it?

BELIAEV: I think it's rather affected. I like funny rhymes, of course, but that's different.

RAKITIN: It is, rather— You prefer novels?

BELIAEV: Oh, yes, I like something that tells a story—

RAKITIN: Do you dabble in writing yourself?

BELIAEV: Lord no, I haven't any gifts for it and I know better than to try. I've got my work cut out trying to fathom what others get on to paper.

RAKITIN: Do you realize, Alexei Nikolaich, that very few young men have your common sense?

BELIAEV: Thank you, sir— [*After a pause.*] I chose the lake because I know how to make Roman candles that'll burn on the water.

RAKITIN: Do you really? That must be a lovely sight— Alexei Nikolaich, do you speak French?

BELIAEV: I'm afraid I don't—my laziness again. I'd give a lot to master George Sand in the original—she's a woman of course, but damn good reading. Thank the Lord other people aren't quite such loafers as I am.

RAKITIN: Now you're exaggerating—

BELIAEV: No, I'm not; you see, I know myself.

RAKITIN: I know something about you that you're not aware of.

BELIAEV: Oh? What is it?

RAKITIN: I know that what you look on as a fault in yourself—your naturalness—is the very thing which attracts people to you.

BELIAEV: Attracts people? Who, for example?

RAKITIN: Natalia Petrovna?

BELIAEV: Natalia Petrovna? Oddly enough, she's the one person with whom I don't feel in the least—natural, as you put it.

RAKITIN: Ah—indeed?

BELIAEV: And when all's said and done, surely the most important asset in a man isn't naturalness, but breeding? It's all very well for you, you've *got* breeding— Excuse me, sir—you're rather an odd character, aren't you?

RAKITIN: Am I?

[*A pause.*]

BELIAEV: Did you hear that? Sounded like a corn-crake—

RAKITIN: Perhaps it was—[*As* BELIAEV *rises quickly.*] What is it?

BELIAEV: I'm going to the greenhouse for my shotgun—

[*He starts to go off to the right, and meets* NATALIA.]

NATALIA: Alexei Nikolaich, where are you tearing off to?

BELIAEV: Oh—I was just—

RAKITIN: He heard a corn-crake, and was fetching his gun.

NATALIA [*to* BELIAEV]: Oh, don't do any shooting in the garden, do you mind? Let the poor bird live—besides, it would scare Kolia's Granny out of her skin.

BELIAEV [*confused*]: I beg pardon, madame, I'm sure—

NATALIA [*laughing*]: Alexei Nikolaich, what a thing to say! "I beg pardon, madame, I'm sure," talking like a servant! Mihail Alexandrovich here and I will take you under our wing—*c'est entendu*—*c'est entendu*—

BELIAEV: It's very good of you—

NATALIA: First lesson—no diffidence. That's very impor-

tant; it doesn't suit you at all— Oh, yes, we'll take you in
hand! You're a young man, while he and I—[*pointing her
parasol at* RAKITIN]—are old people. You get busy on my
little Kolia, and we'll get busy on you!

BELIAEV: It's wonderfully kind of you—

NATALIA: *C'est ça*— What have you done with your kite?

BELIAEV: I left it in the schoolroom. I thought you didn't
like it.

NATALIA [*embarrassed*]: Whatever made you think that?
Because I told Vérochka—because I sent her in? [*With ani-
mation.*] Do you know what we'll do? Kolia must have fin-
ished strumming by now, we'll go over and fetch him, and
Vérochka, and the kite, and all go into a field and fly it!
What do you say?

BELIAEV: It would be wonderful, Natalia Petrovna—

NATALIA: Splendid. Take my hand! [*As he hesitates, hold-
out first one hand, then the other.*] Oh, how awkward you
are—*maladroit*—come along—off we go!

[*She and* BELIAEV *hurry off, hand in hand, to the right.*
RAKITIN *looks after them.*]

RAKITIN: I've never seen that expression on her face before. That smile, soft and yet crystal-clear, a look of—yes
—a look of welcome— [*In a sudden outburst.*] Oh God,
spare me the pangs of jealousy!—Especially when it's as
futile as this— [*The* DOCTOR *strolls on from the left, followed by* BOLSHINTSOV, *who lives up to the* DOCTOR'S *description of him: near fifty, fat, good-natured, slow-witted,
and extremely timid. Jauntily.*] Well, well, it's an ill wind—

THE DOCTOR: The lodge-keeper told us the whole family
was in the garden—so here we are!

RAKITIN: But why didn't you come straight up the drive?

THE DOCTOR: As a matter of fact, Afanasy Ivanych here
wanted to call in at the kitchen garden to have a look at
the mushrooms.

BOLSHINTSOV [*puzzled*]: But I—

THE DOCTOR [*to him*]: Now we all know your passion for
mushrooms—

RAKITIN: If you'd rather stay out of doors, I'll go and tell

Natalia Petrovna where you are—I have to go over, anyway—

THE DOCTOR: Ah, well, in that case we won't detain you. Please don't stand on ceremony—

RAKITIN: Thank you. *Au revoir,* gentlemen. [*He bows and hurries off to the right.*]

THE DOCTOR: *Au revoir.* [*To* BOLSHINTSOV.] Now, Afanasy Ivanych, everything depends on—

BOLSHINTSOV [*agitated*]: Ignaty Illyich, you could have knocked me down with a feather— Mushrooms!

THE DOCTOR: Did you expect me to tell him that you were so goggle-eyed with nerves you begged to go miles out of our way, just to gain time?

BOLSHINTSOV: But I don't think I've ever *seen* a mushroom— It may be very slow of me, but I—

THE DOCTOR: It *is* very slow of you, my old dear, and you're leaving the whole thing to me, because I'm that much quicker— When I think you forced me here at the point of a blunderbuss—

BOLSHINTSOV: I know, my friend, but on my own property I feel ready for anything. But now I *am* here, I feel quite giddy— Ignaty Illyich, you interviewed the older person—what *was* her exact answer, yes or no?

THE DOCTOR: Afanasy Ivanych, what is the span from your village to this august domain?

BOLSHINTSOV: Er—fifteen miles—

THE DOCTOR: During those fifteen miles, Afanasy Ivanych, you have asked me that identical question as regular as clockwork, three times to the mile. I have vouchsafed forty-five answers; and now prick up your ears, my old rabbit, for here comes the forty-sixth, and the last. [*Placing him on the seat and sitting beside him.*] This is, word for word, what Natalia Petrovna said to me—

BOLSHINTSOV [*eagerly*]: Yes?

THE DOCTOR [*quoting, slowly*]: "Doctor, on the—"

BOLSHINTSOV [*avidly*]: Yes, I see—

THE DOCTOR [*irritated*]: What d'you mean, you see, I

haven't told you anything yet! She said, "Doctor, on the one hand I—"

BOLSHINTSOV [*holding out his hand*]: "On the one hand" —yes—

THE DOCTOR: "On the one hand, I know very little about Monsieur Bolshintsov—"

BOLSHINTSOV: Monsieur? But I'm not a Frenchman—

THE DOCTOR: I know you're not, and so does she, but as I've told you forty-five times, she fancies you better in French. We'll have another shot— "Doctor, I know very little about Monsieur Bolshintsov, but he looks kind."

BOLSHINTSOV: "Kind." That's nice—

THE DOCTOR: "On the other hand," she went on—

BOLSHINTSOV [*holding out the other hand, thoughtfully*]: The other hand, yes—

THE DOCTOR: "On the other hand, I will not bring pressure to bear on Vérochka, but again on the other hand— [*as* BOLSHINTSOV *holds out the first hand again*]—and if he comes to win her respect, I shall place no obstacles." In a word, Afanasy Ivanych, it's up to you to convince the young lady that marrying you would make her happy.

BOLSHINTSOV [*after thought*]: It's a tall order.

THE DOCTOR: Of course it's a tall order—but cut a dash, my old friend, cut a dash!

BOLSHINTSOV: Cut a dash, yes, that's it— But there is one thing, Ignaty Illyich; you may not believe me, but I have, from my tenderest years, made little contact with the fair sex.

THE DOCTOR: You stagger me.

BOLSHINTSOV: Well, they say it's the first step that counts, don't they— I wondered if you could think of a witty word or two to start the ball rolling?—And as for paying you back—

THE DOCTOR: *Paying* me? [*Rising, and drawing himself up.*] You do not labor, I trust, under the impression that I am bargaining with you?

BOLSHINTSOV [*rising*]: No no, but just to say that if you pull this off you count on more than I said.

THE DOCTOR: Tch, tch, I have no wish to— [*Sitting, and pulling* BOLSHINTSOV *down with him.*] —How d'you mean, more than you said?

BOLSHINTSOV: You know when your nag broke her leg and you said it was a disgrace for a doctor to be seen trudging about like a peasant?

THE DOCTOR: *And* I meant it, my friend—a doctor has as much right to do his rounds on horseback as any lord of the manor—

BOLSHINTSOV: Well, I'll not only replace your beast, I'll give you the team.

THE DOCTOR: The team? You mean—

BOLSHINTSOV: The three horses, and the wagonette with 'em.

THE DOCTOR [*his eyes shining*]: Wagonette— Now where was I— You have under you—three hundred serfs, is it?

BOLSHINTSOV: Three hundred and twenty.

THE DOCTOR: The most eligible bachelor in all the Russias— Always remembering, of course, that young female persons are partial to a good figure. Now yours, while eminently respectable in every way, is a drawback.

BOLSHINTSOV [*depressed*]: A drawback—

THE DOCTOR: But you have another source to draw from —the gushing spring, my dear Afanasy Ivanych, of your virtues; and—of course—of your three hundred and twenty serfs— To cut a long story, I should simply say to the young person—

BOLSHINTSOV: Yes?

THE DOCTOR: "Vera Alexandrovna!"

BOLSHINTSOV [*muttering, his eyes closed*]: "Vera Alexandrovna—"

THE DOCTOR [*as* BOLSHINTSOV *repeats after him, to himself*]: "I am a simple, mild man, and not poor; I should be obliged if you would take a little more notice of me than heretofore, and having made inquiries, give me your answer."

BOLSHINTSOV [*lost in admiration*]: That was a first-rate speech, Ignaty Illyich.

THE DOCTOR: Not bad, was it?

BOLSHINTSOV: Just one thing, my dear friend— You mentioned the word "mild"—you called me "a mild man."

THE DOCTOR: Well, aren't you mild?

BOLSHINTSOV: Yes, yes, of course—but still—

. THE DOCTOR [*sternly*]: But still what?

BOLSHINTSOV [*after a pause*]: No, just tell her I'm a mild man.

THE DOCTOR: One more thing—you won't take offense?

BOLSHINTSOV: No, no, my dear friend—out with it—

THE DOCTOR: You have a regrettable habit, Afanasy Illyich, of mispronouncing French words, and I think it would be safest not to use them.

BOLSHINTSOV: Oh, dear.

THE DOCTOR: For instance, once when you meant to imply that a certain person was distinguished—"*distinguée*" —I heard you exclaim 'The lady looks distinky.' One knows what you mean, but one is not impressed. [*Looking.*] And here they all are— [*As* BOLSHINTSOV *starts to go.*] Now, now, where are you off to? Mushrooms again?

BOLSHINTSOV [*smiling and blushing*]: Oh dear—

[NATALIA *returns from the right, followed by* VERA, BELIAEV (*carrying the kite*), KOLIA, RAKITIN, *and* LIZAVETA BOGDANOVNA. NATALIA *is in high spirits.*]

NATALIA [*to* BOLSHINTSOV *and* THE DOCTOR]: Ah, gentlemen! How are you, Doctor, an unexpected treat! Oh, by the way, you won't forget our picnic tomorrow for Kolia's birthday, will you? And are you well, Afanasy Ivanych?

BOLSHINTSOV [*raising his hat, perspiring and muttering, acutely embarrassed*]: Thank you, lady—thank you—

NATALIA: And to what do we owe this pleasure, Doctor?

THE DOCTOR: My friend here insisted on bringing me with him.

NATALIA: Oh, ho! So you have to be dragged here, do you?

THE DOCTOR: Dragged? Good heavens—

NATALIA: Now I've got you into a muddle—hurrah!

THE DOCTOR [*as the others laugh*]: It's extremely kind of

you to take it like that, Natalia Petrovna. And if I may pass such a remark, it is very pleasant to find you in such a gay mood.

NATALIA: You find it necessary to comment on it? Is it then so very rare?

THE DOCTOR: Good heavens no—good heavens—

NATALIA: *Monsieur le Diplomate* is getting into more and more of a tangle—

KOLIA [*eagerly*]: *Maman,* when do we fly the kite?

NATALIA: Any time you like, my pet [*To* BELIAEV.] Come along, Alexei Nikolaich— [*as* VERA *runs impulsively forward*] —And you, Vera darling—we'll go into the field. [*To the others.*] I don't think any of you would find it much fun, so I'll leave them in your charge, Lizaveta Bogdanovna.

RAKITIN [*as she starts to go*]: But Natalia Petrovna, why do you think we wouldn't be amused?

NATALIA: Because you're so clever— [*To* BELIAEV *and* VERA.] Ready, children?

[*She hurries off to the left, taking* KOLIA *by the hand, followed by* BELIAEV. VERA *starts to follow;* BOLSHINTSOV *tries to intercept her, but cannot get a word out. She stifles a giggle and follows the others.* RAKITIN *looks after them, puzzled and unhappy.* THE DOCTOR *takes his arm, slyly.*]

THE DOCTOR: Just look at the four of them, tearing up to the field! Let's go and see how they get on, shall we? Even though we are so clever! [*Turning and seeing* BOLSHINTSOV *standing alone, the picture of disconsalation, then calling.*] Lizaveta Bogdanovna!

LIZAVETA [*eagerly*]: Doctor—

THE DOCTOR [*to* BOLSHINTSOV]: Our good Afanasy Ivanych, would you offer your arm to this good lady?

BOLSHINTSOV: Only too pleased—

LIZAVETA: Mutual, I'm sure, mutual—

THE DOCTOR: Afanasy Ivanych, you two in front, what d'you think?

[BOLSHINTSOV *gives* LIZAVETA *his arm, ceremoniously; they walk; the others watch them.*]

BOLSHINTSOV [*stiffly*]: The weather is very pleasant to-day, is it not, in a manner of speaking?

LIZAVETA: Isn't it just—

[*They disappear to the left.*]

THE DOCTOR [*to* RAKITIN]: Mihaïl Alexandrovich—[*As* RAKITIN *laughs.*] What are you laughing at?

RAKITIN: I suppose I'm tickled at our bringing up the rear like this.

THE DOCTOR [*as they cross, arm in arm*]: Ah, but don't forget, my dear friend, that the rear guard can only too easily become the advance guard. Shall I tell you how?

RAKITIN: How?

THE DOCTOR: By everybody turning round and going the other way. Ha ha—

[*They follow the others.*]

[*The curtain falls quickly, rising immediately on the next scene.*]

Scene III

The drawing room, the next morning. Early sunlight. A coffee tray on the footstool before the sofa. RAKITIN *and* THE DOCTOR *come in from the hall, arm in arm.*

THE DOCTOR [*speaking as he enters*]: —And to cut a long story short, Mihaïl Alexandrovich—will you give an old friend a helping hand?

RAKITIN: But my dear Ignaty Illyich, I don't quite—

THE DOCTOR: Now see here, my dear old fellow, just for a moment, put yourself in my place. Mind you, I'm really a looker-on, as I'm only dabbling in this to please a bosom friend— [*Sitting on the sofa.*] Oh, dear, my soft old heart will be the ruin of me!

RAKITAN [*smiling*]: I wouldn't say you were anywhere near ruin at the moment—

THE DOCTOR [*laughing*]: Ah ha! Joking apart, old dear, Natalia Petrovna gave me permission to tell the old boy her answer. And now that I have, she's gone into her sulks as if I'd done the wrong thing entirely; and he hangs round my coat-tails like a dear old sheep-dog.

RAKITIN [*sitting next to him, and pouring out coffee*]: Doesn't it seem a pity, Ignaty Illyich, that you stuck your finger in this pie at all? Old Bolshintsov's a fool, now, isn't he?

THE DOCTOR: Of course he's a fool, but if we only allowed the clever ones to get married the race would die out!—Stuck my finger in the pie, indeed—a bosom friend begged me to put a word in—my finger was stuck in for me, *voilà!* Could I refuse, with my soft heart?

RAKITIN: But nobody's blaming you—though we're all entitled to wonder why you're taking so much trouble.

THE DOCTOR: But because the old boy's a very old friend of mine!

RAKITIN: Is he really?

[*They catch each other's eye, and both laugh.*]

THE DOCTOR: There's no pulling wool over your eyes! The fact is, dear fellow, one of my horses has broken his leg.

RAKITIN: And your old friend is mending it for you?

THE DOCTOR: No.

RAKITIN: He's promised you a new horse?

THE DOCTOR: A team of three, and a wagonette.

RAKITIN: Ah— Now I see daylight!

THE DOCTOR: But I wouldn't like you to think I'd be a go-between if he wasn't of the highest character.

RAKITIN: No, no—

THE DOCTOR: The whole thing, quite frankly, goes very much against the grain with me—snuff?

RAKITIN: No thank you—

THE DOCTOR [*sniffing*]: If only I could squeeze a definite "yes" or "no" out of her— You see, the old boy's as innocent as a babe unborn; and besides, his intentions being of the highest order—

RAKITIN: And his horses—

THE DOCTOR: And his horses—

RAKITIN: But where do I come in?

THE DOCTOR: Do we not all know the esteem in which you are held by the lady in question—be an angel from heaven, my dear old Mihail Alexandrovich, put in a word for me—

RAKITIN: Is it your honest opinion that he's a good match for this girl?

THE DOCTOR: If he isn't, then strike me dead where I stand. The first thing in a marriage is a stable character, and the old boy's more than stable, he—he's immovable. I think I hear Natalia Petrovna now—my dear old friend, my benefactor, remember—two chestnuts and a dream of a brown mare—will you do it for me?

RAKITIN [*smiling*]: All right, I'll do my best—

THE DOCTOR: The Lord will bless you. Two chestnuts, and a brown.

[*He hurries into the ballroom as* NATALIA *enters from the study. She sees* RAKITIN *and stops.*]

NATALIA [*hesitating*]: Oh— I thought you were in the garden.

RAKITIN: You look overjoyed to see me—

NATALIA: Oh, don't— Who was that?

RAKITIN: The Doctor.

NATALIA: That provincial Machiavelli— He's still hovering, is he?

RAKITIN: He's staying on for the picnic to which you invited him. The provincial Machiavelli is out of favor today.

NATALIA: He's good value from time to time, but he's inclined to meddle, which I detest. [*Walking about.*] Besides, with all his fawning, he's very impertinent, *and* a cynic— [*Sharply.*] What was he trying on with you?

RAKITIN: He was telling me about your neighbor.

NATALIA [*sitting next to him*]: Oh, that silly old thing.

RAKITIN: You've changed about him, too.

NATALIA: Today is not yesterday.

RAKITIN: It is, as far as I'm concerned, though, isn't it?

NATALIA: How do you mean?

RAKITIN [*handing her coffee*]: You were unkind to me yesterday, and the same holds good today.

NATALIA: I know, my dear, I'm sorry— [*Suddenly gentle.*] Whatever foolish thoughts may come into my head, there is nobody on whom I rely, as I rely on my Michel. [*Quietly.*] There is nobody in the world whom I love, as I love you. [*After a pause.*] You believe me, don't you?

[VERA *begins to play on the pianoforte in the ballroom: Chopin.*]

RAKITIN: I believe you.

NATALIA: But I've come to think, my dear—that one can never—never really be responsible for one's actions; one can swear to nothing. We often fail to understand the past, how can we make pledges for what is to come? You can't put the future into chains.

RAKITIN: That's true enough.

NATALIA [*after a pause*]: Michel, I'm going to tell you something.

RAKITIN: Yes?

NATALIA: It will hurt you, but I know it would hurt you still more if I kept it from you—. This young man—

RAKITIN: Yes?

NATALIA: I find he is constantly in my thoughts.

[*A pause.*]

RAKITIN [*quietly*]: I know.

NATALIA: You know? Michel, since when?

RAKITIN: Yesterday. In that field— If you could have seen yourself!

NATALIA: Did I look so strange?

RAKITIN: I should never have known it was you: your cheeks were flushed, your eyes shone like diamonds. And you looked at him with an attention so trusting, so brimful of happiness, and then the happiness broke into a smile— Even now, at the mere evocation your face is lighting up— [*He averts his eyes—turns away.*]

NATALIA: I don't mind anything you say, Michel, so long as you don't turn away from me—please— You're exaggerating now, you know; he was so wildly young, in that field— I caught it from him—it went to my head, and it'll pass off just like wine, in fact, it's not worth talking about. [*As he does not move.*] I need your help, Michel— don't turn away from me—please—

[*A pause. The music trails away.*]

RAKITIN: I don't think you know yourself quite what is happening to you.

NATALIA: Don't I?

RAKITIN: One minute you say it's hardly worth discussing, the next you're asking for help. People don't ask for help unless they're desperate. You need mine?

NATALIA: Yes, I do.

RAKITIN [*looks at her, realizing at last that his fears were well founded. A pause. Bitterly*]: I see. I'm willing to live up to your expectations, Natalia Petrovna, but I must first recover my breath.

NATALIA: Recover—? But—you don't think I might so far forget myself as to— You're not imagining—

RAKITIN: I imagine nothing. Shall we talk of something else?— [*After a pause.*] About Vérochka?—The Doctor's still waiting for your answer.

NATALIA: You're angry with me.

RAKITIN: I'm sorry for you.

NATALIA: Sorry? [*Rising, and crossing, angrily.*] Oh, Michel, this is too bad— [*As he does not answer, biting her lips.*] The Doctor's waiting for my answer, did you say? But who asked him to meddle—

RAKITIN: He swore to me that you yourself had hinted—

NATALIA: Perhaps I did, I can't remember— What *does* it matter? The Doctor has so many irons in the fire, it can't be such a calamity if one of them falls out and singes his whiskers.

RAKITIN: He merely wants to know—

NATALIA: Michel, I can't bear this cold polite stare—

please! [*A pause.* VERA *begins to play again, in the ball-room.*] I see, I made a mistake in being honest with you. You never suspected a thing, and now you're imagining Heaven knows what— [*After a pause, as he does not move, in a hard voice.*] —I shan't forget— [*Ingenuously.*] Are you jealous?

RAKITIN: I have no right to be jealous, Natalia Petrovna, you know that— As for the other matter, Vera's in the ballroom now—shall I tell her you wish to see her?

NATALIA: This minute? Just as you like—[*As he rises to go.*] Michel, for the last time—you said just now you're sorry for me—is this the way to show it?

RAKITIN [*coldly*]: Shall I tell her?

NATALIA [*angrily*]: Yes, tell her, tell her—[RAKITIN *goes into the ballroom.* NATALIA *stands a moment without moving.*] Even *he* doesn't understand—. And if I cannot turn to him, then who can— My husband? My poor Arkady, I've not given you one thought, not one—

[*The music stops. She looks round, and disposes herself in the armchair.* VERA *comes in from the ballroom, carrying a piece of music.*]

VERA [*timidly*]: Did you want me, Natalia Petrovna?

NATALIA [*starting*]: Ah, Vérochka!

VERA: Do you feel quite well?

NATALIA: Perfectly, it's a little close, that's all. Vera, I want to have a little talk with you.

VERA [*anxiously, putting down her music*]: Oh?—

NATALIA: A serious talk. Sit down, my dear, will you? [*As* VERA *obeys.*] Now— Vera, one thinks of you as still a child; but it's high time to give a thought to your future. You're an orphan, and not a rich one at that: sooner or later you are bound to tire of living on somebody else's property. Now how would you like suddenly to have control of your very own house?

VERA: I'm afraid I—I don't follow you, Natalia Petrovna—

NATALIA: You are being sought in marriage. [VERA *stares*

at her. A pause.] You didn't expect this? I must confess I didn't either; you are still so young. I refuse to press you in the slightest—but I thought it my duty to let you know. [*As* VERA *suddenly covers her face with her hands.*] Vera! My dear— What is it? [*Taking her hands.*] But you're shaking like a leaf!

VERA: Natalia Petrovna, I'm in your power—

NATALIA: In my power? Vera, what do you take me for? [*Cajoling, as* VERA *kisses her hands.*] In my power, indeed— will you please take that back, this muinte? I command you! [*As* VERA *smiles through her tears.*] That's better— [*Putting an arm around her, and drawing her nearer.*] Vera, my child, I tell you what—you'll make believe I'm your elder sister—and we'll straighten out these strange things together—what do you say?

VERA: If you would like me to—yes—

NATALIA: Good— Move closer—that's better— First of all—as you're my sister, this is your home; so there's no possible question of anybody pining to be rid of you— now is that understood?

VERA [*whispering*]: Yes—

NATALIA: Now one fine day your sister comes to you and says "What do you think, little one? Somebody is asking for your hand!" Well, what would be your first thought? That you're too young?

VERA: Just as you wish—

NATALIA: Now now—does a girl say "just as you wish" to her sister?

VERA [*smiling*]: Well, then, I'd just say "I'm too young."

NATALIA: Good; your sister would agree, the suitor would be given "no" for an answer, *fini*— But suppose he was a very nice gentleman with means, prepared to bide his time, in the hope that one day—what then?

VERA: Who is this suitor?

NATALIA: Ah, you're curious. Can't you guess?

VERA: No.

NATALIA: Bolshintsov.

VERA: Afanasy Ivanych?

NATALIA: Afanasy Ivanych. It's true he's not very young, and not wildly prepossessing—

VERA [*begins to laugh, then stops and looks at* NATALIA]: You're joking—

NATALIA [*after a pause, smiling*]: No, but I see the matter is closed. If you had burst into tears when he was mentioned, there might have been some hope for him; but you laughed— [*Rising, smiling wryly.*] The matter is closed.

VERA: I'm sorry, but you took me completely by surprise— Do people still get married at his age?

NATALIA: But how old do you take him for? He's on the right side of fifty!

VERA: I suppose he is, but he has *such* a peculiar face—

NATALIA: Bolshintsov—my dear, you are dead and buried, may you rest in peace— It was foolish of me to forget that little girls dream of marrying for love.

VERA: But, Natalia Petrovna—didn't *you* marry for love?

NATALIA [*after a pause*]: Yes, of course I did— *Eh, bien, fini!* Bolshintsov, you are dismissed— I must confess I never much fancied that puffy old moon-face next to your fresh young cheek. There!— [*Sitting again, next to* VERA.] And you're not frightened of me any more?

VERA: No, not any more—

NATALIA: Well, then, Vérochka darling, just whisper quietly in my ear—you don't want to marry Bolshintsov because he's too old and far from an Adonis—but is that the only reason?

VERA [*after a pause*]: Natalia Petrovna, isn't it reason enough?

NATALIA: Undoubtedly, my dear—but you haven't answered my question.

[*A pause.*]

VERA: There's no other reason.

NATALIA: Oh— [*After a pause.*] Of course, that puts the matter on rather a different footing.

VERA: How do you mean, Natalia Petrovna?

NATALIA: I realize you can never fall in love with Bolshintsov; but he's an excellent man. And if there is nobody else— Isn't there *anybody* you're fond of?

VERA: Well, there's you, and little Kolia—

NATALIA [*with a hint of impatience*]: Vera, you must know what I mean— Out of the young men you've met— have you formed any attachment at all?

VERA: I quite like one or two, but—

NATALIA: For instance, don't I remember at the Krinitsins' your dancing three times with a tall officer—what was his name—

VERA: With a long mustache? [*Smiling.*] He giggled all the time.

NATALIA: Oh— [*After a pause.*] What about our philosopher Rakitin?

VERA: Mihail Alexandrovich? I'm very fond of him, of course, who wouldn't be—

NATALIA: An elder brother, I see— [*Suddenly.*] And the new tutor?

[*A pause.*]

VERA: Alexei Nikoláich?

NATALIA: Alexei Nikolaich.

VERA: I like him very much.

[*She has blushed;* NATALIA *is watching her narrowly.*]

NATALIA: He is nice, isn't he? Such a pity he's so bashful with everybody—

VERA [*innocently*]: Oh, he isn't bashful with me!

NATALIA [*after a slight pause*]: Isn't he?

VERA: I suppose it's because we're both orphans. I think he must appear shy to you because he's afraid of you. You see, he's had no chance to know you—

NATALIA: Afraid of me? How do you know?

VERA: He told me so.

NATALIA: He told you—

VERA: Don't you like him, Natalia Petrovna?

NATALIA: He seems very kind-hearted.

VERA: Oh, he is! If you only knew— [*Turning to her, en-*

thusiastically.] The whole of this household loves him—
he's so warm, once he's got over his shyness—the other
day an old beggar-woman had to be taken to hospital—do
you know he carried her the whole way? And one day he
picked a flower for me off a cliff—he's as nimble as a rein-
deer. D'you remember yesterday, when he cleared that tremendous ditch? And he's always so good-tempered and
gay—

NATALIA: That doesn't sound a bit like him—when he's
with me, he—

VERA: But that's what I mean, Natalia Petrovna, it's because he doesn't know you! I'll tell him how truly kind you
are—

NATALIA [*rising, ironically*]: Thank you, my dear—

VERA: You'll soon see the difference—because he listens to what I say, though I *am* younger than he is—

NATALIA: I never knew you two were such friends. You
must be careful, Vera.

VERA: Careful?

NATALIA: I know he's a very pleasant young man, but
at your age, it's not quite— People might think— [*As* VERA
blushes, and looks down.] Don't be impatient, my dear,
will you, if I seem to be laying down the law? We older
people regard it as our business to plague the young with
our "don'ts" and "mustn'ts." But as you like him, and nothing more, there's no real need for me to say another word.
[*Sitting next to her again.*] Is there?

VERA [*raising her eyes timidly*]: He—

NATALIA: Vera, is that the way to look at a sister? [*Caress-
ing her.*] If your *real* sister asked you very quietly, "Vérochka, what *exactly* are your feelings toward So-and-So?"
—what would you answer? [*As* VERA *looks at her, hesitating.*] Those eyes are dying to tell me something— [VERA *suddenly presses her head to* NATALIA'S *breast.* NATALIA *bites
her lips. A pause.*] My poor Vera.

VERA [*without raising her head*]: Oh dear—I don't know
what's the matter with me—

NATALIA: My poor sweet— [*As* VERA *presses herself closer to her.*] And he—what of him?

VERA: I don't know—

NATALIA: Vera, what of him?

VERA: I don't know, I tell you— Sometimes I imagine—

NATALIA: You imagine what?

VERA [*her face hidden*]: That I see a look in his eyes—as if he thought of me—as a special person—perhaps— [*Disengaging herself, trying to be calm.*] —Oh, I don't know— [*She raises her head, and sees the expression on* NATALIA'S *face.*] What's the matter, Natalia Petrovna?

NATALIA [*is staring at her, as if she were a stranger*]: The matter?— [*Recovering.*] What did you say? Nothing—

VERA: But there *is* something the matter! [*Rising.*] I'll ring—

NATALIA: No, no—don't ring— [*Louder.*] —Please! It's passed off already. You go back to your music—and we— we'll talk another time.

VERA: You're not angry with me, Natalia Petrovna?

NATALIA: Not in the least—I just want to be by myself.

[VERA *tries to take her hand;* NATALIA *turns away as if she had not noticed her gesture.*]

VERA [*tears in her eyes*]: Natalia Petrovna—

NATALIA: Please— [VERA *goes slowly back into the ballroom.* NATALIA *does not move.*] These children love each other.—Well, it's a touching idea, and may Heaven bless them both. The way she came out with it—and I with no idea—[*laughing feverishly*]—ha! [*Rising, vehement.*] But all is not lost—oh, no— [*Stopping, and collecting herself.*] But I don't know myself any more—what am I doing? [*After a pause, deliberately.*] Shall I tell you, Natalia Petrovna? You're trying to marry a poor orphan girl to a foolish fond old man—you've gone as far as to use that wily old doctor as a go-between— Then there's your philosopher, and then your husband—what is happening— [*Panic-stricken, her hands to her face.*] —What is happening? [*After a pause, slowly.*] Unhappy woman, for the first time in your life—you are in love.

[*In the ballroom,* VERA *begins to play on the piano-forte; the same Chopin mazurka.* NATALIA *listens, and walks slowly and dreamily out into the garden. The music echoes louder as the curtain slowly falls.*]

act 2

Scene I

The drawing room, a few hours later; afternoon. NATALIA *is lying on the sofa, an untouched tray of food beside her. The blinds are down, and she is in a fitful sleep. A pause. A knock at the study door; a pause; another louder knock.* NATALIA *starts and wakes.*

NATALIA [*calling*]: Come in— [KATIA *enters, carrying a bottle of smelling-salts; she goes to* NATALIA, *who takes the bottle and sniffs it.* KATIA *takes the tray of food, curtseys, and goes back into the study, shutting the door behind her.* NATALIA *rises and goes to the French windows. A pause.*] How has it happened? I still don't know—it's like—like a poison. One minute life was ordinary, the next—everything shattered and swept away— He's afraid of me, the same as everybody else, and as for any qualities I possess, how could he appreciate them? Rakitin was right, they're both stupid—how I hate that clever man! Control your-self— [*Deliberating.*] Yes, I'm very much taken with him; very much indeed— [*After a pause.*] He must go away— Love—so this is what it feels like—this—frightening en-chantment— I'll go to Arkady—yes, my sweet trusting hus-band—all the others are strangers, and will remain stran-gers— [*After a pause.*] But could she have made a mis-

take—it might be hero-worship, a sort of calf-love. I'll ask
him myself— [*After a pause, reproachfully.*] What is this,
Natalia Petrovna, you refuse to give up hope? And what,
pray, are you hoping for? Oh, God, don't let me despise
myself! [*She hides her head in her hands.*]

RAKITIN [*comes in from the garden. He is pale and disturbed. He sees her*]: Natalia Petrovna— [*He raises the
blinds; the room is flooded with sunlight.*]

NATALIA [*raising her head*]: Yes, who is it? [*Seeing him.*]
Oh—

RAKITIN: We waited for you at the picnic—Kolia and
everybody were bitterly disappointed—

NATALIA: I had a bad headache. I sent a message—

RAKITIN: I've come to ask you to forgive me.

NATALIA: Forgive you?

RAKITIN: I made a fool of myself this morning— You
see, Natalia Petrovna, however modest a man's hopes—
when they are suddenly snatched away, it's hard not to lose
control, just for a moment. But I am myself again. [*After
a pause, kneeling before her.*] Please don't turn away, as I
did.—I am once more the Michel you've always known,
the man who asks nothing better than to be your servant—
you remember what you said? [*As she sits motionless, gazing at the floor.*] "There's nobody in the world—" —remember? Give me back your trust!

NATALIA [*absently*]: Yes— [*Collecting herself.*] I'm sorry,
I haven't heard a word you've been saying—Michel, what is
the matter with me?

RAKITIN: You are in love
    [*A pause.*]

NATALIA [*slowly*]: But Michel, it's madness—can it happen so suddenly?— [*Brusquely.*] She loves him, you know.
They love each other— Michel, please—please tell me what
to do!

RAKITIN: I will, on one condition: that you'll have complete faith in my disinterested wish to help you.

NATALIA: I will— I will! Michel, I'm standing on the
edge of a precipice. Save me!

RAKITIN: He must go away. [*A pause. She looks at him.*] Right away. I won't drag in—your husband, or your duty, because such sentiments would not come well from me— but if these children love each other—imagine yourself standing between them.

NATALIA: He must go.

RAKITIN: For the sake of your happiness, both he and I— must go away for good.

NATALIA: You—go away too?

RAKITIN: It's the only way out.

NATALIA [*desperately*]: And then—what? What shall I have to live for?

RAKITIN: But—your husband, your son— What have you to live for, indeed!— [*As* NATALIA *looks away, without answering.*] Listen—I'll stay a day or two after he's gone, just to make sure that you—

NATALIA [*somberly*]: I see.

RAKITIN: You see what?

NATALIA: That you are counting on a force of habit— which you call our old friendship—bringing me close to you again—am I right?

RAKITIN: Now you are insulting me. After your promise just now—when all I want on earth is for your good name to shine untarnished before the world—

NATALIA: My good name? But this is something new— why have you never mentioned it before? [*He shakes his head despairingly, and starts to go; she holds out her hand toward him.*] Michel—

RAKITIN [*taking her in his arms, overcome*]: Natalia Petrovna—

NATALIA: Can anyone ever have been so unhappy— [*Leaning against his shoulder.*] —Help me, Michel—without you I am lost—

YSLAEV'S VOICE: Mind you, Mamma, it's always been my firm opinion—

[*He enters from the hall,* ANNA SEMYENOVNA *on his arm. They both see* RAKITIN *and* NATALIA, *and stop in*

amazement. NATALIA *turns her head, sees them, gives a
distracted sob, and hurries into the study.* RAKITIN
stands where he is, acutely embarrassed.]

ANNA: Well, upon my soul! What's the matter with Natalia Petrovna—

RAKITIN: Nothing, I tell you—really nothing—

ANNA: But my dear Mihail Alexandrovich, it couldn't
be nothing! Well, upon my soul— [*Making for the study.*]
I'll go and ask her, point blank—

RAKITIN: No, I beg of you—

YSLAEV: But I should like to be enlightened—what's behind it all?

[ANNA *sits on the sofa, and glares at* RAKITIN.]

RAKITIN: There's nothing behind it, Arkady, I swear to
you. I promise on my word of honor that tomorrow morning I'll explain the whole thing.

YSLAEV: I—I'm right out of my depth—Natalia's never
behaved like this before—it's quite fantastic—

ANNA: But she was crying! I could see the tears—and
dashing out as if we were a couple of perfect strangers—

RAKITIN: Listen, dear people, both of you. Natalia Petrovna and I were in the throes of a discussion, and I must
ask you—just for a moment—to leave us completely alone.

YSLAEV: Alone? But is there a secret between you?

RAKITIN: In a way, yes—but you shall know it.

YSLAEV [*after a pause*]: Very well, Mamma, we'll leave
them to wind up this mysterious duologue in camera—

ANNA: But what on earth—

YSLAEV: Come along, Mamma, *please* don't let it be one
of your obstinate days.

RAKITIN: I beg of you to rest assured—

YSLAEV [*coldly*]: I require no assurance, thank you.

ANNA: I repeat—

YSLAEV [*to* ANNA *sternly*]: Mamma—

[ANNA *rises, takes his arm and they both go into the
ballroom. When he is sure they are out of ear-shot,*
RAKITIN *hurries to the study door.*]

RAKITIN [*calling*]: Natalia Petrovna—

NATALIA [*comes back from the study; she is very pale*]: What did they say?

RAKITIN: I said I'd explain the whole thing tomorrow, which means we have today anyway— [*As she sways, and he leads her to a chair.*]—I'll think of something—you can see now, can't you, that we cannot go on like this? I'll have a word with him presently; I feel sure somehow that he's a boy with the right instinct, and he'll see at once—

NATALIA: A word with him? But what will you say?

RAKITIN: Why, that he and I must leave here at once.

[*A pause.*]

NATALIA: Rakitin, do let us be careful.

RAKITIN: Go on.

NATALIA: Are we not being a little rash? I lost my head for a minute, and made you lose yours—and all for nothing, we may discover—

RAKITIN: For nothing?

NATALIA: I mean it! What are we doing? It seems only a moment ago that this was a house of quiet and peace—and look at us now! Really, this nonsense has gone far enough, we're going to take life up where we left off—and as for this dramatic *rencontre* you're planning with my husband —don't bother, because I'll tell him myself all about our little tea-cup tempest, and we'll sit back together and laugh about it.

RAKITIN: Natalia Petrovna, this is dangerous talk indeed.

NATALIA: What do you mean?

RAKITIN: You're smiling, but you're deathly pale.

NATALIA: You don't think I've changed my mind about —about the young tutor leaving? Because I propose to dismiss him myself.

RAKITIN: Yourself?

NATALIA: He must have come back with the others—send him to me, will you?

RAKITIN: Now?

NATALIA: This minute. You see, I'm so completely recovered, I know I can do it.

RAKITIN: But what will you say to him? He confessed to me himself that he's always tongue-tied with you—

NATALIA [*sharply*]: You've already discussed me with him?—[*As he looks at her, a cold, fixed look.*] I'm sorry, Michel—send him to me, there's a dear; I'll give him his *congé*, and everything will be over and done with, like a bad dream.

RAKITIN: Very well.

NATALIA [*as he goes to the ballroom door*]: Thank you Michel—

RAKITIN [*turning, in an outburst*]: Oh, please—at least spare me your gratitude—

[*He controls himself and hurries into the ballroom. A pause.*]

NATALIA [*touched*]: Michel, you're a truly generous creature— But have I ever really loved you?

RAKITIN'S VOICE [*in the hall*]: Monsieur Beliaev! One moment—

NATALIA [*starts, crosses, and sits on the sofa in readiness for the interview*]: One last effort, and I shall be free. Freedom and peace— [*shutting her eyes*] —How I long for you both—

BELIAEV [*enters from the ballroom. He comes down, inquiringly, and looks at her. A pause*]: Natalia Petrovna. [*As she opens her eyes, and looks at him.*] You sent for me?

NATALIA: I should like an explanation.

BELIAEV: An explanation?

NATALIA [*without looking at him, after a pause*]: I'm afraid—I'm dissatisfied with you.

BELIAEV [*dumbfounded*]: Dissatisfied? [*As she rises and wanders restlessly.*] If I have given any impression of neglecting my duties—

NATALIA: No, no, I've been more than pleased with the way you've been handling Kolia—

BELIAEV: Then—excuse me—what—

NATALIA: Please don't take it too much to heart. You're very young, and never having lived in a strange house before, you could hardly have foreseen— Alexei Nikolaich, it's just this: Vérochka has made a clean breast to me of the whole thing.

[*She looks at him, for the first time. A pause.*]

BELIAEV [*bewildered*]: Vera Alexandrovna?

NATALIA: Yes.

BELIAEV: But made a clean breast of what?

NATALIA: You mean to say you cannot guess?

BELIAEV: No.

NATALIA: Oh— Well, if you really don't know—then please forgive me—let's say no more about it—[*Looking at him again, while he stares at her, still bewildered.*] Do you know that I'm not sure I believe you? Though I understand exactly why you should pretend—

BELIEAV: I'm sorry, Natalia Petrovna, but I have not the faintest idea to what you are referring.

NATALIA: Now come, you can't pretend that you haven't noticed!

BELIAEV: Noticed what?

NATALIA: That she is head over heels in love with you. She told me herself— Well?

BELIAEV: I— But—I've always behaved to Vera Alexandrovna—

NATALIA: I put the question to you as to a man of honor —what are your intentions?

BELIAEV: My—intentions?

NATALIA: Yes.

BELIAEV [*acutely embarrassed*]: Natalia Petrovna, this—this is a bolt from the blue.

NATALIA [*after a pause*]: I'm not doing this at all well— You think I'm angry with you—don't you? I'm not, I'm just—concerned—understandably, I think. Shall we sit down? [*She sits.* BELIAEV *hesitates, and sits next to her.*] Vera loves you—oh, I know that's not your fault, I'm quite ready to believe you had nothing to do with it—but you see Alexei Nikolaich, I'm directly responsible for her future. At her age such upheavals do not last long, and now that I've told you, I know I can rely on you to change *your* attitude toward her.

BELIAEV: But Natalia Petrovna—in what way?

NATALIA: By avoiding her— [*After a pause.*] Mind you, when I told you all that, I took it for granted that on your side there was nothing.

BELIAEV [*perplexed*]: And if there had been?

NATALIA: If there had been— You're not rich, but you're young, you have a future, and if two people love each other—

BELIAEV: But—

NATALIA [*hastily*]: Oh, please don't think I'm trying to extort a confession from you— I must remind you, though, that Vera was under the impression that you were not entirely indifferent to her.

[*A pause.*]

BELIAEV [*rises, acutely perplexed*]: As you have been frank with me, Natalia Petrovna, may I be frank with you?

NATALIA: By all means—

BELIAEV: I have a great affection for Vera Alexandrovna, but not—anything—anything more at all—and if, as you say, she is under the impression that I—that I am not indifferent to her, I must tell her the truth. But having told her, it would create too painful a situation—and it will be impossible for me to stay on here.

NATALIA [*after a pause*]: I see—

BELIAEV: I knew you would— I need not tell you how hard it will be for me to leave your house—

NATALIA: Will it?—

BELIAEV: I shall always think of you with—with the deepest gratitude— [*After a pause.*] Will you excuse me for now? I shall ask the honor of taking my formal leave of you, later on—

NATALIA [*shrugging her shoulders*]: Just as you wish. —But I must confess—

BELIAEV: Yes?

NATALIA: I didn't expect quite this. [*Rising.*] All I intended was to remind you that Vera is still a child. I rather feel now that I've exaggerated—is it absolutely necessary for you to go?

BELIAEV: I'm sorry, but I don't see how I can stay.

NATALIA: I'm not in the habit of pressing people against their will, but I must confess to being a little displeased by this turn of events.

BELIAEV: Displeased?—Natalia Petrovna— [*Hesitating.*] —I—I'll stay.

NATALIA: Ah— [*After a pause.*] You've changed your mind very quickly? [*Another pause, then spasmodically.*] Perhaps you're right, perhaps you ought to go after all.

BELIAEV: Thank you. I am at your service. [*He bows and starts to go.*]

NATALIA: One thing, though—you said you were going to explain something to Vera—I question the wisdom of that, very much.

BELIAEV: I bow to your wishes.

NATALIA [*as he goes*]: As for your going away, I'll let you know this evening. [BELIAEV *inclines his head and goes out into the hall. A pause.*] He does not love her!—Though I can't be proud of an interview that starts off dismissing him, and ends up begging him to stay. [*Going up, and sitting at the table.*] And what right had I to tell him the poor girl's madly in love with him, I who dragged the confession out of her, and in such a heartless, cruel way—not even a confession, a half-avowal— [*Covering her face with her hands.*] —What have I done!—Perhaps he was beginning to fall in love with her? If he was, what right had I to trample such a flower into the mud— But have I trampled it *right* in—perhaps he was deceiving me—after all, I did my best to deceive *him*— No, he's too high-minded; not like me— When I think how crafty I tried to be with him, and how courageously he dealt with me: he was a man, suddenly— If he stays—I forgo any self-respect I ever had. [*Rising.*] He leaves, or Natalia Petrovna—is lost. I'll write to him—before he has time to see her—he must go! [*She clasps her hands and walks swiftly up the stairs and into the hall.*]

CURTAIN

Scene II

A corner of the garden, a few hours later; evening. Fitful sunlight; storm-clouds have gathered.

A pause. KATIA *enters cautiously from the left, looks round, tiptoes quickly across and peers anxiously over to the right.*

KATIA: I can't see him—bother! Then why did they tell me he was coming over to the greenhouse? I wish he'd hurry up, now's the time, while they're all at the schoolroom tea— [*Sighing, sitting on the seat.*] Can it be true, this hasty tale that he's going away?— [*After another sigh.*] Poor little thing—the way she begged and begged me!—Well, the least they can ask for is a last little chat together, the sweet pets— Mercy, what a hot day it's been—but it looks as if the rain might start any minute— [*Looking out, and stepping quickly back.*] My goodness, they're not coming down here—yes, they are—oh, mercy me—

[*She runs off right, as* LIZAVETA *and* THE DOCTOR *enter from the left.*]

THE DOCTOR: Looks like another downpour—we'll shelter in this corner—what d'you say?

LIZAVETA: Oh—[*confused*]—I don't know, I'm sure.

THE DOCTOR: You must admit, Lizaveta Bogdanovna, that the clouds have picked the most awkward moment to gather. [*As they settle on the seat.*] Just as we were getting to a—shall I say a soulful stage?

LIZAVETA: Soulful? [*With downcast eyes.*] Oh, Ignaty Illyich—

THE DOCTOR: But now they're all over in the schoolroom, we can sit here and take up the sentimental cudgels where we left off—

LIZAVETA: Cudgels—the things you think of—

THE DOCTOR: Snuff?

LIZAVETA: Well, just this once—

THE DOCTOR [*as they both sniff*]: By the way, did you say the old tabby was in one of her tantrums today?

LIZAVETA: The master's mother? I should think she is. You know what happened this afternoon, don't you—oh, no, I mustn't, it's scandal—

THE DOCTOR: Oh, yes, you must, or I'll lock you up in a cupboard—

LIZAVETA: Oh, you are a terror! Well, she walked in here and found Natalia Petrovna with her professor as she calls him, with her head on his shoulder—crying!

THE DOCTOR: Crying? You don't say— But take it from me, Rakitin's not to be labeled as a dangerous customer.

LIZAVETA: How very very interesting—why, do you think?

THE DOCTOR: Much too good a conversationalist. Ordinary men may lose their heads and behave like beasts, but with those clever ones the whole thing gushes away down a waste-pipe of talk. It's the quiet ones with eyes like live coals and a broad back of the neck—the world over, that spells red for danger— But shall we leave the riff-raff, bless 'em, and glance at our own affairs? Well?

LIZAVETA [*her eyes fluttering*]: Well, said the echo—

THE DOCTOR: Would you object to my inquiring why, when one puts to you a simple question, you raise and lower your eyeballs as if you were a mechanical doll?

LIZAVETA [*rattled*]: Oh—Doctor—

THE DOCTOR [*rising, and pacing*]: We're neither of us chickens, and all this simpering about the bush doesn't suit us in the least. What d'you say to a down-to-earth chat, in keeping with—with the length of our teeth?

LIZAVETA: Oh, dear—

THE DOCTOR: To start with, we like each other; and in other ways surely, we're well suited. I must, in fairness, describe myself as not exactly of high descent—

LIZAVETA [*tolerantly*]: Ah, but a natural gentleman—

THE DOCTOR: —But then of course you're not exactly

blue blood yourself. I'm not rolling in money; if I were, I'd obviously be flying higher, but still— I've got a respectable enough practice; not all my patients die— And I may take it, I hope, that after fifteen years, the first careless rapture of being a governess is wearing off, and that you're also just about sick of waiting hand over fist on a female dragon, when you're not cheating at cards to make her think she's won. [*Sitting again.*] Eh?

LIZAVETA: Oh, dear—

THE DOCTOR: Then there's me. I can't say I'm tired of being a bachelor—on the contrary, suits me to a T; but I'm not getting any younger, and my cook is robbing me. So everything fits in nicely— But there's one thing, Lizaveta Bogdanovna; you don't know me. I know you, of course, backward.

LIZAVETA [*not sure whether she is on her head or her heels*]: Oh, Doctor, really?

THE DOCTOR: Backward. And I can't say you're entirely free from faults.

LIZAVETA [*stiffly*]: Such as?

THE DOCTOR: For one thing, being a spinster for so long has turned you a little bit sour.

LIZAVETA: Oh.

THE DOCTOR: But that would right itself in a jiffy—in the moral hands of a good husband, a wife is clay— But before the ting-a-ling of wedding bells, I'm more than anxious for you to know me, so you can't turn on me afterward. I won't have any wool over your eyes—see what I mean? For example, it wouldn't surprise me if you took me for a cheerful man?

LIZAVETA: Cheerful? Oh, but of course—I've always known you were one to set the table in a roar—

THE DOCTOR: Exactly. Just because I play the fool, and tell the gentry funny stories, you label me like a shot as a sanguine character. Shall I tell you something? If those gentry weren't being damned useful to me, I wouldn't look at 'em twice. As it is, give me half a chance to poke fun at 'em to their faces without actually flicking 'em on the raw, and I'll take it. I get my own back—ah, yes!

LIZAVETA: D'you include Natalia Petrovna?

THE DOCTOR [*mimicking*]: "Now Doctor, you've a tongue like a rapier, which is what I like and respect you for—" He he he, coo away, my dove, coo away! She's like all the others, that crinkle up their society faces at you in a permanent smile of hail-fellow-well-met, and all the time you can see their eyes writing the word "peasant" flat across your phiz; say what you like, they've no use for us. And just because they drench themselves in eau-de-cologne and drawl every syllable as if they were dropping it accidentally for you to pick up, they think you can't trip 'em by the heels. They're human just like us poor sinners, *and* what's more—[*with meaning*]—they're not saints themselves.

LIZAVETA: Ignaty Illyich, you take my breath away.

THE DOCTOR: I knew I would. Anyway, I must have proved to you that I'm not a sanguine character. Mind you, don't think because I play the fool that any of 'em has ever dared to snub me. They're even scared of me; they know I can bite. There was a big dinner once, and sitting a yard from me a landowner fellow—regular son of the soil suddenly up to his knees in filthy lucre; well, just for a joke, in front of the whole room, he took a radish and stuck it in my hair.

LIZAVETA: He didn't! Heavens, what did you do?

THE DOCTOR: Rose quietly to my full height, removed the offending vegetable from my person, bowed, and with the utmost cool courtesy challenged him to a duel.

LIZAVETA [*thrilled and shocked*]: Oh! What did he do?

THE DOCTOR: Nearly had a stroke. Then in front of the whole room, the host made him ask my pardon; it had the most tremendous effect on everybody. Of course I'd known beforehand he was a martyr to gout and wouldn't fight anyway, but still— What I'm getting at, Lizaveta Bogdanovna, is that although I have an unconscionable amount of self-esteem, my life hasn't really come up to scratch. Nobody could call me well-read, and I'm not a good doctor—it's no use pretending I am, and if you ever fall ill, take a tip from one who knows, and don't call *me* in— I'm good enough for these provincial invalids, of course, but it ends there. And now my personal character.

LIZAVETA [*apprehensively*]: Personal—yes?

THE DOCTOR: In my own home I am extremely morose, abnormally silent, and highly exacting. Have I made myself clear?

LIZAVETA: Yes—oh, yes—

THE DOCTOR: Though in fairness I must add that so long as my habits are observed and good hot food is served consistently before me, I keep my temper. What d'you say?

LIZAVETA: Ignaty Illyich, what can I say? Unless you've been slandering yourself on purpose—

THE DOCTOR [*rising, and pacing*]: But you silly woman, I haven't been slandering myself at all! Kindly keep in mind that any other man would ha' died rather than breathe a word till after the wedding, when it'd be too late—no, I'm too proud to do that.

LIZAVETA [*looking at him*]: Proud?

THE DOCTOR: Yes, you can stare as much as you like— proud. To a stranger I'd bow to the ground for a sack of flour, saying to myself, "What a fool, my friend, how you rise to the bait—*how* you rise!" [*Sitting again.*] But to you, Lizaveta Bogdanovna—[*taking her hand*] my future spouse —I say what I think. At least, I don't say *everything* I think—I must be frank—but near enough not to mislead you. Well, that's me. A funny old stick, eh?

LIZAVETA: A little—ah—eccentric, perhaps—

THE DOCTOR: One of these days I'll tell you the story of my early life, and you'll be amazed that I've come through as well as I have— And now I'll give you a little time to chew the cud, what d'you say?

LIZAVETA: Oh—

THE DOCTOR: You shut yourself up somewhere, go carefully into the whole thing, and let me know. By the way, how old are you?

LIZAVETA [*knocked off her perch*]: Oh. Thirty.

THE DOCTOR: No, you're not, you're forty.

LIZAVETA [*with spirit*]: No, I'm not, I—I'm thirty-six.

THE DOCTOR: Well, thirty-six isn't thirty. That's another habit you'll have to get rid of, Lizaveta Bogdanovna. Anyway a married woman of thirty-six isn't old at all. You shouldn't take snuff either. [*Rising.*] I think it's clearing up.

LIZAVETA [*rising*]: Yes, it seems to have blown over, doesn't it?

THE DOCTOR: So I may expect to hear from you in a day or two?

LIZAVETA [*suddenly practical*]: Tomorrow.

THE DOCTOR: Good! I like that, Lizaveta Bogdanovna— common sense, nothing like it— Oh, just one more thing.

LIZAVETA [*turning*]: Yes?

THE DOCTOR: I haven't kissed your hand, and I believe in these circumstances it's expected— [*She holds out her hand; he kisses it, while she blushes.*] That's over—

[*She takes his arm and they go out to the left.* KATIA *emerges cautiously from the right.*]

KATIA: Mercy, what a spiteful man! And the *things* he said. And now I've missed just what I came down here for— [*Sitting on the seat.*] And so Lizaveta Bogdanovna will be Mrs. Medicine— [*Giggling.*] —Oh dear, it's so funny, I'm glad I'm not in her shoes— It's actually been raining over by the greenhouse—the grass looks as if it's had a wash. And what a lovely smell. Must be the wild cherry. [*Sentimentally.*] Oh, dear— Here he is!— [BELIAEV *appears from over the bridge left. Calling cautiously.*] Alexei Nikolaich!

BELIAEV [*turning*]: Yes, who wants me? [*Coming up to the seat.*] Oh, Katia, it's you!

KATIA: I want to tell you something.

BELIAEV: Tell me something? All right— [*Sitting beside her.*] Ecco! D'you know, Katia, you're looking damned pretty today?

KATIA [*blushing and giggling*]: Oh go on—

BELIAEV: You are. [*Taking a peach from his pocket.*] Peach?

KATIA: No, thank you, really—you have it—

BELIAEV: Did I turn down the red currants you offered me yesterday? Come on, take it—I picked it for you.

KATIA: Oh, did you?— Thank you ever so much—

BELIAEV [*as she takes the peach*]: That's the style— Well, what was it you wanted to whisper in my ear?

KATIA: Oh— It's just that Vera Alexandrovna—that young lady is very anxious to see you.

BELIAEV: Oh— [*His face falling.*] Is she?

KATIA: She's over by the plum tree, waiting for me to fetch her—you wouldn't be disturbed down here, she said, with them all still at the birthday tea—

BELIAEV [*taken aback*]: Oh—I see—

KATIA: She's very fond of you. [*Sighing, deeply, then going.*] I shan't be a minute— [*Stopping, and turning.*] —Alexei Nikolaich, is it true what they say?

BELIAEV: What?

KATIA: That you're leaving us?

BELIAEV: Leaving? I—who told you?

KATIA: So you're not going? [*Delighted.*] Oh, gracious Heaven be thanked! [*Embarrassed, primly.*] We'll be back presently.

[*She runs off right. A pause.*]

BELIAEV: The most fantastic things are happening to me. Vera's a sweet little thing with the kindest of hearts, I'm sure, but— And what would be the meaning of a note like this—[*taking a scrap of paper from his pocket*]—from Natalia Petrovna? [*Reading.*] "Please make no decisions until I have seen you again." What could *she* want to see me about?— [*After a pause, rising.*] The stupidest thoughts will keep coming into my head— Whatever it is, it's all damnably embarrassing. If somebody had told me three weeks ago that I—I— What I still can't make head or tail of is that conversation I had with her— [*Sitting again.*]

Lord, I wish my heart would stop thumping like this—
> [VERA *enters from the right with* KATIA; *she is very pale, and keeps her eyes averted.* BELIAEV *jumps up.*]

KATIA: Don't be frightened, miss—it'll be all right—
> [*She hurries back to the right. A pause.*]

BELIAEV: Vera Alexandrovna, you wished to see me. Won't you sit down? [*Taking her hand, leading her to the seat, and sitting beside her.*] But you've been crying!

VERA: You've been dismissed, haven't you?

BELIAEV: Who told you?

VERA: Natalia Petrovna herself. I had to talk to you, to—ask your pardon.

BELIAEV: Pardon? But what for?

VERA: If you only knew how this has upset me, Alexei Nikolaich—to be the cause of the whole thing—[*Starting to cry, then controlling herself.*]

BELIAEV: You the cause of it? But Vera Alexandrovna, nothing's settled, I assure you. It's quite possible I shall stay—

VERA: No, everything's settled, Alexei Nikolaich—everything's over. When you think how you are with me now, and only yesterday, in the garden—do you remember? [*A pause. She fights back her tears, rises, then turns to him.*] Alexei Nikolaich, is it true that you weren't exactly dismissed—that it was you who were anxious to go?

BELIAEV: Why—

VERA: Answer me!

BELIAEV: I—yes. You were right. She told me everything.

VERA [*faintly*]: That I—was in love with you?

BELIAEV [*stammering*]: Yes.

VERA [*quickly*]: It isn't true—

BELIAEV: But—if it isn't true—why should she—

VERA: At least—I didn't tell her—I don't remember—[*Her hands to her face.*] Oh, how cruel of her— And is that why you wanted to leave?

BELIAEV: I ask you, Vera Alexandrovna, what else could I have done— [*He walks away in despair.*]

VERA: He doesn't love me—

[*She shakes her head, and covers her face again with her hands. He sits beside her.*]

BELIAEV: Vera Alexandrovna, please— Give me your hand— [*Taking it.*] I do love you, Vérochka, because it's impossible not to—

VERA: You—you mean—

BELIAEV: In the same way I love my sister— [*As she turns away.*] I'm sorry—oh, Lord, I've never in my life been in a situation like this— I'd do anything rather than hurt you— [*With resolution.*] The best thing is not to pretend anything to you at all, don't you think so?

VERA: Yes, yes—

BELIAEV: Well, I know that you—you've grown fond of me. But you see, Vérochka, I'm just twenty-one, and haven't a farthing to bless myself with— [*As* VERA *stifles a sob.*] I—oh, Lord, I don't know what to say to you—

VERA: But I haven't asked you to say anything—and suddenly to bring up your prospects—oh, it's so cruel—

BELIAEV: I'm sorry, Vérochka—

VERA: It isn't your fault, Alexei Nikolaich. I don't even blame her; she just lost her head.

BELIAEV [*puzzled*]: Lost her head?

[*A pause.*]

VERA: Yes. I'm not the only one who's given herself away. [*Turning to him.*] She's in love with you.

BELIAEV: Natalia Petrovna?— [*Staggered.*] What—do you know what you're saying?

VERA: Yes. You see, today has made me years older— And she took it into her head to be jealous of me—me!

BELIAEV: I don't believe it.

VERA: Then why did she suddenly try to palm me off on to that old gentleman? If you could have seen her when I broke down and—and confessed—her face changed before my eyes. She's in love with you all right—

BELIAEV [*after a pause*]: I still think you've made a mistake.

VERA [*wearily*]: I haven't. I haven't—what have I ever done for her to torment me like that, unless it's to make her jealous? And now she's dismissed you, because she imagines that you and I— [*Hiding her head again.*]

BELIAEV: But she hasn't even dismissed me, I've told you. Nothing at all is settled, yet.

VERA [*raising her head and looking at him*]: Nothing at all?

BELIAEV: Nothing— Why are you looking at me like that?

[NATALIA *enters from the left; she sees them both, and stops. They have not seen her.*]

VERA: Because it's all perfectly clear to me now. She's come to her senses, and realized that she has nothing to fear from a gawky schoolgirl. And anyway perhaps you're in love with *her.*

BELIAEV: I?

VERA: You've turned quite red.

BELIAEV: Have I?

VERA: *Are* you in love with her? Or may you be, in time? [*After a pause.*] You don't answer me.

BELIAEV: But what do you expect me to say—

VERA [*turning away*]: Oh, please stop talking to me as if I were five years old! And you *will* console me—I just can't bear it—

[*She rises, starts to go out to the left, and finds herself face to face with* NATALIA. BELIAEV *turns, and springs to his feet. A pause.* NATALIA *comes forward, slowly; she is outwardly composed and icily dignified.*]

NATALIA: I'm sorry to see, Vérochka, that you're becoming very head-strong. I've reminded you more than once— and you too, sir, appear to have forgotten that you gave me your word— You have deceived me. Vérochka, I'm just a little cross with you—

VERA: Don't you think it's time you dropped all this as well?

NATALIA [*looks at her in amazement*]: What do you mean?

VERA: I mean this talking to me as if I were still a child. From today on, I'm a woman—a woman like yourself.

NATALIA [*quickly*]: Vera—

VERA: He hasn't deceived you; he doesn't love me, you know. So you've no reason in the world to be jealous of me.

NATALIA [*shocked*]: Vera!

VERA: And will you please not throw any more dust in my eyes, because it just won't be any good— For the simple reason I'm no longer your ward, watched over by a tolerant and mocking elder sister—I'm your rival.

[*A pause.*]

NATALIA: You forget yourself.

VERA: And if I do, who is to blame? I dare talk to you like this, because I've nothing to hope for any more—you've seen to that— But I'm not going to pretend with you, as you did with me. I've told him.

[*A pause.*]

NATALIA: Told him—what?

VERA: Something I noticed. You hoped to worm everything out of me without giving anything away about yourself, didn't you?

NATALIA: Vera—I entreat you—you don't know what you're saying—

VERA: Then will you tell me I'm dreaming? That you don't love him? After all, he's made it perfectly plain that he doesn't love me—

[*She bursts into tears and stumbles out to the left. A pause. It begins to grow dark.* BELIAEV *starts to go, then turns.*]

BELIAEV: Natalia Petrovna, is it any good my assuring you— [*He shakes his head, and starts to go again.*]

NATALIA: She was right, it's no good my pretending any more. The only possible way in which I can hope to regain your respect—and my own—is to be perfectly frank. Besides, as we shall never see each other again—this is the last time I shall ever speak to you. [*Going to him.*] She was telling the truth. I love you.

[*A pause.*]

BELIAEV: You—Natalia Petrovna—

NATALIA [*with a strained and deliberate calm*]: From the very first day, I loved you; though it was only yesterday that I was fully aware of it.

BELIAEV [*almost in a whisper*]: Natalia Petrovna—

NATALIA [*crossing quickly*]: One thing—please understand that it is pride, and pride only, that gives me the courage to tell you this; the farce of pretending revolted me to the marrow—[*sitting on the seat*] and I have been desperately anxious to wipe from your mind this picture of a tyrannical, cunning creature—anxious that the memory of me which you take away, shall not be—too vile— I was jealous of her and I took advantage of my authority—it was all despicably unworthy of me, and we'll leave it at that. I have only one excuse, that I was in the power of something I knew nothing of. [*After a pause, with more emotion.*] You have nothing to say— But then I do understand why, I do: for a man to have to listen to a declaration of love from a woman to whom he is indifferent—there can be nothing more painful, I am even grateful for your silence. You must feel intensely uncomfortable even in my presence—you have my permission to leave it at once, without formality— It seems that we two were never destined to know each other. Good-by forever. [*A pause.* BELIAEV *tries to say something, fails, bows, starts to go, then turns.*] Well?

BELIAEV: I can't go.

[*She turns; they are looking at each other for the first time.*]

NATALIA: You—can't go?

BELIAEV: Not like this—how can I—how can I?—[*Controlling himself.*] Natalia Petrovna—I—I— Oh, God, why can't I find the words to say it— I'm sorry, I don't know how to talk to women— She was right, you know, I was afraid of you—and still am. I'm not exaggerating when I say that I looked upon you as a creature from another planet—a truly heavenly being—and yet, when you said—

NATALIA [*softly*]: Go on.

BELIAEV: When you told me that you—loved me— [*Sitting beside her with an exultant cry.*] Natalia Petrovna, you love me! I can hear my heart beating, as I've never heard it before— [*With sudden feverish decision.*] I cannot go away like this.

NATALIA [*as if to herself*]: What have I done? [*After a pause, recovering.*] I'm glad you told me all that, because it makes it clear that it was nothing in me personally which repelled you, only my position— I'm glad— it makes the parting easier.

[*A pause.*]

BELIAEV [*rises*]: It was madness just now, when I said "I can't go," of course I must go— But you can have no idea of what is going on in my breast— I am seeing you for the first time, hearing your voice for the first time— [*He sits next to her; they look into each other's eyes for the first time.*] Yes, I must go—if I don't, I—I can't answer for what might happen.

NATALIA: Yes, you must go— But can it be, that in spite of the way I've behaved, you still think of me as a—a special sort of person? If I'd known, I would have died rather than confess to you what I did. All I thought I was doing was punishing myself—if I had dreamt— [*Hiding her face in her hands.*]

BELIAEV: This time yesterday I myself could never have imagined—it was only just now, when suddenly—

NATALIA: Yes? [*Her eyes shining with happiness.*] Suddenly—

BELIAEV: It was as if a hand were laid gently on my heart, a warm hand that pressed and pressed, until there was a burning in me that would scorch up my whole being—

NATALIA [*her eyes closed*]: We have no right to forget that tomorrow you are leaving. That we are speaking to each other for the last time.

BELIAEV: Yes, the last time. And whatever happens, one memory will stay with me forever, how Natalia Petrovna came to love me—

NATALIA: But you told me just now that you were still

afraid of me— [*She looks into his eyes; her smile fades, she shudders, and puts her hand to her eyes.*] But what am I saying— [*Recovering, trying to be practical.*] Alexei Nikolaich, listen— I've no more strength to fight, and I count on your help. [*Rapidly, convincing herself.*] It is for the best that all should end quickly, now; we have at least grown in this minute to know each other. Give me your hand, and good-by.

BELIAEV [*takes her hand*]: I am parting from you, Natalia Petrovna, and my heart is so full that I have not a word to say. May Heaven give you—give you— [*He breaks off, overcome, and presses her hand to his lips. In a stifled whisper.*] Good-by—

[RAKITIN *appears from the left, and sees them.*]

NATALIA: If you stay, my love—then Heaven must be our judge—

BELIAEV: Natalia—

RAKITIN: Natalia Petrovna. [*The others start, and look round at him.* BELIAEV *bows, intensely embarrassed, and hurries awkwardly out to the right.*] I'm sorry. I was walking past, and heard your voices.

NATALIA [*collecting herself*]: This seems the day for explanations, does it not?— Who sent you to look for me?

RAKITIN: Your husband.

NATALIA [*after a pause, rising*]: Shall we go back to the schoolroom? [*She starts to go past him.*]

RAKITIN [*anxiously*]: May I ask—what decision you came to—

NATALIA: Decision? [*Affecting surprise.*] I don't understand you.

[*A pause. She faces his look.*]

RAKITIN: You don't? Then I understand everything.

NATALIA: Oh, Rakitin, there you go again, hinting and hinting, really you are provoking! He and I thrashed the whole silly matter out, and anything you've ever discussed with me is dead and forgotten. Puerile nonsense. Do you hear?

RAKITIN: But I haven't said a word, Natalia Petrovna.

Except that I understand everything. How annoyed you must be with yourself.

NATALIA: What for?

RAKITIN: For your frankness to me this morning.

NATALIA [*tries to turn away, hesitates, then looks at him. Uncertainly*]: Michel—you haven't yet spoken to him?

RAKITIN: Your husband?

NATALIA [*in an outburst, sitting on the seat*]: Please don't go on saying "your husband," if his name's Arkady, then call him Arkady!

RAKITIN: I haven't yet had time to prepare my speech to him.

NATALIA: Oh, what a wretched business—it makes me positively ashamed that you should have to intrigue—

RAKITIN [*coldly*]: Please don't lose any sleep over that— A pity, though, that the young gentleman should turn out such a novice.

NATALIA: Novice?

RAKITIN: Taking to his heels like that; I've never seen a man quite so bursting with guilt. Give him time, though, and he'll soon pick up the rudiments— Shall we go?

[YSLAEV *appears from the left, followed by* THE DOCTOR.]

YSLAEV: You saw him go down this path, did you say?

THE DOCTOR: I certainly thought I did—

[NATALIA *draws back.* YSLAEV *sees* RAKITIN.]

YSLAEV: Ah, you were right, my dear fellow— [*Seeing* NATALIA.] Oh— [*After a pause, with forced conviviality.*] You're not still on this morning's talk, are you?

NATALIA: More or less, yes—

YSLAEV: It must be of world-shaking importance—

NATALIA: Oh, it is, cataclysmic!

YSLAEV [*after a pause*]: Tea's ready in the schoolroom. Shall we go across?

NATALIA [*rising, briskly, and taking his arm*]: What a good idea—

YSLAEV [*looking round*]: You know, Doctor, I was just looking at that schoolroom; when our Kolia grows up—to

the credit of both his parents, one hopes—we've only got
to set up a partition, and we'll have two gardener's bedrooms
—what d'you say?

THE DOCTOR: An excellent idea, first-rate—

[YSLAEV *crosses*, NATALIA *on his arm; he has not looked
once at* RAKITIN. *He turns round.*]

YSLAEV: Well, gentlemen? A cup of tea?

[*He and* NATALIA *go out to the left.*]

THE DOCTOR [*to* RAKITIN]: Will you grant me the honor
of taking your arm? [*As they start to go.*] It looks as if you
and I are fated always to bring up the rear—ha!

RAKITIN [*in a sudden burst of temper*]: Allow me to inform you, Doctor, how much you get on my nerves!

[*A pause.*]

THE DOCTOR [*looks at him, startled, then recovers*]: If
you only knew, my friend, how much I get on my own.

[*They follow the others out to the left.*]

QUICK CURTAIN

Scene III

The drawing room, the next morning. Early sunlight.

YSLAEV *is seated at the desk, looking through papers. A
pause. He begins to think, puts down the papers, then makes
an effort to work again. He shakes his head, rises, pulls a
bell rope and walks to the windows.* MATVEI *enters from the
study, carrying a duster.*

MATVEI: You rang, sir?

YSLAEV: Yes—er—send the bailiff to me, will you?—

MATVEI: Very good, sir. [*Going, then remembering something.*] Oh, excuse me, sir—

YSLAEV: Yes?

MATVEI: The workmen digging at the dam—

YSLAEV: What about them?

MATVEI: They're waiting to know what they are to do now.

YSLAEV: Oh. Tell them I shan't be a moment—say I've been delayed—

MATVEI: Very good, sir

YSLAEV [*As* MATVEI *bows and starts to go back*]: Is Monsieur Rakitin in the house?

MATVEI: I just saw him in the billiard room, sir.

YSLAEV [*sitting back at the desk*]: Ask him if he would be so good as to take a glass of wine with me in here.

MATVEI [*after a slight pause*]: Yes, sir.

[*He bows and goes into the ballroom, nearly running into* ANNA SEMYENOVNA *as she enters from the hall; she is in breakfast toilette and carries a cup of chocolate and a card-box. She is in a genuine state of agitation, but appears determined to let everyone know it. She looks at* YSLAEV, *who does not stir. She looks at letters on occasional table behind sofa, moves across and deposits the card-box on the table; he looks up quickly, sees her and goes back to his papers. She sighs explosively, and sits on the stool; he still pays no attention to her.*]

ANNA: Arkasha—

YSLAEV [*turning*]: Oh, Mamma—I didn't see you— [*Rising, crossing, and kissing her on the brow, mechanically.*] How are we this morning?

ANNA [*her voice quavering*]: Well, the Lord be thanked.

YSLAEV [*briskly*]: Good. [*He returns to his paper.*]

ANNA [*with a deep sigh*]: As well as can be expected—Matters might be worse—

[*Seeing that he takes no notice, she draws a deeper breath, almost a sob. He turns to her.*]

YSLAEV: Were you sighing, Mamma?

ANNA: Arkady Sergheich Yslaev, I am your mother.

YSLAEV [*back to his papers*]: Really, Mamma, that's no news to me—

ANNA: You're a great big man, Arkasha, grown up to

Adam's estate—but I am the one who dangled you on my
knee. It's a wonderful word, "Mother."

YSLAEV: Mamma, do please explain what you're hinting
at—

ANNA: My dear, you know perfectly well. Arkasha, you
married an excellent wife—

YSLAEV [*dryly*]: Did I? Good—

ANNA: Whose conduct up till *now* has been beyond reproach—

YSLAEV: You mean that Rakitin—

ANNA [*shocked*]: No, no—God forbid—I don't mean that
at all—no, no—

YSLAEV: Do let me finish, Mamma— You mean that
her relationship with Rakitin is not quite—as straightfor-
ward as it might be?

ANNA: Yes, I do. Arkady, has he given you any idea at
all what those tears and those talks were about?

YSLAEV: I haven't asked him. [*Back to his pages.*] And he
seems in no hurry to satisfy my curiosity.

ANNA: Then what d'you intend to do now?

YSLAEV: Nothing.

ANNA: Nothing?—*Well!* Of course, you're the master—
and who am I to advise you, at your age; I'm only your
mother, it's your bed, and you must lie on it— [*After a
pause*]. What I meant was, I should be only too pleased to
clear the air with a little chat with them both—

YSLAEV [*rising, perturbed*]: Mamma, you'll do nothing of
the sort—I mean—I can't have you worried. Now d'you
promise me, faithfully?

ANNA: You can't say I haven't cautioned you; from now
on I shan't lift a finger. I'll be like an oyster. Not another
syllable.

[*A pause. He sits again.*]

YSLAEV: Are you driving out anywhere today?

ANNA: Still, I *must* give you one word of warning. True
friends get scarcer every day, and my baby's too trusting,
my baby judges everybody else by himself.

YSLAEV: Your baby's more than able to deal with his own life, Mamma—

ANNA: Ah well, an old woman like me— I'm probably out of my mind anyway, old women go out of their minds. [*Rising.*] Then I was brought up on rather different principles, but of course all that's old-fashioned now. You go on working, I shan't lift a finger— [*At the steps.*] I'll just turn into an oyster. [*She goes into the hall.*]

[*A pause.*]

YSLAEV: When you have an open wound, what makes people who really wish you well, prod into it first one finger, and then another? [*He holds his head, crosses and pours out two glasses of wine.* RAKITIN *comes in from the ballroom; he is very much on the defensive.*] Ah, good morning, Mihail Alexandrovich—a glass of wine?

RAKITIN: Thank you—

[*They toast each other. A pause.* YSLAEV *sits on the sofa.*]

YSLAEV [*smiling*]: Michel, haven't you forgotten something?

RAKITIN: I?

YSLAEV: Your promise?

RAKITIN: My promise?

YSLAEV [*charging on*]: You remember—when Mother and I came in here—Natasha in tears—something about a secret—you remember?

RAKITIN: Can I have used the word "secret"? [*Sitting beside him.*] We had a talk, that was all—

YSLAEV: Michel, I can't bear to see you having to act such a shifty part. We've known each other since we were that high—I've no talent for subterfuge, and you've never been anything but aboveboard with me. Will you allow me one question, if I give you my word that I shan't doubt the sincerity of your answer?

RAKITIN: Go on.

YSLAEV: Do you love my wife? [*A pause. They look at each other.*] I must make myself absolutely clear. Do you love her—with the sort of affection which it is hard to confess to her husband?

RAKITIN [*after a pause, quietly*]: Yes, Arkady, I do.

YSLAEV [*taking his hand*]: Michel, your frankness does credit to the man of honor I have always known.

RAKITIN: Thank you.

YSLAEV: But the immediate problem is—what are we to do? [*Walking up and down.*] I know Natasha, the range of her qualities—but I know the range of my own too, and I can't compete with you there, Michel—

RAKITIN: My dear friend—

YSLAEV: No, no, I'm not in your class. You're brainier in every way, and immeasurably better company; there's no getting away from it, I'm a dull stick. I think Natasha's fond of me, but she's got eyes in her head—she was bound to be taken with you, I always appreciated that— But I've always trusted you both, and so long as—er—nothing definite happened—oh, I wish I had your gift of the gab— But after us coming upon you yesterday—what *are* we to do? I'm a simple sort of fellow, but I've enough horse sense to realize that nobody should have the power to ruin other people's lives, and that there are times when to insist on one's rights would be wicked. And I'm not saying that because I've read it somewhere— I've got it out of my conscience; freedom—every single soul should be free, that's always been my idea. Only this *does need thinking over.*

RAKITIN: I've already thought it over.

YSLAEV: You have?

RAKITIN: I'm leaving.

YSLAEV: Leaving? [*After a pause.*] You think you should? For good, you mean?

RAKITIN: For good.

YSLAEV: That's—a big step to take, Michel— Perhaps you're right. There's no doubt that you—my very good friend—have become a menace to me. And when I said that just now about freedom, perhaps I was forgetting my own feelings, if she—you see, for me to be without Natasha, would be like being without—without— And then again, if your going away were to cure this unrest of hers—I haven't been imagining all that, have I?

RAKITIN [*bitterly*]: No, you haven't indeed—

MATVEI [*enters from the hall.*] Excuse me, sir, the bailiff is here.

YSLAEV: I shan't be a moment. [*As* MATVEI *bows and goes back.*] Michel, we'll miss you sorely, of course—you wouldn't be away long? That would be carrying things too far—

RAKITIN: I don't know—quite a time, I think—

YSLAEV: Now you're not going to turn me into Othello, are you?—Upon my soul, I don't think there can have ever been such a conversation between two friends since the world began! [*Putting out his hand.*] We can't part like this—

RAKITIN [*taking his hand*]: Will you let me know when I may come back?

YSLAEV: But which of our neighbors is going to take your place in our hearts? Poor old Bolshintsov?

RAKITIN [*lightly*]: There's—there's the new tutor, of course.

YSLAEV: The new tutor? Oh, a nice boy, but one can't mention him in the same breath with you.

RAKITIN [*sardonically*]: Oh, d'you think so?

[*A knock at the ballroom door.*]

YSLAEV [*calling*]: Just a minute! [*To* RAKITIN, *hurriedly.*] We take it as settled, then, my dear friend, that you're going away—just for a time—no hurry, you know, no hurry— Well, you've taken a weight off my mind— [*Moved.*] My dear boy, God bless you— [*He embraces* RAKITIN *impetuously, on both cheeks. Calling.*] Come in! [BELIAEV *enters from the ballroom. He looks smarter; his customary shyness can hardly hide glimpses of an excited buoyancy. He carries papers.*] Ah, it's you—

BELIAEV: I'm sorry, sir, I've made up Kolia's report, I hope I'm not interrupting—

YSLAEV: Not at all— Well, gentlemen, the devil finds work for idle hands, et cetera, I haven't looked at the dam this morning, this will never do. [*Taking his papers under his arm.*] We shall meet again. [*Calling.*] —Ready, Matvei! Matvei! All right—

[*He goes out into the hall.* BELIAEV *crosses to desk and arranges his papers.*]

BELIAEV: How are you today, Mihail Alexandrovich?

RAKITIN: Surely that's a new coat you have on? And a buttonhole?—

BELIAEV [*blushing, and starting to pluck it out*]: Oh— if it's too much—

RAKITIN: But why, it's charming!— [*After a pause.*] In case you want any messages run, I'm going into the town tomorrow, en route for Moscow.

BELIAEV [*turning*]: Moscow? Tomorrow?

RAKITIN: A matter of business has cropped up.

BELIAEV: Will you be away long?

RAKITIN: Possibly quite a time.

BELIAEV: May I ask—does Natalia Petrovna know?

RAKITIN: No, she doesn't. Why do you ask?

BELIAEV [*somewhat embarrassed*]: No particular reason.

RAKITIN: I don't see anybody else in the room?

BELIAEV [*turning round to him*]: What?— [*following suit.*] —No, there isn't—why?—

RAKITIN: I thought there must be, for us to be acting such a farce. [*As* BELIAEV *rises.*] You mean to say you can't guess why I'm going away?

BELIAEV [*on the defensive*]: No, I can't.

RAKITIN: Oh—well, I'll believe you— Just before you came in then, Arkady Sergheich and I had rather an important talk, man to man, as a result of which I have decided to take my departure: the reason being that he fancied me to be in love with his wife.

BELIAEV [*after a pause, stiffly*]: Indeed—

RAKITIN: Now what would you do in my place? [*After

a pause.] His suspicions were totally unfounded, of course, but it didn't prevent him being tormented by them, and I felt that for a friend's peace of mind, an honorable man must be prepared to sacrifice his own—his own happiness. That is why I am going away. [*With meaning*.] If you were in my place—you'd do the same, wouldn't you? You'd go away?

BELIAEV [*after a pause*]: I suppose I would, yes—

RAKITIN: I'm delighted to hear it. Of course, there's a funny side to my decamping—it implies that I regard myself as a menace. But I feel that a woman's good name— Besides, haven't you known women, innocent of heart and pure as snow—real children in spite of their intelligence— why by very reason of that lack of guile, were the more apt to yield to a sudden infatuation?— [*Suddenly*.] After all that, do you still look upon love as the greatest blessing on earth?

BELIAEV [*with a noncommittal laugh*]: Not having yet fallen a victim, I'm not in a position to say—but I've always understood that to love a woman, and be loved in return, is the—er—the nearest a man can reach to perfect happiness.

RAKITIN: Long may you be soothed by such pleasant lullabies!—Shall I tell you what I think?

BELIAEV: Do.

RAKITIN: Just this. Once you surrender to it, all love— spurned, or returned—becomes a calamity. Mark my words, my friend—the day will come for you to know just how those flowerlike hands can torture, with what exquisite care they can tear your heart to shreds; the day will come for you to discover what a world of hate can smolder underneath the most ardent passion. When you find yourself longing for peace of mind as a sick man pines for health— for any insipid everyday peace—think of me; when you stand shackled to a woman's apron-string, and watch yourself envying, from the bottom of an agonized heart, every carefree stranger on the highway, while the shame of your own slavery seeps into your vitals—the slavery of paying the highest price for the most miserable returns—think of me. [*A pause.* BELIAEV *watches him, fascinated. Collecting himself.*] I mean, think of what I've just said.—I was— philosophizing.

BELIAEV [*soberly*]: With no motive?

RAKITIN [*dryly*]: Exactly— So you don't want anything in town?

BELIAEV: Nothing, thank you. [*Rising.*] May I say how sorry I am you are going?

[NATALIA *is seen walking in the garden from the right, and stands in the French windows; she is followed by* VERA, *who looks pale and woebegone.*]

RAKITIN [*without seeing them*]: May I say, quite sincerely, how glad I am to have made your acquaintance?

[*They shake hands.* NATALIA *watches them.*]

NATALIA [*too lively*]: Well, gentlemen, what has your program been this morning?

RAKITIN [*starting*]: Oh, good day—nothing very exciting so far—

NATALIA [*coming in, followed by* VERA, *as* BELIAEV *bows, embarrassed*]: Vera and I have been in the garden for hours—it's quite heavenly out of doors today. I love the smell of limetrees, don't you? [*Sitting.*] We walked under them for ages, listening to the bees humming, it was perfect.

BELIAEV: No. [*Lamely.*] I wasn't—

RAKITIN [*jauntily, to* NATALIA]: So today it's your turn to pay tribute to the beauties of Nature? [*After an awkward pause.*] As a matter of fact, Alexei Nikolaich here couldn't risk the garden this morning, as he's sporting a new coat, hadn't you noticed?

BELIAEV [*stung*]: You mean that as it must be the only one I have, I couldn't have risked spoiling it?

RAKITIN [*confused*]: Of course not. I was joking. [*An awkward pause.* VERA *sits and takes up some sewing. Non-*

chalantly.] Oh, Natalia Petrovna—I knew there was something—it nearly slipped my mind. I'm leaving today.

NATALIA [*staring at him*]: Leaving?

RAKITIN: I'm going to Moscow, on business.

NATALIA [*after a pause*]: Well, hurry back, won't you— [*To* BELIAEV, *suddenly.*] Alexei Nikolaich, were those your drawings Kolia was showing me?

BELIAEV [*rising*]: Oh—they're nothing much—

NATALIA: Nothing much, but they're charming! You have a distinct flair—

RAKITIN [*As* BELIAEV *bows*]: I observe that every day you discover new virtues in Monsieur Beliaev.

NATALIA: Do I? [*Coldly.*] I'm so glad—

RAKITIN [*who has for the last few moments been on the rack*]: Well, I must prepare for my journey—[*Going.*]— *Au revoir* for the present—

NATALIA [*calling after him*]: You'll come and say good-by, won't you—it won't slip your mind?

RAKITIN: No. It won't slip my mind.

BELIAEV [*suddenly, as* RAKITIN *bows*]: Mihail Alexandrovich, may I come and have a word with you?

RAKITIN: Certainly—by all means—

[*He goes out into the ballroom.* BELIAEV *bows awkwardly and follows him.*]

NATALIA: Vera, *don't* be like this with me— [*As* VERA *does not respond in any way, rising impetuously, going to her, and kneeling, entreating, as* VERA *covers her face with her hands.*] No, Vérochka—it's all my fault—

VERA [*through her sobs*]: Don't kneel to me— I can't bear you to kneel to me—

NATALIA: I shall kneel to you until you say I'm forgiven — My dear, I know how hard it is for you, but is it any easier for me? The difference between us is that you've done nothing wrong to me, while I—

VERA [*in a hard voice*]: There's another difference, Natalia Petrovna, that you haven't noticed. Today I find you gentle, and kind—

NATALIA: And do you know why? Because I realize how wicked I've been—

VERA [*suddenly*]: You are gentle and kind today because you know that you are loved.

[*A pause.*]

NATALIA [*somberly*]: Will you believe me when I tell you that you and I are as unfortunate as each other?

VERA: He loves you!

NATALIA: Vera, it's time we came back to reality. Do remember the position I'm in—the position we're both in—When you think that our secret—entirely my fault, I know—that our secret is already known in this house by two men — Vera, instead of mortifying each other, shouldn't we be trying to rescue ourselves from an impossible situation? Have you forgotten who I am, my position in this house?—But you're not even listening to me.

VERA [*looking before her, tonelessly*]: He loves you—

NATALIA: Vera, he'll be going away—

VERA [*in an outburst*]: Leave me alone!

[NATALIA *looks at her, undecided what to do.*]

YSLAEV'S VOICE [*calling, in the study*]: Natasha, are you in the drawing room?

NATALIA [*calling*]: Yes? Did you want me?

YSLAEV'S VOICE [*calling*]: I've got something to show you —the new plans of the dam, my dear—quick!

NATALIA: Coming—

[*She starts to go, turns, and holds out her hand to* VERA, *who makes no sign.* NATALIA *bites her lip and goes into the study. A pause.*]

VERA: He loves her. And I have to remain in her house—I can't bear it—

[*She puts her hand to her eyes. The ballroom door opens and* THE DOCTOR'S *head appears slowly. He looks round cautiously, and steals across the room to* VERA, *who does not see him. He stands with his arms folded, grinning mischievously from ear to ear.*]

THE DOCTOR [*suddenly*]: Boo!

VERA [*starting*]: Oh— Oh, Doctor, it's you—

THE DOCTOR: What's the complaint this morning? Delirium tremens, gout or St. Vitus' Dance?

VERA: I'm all right, really, thank you—

THE DOCTOR: Your pulse, young lady, stand and deliver— [*Feeling her wrist*] Hmm— Vivace, very vivace, one might say galloping— Now take my advice, as a professional man—

VERA [*looking at him, suddenly resolute*]: Ignaty Illyich, that gentleman, our neighbor—what was his name—

THE DOCTOR: Bolshintsov? Yes?

VERA: Is he really a nice man?

THE DOCTOR: A *nice man?* Young lady, there's only one word for my old Bolly—"paragon."

VERA: Has he a temper?

THE DOCTOR: A temper? My dear, I can only tell you,— he's not a man, he's a mountain of dough; you just dump him on to the kitchen table, roll up your sleeves, and— [*Making graphic gestures of kneading a pliable mass.*]

VERA: You can answer for him?

THE DOCTOR: As I would for myself, hand on heart—

VERA [*after a pause*]: Then will you say—that I am willing to marry him.

THE DOCTOR: Willing to— [*With incredulous amazement.*] No! [*Springing up.*] No! !

VERA: But only if it's as soon as ever possible, do you understand?

THE DOCTOR: But tomorrow, if you like! Bravo, Vera Alexandrovna, bravo! [*Blowing ecstatic kisses to her.*] *There's* spirit for you— He's waiting at the lodge gates— he'll have a fit—what a whirligig—have you *any* idea, Vera Alexandrovna, *how* much he worships you?

VERA [*brusquely*]: We'll take that for granted, Doctor, shall we—

THE DOCTOR: All right, my sugar plum, mum's the word —I'll take the short cut—on the wings o' the wind, I fly. *Au revoir—bonne chance—enchanté!* [*He kisses her hand tempestuously, and races out into the hall.*]

VERA: Anything in the world rather than stay here and

watch her with him. Because she *is* happy, however much she may pretend to be wretched—the way she tried to comfort me— [*Rising.*] I can't—bear it—

BELIAEV [*comes in from the ballroom and nearly runs into her. Quietly*]: Vera.

[*She starts and looks up at him. A pause.*]

VERA: Yes?

BELIAEV: I'm glad you're by yourself. I've come to say good-by.

VERA: To say—good-by?

BELIAEV [*as she sits*]: I've just had a talk in there with Monsieur Rakitin, a serious talk— I can't give you any idea of the sting in his voice— He was right about my new coat, too— I deserved every word. Not only have I disturbed your peace of mind— I still don't know quite how—and Natalia Petrovna's— I've been the cause of old friendship breaking up—anyway, turning the heads of rich women and young girls is *not* my style. [*Sitting next to her.*] When I've gone, everything will simmer down back to normal, you'll see—you'll forget me and wonder how on earth it ever came about—

VERA: Please don't break your heart over me. I shan't be staying here long myself.

BELIAEV: You won't? How d'you mean?

VERA: That's my secret.

BELIAEV [*rising*]: But that's what I mean, how can I *help* leaving this house, when I seem to have started a sort of fever that makes everybody want to disappear one after the other? Anyway, I feel acutely uncomfortable here—I keep thinking everybody's looking at me; I don't mind telling you, Vera Alexandrovna, I'm counting the minutes till I'm up on that dog-cart, bowling along the high road. It's a strange feeling, when your heart aches intolerably, and yet your head is as gay and light as if you were a sailor embarking on a long voyage beyond the seas. You know too well the perils ahead, you're sad at leaving your friends, and yet the waves call so joyously—the wind blows so fresh—that the blood starts dancing like mad through your veins. Yes, I must be off. Back to Moscow—all my old friends— I'll get straight to work—

VERA: You love her—and yet you're leaving—

BELIAEV: Can't you see, that all that's over and done with? It flared up and it went out, like a spark— Let's part friends, for God's sake, shall we?— [*After a pause, awkwardly.*] I shall never forget you, Vera—believe me, I've grown very fond of you— [*Embarrassed, taking a paper from his pocket.*] Would you—would you be so kind as to give this note for me, to Natalia Petrovna?

VERA: A note?

BELIAEV: I—I don't feel able to say good-by to her.

VERA [*taking the note*]: But you are leaving straight away?

BELIAEV: This minute. I'm walking as far as Petroskoye, and waiting there for Monsieur Rakitin. You see, everything's in hand— And when you give that, would you just say—no, what's the point— [*Listening.*] Somebody's coming —good-by—

[*He hurries toward the hall, turns, looks toward the study, hesitates, and runs out into the hall.* NATALIA *enters from the study, and looks at* VERA.]

NATALIA: I heard his voice— [*Seeing her expression.*] What's the matter? [VERA *hands her the note;* NATALIA *looks from it to her.*] Vera, you're frightening me—

VERA: Read it. [NATALIA *opens the note, and sinks to a chair. A pause. She stares before her.*] Natalia Petrovna—

NATALIA: But he said good-by to *you.* He was able to say good-by to *you*—

VERA: Only because he doesn't love me.

NATALIA: But he can't go like this— [*Rising abruptly.*] He has no right—who gave him the idea of this ridiculous gesture—it's too slighting—how does he know that I wouldn't have had the courage— [*Sinking down again.*] What am I to do— [*In a cry.*] —what am I—

VERA [*walking slowly to the steps*]: Not a minute ago you said yourself he would have to go—remember?

NATALIA: Well, he *is* going—and now you're glad. Because it makes us equal— [*Her voice breaks in a sob.*]

VERA [*turning*]: Natalia Petrovna, you said to me just now—

NATALIA [*turning from her, almost in aversion*]: I don't want to hear—

VERA [*inflexibly*]: You said, "Instead of mortifying each other, shouldn't we be saving ourselves?" We're saved now.

[*She goes out into the hall.* NATALIA *recovers.*]

NATALIA: She was speaking the truth—we're saved. It's all over—all put beautifully to rights—

[YSLAEV *enters from the study with papers.* NATALIA *rises abruptly and goes to the French windows. He crosses to the desk, then sees her.*]

YSLAEV [*calling*]: Natasha! [NATALIA *does not answer. He goes up to her. Gently.*] It's me, Natasha— [*She turns; he takes her hand; she attempts to smile at him.*] You're so pale, my dear. It worries me.

NATALIA: It's nothing, Arkady, really—

YSLAEV: Won't you lie down, my darling? Just to please me?

NATALIA: Very well—

[*She takes a step and sways; he catches her.*]

YSLAEV: There, you see? [*As she leans on him.*] Shall I take you upstairs?

NATALIA [*trying to laugh*]: No, really, Arkady, I'm not as bad as all that! I just want some fresh air—just for a minute—

[*She walks slowly into the garden.* RAKITIN *enters from the ballroom.*]

YSLAEV: Michel, what on earth possessed you to do it, when I'd begged you to wait—she was so upset when I came in here—

RAKITIN: To do what?

YSLAEV: To tell her you're leaving like that!

[*A pause.*]

RAKITIN: You think that's what upset her?

YSLAEV [*as* NATALIA *turns, and comes into the room again*]: Are you going up now, my dear?

NATALIA: Yes.

RAKITIN: Between ourselves, Arkady, little Vérochka's fallen in love with him.

YSLAEV: With the tutor? [*Whistling.*] Whew—

RAKITIN: And like an honorable man, he has decided it would be only tactful to take his departure. [*As* YSLAEV *sits, with a gesture of bewilderment.*] So now you understand—

YSLAEV: I don't understand anything at all, and my head's going round like a top. Everybody muttering what honorable men they are, and scurrying off north, south, east and west, like a lot of partridges!

ANNA [*coming to them*]: Now what is all this—something about a tutor, did I hear—

YSLAEV [*holding his head, in a shout*]: Nothing, Mamma, nothing, nothing!

KOLIA: But, Papa—

YSLAEV: Monsieur Shaaf—

SHAAF [*bustling forward, with alacrity*]: *Mein Herr!*

YSLAEV: Would you kindly give Kolia his German lesson now—

KOLIA [*bursting into tears*]: No, I want the other tutor! I want the other tutor— [*As* SHAAF *pilots him, screaming and kicking, into the ballroom.*] —I want the other tutor—

[*A pause.*]

YSLAEV [*to* RAKITIN]: Michel, I'll come part of the way with you. I'll have Favorite saddled, and meet you at the dam. And, Mamma, will you do something for me?

ANNA: My dear, any mortal thing to help—

YSLAEV: Keep away from Natasha, will you? And you too, Doctor, she's not at all well— [*Going into the study, calling.*] Matvei! Matvei!

[ANNA *sits, bristling with wounded dignity, like an old hen.* LIZAVETA, *her eyes round with amazement, takes up her stand behind her, like a shadow. A pause. A great sigh from* ANNA, *as her eyes are raised to Heaven.*]

THE DOCTOR [*to* RAKITIN, *an uncontrollable twinkle in his eye*]: Mihail Alexandrovich, may I have the honor of driving you as far as the main road?

RAKITIN: Driving me? Have you got a horse?

THE DOCTOR [*beaming from ear to ear*]: Three horses, my dear friend, *and* a wagonette.

ANNA: What is all this—

RAKITIN [*bowing*]: Anna Semyenovna.

ANNA [*majestic, without rising*]: Good-by, Mihail Alexandrovich. [*Sepulchrally.*] I wish you as pleasant a journey as can be expected.

RAKITIN: Thank you— Lizaveta Bogdanovna.

[*He bows;* LIZAVETA *drops a frightened curtsey. He hurries out abruptly into the hall.*]

THE DOCTOR [*kissing* ANNA'S *hand*]: *Au revoir*, honored lady—

ANNA: Don't tell me you're going to Moscow too?

THE DOCTOR: No, no, just as far as my own humble abode. My patients, you know, my patients— [*To* LIZAVETA.] Dear lady—

LIZAVETA [*her eyes fluttering*]: Doctor—

THE DOCTOR: *Au revoir*, but not good-by. [*He kisses her hand, peers to see that* ANNA *is not looking, winks broadly at her, and hurries out into the hall.*]

ANNA [*as* LIZAVETA *sits opposite her, with knitting*]: Well, Lizaveta Bogdanovna—and what do *you* make of all this?

LIZAVETA: Anna Semyenovna, I am at a loss.

ANNA: Did you hear what *I* heard? That the tutor boy is leaving too?

LIZAVETA: No!.

ANNA: But what is the world coming to? Ah, well—

LIZAVETA [*her eyes modestly downcast*]: Anna Semyenovna.

ANNA: Yes, dear?

LIZAVETA: *I* may not be staying here much longer either—

[ANNA *sits back, staring at her in amazement.*]

QUICK CURTAIN

The Power of

Darkness

LEO TOLSTOY

Translated by George Rapall Noyes
and George Z. Patrick

CHARACTERS

PETR, *a rich peasant, forty-two years old, married for a second time, in poor health*

ANISYA, *his wife, thirty-two years old, smartly dressed [in Acts 1 and 2]*

AKULINA, *daughter of* PETR *by his first marriage, sixteen years old, hard of hearing and feeble-minded*

ANYUTKA, *daughter of* PETR *and* ANISYA, *ten years old*

NIKITA, *their workman, twenty-five years old, smartly dressed*

AKIM, *father of* NIKITA, *fifty years old, a pious peasant, unattractive in external appearance*

MATRENA, *his wife, fifty years old*

MARINA, *an orphan girl, twenty-two years old*

FRIEND *of* ANISYA

MARFA, *sister of* PETR

MITRICH, *an old laborer, a soldier retired because of age*

NEIGHBOR *[woman]*

MATCHMAKER *[man], a glum peasant*

HUSBAND *of* MARINA

FIRST GIRL

SECOND GIRL

POLICEMAN

COACHMAN

MATCHMAKER *[woman]*

BRIDEGROOM *of* AKULINA

BEST MAN *[at wedding]*

VILLAGE ELDER

PEASANTS: *men, women and girls*

act 1

The action takes place in autumn in a large peasant village. The stage represents PETR'S *spacious cottage.* PETR *is seated on a bench, repairing a horse-collar.* ANISYA *and* AKULINA *are spinning and singing together.*

PETR [*glancing out of the window*]: The horses have got loose again. They'll kill the colt before you know it. Nikita! Hey, Nikita! He's deaf! [*Listens for a moment. To the women.*] Keep still, will you! I can't hear anything.

NIKITA [*from the yard, offstage*]: What?

PETR: Drive in the horses.

NIKITA [*same*]: I'll drive 'em in. Give me time.

PETR [*shaking his head*]: Drat these hired men! If I was well, I'd never think of keeping one. They do nothing but make trouble. [*Rises and sits down again.*] Nikita! I can't make him hear.— One of you go, will you? Akulina, go and drive 'em in.

AKULINA: The horses?

PETR: What do you suppose?

AKULINA: Right away. [*Goes out.*]

PETR: The fellow's a loafer, no good on the farm. If he'd only stir himself!

ANISYA: You're mighty spry yourself—just crawl from the stove to the bench. All you do is boss the rest of us.

PETR: If I didn't boss you, the whole farm'd be ruined in a year. Oh, what a lot you are!

ANISYA: You give us a dozen jobs and then growl. It's easy to lie on the stove and give orders.

PETR [*sighing*]: Oh, if this sickness didn't have hold of me, I wouldn't keep him for a day.

AKULINA [*offstage*]: Shoo! shoo! shoo!

[*One can hear the colt whinny and the horses run into the yard. The gate creaks.*]

PETR: Fancy talk is all he's good for. Honest, I wouldn't keep him.

ANISYA [*mimicking him*]: "I won't keep him." If you'd only get a move on yourself, you might talk.

AKULINA [*coming in*]: I had hard work to drive 'em in. The roan kept—

PETR: Where's that Nikita?

AKULINA: Nikita? He's standing in the street.

PETR: What's he standing there for?

AKULINA: What for? He's standing round the corner and chatting.

PETR: Can't get sense out of her! Who's he chatting with?

AKULINA [*not catching his words*]: What?

[PETR *brandishes his arm at* AKULINA; *she sits down at her spinning.*]

ANYUTKA [*running in. To her mother*]: Nikita's father and mother have come to see him. They're taking him home to marry him—just think!

ANISYA: Aren't you lying?

ANYUTKA: Honest and true, may I die if it ain't! [*Laughs.*] I was going by, and Nikita says to me: "Now good-by, young lady," he says; "come and have some fun at my wedding. I'm leaving you," he says. And then he just laughed.

ANISYA [*to her husband*]: Folks haven't much need of you. You see he was getting ready to leave himself. And you were saying: "I'll turn him out"!

PETR: Let him go; can't I find other men?

ANISYA: But haven't you paid him in advance?

[ANYUTKA *goes toward the door, listens to their words for a moment, and goes out.*]

PETR [*frowning*]: He can work off the money next summer if necessary.

ANISYA: Yes, you're glad to let him go—one less mouth to feed. But during the winter I'll have to tend to things all alone, like a work horse. The girl ain't eager to work, and you'll just lie on the stove. I know you!

PETR: What's the use of wagging your tongue for nothing when you ain't heard anything yet?

ANISYA: The place is crowded with the animals. You haven't sold the cow and you've taken in all the sheep for the winter—it'll be hard enough to store up feed for all of 'em, and to water 'em. And now you want to let the hired man go. I won't do a man's work! I'll lie down on the stove just like you and let things go to smash—and you can do what you please about it.

PETR [to AKULINA]: Go for the fodder, will you? It's time.

AKULINA: For the fodder? All right. [Puts on her coat and takes a rope.]

ANISYA: I won't work for you. I've had enough of it—I won't! Work for yourself.

PETR: Shut up! What are you mad about? You're like a wet hen.

ANISYA: You're a mad dog yourself! There's no work or joy to be got out of you. You're just sucking the life out of me. A mad dog, that's what you are.

PETR [spits and puts on his coat]: Plague take you—Lord forgive me! I'll go and find out how things are. [Goes out.]

ANISYA [shouts after him]: Rotten, long-nosed devil!

AKULINA: What are you scolding dad for?

ANISYA: Shut up, you fool!

AKULINA [going toward the door]: I know what you're scolding him for. You're a fool yourself, you cur. I ain't afraid of you.

ANISYA: What's that? [Jumps up and looks for something with which to strike her.] Look out or I'll take the poker to you.

AKULINA [opening the door]: You're a cur, you're a devil; that's what you are. Devil, cur, cur, devil! [Runs out.]

ANISYA [meditates]: "Come to the wedding," says he. So that's what they're up to—marrying him? Look out, Nikita, if that's your doings, I'll have my say too.... I can't live without him. I won't let him go.

NIKITA [Comes in and glances about. Seeing that ANISYA

is alone, he approaches her quickly. Whispers]: Well, my girl, I'm in trouble! My father's come and wants to take me away—tells me I must go home. "We're marrying you off for good and all," says he, "and you'll have to stay at home."

ANISYA: Well then, marry. What do I care?

NIKITA: Oh, re-ally! I thought it'd be better to talk things over; but this is what he says: he tells me I must marry. What does this mean? [*Winks.*] Have you forgotten?

ANISYA: Go ahead and marry. You needn't—

NIKITA: What are you snorting at? You won't even let me pet you a bit.— Well, what's wrong with you?

ANISYA: I think you want to desert me. And if you do want to desert me, then I've no use for you either. That's the whole story!

NIKITA: Oh, stop, Anisya. Do you think I want to forget you?— Not so long as I live. So I won't leave you for good and all. This is the way I figure it; let 'em marry me, but then I'll come back to you—if only they don't make me stay at home.

ANISYA: Much I'll care for you if you're married.

NIKITA: But remember, my dear girl: I simply can't go against my father's will.

ANISYA: You put the blame on your father, but the scheme's your own. You've been plotting for a long time with your sweetheart, with Marina. She put you up to this. She didn't run over here the other day for nothing.

NIKITA: Marina? Much I care for her! . . . Many of her kind fall for me!

ANISYA: Why did your father come? You told him to! You've been deceiving me! [*Weeps.*]

NIKITA: Anisya, do you believe in God or not? I never even dreamed of any such thing. Honestly, I never thought of it. My old man made the plan out of his own head.

ANISYA: If you don't want to get married yourself, can anyone pull you to it like a jackass?

NIKITA: All the same, I figure a fellow can't oppose his father. And I don't want to.

ANISYA: Just say you won't, and stick to it.

NIKITA: One fellow refused, and they thrashed him in the village jail. Then he understood. I don't want to go through that. I tell you, it's ticklish.

ANISYA: Quit your fooling. Listen, Nikita: if you're going to marry Marina, I don't know what I'll do to myself.... I'll kill myself! I've sinned and broken the law, but now I can't turn back. Just as soon as you leave me, I'll do it.

NIKITA: Why should I leave? If I wanted to leave, I'd have gone long ago. The other day Ivan Semenych offered me a job as coachman ... and what an easy life! Yet I didn't take it. I think that everybody likes me. If you didn't love me, I'd act differently.

ANISYA: Just remember this. The old man may die any day; then I think we can cover up all our sins. I've planned to marry you; then you'll be the master of the house.

NIKITA: No use guessing. What do I care? I do the work as if it was for my own self. The master likes me, and his wife —well, she's in love with me. And if women love me, I'm not to blame; it's a simple matter.

ANISYA: Will you love me?

NIKITA [*embracing her*]: Just this way! You've always been in my heart.

[MATRENA *comes in and for some time stands before the ikon in the corner of the room, crossing herself.* NIKITA *and* ANISYA *move away from each other.*]

MATRENA: Oh, what I've seen, I didn't see; what I've heard, I didn't hear. Been having fun with a nice little woman, have you? What of it? Even calves have their fun, you know. Why shouldn't you? You're still young. But the master is asking for you in the yard, my son.

NIKITA: I came in to get the ax.

MATRENA: I know, my boy; I know what sort of an ax you came for. You're likely to find that kind near a woman.

NIKITA [*bends down and picks up an ax*]: Well, mother, are you really going to marry me? I think there's no reason for that at all. And then I don't want to marry.

MATRENA: Oh, my darling, why should we marry you?

You're living and having a good time; it's only the old man's plan. Go ahead, my boy; we'll settle the whole business without your help.

NIKITA: This is queer: first you want to marry me, and then you say there's no need of it. I can't understand things at all. [*Goes out.*]

ANISYA: Well, Auntie Matrena, do you really want to marry him?

MATRENA: Why should we marry him, my precious? You know what our family's like. My old man keeps mumbling foolish stuff: "Marry him, must marry him." But he hasn't enough sense to judge. Horses don't run away from oats, you know, men don't quit one good thing for another: that's the way to look at it. Don't I see [*winks*] the turn things are taking?

ANISYA: It's no use for me to hide from you, Auntie Matrena. You know everything. I have sinned; I have fallen in love with your son.

MATRENA: Well, this is news! And Auntie Matrena didn't know! Oh, girlie, Auntie Matrena is an old bird, a sly old bird. Auntie Matrena, I can tell you, darling, can see a yard underground. I know everything, precious! I know why young wives need sleeping powders. I've brought some. [*Unties a corner of her kerchief and takes out a packet of powders.*] What I need to, I see; and what I don't need to, I don't know and don't want to know. That's the way. Auntie Matrena was young once herself. I've had to find out how to live with my own fool, you see. I know the whole seventy-seven tricks. I see your old man's withering away, darling, withering away. What sort of life can you have? Stick a pitchfork into him and the blood won't flow. I tell you: you'll be burying him next spring! You must get someone else to be the boss. And ain't my son up to the job? He's no worse than others. So what use would it be for me to pull my son away from a good soft place? Am I my own child's enemy?

ANISYA: If only he don't leave us!

MATRENA: He won't leave you, birdie. That's all non-

MATRENA: I can take 'em back.

ANISYA: Do you dissolve the second sort in water, like the others?

MATRENA: It's better in tea, he says. "You don't notice 'em at all," he says, "there's no smell to 'em, not a bit." He's a clever man.

ANISYA [taking the powders]: Oh! oh! poor me! I'd never meddle with such things if my life wasn't a torment worse than prison.

MATRENA: And don't forget the ruble; I promised to take it to the old man. He has troubles of his own.

ANISYA: Sure! [Goes to the chest and hides the powders.]

MATRENA: And keep 'em tight, darling, so that people won't know. And if he finds 'em—God forbid!—say that they're for cockroaches. [Takes the ruble.] They're good for cockroaches, too. . . . [Stops suddenly.]

[AKIM comes in and crosses himself before the ikon; PETR comes in and sits down.]

PETR: Well, how goes it, Uncle Akim?

AKIM: A bit better, Ignatych, a bit better, y'see; a bit better. Because I was afraid that there might— Foolery, you know. I'd like, y'see, I'd like to get the lad down to business, and if you'd agree, y'see then we might. It'd be better if—

PETR: All right, all right. Sit down and let's talk. [AKIM sits down.] Well then? So you want to marry him?

MATRENA: We can wait about marrying him, Petr Ignatych. You know how hard up we are, Ignatych: If we marry him, we can't make a living ourselves. How can we marry him!

PETR: Decide for yourselves what's better.

MATRENA: Well, there's no haste about the marrying. It'll wait. She's no raspberry; she won't fall off the bush.

PETR: Of course, it'd be a good thing if you married him.

AKIM: I'd like to, y'see. Because, y'see, I've some work in town; I struck a good job, y'see.

MATRENA: Fine job! Cleaning cesspools. When he came home the other day, I puked and puked. Ugh!

AKIM: That's true; at first it just knocks you over, y'see,

the smell of it. But when you get used to it, it's no worse than malt dregs, and after all it suits me. And about the smell, y'see— Men like me needn't mind it. And then we can change our clothes— I wanted to have Nikita at home, you know; he can tend to things there. He can tend to things at home, and I'll make some money in town, y'see.

PETR: You want to keep your son at home: very well then. But how about the pay he took in advance?

AKIM: That's right, Ignatych, that's right; you told the truth there, y'see. He's hired himself out and sold himself, so let the bargain stand. But we must just marry him, y'see; so you just let him off for a while.

PETR: Well, that's possible.

MATRENA: But we two don't agree about it. Petr Ignatych, I'll tell you the truth as I'd tell it to God. You judge between me and my old man. He keeps saying, "Marry him, marry him." But marry him to whom, may I ask? If she was a decent girl, I'd not stand in my boy's way, but she's a low-lived hussy.

AKIM: That's all wrong. You're wrong in slandering the girl, y'see; you're wrong. Because she—that girl, I say— has been injured by my son; she's been injured, I tell you. The girl has, you know.

PETR: What was the injury?

AKIM: She got mixed up with my son, Nikita, y'see. With Nikita, you know.

MATRENA: Don't you speak of it; my tongue's softer, I'll tell the story. Before he came to you, you know, our lad was living on the railroad. And there a girl got hold of him; you know, a stupid hussy named Marina—she was cook for the railroad gang. So she accused him, that hussy did, our own son, and said that it was he, Nikita, that deceived her.

PETR: That's a bad business.

MATRENA: But she's a low-lived creature herself, runs after the men. She's just a streetwalker.

AKIM: Old woman, you're telling wrong stories again, y'see; it ain't a bit so. I tell you it ain't, y'see.

MATRENA: All my old boy can say is: "y'see, y'see"; but

what he means by it he don't know himself. Don't ask me about the hussy, Petr Ignatych, ask other folks; anybody'll tell you. She's just a homeless vagrant.

PETR [*to* AKIM]: Well, Uncle Akim, if that's the case, then there's no use marrying him. The business ain't an old shoe that you can kick off by making him marry her.

AKIM [*getting excited*]: It's an injury to the girl, y'see, old woman, an injury, y'see. Because the girl is a very decent sort, y'see, a very decent sort; and I'm sorry for her, sorry for the girl, you know.

MATRENA: You're just like a silly old woman; you waste your sorrow on the whole world, while your own folks go hungry. You're sorry for the girl, but you ain't sorry for your son. Tie her round your own neck and walk with her! Quit talking nonsense!

AKIM: No, it ain't nonsense.

MATRENA: Don't you get on your ear: I'll say my say.

AKIM [*interrupting*]: No, it ain't nonsense. You turn things your own way—maybe about the girl, maybe about yourself —you turn things your own way, as it's best for you; but, y'see, God will turn 'em his way. That's how it stands.

MATRENA: Bah! No use wasting words on you.

AKIM: The girl's a hard worker, a decent sort, and she knows how to look out for herself, y'see. And we're poor, and she'll be an extra hand, y'see; and the wedding won't cost much. But the main thing's the injury done the girl, you know; she's an orphan, y'see, the girl is. And she's been injured.

MATRENA: Any girl'd say that.

ANISYA: Just you listen to us women, Uncle Akim. We can tell you things.

AKIM: But God, I tell you, God! Ain't she a human being, that girl? So, y'see, God cares for her. What do you think about that?

MATRENA: Oh, he's off again!

PETR: See here, Uncle Akim, you can't much believe those hussies either. And the lad's alive. He's close by! Let's send and ask him straight out whether it's true. He won't perjure his soul. Call the lad here! [ANISYA *rises*.] Tell him his father's calling for him.

[ANISYA *goes out*.]

MATRENA: You've settled the business, my dear, you've cleaned it up: let the lad speak for himself. And these times you can't marry off a lad by force. We must ask him what he thinks. He'll never want to marry her and shame himself. What I think is: he'd better stay with you and work for his master. Even in summer we won't need to take him; we can hire somebody. Just give us ten rubles and he can stay here.

PETR: We'll talk about that later: take things in order. Finish one job before you start another.

AKIM: I'm talking this way, Petr Ignatych, you know, because such things happen sometimes, y'see. You keep trying to better yourself, and you forget about God, y'see; you think it'd be better—you go your own gait, and find the load's on your own shoulders. We think it'll be better for us, you know; and then it's much worse, for we've left out God.

PETR: Of course! We must remember God.

AKIM: All of a sudden, it's worse. But if you act according to the law, and as God wills, then, y'see, somehow everything makes you happy. So that's how you want to do. So I struck the idea, you know: I'll marry the lad and keep him out of sin. He'll be at home, y'see, just as he should be by rights; and I'll just go to work in the town, y'see. It's a pleasant job. Suits me. Do as God wills, y'see, and things are better. And then she's an orphan. For instance, last summer they stole some wood from the clerk—what a trick! They thought they'd fool him. They did fool the clerk, but y'see, they didn't fool God: so, y'see—

[*Enter* NIKITA *and* ANYUTKA.]

NIKITA: Did you ask for me? [*Sits down and takes out his tobacco*.]

PETR: [*in a low voice, reproachfully*]: Look here, don't you know how to behave? Your father is going to ask you questions, and you're fooling with your tobacco, and you've sat down. Get up and come over here.

[NIKITA *takes his stand by the table, jauntily leaning against it, and smiling.*]

AKIM: Well, y'see, there's a complaint against you, Nikita; a complaint, y'see.

NIKITA: Who complained?

AKIM: Who complained? A girl, an orphan complained. It was she, that same Marina, who complained on you, y'see.

NIKITA [*grinning*]: Mighty queer. What's the complaint? Who told you about it? Was it she?

AKIM: Now I'm asking you questions, y'see, and you've got to answer, you know. Did you get mixed up with the girl? Did you get mixed up with her, I say?

NIKITA: I simply don't understand what you're talking about.

AKIM: I mean, was there any foolery, y'see, between you and her? Foolery, foolery, you know.

NIKITA: Of course there was. You have fun with the cook to pass the time away; you play the accordion and she dances. What more foolery do you want?

PETR: Nikita, don't shuffle around: answer straight out what your father's asking you.

AKIM [*solemnly*]: Nikita, you can hide things from men, but you can't hide 'em from God. Nikita, just think it over, y'see; don't you tell me lies! She's an orphan, y'see; it's easy to injure her. An orphan, you know. Tell me plain how it was.

NIKITA: But there's nothing to tell. I'm telling you the whole story, because there's nothing to tell. [*Getting excited.*] She'll say anything. She can spread all the stories she wants, as if a man was dead. What stories didn't she tell of Fedka Mikishkin? So I suppose nowadays you can't have any fun! Let her talk!

AKIM: Eh, Nikita, look out! The truth will be known. Was there something or wasn't there?

NIKITA [*aside*]: They're pressing me hard. [*To* AKIM.] I tell you there wasn't anything. There was nothing between me and her. [*Angrily.*] I swear to Christ, may I die on the spot if there was! [*Crosses himself.*] I don't know anything about the business. [*Silence.* NIKITA *continues still more excitedly.*] How did you get the idea of marrying me to her! What's all this anyhow? It's an outrage. Nowadays you've no right to marry a man by force. It's simple enough. I've just sworn to you—I don't know a thing about it.

MATRENA [*to her husband*]: That's it, you silly old fool: whatever rubbish they tell you, you believe it all. You've just put the lad to shame for nothing. And he'd better just stay on living here with the master. Now the master will give us ten rubles to help us out. And when the time comes—

PETR: Well then, Uncle Akim?

AKIM [*clucks with his tongue. To his son*]: Look out, Nikita; the tear of an injured girl don't flow in vain, y'see; it drops on a man's head. Look out for what's coming.

NIKITA: What's there to look out for? Look out yourself. [*Sits down.*]

ANYUTKA: I'll go tell mama. [*Goes out.*]

MATRENA [*to* PETR]: That's how it always is, Petr Ignatych. My old man just makes trouble with his talk; when he gets a notion in his nut, you can't knock it out. We've just bothered you for nothing. Let the lad stay on living here as he has done. Keep the lad—he's your servant.

PETR: How about it, Uncle Akim?

AKIM: Well, y'see, I didn't want to force the lad—I was just afraid— Y'see, I'd like to have—

MATRENA: You don't know yourself what you're meddling with. Let him live here just as he has. The lad himself don't want to leave. And what use have we for him? We'll manage alone.

PETR: Just one thing, Uncle Akim: if you're going to take him in the summer, I don't want him this winter. If he's to stay here, it must be for a year.

MATRENA: He'll promise for the whole year. At home, when the working time comes, if we need anybody we'll hire him; and let the lad stay here. And now you give us ten rubles.

PETR: Well then, for a year more?

AKIM [*sighing*]: Well, seems like, y'see; I suppose it's so.

MATRENA: One year more, from the feast of St. Dmitry. You won't beat us down on the price—and now give us ten rubles. You'll do us that favor.

[*Rises and bows.* ANISYA *comes in with* ANYUTKA *and sits down at one side.*]

PETR: Well? If that's all right, then—then let's go to the tavern and wet down the bargain. Come on, Uncle Akim, and have a drink of vodka.

AKIM: I don't drink vodka, I don't.

PETR: Well, you'll have some tea.

AKIM: Tea's my sin. Tea, sure.

PETR: The women will have some tea too. Nikita, see that you don't drive the sheep too fast—and rake up the straw.

NIKITA: All right.

[*All go out except* NIKITA. *Darkness is falling.*]

NIKITA [*lights a cigarette*]: They nagged and nagged me to tell about my doings with the girls. Those'd make a long story. He told me to marry her. If I married 'em all, I'd have a lot of wives. No use of my marrying; I'm as well off now as a married man: people envy me. And how lucky it was that something or other just put me up to go and cross myself before the ikon. That way I cut the whole business short. They say it's scary to swear to what ain't true. That's all bosh. Nothing but words anyhow. It's simple enough.

AKULINA [*comes in, lays down the rope, takes off her coat, and goes to the storeroom*]: You might give us a light, anyhow.

NIKITA: To look at you? I can see you without it.

AKULINA: Drat you!

ANYUTKA [*runs in and whispers to* NIKITA]: Nikita, hurry up; somebody's asking for you. Can you imagine!

NIKITA: Who is it?

ANYUTKA: Marina from the railroad. She's standing round the corner.

NIKITA: You lie.

ANYUTKA: Honest!

NIKITA: What's she want?

ANYUTKA: Wants you to come. "I just need to speak one word to Nikita," she says. I began to ask questions, but she won't tell. She just asked if it was true that you're leaving us. "It ain't true," says I, "his father wanted to take him away and marry him, but he refused and he's going to stay another year with us." And she says: "Just send him to me, for Christ's sake. I just must say one word to him," she says. She's been waiting a long time. You go to her.

NIKITA: Plague take her! Why should I go?

ANYUTKA: "If he don't come," she says, "I'll come into the cottage for him. Honest I'll come," she says.

NIKITA: Don't worry: she'll stand there a while and then go away.

ANYUTKA: "Do they want to marry him to Akulina?" she says.

AKULINA [*still spinning, goes up to* NIKITA]: Marry whom to Akulina?

ANYUTKA: Nikita.

AKULINA: Really? Who says so?

NIKITA: Some people say so. [*Looks at her and laughs.*] Akulina, will you marry me?

AKULINA: You? Maybe I'd have married you a little while ago, but now I won't.

NIKITA: Why won't you now?

AKULINA: 'Cause you won't love me.

NIKITA: Why won't I?

AKULINA: They won't let you. [*Laughs.*]

NIKITA: Who won't?

AKULINA: Stepmother, of course. She keeps scolding; she watches you all the time.

NIKITA [*laughing*]: Bright girl! What sharp eyes you have!

AKULINA: I? Course I see. Am I blind? She blew up dad sky-high today. She's a witch with a big snout. [*Goes into the storeroom.*]

ANYUTKA: Nikita, just look! [*She looks out of the window.*] She's coming. Honest, it's she. I'll clear out. [*Goes out.*]

MARINA [*coming in*]: What's this you're doing to me?

NIKITA: What am I doing? I'm not doing anything.

MARINA: You're going to desert me.

NIKITA [*rising angrily*]: Well, what do you mean by coming here?

MARINA: Oh, Nikita!

NIKITA: You girls are a queer lot.... What have you come for?

MARINA: Nikita!

NIKITA: Nikita, you say? I'm Nikita. What do you want? Get out, I tell you.

MARINA: I see you mean to desert me, to forget me.

NIKITA: Why should I remember you? You don't know yourself. You were standing round the corner and sent Anyutka to me, and I didn't come to you. So I haven't any use for you; that's all. Now get out.

MARINA: No use for me! You've no use for me now. I believed you when you said you'd love me. And now you've done this with me and haven't any use for me.

NIKITA: This talk of yours is all no use, don't amount to anything. You even blabbed to my father. Clear out, please!

MARINA: You know yourself that I never loved anybody but you. You might marry me or not, as you please; I shouldn't care. Have I done you any wrong that you've stopped loving me? Why did you?

NIKITA: There's no use of our wasting time talking. Clear out! ... These senseless girls!

MARINA: What hurts ain't that you deceived me and promised to marry me, but that you don't love me any more. And it don't hurt that you don't love me, but that you've changed me off for another woman. For whom? I know!

NIKITA [*steps toward her angrily*]: No use talking with girls like you; they won't listen to reason. Clear out, I tell you, or you'll make me do something bad.

MARINA: Something bad? Well, are you going to beat me? Go on, do! What are you turning away your mug for? Oh, Nikita!

NIKITA: Of course, it won't do; people'd come. But talking's no use.

MARINA: Well, this is the end; what's done is done. You tell me to forget it all! Well, Nikita, remember this. I guarded my honor more than my very eyes. You just ruined me and deceived me. You had no pity for an orphan [*weeps*]: you deserted me. You've killed me, but I don't bear you any grudge. Good-by; I don't care. If you find a better one, you'll forget me; if you find a worse one, you'll remember. You'll remember, Nikita! Good-by, if I must go. But how I *loved* you! Good-by for the last time! [*Tries to embrace him and clasp his head.*]

NIKITA [*tearing himself free*]: Bah! I'm sick of talking with you. If you won't go, I'll go myself and you can stay here.

MARINA [*screams*]: You're a beast! [*In the doorway.*] God won't give you happiness! [*Goes out, weeping.*]

AKULINA [*coming out of the storeroom*]: You're a cur, Nikita!

NIKITA: Well?

AKULINA: How she yelled! [*Weeps.*]

NIKITA: What's the matter with you?

AKULINA: What? You wronged her. You'll wrong me the same way—you cur! [*Goes out into the storeroom.*]

NIKITA [*after an interval of silence*]: It's all a puzzle to me. I love those women like sugar; but if a man sins with them—there's trouble!

act 2

The stage represents a street and PETR'S *cottage. On the spectators' left, a cottage with a porch in the center, and on each side of this a living room; on the right, the yard fence, with a gate. Near the fence* ANISYA *is stripping hemp. Six months have passed since the first act.*

ANISYA [*stopping and listening*]: He's growling once more. Most likely he's got off the stove.[1]

[AKULINA *comes in, carrying pails on a yoke.*]

ANISYA: He's calling. Go and see what he wants. Hear him yell!

AKULINA: Why don't you go yourself?

ANISYA: Go along, I tell you!

[AKULINA *goes into the cottage.*]

ANISYA: He's worn me out: he won't tell where the money is; that's all there is to it. The other day he was in the entry way; most likely he'd hid it there. Now I don't know myself where it is. It's lucky he's afraid to part with it. It's still in the house. If I could only find it! It wasn't on him yesterday. Now I don't know where it is myself. He's clean worn me out.

[AKULINA *comes out, tying on her kerchief.*]

ANISYA: Where are you going?

AKULINA: Where? He told me to call Auntie Marfa. "Send for my sister," he says. "I'm dying," he says, "and I need to tell her something."

ANISYA [*to herself*]: Sending for his sister! Oh, poor me! Oh! oh! Most likely he wants to give it to her. What shall I do? Oh! [*To* AKULINA.] Don't you go! Where are you going?

AKULINA: For auntie.

ANISYA: Don't you go, I tell you; I'll go myself. And you go to the brook with the wash. Otherwise you won't finish it before night.

AKULINA: But he told me to.

ANISYA: Go where I'm sending you. I'll go for Marfa myself, I tell you. Take the shirts off the fence.

AKULINA: The shirts? But I'm afraid you won't go. He told me to.

ANISYA: I've told you I'll go. Where's Anyutka?

AKULINA: Anyutka? She's herding the calves.

ANISYA: Send her here; they won't stray.

[1] In a Russian peasant cottage the best couch is on top of the oven. It is generally reserved for the old or infirm.

[AKULINA *gathers up the clothes and goes out.*]

ANISYA: If I don't go, he'll scold at me. If I go, he'll give his sister the money. All my toil will go for nothing. I don't know myself what to do. My head's all mixed up. [*Continues her work.*]

[MATRENA *comes in with a staff and a small bundle, equipped for traveling on foot.*]

MATRENA: God help you, darling.

ANISYA [*looks around, drops her work, and claps her hands for joy*]: Well, I never expected you, auntie. God has sent me such a guest just in time.

MATRENA: Well then?

ANISYA: I was just going crazy. Trouble!

MATRENA: Well, he's still alive, they tell me?

ANISYA: Don't speak of it. He's half alive and half dead.

MATRENA: Has he given the money to anybody?

ANISYA: He's just sending for Marfa, his own sister. Must be about the money.

MATRENA: Sure thing. But ain't he given it to somebody without your knowing it?

ANISYA: Not much! I've been watching him like a hawk.

MATRENA: But where is it?

ANISYA: He won't tell. And I can't find out anyhow. He hides it first one place and then another. And Akulina hampers me. She's only a silly fool, but she too keeps spying round and watching. Ah, poor me! I'm all worn out.

MATRENA: Eh, darling, if he gives the money to someone without your knowing it, you'll weep forever. They'll turn you out of the house empty-handed. You've worn yourself out, my precious, worn yourself out all your life with a man you don't love, and when you're a widow you'll have to go begging.

ANISYA: Don't speak of it, auntie. My heart aches and I don't know what to do and I've nobody to advise me. I told Nikita. But he's afraid to meddle with the business. He just told me yesterday that it was under the floor.

MATRENA: Well, did you look to see?

ANISYA: I couldn't; he was there himself. I notice sometimes he carries it on him, sometimes he hides it.

MATRENA: Just remember, girlie: if you slip up once, you'll never get straight again. [*In a whisper.*] Well, have you given him the strong tea?

ANISYA: O-oh!

[*Is about to reply, but sees her* FRIEND, *and stops short. Another housewife, a* FRIEND OF ANISYA, *walks past the cottage, and stops to listen to the shouts from within it.*]

FRIEND [*to* ANISYA]: Hey, friend! Anisya, Anisya, I say! Your man seems to be calling you.

ANISYA: He keeps coughing that way, and it sounds as if he was calling. He's pretty low by now.

FRIEND [*coming up to* MATRENA]: Good day, old woman, where in the world did you come from?

MATRENA: From home, of course, my dear. I came to see my son. I've brought him some shirts. He's my boy, you know, and I'm sorry for him.

FRIEND: That's natural. [*To* ANISYA.] I was going to bleach my linen, friend, but I think it's too soon. People haven't begun yet.

ANISYA: No use of hurrying.

MATRENA: Well, have they given him the Communion?

ANISYA: Sure; the priest was here yesterday.

FRIEND [*To* MATRENA]: I had a look at him yesterday myself, my dear; and he seemed hardly alive. He'd just wasted away. And the other day, my friend, he seemed on the point of death; they laid him out under the holy ikons. They were already wailing for him, and getting ready to wash the body.

ANISYA: He's come to life again—got out of bed; now he's walking again.

MATRENA: Well, will you give him extreme unction?

ANISYA: People are urging me to. If he's alive, we're going to send for the priest tomorrow.

FRIEND: Eh, it must be pretty hard for you, Anisya dear. It's a true saying: The bed's soft for the sick man, but hard for those that tend him.

ANISYA: That's so, but there's more to it.

FRIEND: Of course, he's been dying for most a year. He's tied you hand and foot.

MATRENA: A widow's lot is hard too. It's all right when you're young, but when you're old nobody will pity you. Old age is no joy. Take me for instance. I haven't walked far; but I'm tired out—my legs are numb— Where's my son?

ANISYA: Plowing.— But come in, we'll start the samovar. The tea'll refresh you.

MATRENA [*sitting down*]: I'm certainly tired, my dears. But you simply must give him the unction. People say that it's good for the soul.

ANISYA: Yes, we'll send tomorrow.

MATRENA: That's right.— But we're having a wedding down our way, girlie.

FRIEND: What, in the spring?

MATRENA: It's a good old proverb: "A poor man hurries to marry before the night's over." Semyon Matveyevich is going to take Marina.

ANISYA: She's in great luck!

FRIEND: He must be a widower; she'll have to look out for the children.

MATRENA: There are four of 'em. What decent girl would marry him? Well, he took her. And she's glad enough. They were drinking, you know, and the glass was cracked—they spilled the wine.

FRIEND: Just think! Was there gossip? And has the man some property?

MATRENA: They get along pretty well.

FRIEND: It's true, hardly any girl will marry a man with children. . . . Just take our Mikhaylo. My dear, he's a man who—

PEASANT [*offstage*]: Hey, Mavra, what the devil are you up to? Go and drive home the cow.

[FRIEND *goes out.*]

MATRENA [*while the* FRIEND *is going out, she speaks in a calm voice*]: They've got her out of harm's way, girlie; at

any rate my old fool won't think any more about Nikita.
[*Suddenly changes her voice to a whisper.*] She's gone!
[*Whispers.*] Well, I say, did you give him the tea?

ANISYA: Don't speak of it. He'd better die all by himself.
He's not dying anyhow; I've just got the sin of it on my
conscience. O-oh, poor me! Why did you give me those
powders?

MATRENA: Powders? They were sleeping powders, girlie;
why shouldn't I give 'em to you? They won't do any harm.

ANISYA: I don't mean the sleeping powders; I mean the
others, the white ones.

MATRENA: Well, darling, those powders were medicine.

ANISYA [*sighs*]: I know, but I'm afraid. He's worn me out.

MATRENA: Have you used much of it?

ANISYA: I gave it to him twice.

MATRENA: Well, he didn't notice?

ANISYA: I tasted it a bit in the tea, myself; it's a trifle bitter. And he drank it with the tea and said: "I can't stand
that tea." And says I, "Everything's bitter to a sick man."
And I felt my heart sink, auntie.

MATRENA: Don't think about it; thinking makes things
worse.

ANISYA: I wish you hadn't given 'em to me and led me
into sin. When I remember it, it makes me shiver. And why
did you give 'em to me?

MATRENA: Eh, what do you mean, darling! Lord help
you! Why do you throw the blame on me? Look out, girlie,
don't shift the blame to someone else's shoulders. If any
questions are asked, I'm not concerned; I don't know a
thing about it: I'll kiss the cross and say I never gave her
powders, never saw any, never even heard that there were
such powders. Just think for yourself, girlie. We were talking about you the other day, saying how the precious
woman was just tormented to death. Her step-daughter's a
fool, and her husband's no good, just skin and bones. Such
a life'd make a woman do anything.

ANISYA: Well, I don't deny it. My life'd make me do
worse things than these; I'm ready to hang myself or stran-

gle him. 'Tain't being alive.

MATRENA: That's just the point. No time to stand and yawn. Somehow you must find the money and give him some more tea.

ANISYA: O-oh! Poor me! What to do now I don't know myself; it makes me shiver. I wish he'd die all by himself. I don't want to have the guilt on my soul.

MATRENA [angrily]: But why don't he tell where the money is? Does he expect to take it with him and not let anybody have it? Is that right and proper? God forbid that such a lot of money should be wasted. Ain't that a sin? What's he doing? May I have a look at him?

ANISYA: I don't know myself. He's worn me out.

MATRENA: What don't you know? It's a clear case. If you make a slip now, you'll repent of it forever. He'll give the money to his sister, and you'll be left out.

ANISYA: O-oh, he was sending for her—I must go.

MATRENA: Don't go yet awhile: we'll start the samovar first thing. We'll give him the tea and between us we'll find where the money is—we'll manage to get it.

ANISYA: O-oh! Something may happen.

MATRENA: What's the matter? What are you staring at? Are you just going to roll your eyes at the money and not get it in your hands? Get to work.

ANISYA: Then I'll go and start the samovar.

MATRENA: Go on, darling; do the business right, so that you won't be sorry afterward. That's the way. [ANISYA moves away, MATRENA urging her.] Be sure and not tell Nikita about all this business. He's sort of silly. God forbid he find out about the powders. God knows what he'd do. He's very tender-hearted. You know, he never would kill a chicken for me. Don't you tell him. Trouble is, he won't understand it.

[She stops in horror; PETR makes his appearance on the threshold. PETR, holding to the wall, crawls out on the porch and calls in a weak voice.]

PETR: Why can't I make you hear? O-oh! Anisya, who's here? [Falls on the bench.]

ANISYA [coming in from around the corner]: What have you come out for? You ought to lie where you were.

PETR: Well, has the girl gone for Marfa? . . . I feel bad. . . . Oh, if death would only hurry up!

ANISYA: She's busy; I sent her to the brook. Give me time and I'll attend to it. I'll go myself.

PETR: Send Anyutka. Where is she? Oh, I feel bad! Oh, my death!

ANISYA: I've sent for her already.

PETR: O-oh! Where is she?

ANISYA: Where can she be? Plague take her!

PETR: O-oh, I can't stand it! My inside is burning. Seems like an auger was boring me. Why have you deserted me like a dog? . . . There's no one even to give me a drink. . . . O-oh! . . . Send Anyutka to me.

ANISYA: Here she is.—Anyutka, go to your father.

[ANYUTKA runs in and ANISYA retires around the corner.]

PETR: Go and tell—o-oh!—your Aunt Marfa that your father wants to see her; tell her to come here.

ANYUTKA: Is that all?

PETR: Wait. Tell her to hurry up. Tell her I'm almost dead. O-oh!

ANYUTKA: I'll just get my kerchief and go right away. [Runs out.]

MATRENA [winking]: Now, girlie, get down to work. Go into the cottage and rummage everywhere. Look for it like a dog looks for fleas; turn over everything, and I'll search him right away.

ANISYA [to MATRENA]: With you seems like I have more courage. [Goes towards the porch. To PETR.] Shan't I start a samovar for you? Auntie Matrena's come to see her son; you'll have tea with her.

PETR: Go ahead and start it. [ANISYA goes into the cottage. MATRENA comes toward the porch]

PETR: Hello!

MATRENA: Good day, my benefactor! Good day, my precious! I see you're still sick. And my old man is so sorry for you. "Go and inquire," says he. He sent his regards. [*Bows once more.*]

PETR: I'm dying.

MATRENA: Well, when I look at you, Ignatych, I can see that trouble haunts men and not the forest. You've wasted away, my precious, all wasted away; I can see that. Sickness don't bring beauty, I suppose?

PETR: My death's near.

MATRENA: Well, Petr Ignatych, it's God's will. They've given you the Communion, and now, God willing, they'll give the unction. Thank God, your wife's a sensible woman; she'll bury you and have prayers said, all as is proper. And my son too, while he's needed, he'll tend to things about the house.

PETR: There's no one that I can give orders to! The woman's heedless and spends her time on foolery; I know all about it—I know. The girl's half-witted, and young at that. I've gathered a good property, and there's nobody to attend to it. It's too bad. [*Snivels.*]

MATRENA: Well, if it's money or anything like that, you can give directions.

PETR [*calls into the house, to* ANISYA]: Has Anyutka gone yet?

MATRENA [*aside*]: Oh, my, he still remembers!

ANISYA [*from indoors*]: She went right off. Come into the house; I'll help you.

PETR: Let me sit here for the last time. It's close in there. I feel bad.... Oh, my heart's burning! ... If only death would come!

MATRENA: When God won't take a soul, the soul won't leave of itself. God's the judge of life and death, Petr Ignatych. You can never tell when death will come. Sometimes you recover. For instance in our village a peasant was just on the point of death—

PETR: No! I feel that I'll die today; I feel it. [*Leans against the wall and closes his eyes.*]

ANISYA [*coming out of the cottage*]: Well, are you coming in or not? Don't keep me waiting. Petr! Petr, I say!

MATRENA [*walking away and beckoning to* ANISYA]: Well, how about it?

ANISYA [*coming down from the porch, to* MATRENA]: Not there.

MATRENA: But did you look everywhere? Under the floor?

ANISYA: Not there either. Maybe in the shed. He went there yesterday.

MATRENA: Search, search, I tell you. Lick things clean. And it's my notion he'll die today anyhow; his nails are blue and his face like earth. Is the samovar ready?

ANISYA: It'll boil right off.

[NIKITA *comes in from the other side of the stage—if possible on horseback, he comes up to the gate without seeing* PETR.]

NIKITA [*to his mother*]: Hello, mother; are you all well at home?

MATRENA: Thanks to the Lord God, we're still alive; we can still eat.

NIKITA: Well, how's the boss?

MATRENA: Shh—he's sitting there. [*Points to the porch.*]

NIKITA: Well, let him sit. What do I care?

PETR [*opening his eyes*]: Nikita; hey, Nikita, come here!

[NIKITA *goes to him.* ANISYA *and* MATRENA *whisper.*]

PETR: Why have you come home so early?

NIKITA: I finished the plowing.

PETR: Did you plow the strip beyond the bridge?

NIKITA: It was too far to go there.

PETR: Too far? It's still farther from the house. You'll have to go there specially. You ought to have finished it at the same time.

[ANISYA *listens to the conversation without showing herself.*]

MATRENA [*approaching them*]: Oh, sonny, why don't you try to please the master? The master is ill and relies on you; you ought to work for him as for your own father. Just stir yourself and work hard for him as I've told you to so often.

PETR: Then—ugh!—haul out the potatoes; the women—

o-oh!—will sort them over.

ANISYA [*to herself*]: Well, I won't budge. He's trying to send everybody away from him once more; most likely he has the money on him. He wants to hide it somewhere.

PETR: Otherwise—o-oh!— It'll be time to plant 'em, and they'll have sweated. O-oh, I'm exhausted. [*Rises.*]

MATRENA [*runs up on the porch and supports* PETR]: Shall I take you into the room?

PETR: Yes. [*Stops.*] Nikita!

NIKITA [*angrily*]: What next?

PETR: I shan't see you again. . . . I shall die today. . . . Forgive me for Christ's sake if I've sinned against you. . . . Whether in word or deed . . . if I ever sinned. There were many times. Forgive me.

NIKITA: No need to forgive; I'm a sinner myself.

MATRENA: Oh, sonny, take this to heart!

PETR: Forgive me, for Christ's sake! . . . [*Weeps.*]

NIKITA [*in a choked voice*]: God will forgive you, Uncle Petr. I've no cause to bear you a grudge. I've never been ill treated by you. You forgive me; maybe I've sinned more against you. [*Weeps.*]

[PETR *goes out, sniffling, supported by* MATRENA.]

ANISYA: Oh, poor me! He didn't think of that for nothing; it's clear that— [*Goes up to* NIKITA.] Well, you said that the money was under the floor— It ain't there.

NIKITA [*sobs, without replying*]: He was always fair and square to me—and see what I've done!

ANISYA: Well, stop it. Where's the money?

NIKITA [*angrily*]: How should I know? Look for yourself.

ANISYA: You seem to be awful sorry for him?

NIKITA: Yes, I am sorry for him, mighty sorry. How he wept! O-oh!

ANISYA: How kind you are—found somebody to pity! He treated you like a dog, like a dog. Just now he was telling us to turn you out. You might be sorry for me instead.

NIKITA: Why should I be sorry for you?

ANISYA: He'll die and hide the money. . . .

NIKITA: Maybe he won't hide it. . . .

ANISYA: Oh, Nikita dear! He's sent for his sister and wants to give it to her. Bad luck for us! How can we live if he gives away the money? They'll drive me out of the house. You might do something about it. Didn't you tell me he went to the shed last evening?

NIKITA: I saw him coming out of there, but nobody knows where he hid it.

ANISYA: Oh, poor me, I'll go and look there.

[NIKITA *walks away.* MATRENA *comes out of the cottage and goes over to* ANISYA *and* NIKITA.]

MATRENA [*whispers*]: You needn't go anywhere. The money's on him: I felt it; it's on a string around his neck.

ANISYA: Oh, poor me!

MATRENA: If you let it out of your sight now, you can look for it next door to nowhere. His sister'll come and you're done for.

ANISYA: She'll come and he'll give it to her. What shall we do? Oh, poor me!

MATRENA: What shall you do? See here: the samovar's boiling; go make the tea and pour it out for him, and [*in a whisper*] sprinkle in all the powder out of the paper and make him drink it. When he's drunk a cupful, just pull the string. Don't worry; he'll never tell about it.

ANISYA: Oh, I'm afraid!

MATRENA: Don't argue, hurry up about it; and I'll take care of the sister if she comes. Don't make a slip. Pull out the money and bring it here, and Nikita will hide it.

ANISYA: Oh, poor me! How can I ever dare to . . . and and . . . and . . .

MATRENA: Don't argue, I tell you; do as I say. Nikita!

NIKITA: What?

MATRENA: Stay here; sit down on the bench close to the house, in case—you're needed.

NIKITA [*with a wave of his hand*]: Those women are crafty. They make a man dizzy. Plague take you! I'll go haul out the potatoes.

MATRENA [*clutching his arm*]: Stay here, I tell you.

[ANYUTKA *comes in.*]

ANISYA [*to* ANYUTKA]: Well?

ANYUTKA: She was at her daughter's in the garden; she'll come right away.

ANISYA: If she comes, what'll we do?

MATRENA [*to* ANISYA]: Don't bother about her now; do as I tell you.

ANISYA: I don't know myself—I don't know anything; my head's all mixed up. Anyutka, girlie, run off for the calves; they must have strayed away. Oh, I'll never dare!

[ANYUTKA *runs out.*]

MATRENA: Go along; the samovar's boiling over, most likely.

ANISYA: Oh, poor me! [*Goes out.*]

MATRENA [*going up to her son*]: Well, sonny! [*Sits down beside him on the earth bench around the house.*] Now we must think over your business, not just let it drift.

NIKITA: What business?

MATRENA: Why, how you're going to get along and make your living.

NIKITA: Get along? Other people do, and so can I.

MATRENA: The old man's sure to die today.

NIKITA: If he dies, let him go to heaven! What do I care?

MATRENA [*during her speech she keeps glancing at the porch*]: Eh, sonny! The living must think of life. Here you need a lot of sense, my precious. Just think, for your sake I've run around everywhere; I've trotted my legs off working for you. And mind you: don't forget me later.

NIKITA: What sort of work were you doing?

MATRENA: For your sake, for your future. If you don't take pains in time, nothing ever succeeds. You know Ivan Moseich? I called on him too. I went over the other day, you know, and told him about a certain matter; I sat there and we got to talking. "Ivan Moseich," says I, "how could a case like this be fixed up? Suppose," says I, "a peasant is a widower, and suppose he takes another wife; and just suppose," says I, "he has children, one daughter by his first wife and one by the second. Well," says I, "if that peasant dies, is it possible," says I, "for another peasant to marry the widow and get the farm? Is it possible," says I, "for that peasant to marry off the daughters and stay on the farm himself?" "It's possible," says he, "only you need to take a lot of pains; and," says he, "you need to use money to fix things up. Without money," says he, "there's no use meddling with it."

NIKITA [*laughing*]: You needn't tell me that; just give 'em money. Everybody needs money.

MATRENA: Well, darling, I explained everything to him. "First of all," says he, "your son must get himself enrolled legally as a member of that village commune: for this he'll need money, to give a drink to the old men of the village. Then they'll agree to it and sign the paper. Only," says he, "you must do everything with some sense." Look here [*takes a paper from her kerchief*] he wrote out a paper. Read it—you're smart.

[NIKITA *reads, and* MATRENA *listens.*]

NIKITA: The paper is a legal order, of course. No great amount of sense needed here.

MATRENA: But just hear what Ivan Moseich had to say. "The main thing is, auntie," says he, "look out and don't let the money slip past you. If she don't grab the money," says he, "they won't let her marry off her daughter. The money's the root of the whole matter," says he. So look out. The time's coming to act, sonny.

NIKITA: What do I care: the money's hers, let her worry about it.

MATRENA: Is that what you think, sonny! Can a woman make plans? Even if she gets the money, she won't know how to manage it. She's nothing but a woman, and you're a man. So you can hide it and do anything you choose. Anyhow, you have more sense if any hitch comes.

NIKITA: Oh, you women don't understand anything!

MATRENA: Don't we though? You get hold of the money. Then the woman will be in your hands. If she ever happens to growl or grumble, then you can take her down.

NIKITA: Oh, you make me tired! I'm going.

[ANISYA *runs out of the cottage, all pale, and goes around the corner to* MATRENA.]

ANISYA: It was on him. There it is. [*Points under her apron.*]

MATRENA: Give it to Nikita; he'll hide it. Nikita, take it and hide it somewhere.

NIKITA: Well, give it here!

ANISYA: O-oh, poor me! Maybe I'd better do it myself. [*Goes toward the gate.*]

MATRENA [*clutching her by the arm*]: Where are you going? They'll miss it; his sister's coming. Give it to him; he knows what to do. How silly you are!

ANISYA [*stops, undecided*]: Oh, poor me!

NIKITA: Well, give it here; I'll hide it somewhere.

ANISYA: Where'll you hide it?

NIKITA: Are you afraid?

[*Laughs.* AKULINA *comes in with the clothes.*]

ANISYA: O-oh, poor me, poor me! [*Hands him the money.*] Look out, Nikita!

NIKITA: What're you afraid of? I'll tuck it away where I can't find it myself. [*Goes out.*]

ANISYA [*stands terrified*]: O-oh, what if he—

MATRENA: Well, is he dead?

ANISYA: Yes, seems dead. I pulled it out, and he didn't feel it.

MATRENA: Go inside; there's Akulina coming.

ANISYA: Well, I've sinned—and now he's got the money—

MATRENA: That'll do; go inside: there's Marfa coming.

ANISYA: Well, I trusted him. What'll come of it?

[*Goes out.* MARFA *comes in from one side;* AKULINA *approaches from the other.*]

MARFA [*to* AKULINA]: I'd have come long ago, but I'd gone to my daughter's— Well, how's the old man? Is he dying?

AKULINA [*sorting out the clothes*]: How should I know? I've been at the brook.

MARFA [*pointing to* MATRENA]: Where's she from?

MATRENA: I'm from Zuyev; I'm Nikita's mother, from

Zuyev, dearie. Good day to you! Your dear brother is very sick, very sick. He came out here himself. "Send for my sister," says he, "because," says he— Oh! Maybe he's dead already?

[ANISYA *runs out of the cottage with a cry, clutches the post of the porch, and begins to wail.*]

ANISYA: O-o-oh! O-o-oh! Why have you left—o-o-oh!— and why have you deserted—o-o-oh!—your wretched widow?— Forever and ever, he has closed his bright eyes!—

[FRIEND *comes in. The* FRIEND *and* MATRENA *support* ANISYA *under the arms.* AKULINA *and* MARFA *go into the cottage.* PEASANTS, *both men and women, come in.*]

VOICE FROM THE CROWD: Call the old women; they must lay him out.

MATRENA [*rolling up her sleeves*]: Is there any water in the kettle? And I don't believe the samovar's been emptied. I'll help in the work myself.

act 3

PETR'S *cottage. Winter. Nine months have passed since Act 2.* ANISYA, *dressed in shabby workaday clothes, is seated at the loom, weaving.* ANYUTKA *is perched on the stove.* MITRICH, *an old laborer, comes in.*

MITRICH: Oh, the Lord be with you! Well, hasn't the master come home?

ANISYA: What?

MITRICH: Hasn't Nikita come home from town?

ANISYA: No.

MITRICH: Seems like he's been on a spree. Oh, Lord!

ANISYA: Have you fixed up the threshing floor?

MITRICH: Sure. I fixed it all up proper, covered it with straw. I don't like a halfway job. Oh, Lord! Gracious St. Nicholas! [*Pecks at his calluses.*] Yes, it's high time for him to be here.

ANISYA: Why should he hurry? He has money; I suppose he's on a spree with some hussy.

MITRICH: He has money; so why shouldn't he go on a spree? What did Akulina go to town for?

ANISYA: Ask her why the devil took her there!

MITRICH: Why should she go to town? There are all kinds of things in town, if you only have the money. Oh, Lord!

ANYUTKA: Mama, I heard why. "I'll buy you a little shawl," says he, just think; "you can pick it out yourself," says he. And she dressed up just fine; put on her plush wrap and a French kerchief.

ANISYA: That's just it: maiden's modesty as far as the threshold; but when she's crossed it she forgets everything. She's a shameless hussy.

MITRICH: Really! Why be modest? If you have money, go on a spree! Oh, Lord! Is it too soon for supper? [ANISYA *is silent.*] I'll go warm myself meanwhile. [*Climbs on the stove.*] Oh, Lord! Holy Virgin Mother! St. Nicholas the Martyr!

FRIEND [*coming in*]: I see your man ain't back yet?

ANISYA: No.

FRIEND: Time for him. Hasn't he gone to our tavern? Sister Fekla said, my dear, that a lot of sleighs from town were standing there.

ANISYA: Anyutka! Hey, Anyutka!

ANYUTKA: What?

ANISYA: Run over to the tavern, Anyutka, and take a look. See if he's got drunk and gone there.

ANYUTKA [*jumping down from the stove and putting on her coat*]: Right away.

FRIEND: Did he take Akulina with him?

ANISYA: Otherwise he'd have no reason to go. It's she who keeps him busy in town. "I must go to the bank," says he, "there's some money due me"—but she's really the cause of all this mess.

FRIEND [*shaking her head*]: You don't say!

[*Silence.*]

ANYUTKA [*at the door*]: If he's there, what shall I say!

ANISYA: Just see if he's there.

ANYUTKA: All right, I'll fly like a bird.

[*Goes out. A long silence.*]

MITRICH [*bellows*]: Oh, Lord! Gracious St. Nicholas!

FRIEND [*starts from fright*]: Oh, he scared me! Who's that?

ANISYA: Mitrich, our laborer.

FRIEND: O-oh, how he frightened me! I forgot about him. Well, friend, they say people have made proposals for Akulina?

ANISYA [*coming out from behind the loom and sitting down at the table*]: People from Dedlov hinted about it, but they must have heard something—they hinted and then shut up, so the matter dropped. Who wants her?

FRIEND: How about the Lizunovs from Zuyev?

ANISYA: They sent to inquire. But that too came to nothing. He wouldn't receive them.

FRIEND: But you ought to marry her off.

ANISYA: We sure ought. I can hardly wait to get her out of the house, friend, but I've no luck. He don't want to, nor she either. You see he's not had fun enough yet with that beauty of his.

FRIEND: Eh-eh-eh! Sins! The idea of it! Why, he's her stepfather.

ANISYA: Ah, friend! They tied me hand and foot too cleverly for words. Fool that I was, I didn't notice anything, didn't even think of it—and so I married him. I didn't guess one single thing, but they already had an understanding.

FRIEND: O-oh, how sad things are!

ANISYA: More and more, I see, they're hiding things from me. Oh, friend, my life has been miserable, just miserable. It'd be all right if I only didn't love him.

FRIEND: You needn't tell me!

ANISYA: And it hurts me, friend, it hurts me to suffer such an insult from him. Oh, how it hurts!

FRIEND: Well, they say he's even getting rough with his hands. Is that so?

ANISYA: Rough every kind of way. When he was drunk he used to be gentle; even in old times he used to take a drop, but it never made him turn against me. But now, when he gets liquor in him, he just flies at me and wants to trample on me. The other day he got his hands into my hair, and I had hard work to break loose. And the hussy is worse than a snake; I wonder how the earth can bear such spiteful creatures.

FRIEND: O-o-oh! You're in hard luck, friend, the more I think of it! How can you stand it? You took in a beggar, and now he's going to make sport of you like that. Why don't you take him down a bit?

ANISYA: Oh, my dear friend, with a heart like mine what can I do! My dead husband was mighty severe, but all the same I could manage him whatever way I wanted to; but here I can't, friend. When I see him, my heart just melts. Against him I haven't any courage; he makes me feel like a wet hen.

FRIEND: O-oh, friend, I can see that somebody's bewitched you. That Matrena—they say she practices such things. Must be she.

ANISYA: I think so myself, friend. Sometimes I'm fairly ashamed of myself. I feel as if I'd like to tear him in pieces. But when I see him, no, my heart won't rise against him.

FRIEND: There must be a spell on you. It's easy enough to ruin a person, my precious. When I look at you, I can see that something's happened.

ANISYA: My legs are thin as bean poles. But look at that fool Akulina. She was a frowzy, sluttish hussy, and now look at her! What's the reason of this change? He's given her finery. She's swelled up and puffed up like a bubble on water. And then, no matter if she is a fool, she's got notions into her head. "I'm the mistress here," she says, "the house is mine. Dad wanted to marry me to him." And what a temper! God save us! When she gets mad, she fairly tears the straw off the roof.

FRIEND: O-oh, I see what a life you have, friend! And yet people envy you! "They're rich," they say; but, my dear, tears flow even through gold, you know.

ANISYA: Much there is to envy! And even the wealth will scatter like dust. He squanders money something awful.

FRIEND: But haven't you given him a pretty free rein, friend? The money's yours.

ANISYA: If you only knew the whole story! I made one big mistake.

FRIEND: In your place, friend, I'd go straight to the chief of police. The money's yours. How can he squander it? He's no right to.

ANISYA: Nowadays rights don't matter.

FRIEND: Oh, friend, I can see that you've grown weak.

ANISYA: Yes, darling, weak as a rag. He's bound me hand and foot. And I can't see any way out of it. O-oh, poor me!

FRIEND: Isn't somebody coming?

[*She listens. The door opens and* AKIM *comes in.*]

AKIM [*crossing himself, knocking the snow off his bast shoes, and taking off his coat*]: Peace to this house! Are you all well? Good evening, auntie.

ANISYA: Good evening, daddy. Have you come from home?

AKIM: I thought, y'see, I'd come see my son, y'see; I'd call on my son, you know. I didn't start early, had my dinner, you know; I started and it was deep snow, y'see, hard going, hard going; and so, y'see, I'm pretty late, you know. But is sonny at home? Is he home?

ANISYA: No, in town.

AKIM [*sitting down on the bench*]: I have some business with him, y'see; a bit of business. I was telling him the other day, you know; telling him about our needs, y'see: the old horse has given out, you know, the old horse. So we must get some sort of nag, y'see; some kind of nag. And so, y'see, I've come.

ANISYA: Nikita told me: when he comes, you can talk with him. [*Rises and goes to the oven.*] Have supper, and he'll come. Mitrich, hey, Mitrich, come and have supper.

MITRICH: Oh, Lord, merciful St. Nicholas!

ANISYA: Come and have supper.

FRIEND: I'll be going; good-by. [*Goes out.*]

MITRICH [*climbing down*]: I never noticed how I went to sleep. Oh, Lord, St. Nicholas the Martyr!—Good evening, Uncle Akim.

AKIM: Huh! Mitrich! What're you doing here?

MITRICH: I'm working for Nikita now; I'm living with your son.

AKIM: Do say! So, y'see, you're working for my son. Do say!

MITRICH: I was living with a merchant in town, but I ruined myself by drink there. So I came to the country. I'd no home to go to, so I hired myself out. [*Yawns.*] Oh, Lord!

AKIM: Well, y'see, well, what's Nikita doing himself? Is he so fixed, y'see, that he has to hire a workman, you know?

ANISYA: How's he fixed? First he managed by himself, but now he don't want to: so he's hired a laborer.

MITRICH: He has money, so what does he care?

AKIM: That's wrong, y'see; that's all wrong, y'see. It's wrong. He's just lazy.

ANISYA: Yes, he's got lazy, got lazy: that's the trouble.

AKIM: That's it, y'see, you think it'll be better, and, y'see, it turns out worse. When a man's wealthy, he gets lazy, gets lazy.

MITRICH: Fat makes a dog go mad, so why shouldn't fat make a man lazy! Fat was what was the ruin of me. I drank for three weeks without stopping. I drank up my last pair of pants. When I'd nothing more, I just quit. Now I've sworn off. Plague take the stuff!

AKIM: And where's your old woman now, y'see?

MITRICH: My old woman, friend, has found a place of her own. She's in town; sits in the taverns and begs. She's a beauty, too: one eye pulled out and the other knocked in and her mouth twisted sidewise. And—may she always have cakes and pie!—she's never sober.

AKIM: Oh ho! What's that?

MITRICH: But where's there a place for a soldier's wife? She's found her job.

[*Silence.*]

AKIM [*to* ANISYA]: What did Nikita go to town for? Did he take something, y'see? Did he take something to sell, you know?

ANISYA [*setting the table and passing the food*]: He went empty-handed. He went for money, to get some money in the bank.

AKIM [*eating*]: What do you want the money for, y'see? Are you going to make some new use of it?

ANISYA: No, we don't spend much. Only twenty or thirty rubles. We ran short, so we had to get some.

AKIM: Had to get some? What's the use of taking it, y'see, that money? Today you take some, you know; tomorrow you take some, y'see: that way you'll use it all up, you know.

ANISYA: This was just extra. But the money's all there.

AKIM: All there? How can it be all there, y'see? You take it and still it's all there? See here: if you pour meal, y'see, or something, you know, into a chest, y'see, or a storehouse, and then go take the meal out of there—will it still be all there, y'see? That means something is wrong, you know; they're cheating you. You see to it, or they'll cheat you. Much it's all there! You keep on taking it, and it's all there.

ANISYA: I don't know about such things. Ivan Moseich gave us some advice then. "Put your money in the bank," says he, "and the money'll be safer, and you'll get interest."

MITRICH [*finishing his meal*]: That's right. I lived with a merchant. They all do that way. Put your money in and lie on the stove and earn more.

AKIM: That's queer talk of yours, y'see. You say, "earn more," y'see, "earn more," but how do they earn that money, you know; who do they earn it from?

ANISYA: They give 'em the money from the bank.

MITRICH: What a notion! Women can't understand things. Look here and I'll explain the whole thing to you. You pay attention. You, for instance, have money, and I, for instance, when spring comes, have an empty field and nothing to sow on it, or I can't pay my taxes, maybe. So I just come to you, you know: "Akim," says I, "give me ten rubles; and when I harvest my crop, I'll return it to you on St. Mary's Day in October, and I'll help you to harvest your field for your kindness." You, for instance, see that I have something to use as security, a horse or a cow, maybe, and you say: "Give me two or three rubles extra for my kindness and let it go at that." I have the halter round my neck and can't help myself. "All right," says I, "I'll take the ten rubles." In the autumn I make a turnover and bring you the money, and you skin me of those three rubles extra.

AKIM: That means, y'see, those peasants are acting crooked, y'see; that's how it is when a man forgets God, y'see; 'tain't right, you know.

MITRICH: Wait a bit. It'll work out the same way over again. Remember now, that's what you've done, skinned me, you know: well, Anisya too, for instance, has some money on hand. She's nowhere to put it; and, just like a woman, you know, don't know what to do with it. She comes to you and says: "Can't you make some use of my money too?" she says. "Sure I can," says you. And you just wait. Then I come again next spring. "Give me another ten," says I, "and I'll pay you for it." So you just look and see if the skin ain't all peeled off of me, maybe you can tear off a bit more, and you give me Anisya's money. But if, for instance, I haven't a rag left, nothing to seize on, you just know it at a glance, and see that there's nothing to squeeze out of me, and you say right away, "Go somewhere else, my dear man, and may God help you!" and you look for some other fellow: then you lend him your own money once more and Anisya's too, and so you skin him. That's what a bank amounts to. It just goes round and round. It's a clever scheme, friend.

AKIM [getting excited]: What's that? That's just nasty

work, y'see. Peasants do that way; but the peasants, y'see, they feel it's sinful. That ain't lawful, y'see; it ain't lawful. It's nasty work. How do those learned men, y'see—?

MITRICH: That's just what they like best, my friend. Just remember this. If there's a man stupider than the rest of us, or a woman, and he can't make any use of the money himself, he just takes it to the bank; and they—it's fine bread and butter for them—just grab at it; and with that money they skin the people. It's a clever scheme.

AKIM [*sighing*]: Eh, I see, it's hard not to have money, y'see; and it's twice as hard if you have it, y'see. Anyhow God bids us toil. But you, y'see, just put your money in the bank and go to sleep; and the money, y'see, will feed you while you lie idle. That's nasty work, you know; 'tain't lawful.

MITRICH: Not lawful? That ain't what folks think nowadays, my friend. And how they do strip a man bare. That's the point.

AKIM [*sighing*]: That's the kind of times we're coming to, y'see. I've seen privies in town, you know. The new kind, y'see. All polished and polished, you know; made fine as a tavern. But it's no use, no use at all. Oh, they've forgotten God! They've forgotten him, you know! We've forgotten God, forgotten God!— Thank you, friend Anisya, I'm full; I've had enough. [*Gets up and leaves the table;* MITRICH *climbs on the stove.*]

ANISYA [*putting away the dishes and eating*]: If only his father would make him repent of his sins—but I'm ashamed to tell him.

AKIM: What?

ANISYA: I was just talking to myself.

[ANYUTKA *comes in.*]

AKIM [*to* ANYUTKA]: Hello, girlie! Always busy? Got chilled, didn't you?

ANYUTKA: Just awful chilled. Hello, grandpa!

ANISYA: Well? Is he there?

ANYUTKA: No. Only Andrian was there, just come from

town; he said he'd seen 'em in town, in a tavern. He said dad was drunk, drunk as a fish.

ANISYA: Are you hungry? There's something for you.

ANYUTKA [*going to the stove*]: I'm so cold. My hands are numb.

[AKIM *takes off his bast shoes*, ANISYA *washes the dishes.*]

ANISYA: Daddy!

AKIM: What do you want?

ANISYA: Tell me: is Marina getting on well?

AKIM: All right. She's getting on. She's a sensible, quiet little woman, y'see; she gets on, y'see; she tries hard. She's a good sort of woman, you know; clever and hard-working and patient, y'see. She's a good sort of little woman, you know.

ANISYA: Well, people from your village tell me, the kins-folk of Marina's husband want to ask for our Akulina in marriage. Have you heard of it?

AKIM: The Mironovs? The women were saying something about it. But I didn't pay attention, you know. I don't know whether it's true, y'see. The old women were talking about it. But I've a poor memory, poor memory, y'see. Well, the Mironovs, y'see, are decent sort of folks, y'see.

ANISYA: I wish that we could marry her off in a hurry.

AKIM: Why so?

ANYUTKA [*listening*]: They've come.

ANISYA: Well, let 'em alone.

[*Continues to wash the dishes, without turning her head. Enter* NIKITA.]

NIKITA: Anisya, wife, who's come?

[ANISYA *glances at him and turns away in silence.*]

NIKITA [*threateningly*]: Who's come? Have you forgot-ten?

ANISYA: Quit your bullying. Come in.

NIKITA [*still more threateningly*]: Who's come?

ANISYA [*going to him and taking his arm*]: Well, my hus-band's come. Come into the room.

NIKITA [*resisting*]: So that's it! Your husband. And what's your husband's name? Say it right.

ANISYA: Confound you: Nikita.

NIKITA: So that's it! Booby! Say the full name.

ANISYA: Akimych. Well!

NIKITA [*still in the doorway*]: So that's it! No, tell me what's the last name.

ANISYA [*laughing and pulling at his arm*]: Chilikin. How drunk you are!

NIKITA: That's so! [*Holds to the door jamb.*] No, tell me what foot Chilikin puts into the room first.

ANISYA: Oh, stop, you'll cool off the room.

NIKITA: Say what foot he puts into the room first. You must tell me.

ANISYA [*to herself*]: I'm sick of this. [*Aloud.*] Well, the left. Come in, will you?

NIKITA: So that's it!

ANISYA: Just see who's in the room.

NIKITA: Father? Well, I don't despise my father. I can show respect to my father. Good evening, daddy. [*Bows to him and offers his hand.*] My respects to you!

AKIM [*not replying to him*]: Liquor, liquor, that's what it does. Nasty business.

NIKITA: Liquor? Have I had a drink? I'm certainly guilty; I had a drink with a friend—drank his health.

ANISYA: You'd better go lie down

NIKITA: Wife, where am I standing? Tell me!

ANISYA: Oh, that's all right. Go lie down.

NIKITA: I'm going to have some tea with my father. Start the samovar. Akulina, come in, will you?

[AKULINA, *gayly dressed, comes in with packages she has bought and goes to* NIKITA.]

AKULINA: You've mislaid everything. Where's the yarn?

NIKITA: The yarn? The yarn's over there— Hey, Mitrich, what're you doing there? Gone to sleep? Go and unharness the horse.

AKIM [*without noticing* AKULINA, *looks at his son*]: Just see how he's acting. The old man's tired out, y'see; been thrashing, you know; and he's showing his authority, you know. "Unharness the horse!" Bah! nasty!

MITRICH [*climbs down from the stove and puts on his felt boots*]: Oh, merciful Lord! Is the horse in the yard? It sure must be tired. How drunk he is, confound him! Beats all! Oh, Lord! St. Nicholas the Martyr! [*Puts on his sheepskin and goes outdoors.*]

NIKITA [*sitting down*]: Forgive me, daddy. I had a drink, that's true; but how can a man help it? Even a hen drinks. Ain't that so? And you forgive me? What about Mitrich? He don't take it ill; he'll unharness.

ANISYA: Shall I really start the samovar?

NIKITA: Yes. My father's come, I want to talk with him; I'll have tea. [*To* AKULINA.] Have you brought in all the packages?

AKULINA: Packages? I took my own, but there àre some left in the sleigh— Here, this ain't mine.

> [*She tosses a bundle on the table and puts away the rest of the packages in the chest.* ANYUTKA *watches her do so.* AKIM, *without looking at his son, sets his leg wrappers and bast shoes on the stove.*]

ANISYA [*going out with the samovar*]: The chest was full already, and he's bought more.

NIKITA [*assuming a sober air*]: Don't be cross with me, dad. You think I'm drunk? I'm equal to anything whatever, because I can drink and not lose my senses. I can talk things over with you this very minute, dad. I remember the whole business. You gave directions about money; the horse was worn out—I remember. I can do the whole thing. I have it right on hand. If you needed a huge sum of money, then you might have to wait a bit; but I can attend to all this! Here it is!

AKIM [*continues to fuss with the leg wrappers*]: Eh, my boy, y'see, spring's coming on, y'see; bad traveling.

NIKITA: What're you saying that for? There's no talking with a man that's drunk. But don't you worry; we'll have some tea. And I can do everything; I can fix up absolutely the whole business.

AKIM [*shaking his head*]: Eh-eh-eh!

NIKITA: Here's the money. [*Puts his hand in his pocket and takes out his purse; he turns over the bills and pulls out a ten-ruble note.*] Take that for the horse. Take it for the horse; I can't neglect my father. I certainly won't desert you, for you're my father. Here, take it. It's easy enough; I don't grudge it.

[*He comes up and thrusts the money at* AKIM; AKIM *does not take the money.*]

NIKITA [*clutching his hand*]: Take it, I say, when I give it to you—I don't grudge it.

AKIM: I can't take it, my boy, y'see; and I can't talk with you, you know, because there's no decency in you, y'see.

NIKITA: I won't let you off. Take it. [*Stuffs the money into* AKIM's *hands.*]

ANISYA [*comes in and stops suddenly*]: Go ahead and take it. He won't let up, you know.

AKIM [*taking the money and shaking his head*]: Oh, that liquor! A drunkard's not a man, you know.

NIKITA: There, that's better. If you return it, all right; and if you don't return it, I don't care. That's my way! [*Sees* AKULINA.] Akulina, show 'em your presents.

AKULINA: What?

NIKITA: Show 'em your presents.

AKULINA: Presents? Why should I show 'em? I've put 'em away already.

NIKITA: Get 'em out, I tell you; Anyutka'll like to see 'em. Show 'em to Anyutka, I tell you. Untie that little shawl. Give it here.

AKIM: O-oh, makes me sick to watch! [*Climbs on the stove.*]

AKULINA [*getting her presents and laying them on the table*]: There! What's the use of looking at 'em?

ANYUTKA: That's pretty! Good as Stepanida's.

AKULINA: Stepanida's? Stepanida's is nothing to this. [*Becoming animated and spreading out the things.*] Look here at the quality! It's French.

ANYUTKA: And what gay chintz! Mashutka has one like it, only hers is lighter-colored, with a blue background. That's awful pretty.

NIKITA: That's right.

[ANISYA *goes angrily into the storeroom, comes back with the tablecloth and the chimney for the samovar, and goes to the table.*]

ANISYA: Confound you! You've covered up all the table.

NIKITA: Just look here!

ANISYA: Why should I look! Haven't I seen 'em? Take 'em away. [*Brushes off the shawl on the floor with her hand.*]

AKULINA: What are you slinging round? Sling round your own things. [*Picks it up.*]

NIKITA: Anisya! Look out!

ANISYA: What should I look out for?

NIKITA: Do you think I forgot you? Look here! [*Shows her the roll and sits down on it.*] There's a present for you. Only you must earn it. Wife, where am I sitting?

ANISYA: Quit your bullying. I'm not afraid of you. Whose money have you spent on your spree, and on your presents for your fat hussy? Mine.

AKULINA: Much it's yours! You wanted to steal it and couldn't. Get out of my way. [*Tries to pass by her and bumps into her.*]

ANISYA: Who are you shoving? I'll give you a push.

AKULINA: A push? Come on now! [*Pushes against her.*]

NIKITA: Here, women, women! Stop it! [*Stands between them.*]

AKULINA: She picks on me. She'd better shut up and remember what she did. Do you think people don't know?

ANISYA: What do they know? Tell us, tell us what they know.

AKULINA: They know something about you.

ANISYA: You're a slut; you're living with another woman's husband.

AKULINA: And you put yours out of the way.

ANISYA [*rushes at* AKULINA]: You lie!

NIKITA [*holding her back*]: Anisya! Have you forgotten?

ANISYA: Are you trying to scare me? I'm not afraid of you.

NIKITA: Get out! [*Turns* ANISYA *around and starts to push her out.*]

ANISYA: Where'll I go? I won't leave my own house.

NIKITA: Get out, I tell you! And don't you dare come back!

ANISYA: I won't go. [NIKITA *pushes her;* ANISYA *weeps and shrieks, clutching at the door.*] What, are you going to kick me out of my own house? What are you doing, you villain? Do you think there's no law for you? You just wait!

NIKITA: Come, come!

ANISYA: I'll go to the village elder, to the policeman.

NIKITA: Get out, I tell you. [*Pushes her out.*]

ANISYA [*outside*]: I'll hang myself!

NIKITA: Don't worry!

ANYUTKA: Oh, oh, oh! Dear, darling mother. [*Weeps.*]

NIKITA: Well, I was awful scared of her. What are you crying for? She'll come home all right! Go and see to the samovar.

[ANYUTKA *goes out.*]

AKULINA [*gathering up and folding the presents*]: Nasty woman, how she dirtied it! Just you wait, I'll slit her frock for her. I sure will.

NIKITA: I've turned her out. What more do you want?

AKULINA: She's soiled my new shawl. The bitch—if she hadn't left I'd sure have clawed her eyes out.

NIKITA: Just calm down. What's there for you to be angry at? Think I love her?

AKULINA: Love her? Could anybody love that broad mug? If you'd only quit her then, nothing'd have happened. You ought to have sent her to the devil. But the house is mine anyhow and the money's mine. And then she says she's the mistress. Mistress! She was a fine mistress for her husband! She's a murderess; that's what she is. She'll do the same to you!

NIKITA: Oh, you can't stop up a woman's throat. Do you know yourself what you're talking about?

AKULINA: Yes, I know. I won't live with her. I'll turn her off the place. She can't live with me. She the mistress! She ain't the mistress; she's a prison rat.

NIKITA: Stop it. You needn't meddle with her. Don't even look at her. Look at me. I'm the master. What I wish, I do. I don't love her any more; I love you. I love whoever I want to. I'm the boss. And she'll have to mind. That's where I've got her. [*Points under his feet.*] Oh, I haven't my accordion! [*Sings.*]

> On the stove are buns,
> Porridge in the oven;
> Now we'll live gaily,
> We'll take our pleasure.
> And then when death comes,
> Then we'll just be dying.
> On the stove are buns,
> Porridge in the oven

[MITRICH *comes in, takes off his coat, and climbs on the stove.*]

MITRICH: I see the women have been fighting again! Another quarrel! Oh, Lord! Gracious St. Nicholas!

AKIM [*sits up on the edge of the stove, gets his leg wrappers and bast shoes, and puts them on*]: Crawl in, crawl into the corner there.

MITRICH [*crawls in*]: I see they're still arguing over their property. Oh, Lord!

NIKITA: Get out the brandy; we'll drink it with the tea.

ANYUTKA [*coming in, to* AKULINA]: Sister, the samovar's going to boil over.

NIKITA: Where's your mother?

ANYUTKA: She's standing in the hall, crying.

NIKITA: All right: call her in, tell her to bring the samovar. And give us the dishes, Akulina.

AKULINA: Dishes? Well, all right. [*Takes out the dishes.*]

NIKITA [*brings brandy, biscuits, and salt herring*]: This is for me, this is yarn for the woman, the kerosene's there in the hall. And here's the money. Wait. [*Takes the counting frame.*] I'll reckon it up right away. [*Moves the counters on the frame.*] Wheat flour, eighty kopecks, vegetable oil . . . Ten rubles for dad. Dad, come and have tea.

[*Silence.* AKIM *sits on the stove and puts on his leg wrappers.*]

ANISYA [*bringing in the samovar*]: Where shall I put it?

NIKITA: Put it on the table. Well, did you go to the village elder? Now, then, talk ahead and have a bit to eat. Just quit being cross. Sit down and drink. [*He pours her out a glass of brandy.*] And here I've brought a present for you.

[*Hands her the roll on which he has been sitting.* ANISYA *takes it in silence, shaking her head.*]

AKIM [*climbs down and puts on his coat. Goes to the table and puts the ten-ruble note on it*]: Here, that's your money. Take it.

NIKITA [*not seeing the note*]: Where're you going to now you're all dressed?

AKIM: I'm going, I'm going, y'see. Bid me good-by, for Christ's sake. [*Takes his hat and girdle.*]

NIKITA: Do say! Where are you going by night?

AKIM: I can't stay in your house, y'see; I can't stay, you know. Bid me good-by.

NIKITA: But you are running away from tea?

AKIM [*tying on his girdle*]: I'm going, y'see, because it ain't good in your house, you know; it ain't good in your house, Nikita, you know. Your life is bad, Nikita, y'see; it's bad. I'm going.

NIKITA: Come, quit your talk; sit down and have tea.

ANISYA: Why, daddy, we'll be ashamed to face folks. What're you taking offense at?

AKIM: I'm not offended at all, y'see, not at all; but I can just see, you know, that my son's going to ruin, you know, going to ruin.

NIKITA: What ruin? Show me.

AKIM: To ruin, to ruin, you're ruined now. What did I tell you last summer?

NIKITA: You told me a lot of stuff.

AKIM: I told you, y'see, about the orphan; that you injured the orphan: you injured Marina, you know.

NIKITA: The old story! Don't talk twice about last year's snow: that thing's past and gone.

AKIM: Past and gone? No, my boy, it ain't gone. One sin brings another, you know; it brings more; and you're stuck fast in sin, Nikita boy. You're stuck fast in sin, I see. You're stuck fast, deep in it, you know.

NIKITA: Sit down and drink tea; that's all I have to say.

AKIM: I can't drink tea, y'see. Because your wicked ways make me sick, you know, awful sick. I can't drink tea with you, y'see.

NIKITA: Oh! . . . He's just talking silly. Sit down at the table.

AKIM: Your wealth, y'see, has caught you in a net; in a net, you know. Ah, Nikita, you need a soul.

NIKITA: What sort of right have you to reproach me in my own house? And what are you bothering me for anyhow? Am I just a kid for you to pull my hair? The time for such things has past.

AKIM: That's true; I've heard that nowadays, y'see, men pull their fathers' beards, you know; and that brings ruin, you know, brings ruin.

NIKITA [angrily]: We make our living and don't beg of you, and you come to us in distress.

AKIM: Money? There's your money. I'll go begging, you know; but that money I won't take, y'see.

NIKITA: Stop that. What are you cross for, breaking up the party? [Holds him back by the arm.]

AKIM [screaming]: Let me go; I won't stay. I'd rather spend the night under a fence than in this filth of yours. Bah, God forgive me! [Goes out.]

NIKITA: Well, well!

AKIM [opening the door]: Come to your senses, Nikita! You need a soul. [Goes out.]

AKULINA [taking the cups]: Well, shall I pour the tea?
  [All are silent.]

MITRICH [bellows]: O Lord, be merciful to me a sinner!

[*All start with terror.*]

NIKITA [*lying down on the bench*]: Oh, life is hard, hard! Akulina! Where's my accordion?

AKULINA: Your accordion? Don't you know that you took it to be fixed? I've poured the tea. Drink it.

NIKITA: I don't want it. Put out the light. . . . Oh, life is hard for me, awful hard! [*Weeps.*]

act 4

A moonlight evening in autumn. The yard behind the cottage. In the center of the stage is the hall, to the right the warm side of the house and a gate, to the left the cold side of the house and the cellar. From within the house can be heard talking and drunken shouts. A NEIGHBOR *comes out of the house and beckons to* ANISYA'S FRIEND.

NEIGHBOR: Why hasn't Akulina joined the company?

FRIEND: Why not? She'd have been glad to, but it was no time for her, believe me. The matchmakers have come to look at the bride; and she, my dear woman, just lies in the cold room and don't show herself at all, the darling.

NEIGHBOR: Why so?

FRIEND: They say the evil eye has lighted on her belly.

NEIGHBOR: Really!

FRIEND: And you know— [*Whispers in her ear.*]

NEIGHBOR: What? That's a sin. But the matchmakers will find out.

FRIEND: How can they find out? They're all drunk. And they're mostly concerned with the dowry. It's no small amount, my dear, they're giving with the hussy: two coats, six silk gowns, a French shawl, and then a whole lot of linen, and—so they say—two hundred in cash.

NEIGHBOR: Well, in a case like this even money won't make a man happy. Such a disgrace!

FRIEND: Sh! There's the matchmaker. [*They stop talking and withdraw into the vestibule of the cottage.*]

MATCHMAKER (*man*) [*coming out of the vestibule, alone, hiccuping*]: I'm all in a sweat. Awful hot! I want to cool off a bit. [*Stands and catches his breath.*] And the Lord knows—! Something's wrong. It don't make me happy. Well, here's the old woman.

[MATRENA *comes out of the vestibule.*]

MATRENA: And I was gazing round! "Where's the matchmaker? Where's the matchmaker?" says I. So here's where you are, my man. Well, friend, thank the Lord, all's going fine. Wooing's not boasting. And I never learned how to boast. But as you came on a good errand, so, God grant, you'll always be grateful. And the bride, you know, is a marvel. Hard to find such a girl in the district.

MATCHMAKER: That's all right, but we mustn't forget about the money.

MATRENA: Don't you worry about the money. All her parents ever gave her, she still has. By now it must amount to a hundred and fifty.

MATCHMAKER: We're well enough satisfied; but he's our own child, you know. We must do the best we can for him.

MATRENA: I'm telling you the truth, friend: if it wasn't for me, you'd never have found the girl. There was a party from the Kormilins that wanted to get her, but I held out against it. And as for the money I can tell you true and honest: When the deceased—heaven's peace be with him!—was dying, he gave directions that his widow should take Nikita into the house—I know all this through my son—but that the money should be Akulina's. Another man would have made his profit out of the thing, but Nikita is giving them up, every kopeck. Just think what a lot of money!

MATCHMAKER: Folks say she was left more money. He's a sly fellow.

MATRENA: Oh, fiddle-faddle! The other man's slice always looks big: they're giving you all there was. I tell you:

quit your reckonings. Make it a firm bargain. The girl's pretty as a spring cherry.

MATCHMAKER: That's so. My old woman and I were wondering about one thing in the girl: Why didn't she show herself? We think she may be sickly.

MATRENA: Huh? She sickly? There ain't her like in the district. The girl's so plump you can't pinch her. You saw her the other day yourself. And she's a marvel at working. She's a bit deaf, that's true. Well, one little wormhole don't spoil a red apple. And the reason she didn't show herself, you know, was because of the evil eye. There's a spell on her. I know what bitch contrived it. They knew a charm, you see, and worked it on her. But I know a cure for it. The girl will get up tomorrow. Don't you worry about the girl.

MATCHMAKER: Well, the bargain's made.

MATRENA: That's right—and now don't go back on it. And don't forget me. I worked hard on it too. Don't you leave me out.

[*The voice of a woman is heard from the vestibule:* "We must be going: come along, Ivan."]

MATCHMAKER: Right away.

[*Goes out.* PEASANTS *throng the vestibule and take their departure.* ANYUTKA *runs out of the vestibule and beckons* ANISYA *to follow her.*]

ANYUTKA: Mama!

ANISYA [*from the vestibule*]: What?

ANYUTKA: Mama, come here, or they'll hear us. [*Goes off with her to the side of the cart shed.*]

ANISYA: Well, what? Where's Akulina?

ANYUTKA: She's gone into the grain shed. It's awful what she's doing there! Just think, "No," says she, "I can't stand it. I'll scream with all my might," she says. Just think!

ANISYA: She can wait. We must see the guests off, you know.

ANYUTKA: Oh, mama! It's so hard for her. And she's cross. "They needn't drink me out of the house," she says.

"I won't marry," she says. "I'm going to die," she says. Mama, what if she died? It's awful! I'm afraid!

ANISYA: It ain't likely she'll die; don't you go near her. Get along.

[ANISYA *and* ANYUTKA *go out.* MITRICH *comes in from the gate and sets to raking up the hay that is strewn about.*]

MITRICH: Oh, Lord! Merciful St. Nicholas! What a lot of liquor they put down! And they did raise a smell. Stinks even out of doors. No, I won't—I won't touch it. See how they've scattered the hay! They're like a dog in the manger. Just look at this bundle! What a smell! Right under your nose. Plague take it! [*Yawns.*] Time to go to sleep! But I don't want to go into the room. It fills up a man's nose. How it smells, damn it! [*One can hear the guests driving away.*] Well, they've gone. Oh, Lord! Merciful St. Nicholas! They hug each other and make fools of each other. But it don't amount to nothing.

NIKITA [*coming in*]: Mitrich! Go lie down on the stove; I'll rake it up.

MITRICH: All right; give some to the sheep.— Well, did you see 'em off?

NIKITA: We saw 'em off, but things didn't go well. I don't know what'll happen.

MITRICH: Rotten business! Too bad we have it here; that's what the Foundling Asylum's for. There you can spill anything you like, they'll pick it up. Give 'em anything; they ask no questions. And they give money too. But the girl has to turn wet nurse. It's simple nowadays.

NIKITA: Look out, Mitrich: if anything happens, don't blab.

MITRICH: What do I care? Cover your tracks as you like. Eh, how you stink of liquor! I'll go in the house. [*Goes out, yawning.*] Oh, Lord!

NIKITA [*after a long silence, sitting down on a sleigh*]: What a life!

ANISYA [*coming out of the house*]: Where are you?

NIKITA: Here!

ANISYA: What are you sitting still for? There's no time to wait. You must take it away right off.

NIKITA: What are we going to do?

ANISYA: I'll tell you what—and you do it.

NIKITA: You women might take it to the Foundling Asylum, maybe.

ANISYA: Take it and carry it, if you want to. You're ready enough to do anything nasty, but you don't know how to get rid of it. I can see that.

NIKITA: Well, what's to be done?

ANISYA: Go in the cellar, I tell you, and dig a hole.

NIKITA: But you women might manage somehow.

ANISYA [mimicking]: Yes, "somehow." You can't let things just slide. You ought to have thought of it in time. Go where you're sent.

NIKITA: Oh, what a life! What a life!

[Enter ANYUTKA.]

ANYUTKA: Mama! Grandma's calling you. Sister must have a baby; just think—it cried.

ANISYA: What lies are you telling, plague take you! The kittens are squealing in there. Go into the house and go to sleep. Or I'll thrash you!

ANYUTKA: Mama dear, honest to God!

ANISYA [brandishing her arm at her]: I'll give it to you. Get out of here and don't show yourself again. [ANYUTKA runs out.] Go and do what you're told. Otherwise, look out! [Goes out.]

NIKITA [after a long silence]: What a life! Oh, those women! What a mess! "Ought to have thought of it in time," she says. How could I have thought of it in time? When could I have thought of it? Well, last summer, when that Anisya began to nag me about it. What of it? Am I a monk? The master died, and so then I covered up the sin as was proper. I wasn't to blame for that. Such things often happen. And then those powders. Did I set her up to that? If I'd known of it, I'd have killed her on the spot, the bitch. I'd sure have killed her! She made me her partner in that dirty work, the good-for-nothing! And from that time on she was hateful to me. When my mother told me of it at the time, I began to hate her, to hate her; I didn't want to look at her. Well, how could I live with her? And then this thing started! . . . That hussy began to make up to me. What did I care? If it hadn't been me, it'd been somebody else. And this business now! Again I'm not to blame for it a bit. Oh, what a life! [*He sits down and reflects.*] Those women are nervy—see what they've thought of! But I won't join in.

[MATRENA *comes in out of breath, with a lantern and spade.*]

MATRENA: What're you sitting here for like a hen on a perch? What did your wife tell you? Get down to work.

NIKITA: What're you women going to do?

MATRENA: We know what to do. You just attend to your share.

NIKITA: You're getting me mixed up in it.

MATRENA: What's that? Do you think of backing out? So it's come to this: you're trying to back out!

NIKITA: But think what this means! It's a living soul.

MATRENA: Eh, a living soul! Anyhow, it's barely alive. And what can we do with it? If you go and carry it to the Foundling Asylum, it'll die all the same, and there'll be talk; they'll spread the news and that girl'll be left on our hands.

NIKITA: But what if they find out?

MATRENA: We can do what we like in our own house. We'll do it so there won't be a trace. Just do what I tell you. It's our woman's work, but we can't manage it without a man. Here's the spade: now climb down and attend to things there. I'll hold the lantern.

NIKITA: What shall I do?

MATRENA [*whispers*]: Dig a hole. And then we'll bring it out and stuff it in there quick. There she is calling again. Go on, will you! And I'll be going.

NIKITA: Well, is it dead?

MATRENA: Of course it's dead. Only you must hurry up. Folks haven't gone to bed yet. They may hear and see; the scoundrels meddle with everything. And the policeman passed by this evening. This is for you. [*Hands him the spade*.] Get down into the cellar. Dig a hole there in the corner, the earth's soft, and you can even it off again. Mother earth won't tell anyone; she'll lick it clean as a cow with her tongue. Go on, go on, my boy.

NIKITA: You're getting me mixed up in it. Plague take you! I'm going off. Do the thing alone, as you please.

ANISYA [*from the door*]: Well, has he dug the hole?

MATRENA: What've you come out for? Where did you put it?

ANISYA: Covered it with some burlap. Nobody'll hear it. Well, has he dug it?

MATRENA: He don't want to!

ANISYA [*pushing out in a rage*]: Don't want to! Does he want to feed lice in prison? . . . I'll go right away and tell the whole thing to the policeman. We can go to ruin together. I'll tell it all right off!

NIKITA [*panic-stricken*]: What'll you tell?

ANISYA: What? I'll tell everything! Who took the money? You! [NIKITA *is silent*.] And who gave him the poison? I gave it to him! But you knew it, knew it! I was in conspiracy with you!

MATRENA: Oh, stop it! Nikita, why are you so stubborn? See here, what's to be done? You must get to work. Come on, darling.

ANISYA: Look what an innocent you are! Don't want to! You've been abusing me long enough. You've been riding over me, but my turn's come now. Go along, I tell you, or I'll do what I said! . . . Here's the spade: take it! Get along!

NIKITA: Well, what are you nagging me for? [*Takes the spade, but falters.*] If I don't want to, I won't go.

ANISYA: Won't go? [*Begins to shout.*] Hey, folks!

MATRENA [*stopping her mouth*]: What are you doing? Are you daft! He'll go. . . . Go along, sonny; go along, my dear boy.

ANISYA: I'll cry for help right off.

NIKITA: Stop it! Oh, what a lot you women are! But you'd better hurry up. The sooner the better. [*Goes toward the cellar.*]

MATRENA: Yes, that's the way it is, darling; if you've had your fun, you must know how to cover up your tracks.

ANISYA [*still agitated*]: He and his hussy have been taking out their spite on me, and I've had enough of it! I'm not going to be the only one. Let him be a murderer too. He'll find out how it feels.

MATRENA: Well, well, you're excited. Now, girlie, don't be cross: take it slow and easy, and it'll be better. You go in to the hussy. He'll do the work.

[*She follows Nikita with the lantern; he climbs down into the cellar.*]

ANISYA: I'll tell him to strangle his dirty brat. [*Still excited.*] I had my torture all alone, pulling Petr's bones. Let him find out, too. I'll do my best to make him; I tell you, I will.

NIKITA [*from the cellar*]: Give me a light, will you!

MATRENA [*holding the light, to* ANISYA]: He's digging; go and bring it.

ANISYA: You just watch him. Otherwise he'll run away, the wretch. And I'll go bring it out.

MATRENA: See that you don't forget to put a cross on it. Or I'll attend to that. Is there a cross for it?

ANISYA: I'll find one; I know about that. [*Goes out.*][2]

MATRENA: How the woman did get worked up! And I must say, it was rough on her. Well, thank God, we'll just hush up this business and hide the traces. We'll get rid of the girl without scandal. My son will rest easy now. The house, thank God, is rich and well-stocked. He won't forget me either. They couldn't get along without Matrena. They couldn't attend to things. [*Calls into the cellar.*] All ready, sonny?

NIKITA [*climbs up; only his head can be seen*]: What are you doing there? Bring it, will you! What are you dawdling for? If you're going to do it, go ahead.

[MATRENA *goes toward the house door and meets*

[2]For variant ending of Act 4, see p. 281.

ANISYA. ANISYA *comes out with the baby, wrapped in rags.*]

MATRENA: Well, did you put the cross on?

ANISYA: Sure! I had hard work to get the brat; she wouldn't give it to me. [*Comes up and holds out the baby to* NIKITA.]

NIKITA [*not taking it*]: Bring it down here yourself.

ANISYA: Here, take it, I tell you. [*Throws the baby to him.*]

NIKITA [*picking it up*]: It's alive! Darling mother, it's moving! It's alive! What shall I do with it?

ANISYA [*snatching the baby out of his hands and throwing it into the cellar*]: Hurry up and strangle it and it won't be alive. [*Pushing* NIKITA *down.*] It's your business; finish it.

MATRENA: He's too kind-hearted. It's hard for him, the dear boy. Well, no help for it! It's his sin too. [ANISYA *stands over the cellar.* MATRENA *sits down on the house step, watches her, and reflects.*] Eh, eh, eh! How scared he was! Well, even if it is hard, you couldn't do anything else. No way out. And then just think how sometimes people beg for children! And then, y'see, God don't give 'em; they're all born dead. Take the priest's wife for instance. . . . But here it wasn't wanted, and it's alive. [*Looks toward the cellar.*] He must have finished. [*To* ANISYA.] Well?

ANISYA [*looking into the cellar*]: He's covered it with a board and sat down on the board. Must've finished.

MATRENA: O-oh! He'd be glad not to sin, but what can you do?

NIKITA [*climbing out, shaking all over*]: It's still alive! I can't! It's alive!

ANISYA: If it's alive, where are you going? [*Tries to stop him.*]

NIKITA [*rushing at her*]: Get out; I'll kill you!

[*He clutches her by the arm, she tears herself free; he runs after her with the spade.* MATRENA *rushes toward him and stops him.* ANISYA *runs off to the house.* MATRENA *tries to take the spade from* NIKITA.]

NIKITA [*to* MATRENA]: I'll kill you; I'll kill you too! Get out! [MATRENA *runs to the house, to* ANISYA. NIKITA *stops.*] I'll kill you; I'll kill you all!

MATRENA: That's because he's scared. Never mind; it'll pass off!

NIKITA: What's this they've done? What have they done to me? How it wailed! . . . How it cracked underneath me! What have they done to me! And it's still alive, alive sure enough! [*Is silent and listens.*] It's wailing! . . . Hear it wail! [*He runs toward the cellar.*]

MATRENA [*to* ANISYA]: He's going; he must mean to bury it. Nikita, you need a lantern.

NIKITA [*listens at the cellar, without answering her*]: I can't hear it. I just fancied. [*Walks away and stops.*] And how the little bones cracked underneath me! . . . Krr . . . krr. . . . What have they done to me? [*Listens once more.*] It's wailing again; it's sure wailing. What's this? Mother! Mother, I say! [*Goes up to her.*]

MATRENA: What, sonny?

NIKITA: Mother, darling, I can't do any more. I can't do anything. Mother, darling, have pity on me!

MATRENA: Oh, you're frightened, my dear boy. Come, come, drink a drop to give you courage.

NIKITA: Mother, darling, my time must have come. What have you done to me? How those little bones cracked, and how it wailed! Mother, darling, what have you done to me! [*Goes off and sits down on a sleigh.*]

MATRENA: Go have a drink, my lad. It's true enough, nighttime makes you shiver. But just wait, the dawn will come; and then, you know, a day or two will pass, and you'll forget to think about it. Just wait, we'll get rid of the girl and forget to think about it. But you have a drink, go have a drink. I'll attend to things in the cellar myself.

NIKITA [*shaking himself*]: Is any liquor left in there? Can't I drink this down! [*He goes out.* ANISYA, *who has been standing by the door all this time, silently stands aside to let him pass.*]

MATRENA: Come, come, darling, I'll get to work myself, I'll climb down and bury it. Where did he throw the spade?

[*She finds the spade and descends halfway into the cellar.*] Anisya, come here; give me a light.

ANISYA: But what's the matter with him?

MATRENA: He got awful scared. You gave it to him pretty hard. Don't meddle with him; he'll come to himself. Let him alone; I'll get to work myself. Set the lantern here. Then I can see. [MATRENA *disappears into the cellar.*]

ANISYA [*shouts at the door by which* NIKITA *has departed*]: Well, is your fun over? You've had your fling: now just wait, you'll find out yourself how it feels. You won't be so lofty.

[NIKITA *rushes out of the house toward the cellar.*]

NIKITA: Mother! Hey, mother!

MATRENA [*emerging from the cellar*]: What, sonny?

NIKITA [*listening*]: Don't bury it; it's alive! Don't you hear it? It's alive! There, it's wailing! ... There ... plainly. ...

MATRENA: How could it wail? You squashed it into a pancake. You crushed its head.

NIKITA: What's that? [*Stops his ears.*] It's still wailing! I've ruined my life, ruined it! What have they done to me? ... Where shall I go! ... [*Sits down on the steps.*]

Variant ending for

Act 4

The same scene as in Act 1.

ANYUTKA, *undressed, is lying on a bench with a coat spread over her.* MITRICH *is sitting on a bunk at the head of the room, smoking.*

MITRICH: Pah! They've raised a smell, good luck to 'em for it! They spilled the goods. You can't drown it with tobacco. It gets into a man's nose. Oh, Lord! I'd better go to sleep. [*Goes to the lamp and is about to turn it out.*]

ANYUTKA [*sitting up with a start*]: Granddad, dear, don't put it out.

MITRICH: Why not put it out?

ANYUTKA: They're up to something in the yard. [*Listens.*] Do you hear? They've gone into the grain shed again.

MITRICH: What do you care? They aren't asking you about it. Lie down and go to sleep. And I'll turn down the light. [*Turns it down.*]

ANYUTKA: Granddad, precious! Don't put it way out. Leave just a tiny bit, or I'll feel creepy.

MITRICH [*laughing*]: All right, all right. [*Sits down beside her.*] What makes you creepy?

ANYUTKA: I can't help feeling creepy, granddad! How sister struggled. She kept knocking her head against the chest. [*Whispers.*] I know—she's going to have a baby.... Maybe it's born already.

MITRICH: What a little imp, confound you! You want to know everything. Lie down and go to sleep. [ANYUTKA *lies down.*] That's the way. [*Covers her up.*] That's the way. If you know too much, you'll grow old too soon.

ANYUTKA: Are you going up on the stove?

MITRICH: Of course I am.... You're a silly little girl, I see. You want to know everything. [*Covers her up and rises to go.*] Just lie there like that and go to sleep. [*Goes to the stove.*]

ANYUTKA: It cried just once, but now I can't hear it.

MITRICH: Oh, Lord! Merciful St. Nicholas!... What can't you hear?

ANYUTKA: The baby.

MITRICH: There isn't any, so you can't hear it.

ANYUTKA: But I heard it; just think, I heard it. A little shrill voice.

MITRICH: You heard a lot. Did you hear how the bogyman put a naughty little girl like you in a sack and carried her off?

ANYUTKA: What's the bogy-man?

MITRICH: Just the bogy-man. [*Climbs on the stove.*] The stove's fine and warm now. Nice! Oh, Lord! Merciful St. Nicholas!

ANYUTKA: Granddad! Are you going to sleep?

MITRICH: What do you think? That I'm going to sing songs?

[*Silence.*]

ANYUTKA: Granddad! Oh, granddad! They're digging! Honest to God they're digging! Do you hear? Just think, they're digging!

MITRICH: What notions you have! Digging? Digging at night? Who's digging? It's the cow scratching herself. And you say, digging! Go to sleep, I tell you, or I'll put out the light right away.

ANYUTKA: Granddad, darling, don't put it out. I'll stop. Honest to God, I'll stop. It scares me.

MITRICH: Scares you? Don't be afraid of anything, and then you won't be scared. Now you just feel afraid and you say that it scares you. Of course it scares you when you're afraid. What a silly little girl!

[*Silence. The cricket chirps.*]

ANYUTKA [*whispers*]: Granddad! Hey, granddad! Are you asleep?

MITRICH: Well, what do you want?

ANYUTKA: What's the bogy-man like?

MITRICH: I'll tell you what he's like. Whenever there's any little girl like you, who won't go to sleep, he comes along with his sack, and he pops the little girl into the sack; and then he pops his own head in and lifts up her little shirtie, and he gives her a spanking.

ANYUTKA: What does he spank her with?

MITRICH: He takes a broom.

ANYUTKA: But he can't see, himself, can he, in the sack?

MITRICH: He'll see all right.

ANYUTKA: But I'll bite him.

MITRICH: No, girlie, you won't bite him.

ANYUTKA: Granddad, somebody's coming! Who is it? Oh, holy saints, who is it?

MITRICH: If somebody's coming, let him come. What do you care? . . . I think it's your mother coming.

[ANISYA *comes in.*]

ANISYA: Anyutka! [ANYUTKA *pretends to be asleep*.] Mitrich!

MITRICH: What?

ANISYA: What have you a light burning for? We'll go to bed in the cold half.

MITRICH: I've just finished my work. I'll put it out.

ANISYA [*searching in the chest and grumbling*]: When you want something, you can't find it.

MITRICH: What are you looking for?

ANISYA: I'm looking for a cross, I must put one on him. He'll die unchristened, God have mercy on him! Without a cross! It's a sin, you know!

MITRICH: Of course, you must do things properly.... Well, have you found it?

ANISYA: Yes. [*Goes out.*]

MITRICH: That's lucky—otherwise I'd have given her my own. Oh, Lord!

ANYUTKA [*jumps up, trembling*]: O-oh, granddad! Don't go to sleep, for Christ's sake! I'm so scared!

MITRICH: What are you scared of?

ANYUTKA: Won't the baby die, most likely? Grandma put a cross on Auntie Arina's too—and it died.

MITRICH: If it dies, they'll bury it.

ANYUTKA: But maybe it wouldn't die if Grandma Matrena wasn't here. You know I heard what grandma was saying; just think, I heard it.

MITRICH: What did you hear? Go to sleep, I tell you. Pull things over your head: that's all.

ANYUTKA: But if it was alive, I'd nurse it.

MITRICH [*bellows*]: Oh, Lord!

ANYUTKA: Where'll they put it?

MITRICH: They'll put it where it's proper. It's not your business. Go to sleep, I tell you. Your mother'll come—she'll give it to you!

[*Silence.*]

ANYUTKA: Granddad! That little girl you were telling about—they didn't kill her?

MITRICH: That one? Oh, that girl came out all right.

ANYUTKA: How was it you were telling me they found her, granddad?

MITRICH: They just found her.

ANYUTKA: But where did they find her? Tell me.

MITRICH: They found her in a house over there. The soldiers came to a village and began to search the house; and there that same little girl was lying on her belly. They were going to smash her. But I just felt lonesome and I took her in my arms—she struggled. She was as heavy as if she had two hundred pounds inside her; and she clutched at everything with her hands—you could hardly tear her away. Well, I took her and stroked her head, stroked her head. And she was bristly as a hedgehog. I stroked her and stroked her, and she quieted down. I soaked a biscuit and gave it to her. She caught on. She chewed it. What could we do with her? We took her with us. We took her and just fed her and fed her, and she got so used to us we took her with us on the march: she just went with us. She was a nice little girl.

ANYUTKA: Well, she wasn't christened, was she?

MITRICH: Nobody knows. Not altogether, they said. For her people weren't ours.

ANYUTKA: Germans?

MITRICH: "German," you say? Not Germans, but Asiatics. They are just the same as Jews, but they aren't Jews either. They're Poles, but they're Asiatics. They're called Krudly or Krugly: I've forgotten the name— We called the little girl Sashka. Sashka—and she was pretty. I've forgotten everything else, you see; but that little girl—Lord bless her! —I can see before my eyes right now. That's all I remember of life in the army. I recollect how they flogged me, and then I remember that little girl. She used to hang round your neck when you carried her. You couldn't have found a nicer little girl nowhere. Later we gave her away. The sergeant's wife adopted her as her daughter. And she came out all right. How sorry the soldiers were!

ANYUTKA: See here, granddad, I remember how daddy died too. You hadn't come to live with us then. He called

Nikita and says to him: "Forgive me, Nikita," he says—and he began to cry himself. [*Sighs.*] That made me sad too.

MITRICH: Well, that's the way things go.

ANYUTKA: Granddad; oh, granddad! They're making a noise again in the cellar. Oh, dearie me, holy saints! Oh, granddad, they'll do something to him. They'll destroy him. He's just a little thing.—Oh! oh! [*Pulls the clothes over her head and weeps.*]

MITRICH [*listening*]: They really are up to something nasty —curse 'em! Those women are a nasty lot. The men ain't much to boast of, but the women—they're like beasts of the woods. They ain't afraid of anything.

ANYUTKA [*getting up*]: Granddad! Hey, granddad!

MITRICH: Well, what next?

ANYUTKA: The other day, a passer-by spent the night here. He was saying that when a child dies its soul goes straight to heaven. Is that true?

MITRICH: How should I know? Most likely. What of it?

ANYUTKA: Why, then I'd like to die too. [*Whimpers.*]

MITRICH: If you die, nobody'll miss you.

ANYUTKA: Till you're ten years old you're still a child, and maybe your soul'll still go to God. After that you get spoiled, you know.

MITRICH: You certainly do get spoiled! How can girls like you help getting spoiled? Who teaches you anything? What do you ever see? What do you hear? Nothing but nastiness. I'm not very learned, but still I know something; not very well, but anyhow better than a village woman— What is a village woman? Just mud. There's huge millions of your sort in Russia, and you're all like blind moles—don't know anything. How to keep cows safe from the evil eye—all kinds of charms—how to cure children by putting 'em under the hen roost—that's what women know how to do.

ANYUTKA: Mama used to put 'em there.

MITRICH: That's just it. How many millions of you women and girls there are, and you're all like beasts of the forest. You grow up and then you die. You don't see anything and don't hear anything. A man—even if it's in a tavern, or

maybe in a fortress, accidentally, or in the army, like me—
he learns something or other. But what about a woman?
Don't ask her about God and what's right! She don't even
know sensibly what Good Friday is. Friday's Friday, but
ask her anything about it and she don't know. They crawl
round just like blind pups and stick their noses in the ma-
nure— All they know is their silly songs: "Ho, ho! Ho, ho!"
And they don't know themselves what "Ho, ho!" means.

ANYUTKA: But, granddad, I know "Our Father" halfway
through.

MITRICH: You know a lot! But then one can't expect much
of you. Who teaches you? Only a drunken peasant teaches
you now and then with a strap. That's all your training. I
don't know who'll ever answer for you. They put a sergeant
in charge of recruits and hold him responsible for 'em.
But nobody's responsible for you girls. So you women are
just like a herd of cattle—without a herdsman—that run
wild; your kind is the stupidest that's made. Your kind is
just hopeless.

ANYUTKA: But what can you do about it?

MITRICH: Not much. . . . Now pull the clothes over your
head and go to sleep. Oh, Lord!

[Silence. The cricket chirps.]

ANYUTKA [jumping up]: Granddad! Somebody's shouting,
somebody's just yelling! Honest to God, he's shouting.
Granddad, dear, he's coming this way.

MITRICH: I tell you, pull the clothes over your head.

NIKITA [coming in]: What have they done to me? What
have they done to me!

MATRENA: Have a drink, have a drink, darling. What's
the matter? [Gets liquor and sets it before him.]

NIKITA: Give it here: I guess I'd better take some.

MATRENA: Shh! They aren't asleep, you know. Here,
drink it.

NIKITA: What does this mean? Why did you want to act
that way? You might have carried it off.

MATRENA [in a whisper]: Sit here, sit here; have another
drink, and then smoke a bit. That'll divert your thoughts.

NIKITA: Mother darling, my time must have come. When it wailed, and when those little bones cracked, krr...krr... my strength gave out.

MATRENA: E-eh! You're just talking silly stuff. It's true enough, nighttime makes you shiver. But just wait till the day comes; a day or two will pass and you'll forget to think about it. [*Goes to* NIKITA *and puts her hand on his shoulder.*]

NIKITA: Get away from me! What have you done to me?

MATRENA: What do you mean, sonny, anyhow? [*Takes him by the hand.*]

NIKITA: Get away from me! I'll kill you! I don't care for anything now. I'll kill you!

MATRENA: Oh, oh, how scared you are! Now go away and go to bed.

NIKITA: I've nowhere to go to. I'm a lost man.

MATRENA [*shaking her head*]: Oh! oh! I'd better go fix things up myself; and let him sit here for a while till he gets rid of all this.

   [*Goes out.* NIKITA *sits still, covering his face with his hands.* MITRICH *and* ANYUTKA *are stiff with terror.*]

NIKITA: It's wailing, it's sure wailing: hark, hark, you can hear it. . . . She'll bury it, she'll bury it! [*Runs to the door.*] Mother, don't bury it, it's alive! . . .

MATRENA [*returning, in a whisper*]: What do you mean, Christ help you! What fancies you have! How can it be alive! All its bones are crushed.

NIKITA: Give me some more liquor! [*Drinks.*]

MATRENA: Go along, sonny. Now you'll go to sleep and it'll be all right.

NIKITA [*standing and listening*]: It's still alive. . . . Hark! . . . It's wailing. Don't you hear it? Hark!

MATRENA [*in a whisper*]: Not a bit of it!

NIKITA: Mother dear! I've ruined my life. What have you done to me? Where shall I go?

   [*Runs out of the house,* MATRENA *following him.*]

ANYUTKA: Granddad, dear, darling, they've strangled him!

MITRICH [*angrily*]: Go to sleep, I tell you! Bother you,

confound you! I'll take a broom to you! Go to sleep, I tell you.

ANYUTKA: Granddad, precious. Somebody's grabbing me by the shoulders, somebody's grabbing me, grabbing me with his paws. Dear granddad, just think: I'll be gone right away. Granddad, precious, let me up on the stove! Let me up for Christ's sake! ... He's grabbing me ... grabbing. ... O-o-oh! [*Runs to the stove.*]

MITRICH: See how they've scared the poor little girl—those nasty women, confound 'em! Well, come up if you want to.

ANYUTKA [*climbing on the stove*]: And don't you go away.

MITRICH: Where should I go to? Climb up, climb up! Oh, Lord! St. Nicholas the Martyr! Holy Virgin Mother of Kazan! ... How they scared the little girl! [*Covers her up.*] You're a little fool, just a little fool. ... They sure scared you, those nasty women, much good may it do 'em!

act 5

Scene I

In the foreground, on the left, a threshing floor, and near it a stack of straw; on the right, a cart shed. The doors of the shed are open; straw is scattered about in the doorway. In the background farm buildings can be seen; songs and the tinkling of tambourines are heard. Two PEASANT GIRLS *come walking along the path past the shed toward the farm buildings.*

FIRST GIRL: You see how well we got across, we didn't even soil our boots; but on the road it was awful, so dirty! [*They stop and wipe their feet with straw.*]

FIRST GIRL [*looks at the straw and sees something*]: What's that there?

SECOND GIRL [*taking a look*]: It's Mitrich, their workman. He's dead drunk.

FIRST GIRL: But he didn't use to drink at all, did he?

SECOND GIRL: Not till today, so it seems.

FIRST GIRL: Just look: he must have come here for straw. You see he has a rope in his hands, but he just went to sleep.

SECOND GIRL [*listening*]: They're still singing the wedding songs. Most likely they haven't given 'em the blessing yet. They say Akulina didn't wail a bit.

FIRST GIRL: Mama told me she didn't want to be married. Her stepfather threatened her; otherwise she'd never have consented. You know what talk there was about her!

MARINA [*overtaking the girls*]: Hello, girls!

GIRLS: Hello, auntie!

MARINA: Going to the wedding, darlings?

FIRST GIRL: It must be over by now. We just came to look around.

MARINA: Call my old man for me, Semyon of Zuyev. You know him, don't you?

FIRST GIRL: Of course we know him. He's some relative of the bridegroom, it seems.

MARINA: Sure: the bridegroom is a nephew of my boss.

SECOND GIRL: Why don't you go yourself? How can you miss the wedding!

MARINA: I don't feel like going, girlie; and then I haven't the time. I must be riding off. We weren't on our way to the wedding. We were carting oats to town. We stopped to feed the horses, and they called in my old man.

FIRST GIRL: Whose house did you stop at? Fedorych's?

MARINA: Yes. So I'll stand here a bit, and you go call my old man, darling. Make him come, precious. Say: "Your wife Marina says you must be going: the fellows are harnessing already."

FIRST GIRL: All right, very well, if you won't go yourself.

[*The girls go out along the path toward the farm buildings. Songs and the tinkling of tambourines are heard.*]

MARINA [*muses*]: It'd be all right to go, but I don't want to, for I haven't seen him since the very time that he refused me. That's more than a year ago. But I'd like to peep in and see how he gets along with his Anisya. Folks say they don't agree. She's a coarse, ill-tempered woman. He's remembered me many a time, I'll warrant. He must have had a liking for an easy life. He gave me the go-by. Well, God help him, I bear no grudge. It hurt then. Oh, how it pained me! But now it's worn off and I've forgotten. But I'd like to see him. . . . [*Looks towards the house and sees* NIKITA.] Just look! What's he coming here for? Did the girls tell him? Why's he left the guests? I'll be going.

[NIKITA *comes in, at first hanging his head, waving his arms, and muttering to himself.*]

MARINA: How gloomy he looks!

NIKITA [*seeing* MARINA *and recognizing her*]: Marina! My dear, darling Marina! What are you here for?

MARINA: I've come for my old man.

NIKITA: Why didn't you come to the wedding? You'd have looked on and laughed at me.

MARINA: What do I want to laugh for? I've come for my boss.

NIKITA: Oh Marina dear! [*Tries to embrace her.*]

MARINA [*turning away angrily*]: Nikita, you quit those tricks. That's been and gone. I've come for my boss. Is he at your house?

NIKITA: So we can't call to mind old times? You won't let me?

MARINA: No use remembering old times. That's been and gone.

NIKITA: So you can't bring it back?

MARINA: It won't come back. But what have you strayed off for? You're the master, and you've deserted the wedding.

NIKITA [*sitting down on the straw*]: Why have I strayed off? Oh, if you only knew and understood! . . . My life's hard, Marina, so hard that I don't want to look at it. I got up from the table and came away, came away from people so that I needn't see anybody.

MARINA [*coming nearer to him*]: How's that?

NIKITA: Well, it's that I have no joy in food or drink, no

rest in sleep. Oh, I'm sick of life, just sick of it! And what makes me sickest of all, Marina dear, is that I'm all alone, and have nobody that I can share my grief with.

MARINA: You can't live without grief, Nikita. I cried over mine and now it's gone.

NIKITA: You're talking about old, old times. Just think, dear! You've done crying over yours, and now it's come my turn.

MARINA: But how's that?

NIKITA: It's that I loathe my whole life. I loathe myself. Ah, Marina, you could not hold me fast, and so you ruined me and yourself too! Well, is this a life worth living?

MARINA [stands by the shed, weeps, but restrains herself]: I don't complain of my own life, Nikita. God grant that everybody had as good as mine! I don't complain. I confessed right off to my old man. He forgave me. And he don't reproach me. I'm satisfied with my own life. He's a gentle old man. And I like him; I wash and dress his children! And he's kind to me too. I've no reason to complain. It must be what God intended for me— But what about your life? You're a rich man.

NIKITA: My life! . . . I just don't want to break up the wedding, or I'd take a rope—this one [takes up a rope from the straw]—and I'd throw it right over that crossbeam. And I'd fix up a nice noose, and I'd climb on the crossbeam and put my head in it. That's what my life is like!

MARINA: Stop, Christ help you!

NIKITA: You think I'm joking? You think I'm drunk? I'm not drunk. Nowadays even liquor don't affect me. But I'm sick of life, sick to death of it! I'm done for, in such misery that I care for nothing! Oh, Marina dear, do you remember how we lived together, how we spent happy nights on the railroad?

MARINA: Nikita, don't rub my sore spot. I'm married now and you are too. My sin's forgiven; don't bring back the past.

NIKITA: What can I do with my heart? To whom can I give it?

MARINA: What should you do? You have a wife: don't lust after other women, but care for your own. You loved Anisya; keep on loving her.

NIKITA: Ah, that Anisya is bitter wormwood to me. She's just tangled up my legs like witchgrass.

MARINA: Whatever she is, she's your wife— But it's no use talking! You'd better go to the guests and call my husband.

NIKITA: Oh, if you knew everything!— But why talk about it!

HUSBAND [*coming in from the farm buildings, red-faced and drunken, accompanied by* ANYUTKA]: Marina! Wife! Old lady! Are you here?

NIKITA: Here's your boss coming and calling for you. Go along!

MARINA: And what'll you do?

NIKITA: I? I'll lie down here. [*Lies down in the straw.*]

HUSBAND: Where is she?

ANYUTKA: There she is, uncle, close to the shed.

HUSBAND: What are you standing here for? Come to the wedding! The hosts want you to come and pay your respects. The marriage party will soon start out: then we'll go.

MARINA [*coming to meet her husband*]: But I didn't want to.

HUSBAND: Come on, I tell you. We'll have a glass; you'll congratulate that rogue Petrunka. The hosts are taking offense—and we'll have time enough for everything.

[MARINA'S HUSBAND *embraces her and goes out with her, staggering.*]

NIKITA [*sitting up on the straw*]: Oh, when I saw her, I felt sicker than ever. The only real life I ever had was with her. I've wasted my days for nothing at all; I've ruined my happiness! [*Lies down.*] What shall I do with myself? Oh, if only damp mother earth would open!

ANYUTKA [*sees* NIKITA *and runs to him*]: Daddy! Oh, daddy! They're looking for you. Godfather and everybody have given their blessing. Just think, they've given their blessing; they're cross.

NIKITA [*to himself*]: What shall I do with myself?

ANYUTKA: What's that? What are you saying?

NIKITA: I'm not saying anything. Don't bother me!

ANYUTKA: Daddy! Come on, will you! [NIKITA *is silent;* ANYUTKA *pulls at his arm.*] Daddy, go and give your blessing! Honest, they're cross; they're scolding.

NIKITA [*pulls away his arm*]: Let me alone!

ANYUTKA: Come on!

NIKITA [*threatening her with the rope*]: Get out, I tell you. I'll give it to you!

ANYUTKA: Then I'll send mother. [*Runs out.*]

NIKITA [*sitting up*]: How can I go in there? How can I take the holy ikon in my hands? How can I look her in the eyes? [*Lies down again.*] Oh, if there were a hole in the earth, I'd crawl into it. People wouldn't see me; I'd see nobody. [*Sits up again.*] But I won't go. . . . Let 'em go to thunder. I won't go. [*Removes his boots and takes up the rope; he makes a noose and puts it around his neck.*] That's the way.

[MATRENA *comes in hurriedly.* NIKITA *sees her, takes the rope off his neck, and again lies down on the straw.*]

MATRENA: Nikita! Hey, Nikita! There you are, and you won't answer. Nikita, what's the matter with you? Are you drunk? Come on, Nikita dear; come on, my precious! Folks are tired of waiting.

NIKITA: Oh, what have you done to me? I'm no longer a man.

MATRENA: What do you mean? Come on, my boy; give the blessing as is proper, and then it'll all be over. Folks are waiting for you.

NIKITA: How can I give a blessing?

MATRENA: Just as usual. Don't you know how?

NIKITA: I know, I know. But who am I going to bless? What have I done to her?

MATRENA: What have you done? The idea of remembering that! Nobody knows: not the cat, nor the mouse, nor the louse in the house. And then the girl herself is willing to marry.

NIKITA: But how is she willing?

MATRENA: Of course, she's doing it out of fear. But she's willing all the same. What else can she do? She ought to have thought of it then. But now she has no other choice. And the matchmakers feel satisfied. They've seen the girl twice, and the money goes with her. All's covered up clean.

NIKITA: But what's in the cellar?

MATRENA [*laughing*]: What's in the cellar? Cabbage, mushrooms, and potatoes, I suppose. Let bygones be bygones.

NIKITA: I'd be glad to, but I can't. Whenever you make me think, I can hear things. Oh, what have you women done to me?

MATRENA: What are you acting so queer for anyhow?

NIKITA [*turning over flat on his face*]: Mother, don't torture me! I can't stand it any longer.

MATRENA: But you must, all the same. There's talk among the people anyhow—and then all of a sudden the father goes off and won't come back, don't dare give his blessing. They'll put two and two together right away. If you shrink from it, they'll guess what's up right away. If you walk the beaten path, nobody thinks you a thief. But if you run away from a wolf, you run into a bear. Above all, don't betray yourself; don't be timid, my boy, or they'll think worse of it.

NIKITA: Oh, you've tied me tight!

MATRENA: Stop it, come along. Come into the company and give your blessing; everything must be as is proper and usual, and then the thing's over.

NIKITA [*still lying on his face*]: I can't.

MATRENA [*to herself*]: What's happened? Everything was all right, all right, and all of a sudden it struck him. There must be a spell on him.— Nikita, get up! Look, there's Anisya coming; she's left the guests.

[ANISYA *comes in gayly dressed and flushed with drink.*]

ANISYA: Ain't this fine, mother! So fine and proper! And how happy folks are over it! ... Where is he?

MATRENA: Here, darling, here. He lay down in the straw and there he lies. He won't come.

NIKITA [*looking at his wife*]: Huh, she's drunk too. When I see her, it makes my heart sick. How can I live with her? [*Turns over on his face.*] I'll kill her some day. It'll be still worse!

ANISYA: Look where he is, buried in the straw! Has he got over his drunk? [*Laughs.*] I'd like to lie down there with you, but I haven't the time. Come on; I'll lead you. And it's so nice in the house! It's a pleasure to see 'em. And the accordion! The women are singing songs, just splendid. Everybody's drunk; all's fine and proper!

NIKITA: What's fine?

ANISYA: The wedding, the merry wedding. Everybody says that it's just a marvel of a wedding. Everything's so fine and lovely. Come on! We'll go together. . . . I've had a drink, but I can lead you. [*Takes his arm.*]

NIKITA [*pulling away from her, with revulsion*]: Go on alone. I'll come later.

ANISYA: What're you in such a temper for! All our troubles are over, we've got rid of the girl that stood between us, we can just live and enjoy ourselves. All's nice and proper, according to the law. I'm so happy over it that I can't tell you. It's just as if I was marrying you a second time. Ha ha! Folks are so pleased! They'll all thank us. And the guests are all nice people. Ivan Moseich is there too, and the policeman. They joined in on the songs.

NIKITA: Well, go sit with them. What did you come out here for?

ANISYA: But you must come along. Otherwise it ain't decent: the hosts have left and deserted the guests. And the guests are all nice people.

NIKITA [*rising and brushing off the straw*]: Go on; I'll come directly.

MATRENA: The night cuckoo sings louder than the day bird. He wouldn't heed me, but he followed his wife right away.

[MATRENA *and* ANISYA *move away.*]

MATRENA: Are you coming?

NIKITA: I'll come right away. You go along, and I'll follow. I'll come and give my blessing.... [*The women pause.*] Go on, and—I'll follow. Go along.

[*The women go out.* NIKITA *gazes after them, musing.*]

NIKITA [*sitting down and taking off his boots*]: Not much I won't go! No indeed! No, you'd better look for me on the crossbeam. I'll straighten the noose and jump from the crossbeam, and then you can look for me. And here are some rope reins, that's lucky. [*Meditates.*] I'd get over my grief, however heavy it was; I'd get over it. But it's right here, it's in my heart; I can't drive it out. [*Looks toward the house.*] Looks like she was coming again. [*Mimics* ANISYA.] "Fine, just fine! I'll lie down with you!" Ugh! the nasty hag! Wait a bit: embrace me when they take me off the beam! That's all that's left. [*Seizes the rope and pulls it.*]

MITRICH [*drunken, sits up, but does not let go of the rope*]: I won't let you have it. I won't let anybody have it. I'll bring it myself. I said I'd bring the straw, and I'll bring it. Is that you, Nikita? [*Laughs*] Oh, the devil! Did you come for straw?

NIKITA: Give me the rope.

MITRICH: No, you wait. The folks sent me. I'll bring it. ... [*He rises to his feet and begins to rake up the straw, but staggers, recovers himself, and finally falls down.*] The liquor's got the best of me. Too much for me!

NIKITA: Give me the reins.

MITRICH: I told you I wouldn't. Oh, Nikita, you're stupid as a blind jackass. [*Laughs.*] I like you, but you're stupid. You think I've been drinking. To hell with you! You think I need you.... Just look at me! I'm a corporal! You fool, you can't even say it, "Corporal of Her Majesty's very First Regiment of Grenadiers." I served tsar and country with faith and truth. But who am I? You think I'm a soldier? No, I'm not a soldier, but the very least of men; I'm an orphan, a vagrant. I swore off drinking. And now I've started in again! ... Well, do you think I'm afraid of you? Not much! I ain't afraid of nobody. When I start to drink, I drink!

Now I'll swill for two weeks and raise the devil. I'll drink away everything down to my cross, I'll drink away my hat, I'll pawn my passport—and I ain't afraid of nobody! They flogged me in the regiment to keep me from drinking! They laid it on and laid it on. "Well," says they, "will you drink any more?" "Yes," says I. Why should I be afraid of 'em: that's the kind of man I am! I'm the way God made me. I swore off drinking, and I didn't drink. Now I've started again, and I drink! And I ain't afraid of nobody. I'm not lying; that's the way it is. . . . Why should I be afraid of 'em, such rot! "There," says I, "that's the kind of man I am!" A priest was telling me: "The devil is the worst boaster. As soon as you begin to boast," says he, "then you'll feel afraid right away. And when you begin to be afraid of people, then the devil, with his cloven hoof, will snatch you up right away and stick you wherever he wants to." But seeing I'm not afraid of people, it's easy for me. I spit on his beard, the lame cuss, the son of a swine. He won't harm me. "Does my fist taste good?" says I.

NIKITA [*crossing himself*]: But what's this I'm doing, anyhow? [*Throws away the rope.*]

MITRICH: What?

NIKITA [*getting up*]: You say not to be afraid of people?

MITRICH: Much you need to be afraid of 'em, such rot! Just you look at 'em in the bath. They're all of the same dough. One has a fatter belly, and the other a thinner; that's all the difference between 'em. They're a fine lot to be afraid of, good luck to 'em!

[MATRENA *approaches from the house.*]

MATRENA [*shouts*]: Well, are you coming?

NIKITA: Ugh! It *is* better that way. I'm coming! [*Goes off toward the house.*]

Change of Scene

The cottage of Act 1, filled with people, some sitting at tables, others standing. In the front corner are AKULINA *and the* BRIDEGROOM. *On the table are the ikons and bread. Among the guests are* MARINA, *her* HUSBAND, *the* POLICE-MAN, COACHMAN, MATCHMAKER [woman], *Bridegroom's* BEST MAN, MATRENA, *and* PEASANTS. *The women are singing songs.* ANISYA *is passing wine. The songs subside.*

COACHMAN: It's high time we were going; the church is a long way off.

BEST MAN: Just wait a while; the stepfather will give his blessing. But where is he?

ANISYA: He's coming, he's coming directly, my dears. Have another glass all around; don't hurt our feelings.

MATCHMAKER [*woman*]: What makes him so slow? We've been waiting a long time already.

ANISYA: He's coming. He's coming directly. He'll be here in two shakes of a lamb's tail. Have some more, my dears. [*Passes wine.*] He'll be here, directly. Sing some more, my beauties, while you wait.

COACHMAN: They've sung all their songs while we've been waiting.

[*The women sing; in the middle of the song* NIKITA *and* AKIM *come in.*]

NIKITI [*holding* AKIM *by the arm and pushing him in front of him*]: Go on, daddy; I can't do it without you.

AKIM: I don't like it, y'see.

NIKITA [*to the women*]: That's enough; keep still. [*Looks around at everybody in the room.*] Marina, are you here?

MATCHMAKER [*woman*]: Come, take the ikon and give us your blessing.

NIKITA: Wait a while, give me time. [*Looking around.*] Akulina, are you here?

MATCHMAKER [*woman*]: What are you calling the roll for? Where should she be?— What a freak he is!

ANISYA: Holy saints! Why's he taken off his boots?

NIKITA: Daddy! Are you here? Look at me! Orthodox people, you are here, and I'm here! Here I am! [*Falls on his knees.*]

ANISYA: Nikita dear, what are you up to? Oh, poor me!

MATCHMAKER [*woman*]: Well, well!

MATRENA: I'll tell you what: he's had too much of that French wine. Come to your senses, will you?

[*She tries to raise him up. He pays no attention to any-body, but looks straight ahead.*]

NIKITA: Orthodox people! I am guilty; I wish to repent.

MATRENA [*pulling him by the shoulder*]: What's the matter with you? Have you gone crazy? Friends, his head's turned; we must take him away.

NIKITA [*shoving her aside with his shoulder*]: Let me alone! And you, daddy, listen to me. To begin with! Marina, look here! [*He bows down to her feet and rises again.*] I did you wrong; I promised to marry you, I seduced you. I de-ceived you, I cast you off: forgive me for Christ's sake! [*Bows down to her feet once more.*]

ANISYA: What are you prating about? This ain't decent. Nobody's questioning you. Get up: what are you making a row for?

MATRENA: O-oh, he's bewitched! How did it happen? He's out of his head— Get up, what are you talking non-sense for? [*Pulls at him.*]

NIKITA [*shaking his head*]: Don't touch me! Forgive me, Marina! Forgive my sins against you for Christ's sake!

[MARINA *covers her face with her hands and is silent.*]

ANISYA: Get up, I tell you: what are you making a row for? No use mentioning bygones. Stop your foolery. Shame on you! Oh, poor me! He's gone clean daft.

NIKITA [*pushing away his wife and turning to* AKULINA]: Akulina, I'll talk to you now. Listen, orthodox people! I am an accursed man. Akulina, I did you wrong! Your father did not die a natural death. He was poisoned.

ANISYA [*shrieks*]: Poor me! What does he mean?

MATRENA: The man's out of his head. Take him away, will you!

[*Several men approach and are about to seize him.*]

AKIM [*shielding him with his arms*]: Wait! Here, fellows, wait, y'see; wait, I tell you!

NIKITA: Akulina, I poisoned him. Forgive me, for Christ's sake!

AKULINA [*jumping up*]: He lies! I know who did it.

MATCHMAKER [*woman*]: What are you doing? Sit still.

AKIM: O, Lord! What a sin! What a sin!

POLICEMAN: Seize him! And send for the village elder, and witnesses. We must draw up the document. Get up and come here.

AKIM [*to the* POLICEMAN]: But you, you know— Brass Buttons, y'see—just wait a bit, you know. Just let him tell the story, y'see.

POLICEMAN [*to* AKIM]: Look out, old man; don't meddle. I must draw up the document.

AKIM: What a fellow you are, y'see. Wait, I tell you. Don't fuss about the document, y'see. God's work's going on here, you know. A man is repenting, y'see; and you talk about a document, you know.

POLICEMAN: Call the elder!

AKIM: Let God's work go on, you know; when it's over, y'see, then you do your business, y'see.

NIKITA: I did you another great wrong, Akulina; I seduced you. Forgive me for Christ's sake! [*Bows down to her feet.*]

AKULINA [*coming out from behind the table*]: Let me go; I won't get married. He told me to, but now I won't.

POLICEMAN: Repeat what you have said.

NIKITA: Wait, please, policeman; let me finish.

AKIM [*in ecstasy*]: Speak on, my lad; tell it all; it'll be easier for you. Repent in the sight of God; do not fear men. God! God! This is His work!

NIKITA: I poisoned the father; I ruined, cur that I am,

the daughter. I had power over her; I ruined her and her baby.

AKULINA: It's true, it's true.

NIKITA: I crushed her child in the cellar with a plank. I sat on it. . . . I crushed it . . . and the little bones in it cracked. [*Weeps.*] And I buried it in the earth. I did it, nobody but me!

AKULINA: He lies! I told him to. . . .

NIKITA: Don't shield me! I'm not afraid of anybody now! Forgive me, orthodox people! [*Bows down to the earth. Silence.*]

POLICEMAN: Bind him. Your marriage is broken up, that's plain.

[*Men approach* NIKITA *with sashes.*]

NIKITA: Wait, you'll have time. . . . [*Bows down to his father's feet.*] Dearest father! Forgive me, accursed sinner that I am—you also! You said to me in the very beginning, when I began to meddle with this nasty whoredom, you said to me: "If a claw is caught, the whole bird is lost." I did not listen to you, cur that I was, and it has come out as you said. Forgive me, for Christ's sake!

AKIM [*in ecstasy*]: God will forgive you, my beloved child! [*Embraces him.*] You have not spared yourself, He will spare you. God! God! This is His work!

ELDER [*coming in*]: There are plenty of witnesses here already.

POLICEMAN: We'll have the examination right away.

[*They bind* NIKITA.]

AKULINA [*coming up and standing beside him*]: I'll tell the truth. Question me too.

NIKITA [*bound*]: No use questioning. I did it all by myself. I planned it and I did it. Lead me wherever you want to. I shall say nothing more.

CURTAIN

The Cherry

Orchard

ANTON CHEKHOV

Translated by Constance Garnett

CHARACTERS

MADAME RANEVSKY [LYUBOV ANDREYEVNA], *the owner of the Cherry Orchard*

ANYA, *her daughter, aged 17*

VARYA, *her adopted daughter, aged 24*

GAEV [LEONID ANDREYEVITCH], *brother of Madame Ranevsky*

LOPAHIN [YERMOLAY ALEXEYEVITCH], *a merchant*

TROFIMOV [PYOTR SERGEYEVITCH], *a student*

SEMYONOV-PISHTCHIK, *a landower*

CHARLOTTA IVANOVNA, *a governess*

EPIHODOV [SEMYON PANTALEYEVITCH], *a clerk*

DUNYASHA, *a maid*

FIRS, *an old valet, aged 87*

YASHA, *a young valet*

A WAYFARER

THE STATION MASTER

A POST-OFFICE CLERK

VISITORS, SERVANTS

The action takes place on the estate of
MADAME RANEVSKY.

act 1

A room, which has always been called the nursery. One of the doors leads into ANYA'S *room. Dawn, sun rises during the scene. May, the cherry trees in flower, but it is cold in the garden with the frost of early morning. Windows closed.*

Enter DUNYASHA *with a candle and* LOPAHIN *with a book in his hand.*

LOPAHIN: The train's in, thank God. What time is it?

DUNYASHA: Nearly two o'clock. [*Puts out the candle.*] It's daylight already.

LOPAHIN: The train's late! Two hours, at least. [*Yawns and stretches.*] I'm a pretty one; what a fool I've been. Came here on purpose to meet them at the station and dropped asleep.... Dozed off as I sat in the chair. It's annoying.... You might have waked me.

DUNYASHA: I thought you had gone. [*Listens.*] There, I do believe they're coming!

LOPAHIN [*listens*]: No, what with the luggage and one thing and another. [*A pause.*] Lyubov Andreyevna has been abroad five years; I don't know what she is like now.... She's a splendid woman. A good-natured, kind-hearted woman. I remember when I was a lad of fifteen, my poor father—he used to keep a little shop here in the village in those days—gave me a punch in the face with his fist and made my nose bleed. We were in the yard here, I forget what we'd come about—he had had a drop. Lyubov Andreyevna—I can see her now—she was a slim young girl then—took me to wash my face, and then brought me into this very room, into the nursery. "Don't cry, little peasant," says she, "it will be well in time for your wedding day." ... [*A pause.*] Little peasant. ... My father was a peasant, it's true, but here am I in a white waistcoat and brown shoes, like a pig in a bun shop. Yes, I'm a rich man, but for all my money, come to think, a peasant I was, and a peasant I am. [*Turns over the pages of the book.*] I've been reading this book and I can't make head or tail of it. I fell asleep over it.

[*A pause.*]

DUNYASHA: The dogs have been awake all night, they feel that the mistress is coming.

LOPAHIN: Why, what's the matter with you, Dunyasha?

DUNYASHA: My hands are all of a tremble. I feel as though I should faint.

LOPAHIN: You're a spoilt soft creature, Dunyasha. And dressed like a lady too, and your hair done up. That's not the thing. One must know one's place.

[*Enter* EPIHODOV *with a nosegay; he wears a pea-jacket and highly polished creaking top-boots; he drops the nosegay as he comes in.*]

EPIHODOV [*picking up the nosegay*]: Here! the gardener's sent this, says you're to put it in the dining-room. [*Gives* DUNYASHA *the nosegay.*]

LOPAHIN: And bring me some kvass.

DUNYASHA: I will. [*Goes out.*]

EPIHODOV: It's chilly this morning, three degrees of frost, though the cherries are all in flower. I can't say much for our climate. [*Sighs.*] I can't. Our climate is not often propitious to the occasion. Yermolay Alexeyevitch, permit me to call your attention to the fact that I purchased myself a pair of boots the day before yesterday, and they creak, I venture to assure you, so that there's no tolerating them. What ought I to grease them with?

LOPAHIN: Oh, shut up! Don't bother me.

EPIHODOV: Every day some misfortune befalls me. I don't complain, I'm used to it, and I wear a smiling face.

[DUNYASHA *comes in, hands* LOPAHIN *the kvass.*]

EPIHODOV: I am going. [*Stumbles against a chair, which*

falls over.] There! [*As though triumphant.*] There you see now, excuse the expression, an accident like that among others. . . . It's positively remarkable. [*Goes out.*]

DUNYASHA: Do you know, Yermolay Alexeyevitch, I must confess, Epihodov has made me a proposal.

LOPAHIN: Ah!

DUNYASHA: I'm sure I don't know. . . . He's a harmless fellow, but sometimes when he begins talking, there's no making anything of it. It's all very fine and expressive, only there's no understanding it. I've a sort of liking for him too. He loves me to distraction. He's an unfortunate man; every day there's something. They tease him about it—two and twenty misfortunes they call him.

LOPAHIN [*listening*]: There! I do believe they're coming.

DUNYASHA: They are coming! What's the matter with me? . . . I'm cold all over.

LOPAHIN: They really are coming. Let's go and meet them. Will she know me? It's five years since I saw her.

DUNYASHA [*in a flutter*]: I shall drop this very minute. . . . Ah, I shall drop.

[*There is a sound of two carriages driving up to the house.* LOPAHIN *and* DUNYASHA *go out quickly. The stage is left empty. A noise is heard in the adjoining rooms.* FIRS, *who has driven to meet* MADAME RANEVSKY, *crosses the stage hurriedly leaning on a stick. He is wearing old-fashioned livery and a high hat. He says something to himself, but not a word can be distinguished. The noise behind the scenes goes on increasing. A voice:* "Come, let's go in here." *Enter* LYUBOV ANDREYEVNA, ANYA, *and* CHARLOTTA IVANOVNA *with a pet dog on a chain, all in traveling dresses.* VARYA *in an out-door coat with a kerchief over her head,* GAEV, SEMYONOV-PISHTCHIK, LOPAHIN, DUNYASHA *with bag and parasol, servants with other articles. All walk across the room.*]

ANYA: Let's come in here. Do you remember what room this is, mamma?

LYUBOV [*joyfully, through her tears*]: The nursery!

VARYA: How cold it is, my hands are numb. [*To* LYUBOV ANDREYEVNA.] Your rooms, the white room and the lavender one, are just the same as ever, mamma.

LYUBOV: My nursery, dear delightful room. . . . I used to sleep here when I was little. . . . [*Cries.*] And here I am, like a little child. . . . [*Kisses her brother and* VARYA, *and then her brother again.*] Varya's just the same as ever, like a nun. And I knew Dunyasha. [*Kisses* DUNYASHA.]

GAEV: The train was two hours late. What do you think of that? Is that the way to do things?

CHARLOTTA [*to* PISHTCHIK]: My dog eats nuts, too.

PISHTCHIK [*wonderingly*]: Fancy that!

[*They all go out except* ANYA *and* DUNYASHA.]

DUNYASHA: We've been expecting you so long. [*Takes* ANYA'S *hat and coat.*]

ANYA: I haven't slept for four nights on the journey. I feel dreadfully cold.

DUNYASHA: You set out in Lent, there was snow and frost, and now? My darling! [*Laughs and kisses her.*] I *have* missed you, my precious, my joy. I must tell you . . . I can't put it off a minute. . . .

ANYA [*wearily*]: What now?

DUNYASHA: Epihodov, the clerk, made me a proposal just after Easter.

ANYA: It's always the same thing with you. . . . [*Straightening her hair.*] I've lost all my hairpins. [*She is staggering from exhaustion.*]

DUNYASHA: I don't know what to think, really. He does love me, he does love me so!

ANYA [*looking toward her door, tenderly*]: My own room, my windows just as though I had never gone away. I'm home! Tomorrow morning I shall get up and run into the garden. . . . Oh, if I could get to sleep! I haven't slept all the journey, I was so anxious and worried.

DUNYASHA: Pyotr Sergeyevitch came the day before yesterday.

ANYA [*joyfully*]: Petya!

DUNYASHA: He's asleep in the bath house, he has settled in there. I'm afraid of being in their way, says he. [*Glancing at her watch.*] I was to have waked him, but Varvara Mihalovna told me not to. Don't you wake him, says she.

[*Enter* VARYA *with a bunch of keys at her waist.*]

VARYA: Dunyasha, coffee and make haste... Mamma's asking for coffee.

DUNYASHA: This very minute. [*Goes out.*]

VARYA: Well, thank God, you've come. You're home again. [*Petting her.*] My little darling has come back! My precious beauty has come back again!

ANYA: I have had a time of it!

VARYA: I can fancy.

ANYA: We set off in Holy Week—it was so cold then, and all the way Charlotta would talk and show off her tricks. What did you want to burden me with Charlotta for?

VARYA: You couldn't have traveled all alone, darling. At seventeen!

ANYA: We got to Paris at last, it was cold there—snow. I speak French shockingly. Mamma lives on the fifth floor, I went up to her and there were a lot of French people, ladies, an old priest with a book. The place smelt of tobacco and so comfortless. I felt sorry, oh! so sorry for mamma all at once, I put my arms round her neck, and hugged her and wouldn't let her go. Mamma was as kind as she could be, and she cried....

VARYA [*through her tears*]: Don't speak of it, don't speak of it!

ANYA: She had sold her villa at Mentone, she had nothing left, nothing. I hadn't a farthing left either, we only just had enough to get here. And mamma doesn't understand! When we had dinner at the stations, she always ordered the most expensive things and gave the waiters a whole ruble. Charlotta's just the same. Yasha too must have the same as we do; it's simply awful. You know Yasha is mamma's valet now, we brought him here with us.

VARYA: Yes, I've seen the young rascal.

ANYA: Well, tell me—have you paid the arrears on the mortgage?

VARYA: How could we get the money?

ANYA: Oh, dear! Oh, dear!

VARYA: In August the place will be sold.

ANYA: My goodness!

LOPAHIN [*peeps in at the door and moos like a cow*]: Moo! [*Disappears.*]

VARYA [*weeping*]: There, that's what I could do to him. [*Shakes her fist.*]

ANYA [*embracing* VARYA, *softly*]: Varya, has he made you an offer? [VARYA *shakes her head.*] Why, but he loves you. Why is it you don't come to an understanding? What are you waiting for?

VARYA: I believe that there never will be anything between us. He has a lot to do, he has no time for me . . . and takes no notice of me. Bless the man, it makes me miserable to see him. . . . Everyone's talking of our being married, everyone's congratulating me, and all the while there's really nothing in it; it's all like a dream. [*In another tone.*] You have a new brooch like a bee.

ANYA [*mournfully*]: Mamma bought it. [*Goes into her own room and talks in a light-hearted childish tone.*] And you know, in Paris I went up in a balloon!

VARYA: My darling's home again! My pretty is home again!

[DUNYASHA *returns with the coffee-pot and is making the coffee.*]

VARYA [*standing at the door*]: All day long, darling, as I go about looking after the house, I keep dreaming all the time. If only we could marry you to a rich man, then I should feel more at rest. Then I would go off by myself on a pilgrimage to Kiev, to Moscow . . . and so I would spend my life going from one holy place to another. . . . I would go on and on. . . . What bliss!

ANYA: The birds are singing in the garden. What time is it?

VARYA: It must be nearly three. It's time you were asleep, darling. [*Going into* ANYA'S *room*.] What bliss!

[YASHA *enters with a rug and a traveling bag.*]

YASHA [*crosses the stage, mincingly*]: May one come in here, pray?

DUNYASHA: I shouldn't have known you, Yasha. How you have changed abroad.

YASHA: H'm! . . . And who are you?

DUNYASHA: When you went away, I was that high. [*Shows distance from floor.*] Dunyasha, Fyodor's daughter. . . . You don't remember me!

YASHA: H'm! . . . You're a peach! [*Looks round and embraces her: she shrieks and drops a saucer.* YASHA *goes out hastily.*]

VARYA [*in the doorway, in a tone of vexation*]: What now?

DUNYASHA [*through her tears*]: I have broken a saucer.

VARYA: Well, that brings good luck.

ANYA [*coming out of her room*]: We ought to prepare mamma: Petya is here.

VARYA: I told them not to wake him.

ANYA [*dreamily*]: It's six years since father died. Then only a month later little brother Grisha was drowned in the river, such a pretty boy he was, only seven. It was more than mamma could bear, so she went away, went away without looking back. [*Shuddering.*] . . . How well I understand her, if only she knew! [*A pause.*] And Petya Trofimov was Grisha's tutor, he may remind her.

[*Enter* FIRS; *he is wearing a pea-jacket and a white waistcoat.*]

FIRS [*goes up to the coffee-pot, anxiously*]: The mistress will be served here. [*Puts on white gloves.*] Is the coffee ready? [*Sternly to* DUNYASHA.] Girl! Where's the cream?

DUNYASHA: Ah, mercy on us! [*Goes out quickly.*]

FIRS [*fussing round the coffee-pot*]: Ech! you good-for-nothing! [*Muttering to himself.*] Come back from Paris. And the old master used to go to Paris too . . . horses all the way. [*Laughs.*]

VARYA: What is it, Firs?

FIRS: What is your pleasure? [*Gleefully.*] My lady has come home! I have lived to see her again! Now I can die. [*Weeps with joy. Enter* LYUBOV ANDREYEVNA, GAEV *and* SEMYONOV-PISHTCHIK; *the latter is in a short-waisted full coat of fine cloth, and full trousers.* GAEV, *as he comes in, makes a gesture with his arms and his whole body, as though he were playing billiards.*]

LYUBOV: How does it go? Let me remember. Cannon off the red!

GAEV: That's it—in off the white! Why, once, sister, we used to sleep together in this very room, and now I'm fifty-one, strange as it seems.

LOPAHIN: Yes, time flies.

GAEV: What do you say?

LOPAHIN: Time, I say, flies.

GAEV: What a smell of patchouli!

ANYA: I'm going to bed. Good night, mamma. [*Kisses her mother.*]

LYUBOV: My precious darling. [*Kisses her hands.*] Are you glad to be home? I can't believe it.

ANYA: Good night, uncle.

GAEV [*kissing her face and hands*]: God bless you! How like you are to your mother! [*To his sister.*] At her age you were just the same, Lyuba.

[ANYA *shakes hands with* LOPAHIN *and* PISHTCHIK, *then goes out, shutting the door after her.*]

LYUBOV: She's quite worn out.

PISHTCHIK: Aye, it's a long journey, to be sure.

VARYA [*to* LOPAHIN *and* PISHTCHIK]: Well, gentlemen? It's three o'clock and time to say good-by.

LYUBOV [*laughs*]: You're just the same as ever, Varya. [*Draws her to her and kisses her.*] I'll just drink my coffee and then we will all go and rest. [FIRS *puts a cushion under her feet.*] Thanks, friend. I am so fond of coffee, I drink it day and night. Thanks, dear old man. [*Kisses* FIRS.]

VARYA: I'll just see whether all the things have been brought in. [*Goes out.*]

LYUBOV: Can it really be me sitting here? [*Laughs.*] I want to dance about and clap my hands. [*Covers her face with her hands.*] And I could drop asleep in a moment! God knows I love my country, I love it tenderly; I couldn't look out of the window in the train, I kept crying so. [*Through her tears.*] But I must drink my coffee, though. Thank you, Firs, thanks, dear old man. I'm so glad to find you still alive.

FIRS: The day before yesterday.

GAEV: He's rather deaf.

LOPAHIN: I have to set off for Harkov directly, at five o'clock. . . . It is annoying! I wanted to have a look at you, and a little talk. . . . You are just as splendid as ever.

PISHTCHIK [*breathing heavily*]: Handsomer, indeed. . . . Dressed in Parisian style . . . completely bowled me over.

LOPAHIN: Your brother, Leonid Andreyevitch here, is always saying that I'm a low-born knave, that I'm a money-grubber, but I don't care one straw for that. Let him talk. Only I do want you to believe in me as you used to. I do want your wonderful tender eyes to look at me as they used to in the old days. Merciful God! My father was a serf of your father and of your grandfather, but you—you —did so much for me once, that I've forgotten all that; I love you as though you were my kin . . . more than my kin.

LYUBOV: I can't sit still, I simply can't. . . . [*Jumps up and walks about in violent agitation.*] This happiness is too much for me. . . . You may laugh at me, I know I'm silly. . . . My own bookcase. [*Kisses the bookcase.*] My little table.

GAEV: Nurse died while you were away.

LYUBOV [*sits down and drinks coffee*]: Yes, the Kingdom of Heaven be hers! You wrote me of her death.

GAEV: And Anastasy is dead. Squinting Petruchka has left me and is in service now with the police captain in the town. [*Takes a box of caramels out of his pocket and sucks one.*]

PISHTCHIK: My daughter, Dashenka, wishes to be remembered to you.

LOPAHIN: I want to tell you something very pleasant and

cheering. [*Glancing at his watch.*] I'm going directly ...
there's no time to say much ... well, I can say it in a couple
of words. I needn't tell you your cherry orchard is to be
sold to pay your debts; the 22nd of August is the date fixed
for the sale; but don't you worry, dearest lady, you may
sleep in peace, there is a way of saving it. ... This is what
I propose. I beg your attention! Your estate is not twenty
miles from the town, the railway runs close by it, and if the
cherry orchard and the land along the river bank were cut
up into building plots and then let on lease for summer
villas, you would make an income of at least 25,000 rubles
a year out of it.

GAEV: That's all rot, if you'll excuse me.

LYUBOV: I don't quite understand you, Yermolay Alexeyevitch.

LOPAHIN: You will get a rent of at least twenty-five rubles a year for a three-acre plot from summer visitors, and
if you say the word now, I'll bet you what you like there
won't be one square foot of ground vacant by the autumn,
all the plots will be taken up. I congratulate you; in fact,
you are saved. It's a perfect situation with that deep river.
Only, of course, it must be cleared—all the old buildings,
for example, must be removed, this house too, which is
really good for nothing, and the old cherry orchard must
be cut down.

LYUBOV: Cut down? My dear fellow, forgive me, but
you don't know what you are talking about. If there is one
thing interesting—remarkable indeed—in the whole province, it's just our cherry orchard.

LOPAHIN: The only thing remarkable about the orchard
is that it's a very large one. There's a crop of cherries every
alternate year, and then there's nothing to be done with
them, no one buys them.

GAEV: This orchard is mentioned in the *Encyclopædia*.

LOPAHIN [*glancing at his watch*]: If we don't decide on
something and don't take some steps, on the 22nd of August the cherry orchard and the whole estate too will be sold

by auction. Make up your minds! There is no other way of saving it, I'll take my oath on that. No, No!

FIRS: In old days, forty or fifty years ago, they used to dry the cherries, soak them, pickle them, make jam too, and they used—

GAEV: Be quiet, Firs.

FIRS: And they used to send the preserved cherries to Moscow and to Markov by the wagon-load. That brought the money in! And the preserved cherries in those days were soft and juicy, sweet and fragrant. . . . They knew the way to do them then. . . .

LYUBOV: And where is the recipe now?

FIRS: It's forgotten. Nobody remembers it.

PISHTCHIK [to LYUBOV ANDREYEVNA]: What's it like in Paris? Did you eat frogs there?

LYUBOV: Oh, I ate crocodiles.

PISHTCHIK: Fancy that now!

LOPAHIN: There used to be only the gentlefolks and the peasants in the country, but now there are these summer visitors. All the towns, even the small ones, are surrounded, nowadays by these summer villas. And one may say for sure, that in another twenty years there'll be many more of these people and that they'll be everywhere. At present the summer visitor only drinks tea in his veranda, but maybe he'll take to working his bit of land too, and then your cherry orchard would become happy, rich and prosperous. . . .

GAEV [indignant]: What rot!

[Enter VARYA and YASHA.]

VARYA: There are two telegrams for you, mamma. [Takes out keys and opens an old-fashioned bookcase with a loud crack.] Here they are.

LYUBOV: From Paris. [Tears the telegrams, without reading them.] I have done with Paris.

GAEV: Do you know, Lyuba, how old that bookcase is? Last week I pulled out the bottom drawer and there I found the date branded on it. The bookcase was made just a hundred years ago. What do you say to that? We might have celebrated its jubilee. Though it's an inanimate object, still it is a *book*case.

PISHTCHIK [*amazed*]: A hundred years! Fancy that now.

GAEV: Yes. . . . It is a thing. . . . [*Feeling the bookcase.*] Dear, honored, bookcase! Hail to thee who for more than a hundred years hast served the pure ideals of good and justice; thy silent call to fruitful labor has never flagged in those hundred years, maintaining [*in tears*] in the generations of man, courage and faith in a brighter future and fostering in us ideals of good and social consciousness.

[*A pause.*]

LOPAHIN: Yes . . .

LYUBOV: You are just the same as ever, Leonid.

GAEV [*a little embarrassed*]: Cannon off the right into the pocket!

LOPAHIN [*looking at his watch*]: Well, it's time I was off.

YASHA [*handing LYUBOV ANDREYEVNA medicine*]: Perhaps you will take your pills now.

PISHTCHIK: You shouldn't take medicines, my dear madam . . . they do no harm and no good. Give them here . . . honored lady. [*Takes the pillbox, pours the pills into the hollow of his hand, blows on them, puts them in his mouth and drinks off some kvass.*] There!

LYUBOV [*in alarm*]: Why, you must be out of your mind!

PISHTCHIK: I have taken all the pills.

LOPAHIN: What a glutton!

[*All laugh.*]

FIRS: His honor stayed with us in Easter week, ate a gallon and a half of cucumbers. . . . [*Mutters.*]

LYUBOV: What is he saying?

VARYA: He has taken to muttering like that for the last three years. We are used to it.

YASHA: His declining years!

[CHARLOTTA IVANOVNA, *a very thin, lanky figure in a white dress with a lorgnette in her belt, walks across the stage.*]

LOPAHIN: I beg your pardon, Charlotta Ivanovna, I have not had time to greet you. [*Tries to kiss her hand.*]

CHARLOTTA [*pulling away her hand*]: If I let you kiss my hand, you'll be wanting to kiss my elbow, and then my shoulder.

LOPAHIN: I've no luck today! [*All laugh.*] Charlotta Ivanovna, show us some tricks!

LYUBOV: Charlotta, do show us some tricks!

CHARLOTTA: I don't want to. I'm sleepy. [*Goes out.*]

LOPAHIN: In three weeks' time we shall meet again. [*Kisses* LYUBOV ANDREYEVNA'S *hand.*] Good-by till then—I must go. [*To* GAEV.] Good-by. [*Kisses* PISHTCHIK] Good-by. [*Gives his hand to* VARYA, *then to* FIRS *and* YASHA.] I don't want to go. [*To* LYUBOV ANDREYEVNA.] If you think over my plan for the villas and make up your mind, then let me know; I will lend you 50,000 rubles. Think of it seriously.

VARYA [*angrily*]: Well, do go, for goodness' sake.

LOPAHIN: I'm going, I'm going. [*Goes out.*]

GAEV: Low-born knave! I beg pardon, though . . . Varya is going to marry him, he's Varya's fiancé.

VARYA: Don't talk nonsense, uncle.

LYUBOV: Well, Varya, I shall be delighted. He's a good man.

PISHTCHIK: He is, one must acknowledge, a most worthy man. And my Dashenka . . . says too that . . . she says . . . various things. [*Snores, but at once wakes up.*] But all the same, honored lady, could you oblige me . . . with a loan of 240 rubles . . . to pay the interest on my mortgage tomorrow?

VARYA [*dismayed*]: No, no.

LYUBOV: I really haven't any money.

PISHTCHIK: It will turn up. [*Laughs.*] I never lose hope. I thought everything was over, I was a ruined man, and lo and behold—the railway passed through my land and . . . they paid me for it. And something else will turn up again, if not today, then tomorrow . . . Dashenka'll win two hundred thousand . . . she's got a lottery ticket.

LYUBOV: Well, we've finished our coffee, we can go to bed.

FIRS [*brushes* GAEV, *reprovingly*]: You have got on the wrong trousers again! What am I to do with you?

VARYA [*softly*]: Anya's asleep. [*Softly opens the window.*] Now the sun's risen, it's not a bit cold. Look, mamma, what exquisite trees! My goodness! And the air! The starlings are singing!

GAEV [*opens another window*]: The orchard is all white. You've not forgotten it, Lyuba? That long avenue that runs straight, straight as an arrow, how it shines on a moonlight night. You remember? You've not forgotten?

LYUBOV [*looking out of the window into the garden*]: Oh, my childhood, my innocence! It was in this nursery I used to sleep, from here I looked out into the orchard, happiness waked with me every morning and in those days the orchard was just the same, nothing has changed. [*Laughs with delight.*] All, all white! Oh, my orchard! After the dark gloomy autumn, and the cold winter; you are young again and full of happiness, the heavenly angels have never left you. . . . If I could cast off the burden that weighs on my heart, if I could forget the past!

GAEV: H'm! and the orchard will be sold to pay our debts; it seems strange. . . .

LYUBOV: See, our mother walking . . . all in white, down the avenue! [*Laughs with delight.*] It is she!

GAEV: Where?

VARYA: Oh, don't, mamma!

LYUBOV: There is no one. It was my fancy. On the right there, by the path to the arbor, there is a white tree bending like a woman. . . .

[*Enter* TROFIMOV *wearing a shabby student's uniform and spectacles.*]

LYUBOV: What a ravishing orchard! White masses of blossom, blue sky. . . .

TROFIMOV: Lyubov Andreyevna! [*She looks round at him.*] I will just pay my respects to you and then leave you at once. [*Kisses her hand warmly.*] I was told to wait until morning, but I hadn't the patience to wait any longer. . . .

[LYUBOV ANDREYEVNA *looks at him in perplexity.*]

VARYA [*through her tears*]: This is Petya Trofimov.

TROFIMOV: Petya Trofimov, who was your Grisha's tutor. . . . Can I have changed so much?

[LYUBOV ANDREYEVNA *embraces him and weeps quietly*.]

GAEV [*in confusion*]: There, there, Lyuba.

VARYA [*crying*]: I told you, Petya, to wait till tomorrow.

LYUBOV: My Grisha . . . my boy . . . Grisha . . . my son!

VARYA: We can't help it, mamma, it is God's will.

TROFIMOV [*softly through his tears*]: There . . . there.

LYUBOV [*weeping quietly*]: My boy was lost . . . drowned. Why? Oh, why, dear Petya? [*More quietly*.] Anya is asleep in there, and I'm talking loudly . . . making this noise. . . . But, Petya? Why have you grown so ugly? Why do you look so old?

TROFIMOV: A peasant-woman in the train called me a mangy-looking gentleman.

LYUBOV: You were quite a boy then, a pretty little student, and now your hair's thin—and spectacles. Are you really a student still? [*Goes toward the door*.]

TROFIMOV: I seem likely to be a perpetual student.

LYUBOV [*kisses her brother, then* VARYA]: Well, go to bed. . . . You are older too, Leonid.

PISHTCHIK [*follows her*]: I suppose it's time we were asleep. . . . Ugh! my gout. I'm staying the night! Lyubov Andreyevna, my dear soul, if you could . . . tomorrow morning . . . 240 rubles.

GAEV: That's always his story.

PISHTCHIK: 240 rubles . . . to pay the interest on my mortgage.

LYUBOV: My dear man, I have no money.

PISHTCHIK: I'll pay it back, my dear . . . a trifling sum.

LYUBOV: Oh, well, Leonid will give it you. . . . You give him the money, Leonid.

GAEV: Me give it him! Let him wait till he gets it!

LYUBOV: It can't be helped, give it him. He needs it. He'll pay it back.

[LYUBOV ANDREYEVNA, TROFIMOV, PISHTCHIK *and*

FIRS *go out.* GAEV, VARYA *and* YASHA *remain.*]

GAEV: Sister hasn't got out of the habit of flinging away her money. [*To* YASHA.] Get away, my good fellow, you smell of the hen-house.

YASHA [*with a grin*]: And you, Leonid Andreyevitch, are just the same as ever.

GAEV: What's that? [*To* VARYA.] What did he say?

VARYA [*to* YASHA]: Your mother has come from the village; she has been sitting in the servants' room since yesterday, waiting to see you.

YASHA: Oh, bother her!

VARYA: For shame!

YASHA: What's the hurry? She might just as well have come tomorrow. [*Goes out.*]

VARYA: Mamma's just the same as ever, she hasn't changed a bit. If she had her own way, she'd give away everything.

GAEV: Yes. [*A pause.*] If a great many remedies are suggested for some disease, it means that the disease is incurable. I keep thinking and racking my brains; I have many schemes, a great many, and that really means none. If we could only come in for a legacy from somebody, or marry our Anya to a very rich man, or we might go to Yaroslavl and try our luck with our old aunt, the Countess. She's very, very rich, you know.

VARYA [*weeps*]: If God would help us.

GAEV: Don't blubber. Aunt's very rich, but she doesn't like us. First, sister married a lawyer instead of a nobleman. . . .

[ANYA *appears in the doorway.*]

GAEV: And then her conduct, one can't call it virtuous. She is good, and kind, and nice, and I love her, but, however one allows for extenuating circumstances, there's no denying that she's an immoral woman. One feels it in her slightest gesture.

VARYA [*in a whisper*]: Anya's in the doorway.

GAEV: What do you say? [*A pause.*] It's queer, there

seems to be something wrong with my right eye. I don't see as well as I did. And on Thursday when I was in the district Court . . .

[*Enter* ANYA.]

VARYA: Why aren't you asleep, Anya?

ANYA: I can't get to sleep.

GAEV: My pet. [*Kisses* ANYA'S *face and hands.*] My child. [*Weeps.*] You are not my niece, you are my angel, you are everything to me. Believe me, believe. . . .

ANYA: I believe you, uncle. Everyone loves you and respects you . . . but, uncle dear, you must be silent . . . simply be silent. What were you saying just now about my mother, about your own sister? What made you say that?

GAEV: Yes, yes. . . . [*Puts his hand over his face.*] Really, that was awful! My God, save me! And today I made a speech to the bookcase . . . so stupid! And only when I had finished, I saw how stupid it was.

VARYA: It's true, uncle, you ought to keep quiet. Don't talk, that's all.

ANYA: If you could keep from talking, it would make things easier for you, too.

GAEV: I won't speak. [*Kisses* ANYA'S *and* VARYA'S *hands.*] I'll be silent. Only this is about business. On Thusrday I was in the district Court; well, there was a large party of us there and we began talking of one thing and another, and this and that, and do you know, I believe that it will be possible to raise a loan on an I.O.U. to pay the arrears on the mortgage.

VARYA: If the Lord would help us!

GAEV: I'm going on Tuesday; I'll talk of it again. [*To* VARYA.] Don't blubber. [*To* ANYA.] Your mamma will talk to Lopahin; of course, he won't refuse her. And as soon as you're rested you shall go to Yaroslavl to the Countess, your great-aunt. So we shall all set to work in three directions at once, and the business is done. We shall pay off arrears. I'm convinced of it. [*Puts a caramel in his mouth.*] I swear on my honor, I swear by anything you like, the estate shan't be sold. [*Excitedly.*] By my own happiness, I swear it! Here's my hand on it, call me the basest, vilest of men, if I let it come to an auction! Upon my soul I swear it!

ANYA [*her equanimity has returned, she is quite happy*]: How good you are, uncle, and how clever! [*Embraces her uncle.*] I'm at peace now! Quite at peace! I'm happy!

[*Enter* FIRS.]

FIRS [*reproachfully*]: Leonid Andreyevitch, have you no fear of God? When are you going to bed?

GAEV: Directly, directly. You can go, Firs. I'll ... yes, I will undress myself. Come, children, by-by. We'll go into details tomorrow, but now go to bed. [*Kisses* ANYA *and* VARYA.] I'm a man of the eighties. They run down that period, but still I can say I have had to suffer not a little for my convictions in my life, it's not for nothing that the peasant loves me. One must know the peasant! One must know how. ...

ANYA: At it again, uncle!

VARYA: Uncle dear, you'd better be quiet!

FIRS [*angrily*]: Leonid Andreyevitch!

GAEV: I'm coming. I'm coming. Go to bed. Potted the shot—there's a shot for you! A beauty! [*Goes out,* FIRS *hobbling after him.*]

ANYA: My mind's at rest now. I don't want to go to Yaroslavl, I don't like my great-aunt, but still my mind's at rest. Thanks to uncle. [*Sits down.*]

VARYA: We must go to bed. I'm going. Something unpleasant happened while you were away. In the old servants' quarters there are only the old servants, as you know —Efimyushka, Polya and Yevstigney—and Karp too. They began letting stray people in to spend the night—I said nothing. But all at once I heard they had been spreading a report that I gave them nothing but pease pudding to eat. Out of stinginess, you know. ... And it was all Yevstigney's doing. ... Very well, I said to myself. ... If that's how it is, I thought, wait a bit. I sent for Yevstigney. ... [*Yawns.*] He comes. ... "How's this, Yevstigney," I said, "you could

be such a fool as to?..." [*Looking at* ANYA.] Anitchka!
[*A pause.*] She's asleep. [*Puts her arm around* ANYA.] Come
to bed ... come along! [*Leads her.*] My darling has fallen
asleep! Come ...

> [*They go. Far away beyond the orchard a shepherd
> plays on a pipe.* TROFIMOV *crosses the stage and, seeing*
> VARYA *and* ANYA, *stands still.*]

VARYA: Sh! asleep, asleep. Come, my own.

ANYA [*softly, half asleep*]: I'm so tired. Still those bells.
Uncle ... dear ... mamma and uncle....

VARYA: Come, my own, come along.

> [*They go into* ANYA'S *room.*]

TROFIMOV [*tenderly*]: My sunshine! My spring.

CURTAIN

act 2

*The open country. An old shrine, long abandoned and fallen
out of the perpendicular; near it a well, large stones that
have apparently once been tombstones, and an old garden
seat. The road to* GAEV'S *house is seen. On one side rise
dark poplars; and there the cherry orchard begins. In the
distance a row of telegraph poles and far, far away on the
horizon there is faintly outlined a great town, only visible
in very fine clear weather. It is near sunset.* CHARLOTTA,
YASHA *and* DUNYASHA *are sitting on the seat.* EPIHODOV *is
standing near, playing something mournful on a guitar. All
sit plunged in thought.* CHARLOTTA *wears an old forage cap;
she has taken a gun from her shoulder and is tightening the
buckle on the strap.*

CHARLOTTA [*musingly*]: I haven't a real passport of my own, and I don't know how old I am, and I always feel that I'm a young thing. When I was a little girl, my father and mother used to travel about to fairs and give performances—very good ones. And I used to dance *salto mortale* and all sorts of things. And when papa and mamma died, a German lady took me and had me educated. And so I grew up and became a governess. But where I came from, and who I am, I don't know.... Who my parents were, very likely they weren't married.... I don't know. [*Takes a cucumber out of her pocket and eats.*] I know nothing at all. [*A pause.*] One wants to talk and has no one to talk to. ... I have nobody.

EPIHODOV [*plays on the guitar and sings*]: "What care I for the noisy world! What care I for friends or foes!" How agreeable it is to play on the mandolin!

DUNYASHA: That's a guitar, not a mandolin. [*Looks in a hand-mirror and powders herself.*]

EPIHODOV: To a man mad with love, it's a mandolin. [*Sings.*] "Were her heart but aglow with love's mutual flame."

[YASHA *joins in.*]

CHARLOTTA: How shockingly these people sing! Foo! Like jackals!

DUNYASHA [*to* YASHA]: What happiness, though, to visit foreign lands.

YASHA: Ah, yes! I rather agree with you there. [*Yawns, then lights a cigar.*]

EPIHODOV: That's comprehensible. In foreign lands everything has long since reached full complexion.

YASHA: That's so, of course.

EPIHODOV: I'm a cultivated man, I read remarkable books of all sorts, but I can never make out the tendency I am myself precisely inclined for, whether to live or to shoot myself, speaking precisely, but nevertheless I always carry a revolver. Here it is.... [*Shows revolver.*]

CHARLOTTA: I've had enough, and now I'm going. [*Puts on the gun.*] Epihodov, you're a very clever fellow, and a very terrible one too, all the women must be wild about you. Br-r-r! [*Goes.*] These clever fellows are all so stupid; there's not a creature for me to speak to.... Always alone, alone, nobody belonging to me ... and who I am, and why I'm on earth, I don't know. [*Walks away slowly.*]

EPIHODOV: Speaking precisely, not touching upon other subjects, I'm bound to admit about myself, that destiny behaves mercilessly to me, as a storm to a little boat. If, let us suppose, I am mistaken, then why did I wake up this morning, to quote an example, and look round, and there on my chest was a spider of fearful magnitude ... like this. [*Shows with both hands.*] And then I take up a jug of kvass, to quench my thirst, and in it there is something in the highest degree unseemly of the nature of a cockroach. [*A pause.*] Have you read Buckle? [*A pause.*] I am desirous of troubling you, Dunyasha, with a couple of words.

DUNYASHA: Well, speak.

EPIHODOV: I should be desirous to speak with you alone. [*Sighs.*]

DUNYASHA [*embarrassed*]: Well—only bring me my mantle first. It's by the cupboard. It's rather damp here.

EPIHODOV: Certainly. I will fetch it. Now I know what I must do with my revolver. [*Takes guitar and goes off playing on it.*]

YASHA: Two and twenty misfortunes! Between ourselves, he's a fool. [*Yawns.*]

DUNYASHA: God grant he doesn't shoot himself! [*A pause.*] I am so nervous, I'm always in a flutter. I was a little girl when I was taken into our lady's house, and now I have quite grown out of peasant ways, and my hands are white, as white as a lady's. I'm such a delicate, sensitive creature, I'm afraid of everything. I'm so frightened. And if you deceive me, Yasha, I don't know what will become of my nerves.

YASHA [*kisses her*]: You're a peach! Of course a girl must never forget herself; what I dislike more than anything is a girl being flighty in her behavior.

DUNYASHA: I'm passionately in love with you, Yasha;

you are a man of culture—you can give your opinion about anything.

[*A pause.*]

YASHA [*yawns*]: Yes, that's so. My opinion is this: if a girl loves anyone, that means that she has no principles. [*A pause.*] It's pleasant smoking a cigar in the open air. [*Listens.*] Someone's coming this way . . . it's the gentlefolk. [DUNYASHA *embraces him impulsively.*] Go home, as though you had been to the river to bathe; go by that path, or else they'll meet you and suppose I have made an appointment with you here. That I can't endure.

DUNYASHA [*coughing softly*]: The cigar has made my head ache. . . .

[*Goes off.* YASHA *remains sitting near the shrine. Enter* LYUBOV ANDREYEVNA, GAEV *and* LOPAHIN.]

LOPAHIN: You must make up your mind once for all— there's no time to lose. It's quite a simple question, you know. Will you consent to letting the land for building or not? One word in answer: Yes or no? Only one word!

LYUBOV: Who is smoking such horrible cigars here? [*Sits down.*]

GAEV: Now the railway line has been brought near, it's made things very convenient. [*Sits down.*] Here we have been over and lunched in town. Cannon off the white! I should like to go home and have a game.

LYUBOV: You have plenty of time.

LOPAHIN: Only one word! [*Beseechingly.*] Give me an answer!

GAEV [*yawning*]: What do you say?

LYUBOV [*looks in her purse*]: I had quite a lot of money here yesterday, and there's scarcely any left today. My poor Varya feeds us all on milk soup for the sake of economy; the old folks get nothing but pease pudding, while I waste my money in a senseless way. [*Drops purse, scattering gold pieces.*] There, they have all fallen out! [*Annoyed.*]

YASHA: Allow me. I'll soon pick them up. [*Collects the coins.*]

LYUBOV: Pray do, Yasha. And what did I go off to the town to lunch for? Your restaurant's a wretched place with its music and the tablecloth smelling of soap. . . . Why drink so much, Leonid? And eat so much? And talk so much? Today you talked a great deal again in the restaurant, and all so inappropriately. About the era of the seventies, about the decadents. And to whom? Talking to waiters about decadents!

LOPAHIN: Yes.

GAEV [*waving his hand*]: I'm incorrigible; that's evident. [*Irritably to* YASHA.] Why is it you keep fidgeting about in front of us!

YASHA [*laughs*]: I can't help laughing when I hear your voice.

GAEV [*to his sister*]: Either I or he. . . .

LYUBOV: Get along! Go away, Yasha.

YASHA [*gives* LYUBOV ANDREYEVNA *her purse*]: Directly. [*Hardly able to suppress his laughter.*] This minute. . . . [*Goes off.*]

LOPAHIN: Deriganov, the millionaire, means to buy your estate. They say he is coming to the sale himself.

LYUBOV: Where did you hear that?

LOPAHIN: That's what they say in town.

GAEV: Our aunt in Yaroslavl has promised to send help; but when, and how much she will send, we don't know.

LOPAHIN: How much will she send? A hundred thousand? Two hundred?

LYUBOV: Oh, well! . . . Ten or fifteen thousand, and we must be thankful to get that.

LOPAHIN: Forgive me, but such reckless people as you are—such queer, unbusinesslike people—I never met in my life. One tells you in plain Russian your estate is going to be sold, and you seem not to understand it.

LYUBOV: What are we to do? Tell us what to do.

LOPAHIN: I do tell you every day. Every day I say the same thing. You absolutely must let the cherry orchard and the land on building leases; and do it at once, as quick as may be—the auction's close upon us! Do understand! Once make up your mind to build villas, and you can raise as much money as you like, and then you are saved.

LYUBOV: Villas and summer visitors—forgive me saying so—it's so vulgar.

GAEV: There I perfectly agree with you.

LOPAHIN: I shall sob, or scream, or fall into a fit. I can't stand it! You drive me mad! [*To* GAEV.] You're an old woman!

GAEV: What do you say?

LOPAHIN: An old woman! [*Gets up to go.*]

LYUBOV [*in dismay*]: No, don't go! Do stay, my dear friend! Perhaps we shall think of something.

LOPAHIN: What is there to think of?

LYUBOV: Don't go, I entreat you! With you here it's more cheerful, anyway. [*A pause.*] I keep expecting something, as though the house were going to fall about our ears.

GAEV [*in profound dejection*]: Potted the white! It fails—a kiss.

LYUBOV: We have been great sinners. . . .

LOPAHIN: You have no sins to repent of.

GAEV [*puts a caramel in his mouth*]: They say I've eaten up my property in caramels. [*Laughs.*]

LYUBOV: Oh, my sins! I've always thrown my money away recklessly like a lunatic. I married a man who made nothing but debts. My husband died of champagne—he drank dreadfully. To my misery I loved another man, and immediately—it was my first punishment—the blow fell upon me, here, in the river . . . my boy was drowned and I went abroad—went away forever, never to return, not to see that river again . . . I shut my eyes, and fled, distracted, and *he* after me . . . pitilessly, brutally. I bought a villa at Mentone, for *he* fell ill there, and for three years I had no rest day or night. His illness wore me out, my soul was dried up. And last year, when my villa was sold to pay my debts, I went to Paris and there he robbed me of everything and abandoned me for another woman; and I tried to poison myself. . . . So stupid, so shameful! . . . And suddenly I felt a yearning for Russia, for my country, for my little girl. . . . [*Dries her tears.*] Lord, Lord, be merciful! Forgive my sins! Do not chastise me more! [*Takes a telegram out of her pocket.*] I got this today from Paris. He implores forgiveness, entreats me to return. [*Tears up the telegram.*] I fancy there is music somewhere. [*Listens.*]

GAEV: That's our famous Jewish orchestra. You remember, four violins, a flute and a double bass.

LYUBOV: That still in existence? We ought to send for them one evening, and give a dance.

LOPAHIN [*listens*]: I can't hear. . . . [*Hums softly.*] "For money the Germans will turn a Russian into a Frenchman." [*Laughs.*] I did see such a piece at the theater yesterday! It was funny!

LYUBOV: And most likely there was nothing funny in it. You shouldn't look at plays, you should look at yourselves a little oftener. How gray your lives are! How much nonsense you talk.

LOPAHIN: That's true. One may say honestly, we live a fool's life. [*Pause.*] My father was a peasant, an idiot; he knew nothing and taught me nothing, only beat me when he was drunk, and always with his stick. In reality I am just such another blockhead and idiot. I've learnt nothing properly. I write a wretched hand. I write so that I feel ashamed before folks, like a pig.

LYUBOV: You ought to get married, my dear fellow.

LOPAHIN: Yes . . . that's true.

LYUBOV: You should marry our Varya, she's a good girl.

LOPAHIN: Yes.

LYUBOV: She's a good-natured girl, she's busy all day long, and what's more, she loves you. And you have liked her for ever so long.

LOPAHIN: Well? I'm not against it. . . . She's a good girl.
   [*Pause.*]

GAEV: I've been offered a place in the bank: 6,000 rubles a year. Did you know?

LYUBOV: You would never do for that! You must stay as you are.

[*Enter* FIRS *with overcoat.*]

FIRS: Put it on, sir, it's damp.

GAEV [*putting it on*]: You bother me, old fellow.

FIRS: You can't go on like this. You went away in the morning without leaving word. [*Looks him over.*]

LYUBOV: You look older, Firs!

FIRS: What is your pleasure?

LOPAHIN: You look older, she said.

FIRS: I've had a long life. They were arranging my wedding before your papa was born.... [*Laughs.*] I was the head footman before the emancipation came. I wouldn't consent to be set free then; I stayed on with the old master. ... [*A pause.*] I remember what rejoicings they made and didn't know themselves what they were rejoicing over.

LOPAHIN: Those were fine old times. There was flogging anyway.

FIRS [*not hearing*]: To be sure! The peasants knew their place, and the masters knew theirs; but now they're all at sixes and sevens, there's no making it out.

GAEV: Hold your tongue, Firs. I must go to town to-morrow. I have been promised an introduction to a general, who might let us have a loan.

LOPAHIN: You won't bring that off. And you won't pay your arrears, you may rest assured of that.

LYUBOV: That's all his nonsense. There is no such general.

[*Enter* TROFIMOV, ANYA *and* VARYA.]

GAEV: Here come our girls.

ANYA: There's mamma on the seat.

LYUBOV [*tenderly*]: Come here, come along. My darlings! [*Embraces* ANYA *and* VARYA.] If you only knew how I love you both. Sit beside me, there, like that. [*All sit down.*]

LOPAHIN: Our perpetual student is always with the young ladies.

TROFIMOV: That's not your business.

LOPAHIN: He'll soon be fifty, and he's still a student.

TROFIMOV: Drop your idiotic jokes.

LOPAHIN: Why are you so cross, you queer fish?

TROFIMOV: Oh, don't persist!

LOPAHIN [*laughs*]: Allow me to ask you what's your idea of me?

TROFIMOV: I'll tell you my idea of you. Yermolay Alexeyevitch; you are a rich man, you'll soon be a millionaire. Well, just as in the economy of nature a wild beast is of use, who devours everything that comes in his way, so you too have your use.

[*All laugh.*]

VARYA: Better tell us something about the planets, Petya.

LYUBOV: No, let us go on with the conversation we had yesterday.

TROFIMOV: What was it about?

GAEV: About pride.

TROFIMOV: We had a long conversation yesterday, but we came to no conclusion. In pride, in your sense of it, there is something mystical. Perhaps you are right from your point of view; but if one looks at it simply, without subtlety, what sort of pride can there be, what sense is there in it, if man in his physiological formation is very imperfect, if in the immense majority of cases he is coarse, dull-witted, profoundly unhappy? One must give up glorification of self. One should work, and nothing else.

GAEV: One must die in any case.

TROFIMOV: Who knows? And what does it mean—dying? Perhaps man has a hundred senses, and only the five we know are lost at death, while the other ninety-five remain alive.

LYUBOV: How clever you are, Petya!

LOPAHIN [*ironically*]: Fearfully clever!

TROFIMOV: Humanity progresses, perfecting its powers. Everything that is beyond its ken now will one day become familiar and comprehensible; only we must work, we must with all our powers aid the seeker after truth. Here among us in Russia the workers are few in number as yet. The vast majority of the intellectual people I know, seek nothing, do nothing, are not fit as yet for work of any kind. They call themselves intellectual, but they treat their servants as inferiors, behave to the peasants as though they were animals, learn little, read nothing seriously, do practically nothing, only talk about science and know very little about art. They are all serious people, they all have severe faces, they all talk of weighty matters and air their theories, and yet the vast majority of us—ninety-nine per cent—live like savages, at the least thing fly to blows and abuse, eat piggishly, sleep in filth and stuffiness, bugs everywhere, stench and damp and moral impurity. And it's clear all our fine talk is only to divert our attention and other people's. Show me where to find the *crèches* there's so much talk about, and the reading-rooms? They only exist in novels: in real life there are none of them. There is nothing but filth and vulgarity and Asiatic apathy. I fear and dislike very serious faces. I'm afraid of serious conversation. We should do better to be silent.

LOPAHIN: You know, I get up at five o'clock in the morning, and I work from morning to night; and I've money, my own and other people's, always passing through my hands, and I see what people are made of all round me. One has only to begin to do anything to see how few honest decent people there are. Sometimes when I lie awake at night, I think: "Oh! Lord, thou hast given us immense forests, boundless plains, the widest horizons, and living here we ourselves ought really to be giants."

LYUBOV: You ask for giants! They are no good except in story-books; in real life they frighten us.

[EPIHODOV *advances in the background, playing on the guitar.*]

LYUBOV [*dreamily*]: There goes Epihodov.

ANYA [*dreamily*]: There goes Epihodov.

GAEV: The sun has set, my friends.

TROFIMOV: Yes.

GAEV [*not loudly, but, as it were, declaiming*]: O nature, divine nature, thou art bright with eternal luster, beautiful and indifferent! Thou, whom we call mother, thou dost unite within thee life and death! Thou dost give life and dost destroy!

VARYA [*in a tone of supplication*]: Uncle!

ANYA: Uncle, you are at it again!

TROFIMOV: You'd much better be cannoning off the red!

GAEV: I'll hold my tongue, I will.

[*All sit plunged in thought. Perfect stillness. The only thing audible is the muttering of* FIRS. *Suddenly there is a sound in the distance, as it were from the sky—the sound of a breaking harp-string, mournfully dying away.*]

LYUBOV: What is that?

LOPAHIN: I don't know. Somewhere far away a bucket fallen and broken in the pits. But somewhere very far away.

GAEV: It might be a bird of some sort—such as a heron.

TROFIMOV: Or an owl.

LYUBOV [*shudders*]: I don't know why, but it's horrid.

[*A pause.*]

FIRS: It was the same before the calamity—the owl hooted and the samovar hissed all the time.

GAEV: Before what calamity?

FIRS: Before the emancipation.

[*A pause.*]

LYUBOV: Come, my friends, let us be going; evening is falling. [*To* ANYA.] There are tears in your eyes. What is it, darling? [*Embraces her.*]

ANYA: Nothing, mamma; it's nothing.

TROFIMOV: There is somebody coming.

[*The* WAYFARER *appears in a shabby white forage cap and an overcoat; he is slightly drunk.*]

WAYFARER: Allow me to inquire, can I get to the station this way?

GAEV: Yes. Go along that road.

WAYFARER: I thank you most feelingly. [*Coughing.*] The weather is superb. [*Declaims.*] My brother, my suffering brother! . . . Come out to the Volga! Whose groan do you hear? . . . [*To* VARYA.] Mademoiselle, vouchsafe a hungry Russian thirty kopecks.

[VARYA *utters a shriek of alarm.*]

LOPAHIN [*angrily*]: There's a right and a wrong way of doing everything!

LYUBOV [*hurriedly*]: Here, take this. [*Looks in her purse.*] I've no silver. No matter—here's gold for you.

WAYFARER: I thank you most feelingly! [*Goes off.*]

[*Laughter.*]

VARYA [*frightened*]: I'm going home—I'm going. . . . Oh, mamma, the servants have nothing to eat, and you gave him gold!

LYUBOV: There's no doing anything with me. I'm so silly! When we get home, I'll give you all I possess, Yermolay Alexeyevitch, you will lend me some more! . . .

LOPAHIN: I will.

LYUBOV: Come, friends, it's time to be going. And Varya, we have made a match of it for you. I congratulate you.

VARYA [*through her tears*]: Mamma, that's not a joking matter.

LOPAHIN: "Ophelia, get thee to a nunnery!"

GAEV: My hands are trembling; it's a long while since I had a game of billiards.

LOPAHIN: "Ophelia! Nymph, in thy orisons be all my sins remember'd."

LYUBOV: Come, it will soon be supper-time.

VARYA: How he frightened me! My heart's simply throbbing.

LOPAHIN: Let me remind you, ladies and gentlemen: on the 22nd of August the cherry orchard will be sold. Think about that! Think about it!

[*All go off, except* TROFIMOV *and* ANYA.]

ANYA [*laughing*]: I'm grateful to the wayfarer! He frightened Varya and we are left alone.

TROFIMOV: Varya's afraid we shall fall in love with each other, and for days together she won't leave us. With her narrow brain she can't grasp that we are above love. To eliminate the petty and transitory which hinder us from being free and happy—that is the aim and meaning of our life. Forward! We go forward irresistibly toward the bright

THE CHERRY ORCHARD 335

star that shines yonder in the distance. Forward! Do not lag behind, friends.

ANYA [*claps her hands*]: How well you speak! [*A pause.*] It is divine here today.

TROFIMOV: Yes, it's glorious weather.

ANYA: Somehow, Petya, you've made me so that I don't love the cherry orchard as I used to. I used to love it so dearly. I used to think that there was no spot on earth like our garden.

TROFIMOV: All Russia is our garden. The earth is great and beautiful—there are many beautiful places in it. [*A pause.*] Think only, Anya, your grandfather, and great-grandfather, and all your ancestors were slave-owners—the owners of living souls—and from every cherry in the orchard, from every leaf, from every trunk there are human creatures looking at you. Cannot you hear their voices? Oh, it is awful! Your orchard is a fearful thing, and when in the evening or at night one walks about the orchard, the old bark on the trees glimmers dimly in the dusk, and the old cherry trees seem to be dreaming of centuries gone by and tortured by fearful visions. Yes! We are at least two hundred years behind, we have really gained nothing yet, we have no definite attitude to the past, we do nothing but theorize or complain of depression or drink vodka. It is clear that to begin to live in the present, we must first expiate our past; we must break with it; and we can expiate it only by suffering, by extraordinary unceasing labor. Understand that, Anya.

ANYA: The house we live in has long ceased to be our own, and I shall leave it, I give you my word.

TROFIMOV: If you have the house keys, fling them into the well and go away. Be free as the wind.

ANYA [*in ecstasy*]: How beautifully you said that!

TROFIMOV: Believe me, Anya, believe me! I am not thirty yet. I am young. I am still a student, but I have gone through so much already! As soon as winter comes I am hungry, sick, careworn, poor as a beggar, and what ups and downs of fortune have I not known! And my soul was always, every minute, day and night, full of inexplicable forebodings. I have a foreboding of happiness, Anya. I see glimpses of it already.

ANYA [*pensively*]: The moon is rising.

[EPIHODOV *is heard playing still the same mournful song on the guitar. The moon rises. Somewhere near the poplars* VARYA *is looking for* ANYA *and calling* "Anya! where are you?"]

TROFIMOV: Yes, the moon is rising. [*A pause.*] Here is happiness—here it comes! It is coming nearer and nearer; already I can hear its footsteps. And if we never see it—if we may never know it—what does it matter? Others will see it after us.

VARYA'S VOICE: Anya! Where are you?

TROFIMOV: That Varya again! [*Angrily.*] It's revolting!

ANYA: Well, let's go down to the river. It's lovely there.

TROFIMOV: Yes, let's go.

[*They go.*]

VARYA'S VOICE: Anya! Anya!

CURTAIN

act 3

A drawing room divided by an arch from a larger drawing room. A chandelier burning. The Jewish orchestra, the same that was mentioned in Act 2, is heard playing in the anteroom. It is evening. In the larger drawing room they are dancing the grand chain. The voice of SEMYONOV-PISH-TCHIK: "Promenade à une paire!" *Then enter the drawing room in couples, first* PISHTCHIK *and* CHARLOTTA IVANOVNA, *then* TROFIMOV *and* LYUBOV ANDREYEVNA, *thirdly* ANYA *with the* POST-OFFICE CLERK, *fourthly* VARYA *with the* STATION MASTER, *and other guests.* VARYA *is quietly weeping and wiping away her tears as she dances. In the last couple is* DUNYASHA. *They move across the drawing room.* PISH-TCHIK *shouts:* "Grand rond, balancez!" *and* "Les Cavaliers à genou et remerciez vos dames."

FIRS *in a swallow-tail coat brings in seltzer water on a tray.* PISHTCHIK *and* TROFIMOV *enter the drawing room.*

PISHTCHIK: I am a full-blooded man; I have already had two strokes. Dancing's hard work for me, but as they say, if you're in the pack, you must bark with the rest. I'm as strong, I may say, as a horse. My parent, who would have his joke—may the Kingdom of Heaven be his!—used to say about our origin that the ancient stock of the Semyonov-Pishtchiks was derived from the very horse that Caligula made a member of the senate. [*Sits down.*] But I've no money, that's where the mischief is. A hungry dog believes in nothing but meat. [*Snores, but at once wakes up.*] That's like me ... I can think of nothing but money.

TROFIMOV: There really is something horsy about your appearance.

PISHTCHIK: Well ... a horse is a fine beast ... a horse can be sold.

[*There is the sound of billiards being played in an adjoining room.* VARYA *appears in the arch leading to the larger drawing room.*]

TROFIMOV [*teasing*]: Madame Lopahin! Madame Lopahin!

VARYA [*angrily*]: Mangy-looking gentleman!

TROFIMOV: Yes, I am a mangy-looking gentleman, and I'm proud of it!

VARYA [*pondering bitterly*]: Here we have hired musicians and nothing to pay them! [*Goes out.*]

TROFIMOV [*to* PISHTCHIK]: If the energy you have wasted

during your lifetime in trying to find the money to pay
your interest had gone to something else, you might in the
end have turned the world upside down.

PISHTCHIK: Nietzsche, the philosopher, a very great and
celebrated man ... of enormous intellect ... says in his
works, that one can make forged banknotes.

TROFIMOV: Why, have you read Nietzsche?

PISHTCHIK: What next ... Dashenka told me.... And
now I am in such a position, I might just as well forge
banknotes. The day after tomorrow I must pay 310 rubles
—130 I have procured. [*Feels in his pockets, in alarm.*]
The money's gone! I have lost my money! [*Through his
tears.*] Where's the money? [*Gleefully.*] Why, here it is behind the lining. ... It has made me hot all over.

[*Enter* LYUBOV ANDREYEVNA *and* CHARLOTTA IVA-
NOVNA.]

LYUBOV [*hums the Lezginka*]: Why is Leonid so long?
What can he be doing in town? [*To* DUNYASHA.] Offer the
musicians some tea. .

TROFIMOV: The sale hasn't taken place, most likely.

LYUBOV: It's the wrong time to have the orchestra, and
the wrong time to give a dance. Well, never mind. [*Sits
down and hums softly*]

CHARLOTTA [*gives* PISHTCHIK *a pack of cards*]: Here's a
pack of cards. Think of any card you like.

PISHTCHIK: I've thought of one.

CHARLOTTA: Shuffle the pack now. That's right. Give it
here, my dear Mr. Pishtchik. *Ein, zwei, drei*—now look,
it's in your breast pocket.

PISHTCHIK [*taking a card out of his breast pocket*]: The
eight of spades! Perfectly right! [*Wonderingly.*] Fancy that
now!

CHARLOTTA [*holding pack of cards in her hands, to* TROFI-
MOV]: Tell me quickly which is the top card.

TROFIMOV: Well, the queen of spades.

CHARLOTTA: It is! [*To* PISHTCHIK.] Well, which card is
uppermost?

PISHTCHIK: The ace of hearts.

CHARLOTTA: It is! [*Claps her hands, pack of cards disappears.*] Ah! what lovely weather it is today!

[*A mysterious feminine voice which seems coming out of the floor answers her.* "Oh, yes, it's magnificent weather, madam."

CHARLOTTA: You are my perfect ideal.

VOICE: And I greatly admire you too, madam.

STATION MASTER [*applauding*]: The lady ventriloquist— bravo!

PISHTCHIK [*wonderingly*]: Fancy that now! Most enchanting, Charlotta Ivanovna. I'm simply in love with you.

CHARLOTTA: In love? [*Shrugging shoulders.*] What do you know of love, *guter Mensch, aber schlechter Musikant*.

TROFIMOV [*pats* PISHTCHIK *on the shoulder*]: You dear old horse. . . .

CHARLOTTA: Attention, please! Another trick! [*Takes a traveling rug from a chair.*] Here's a very good rug; I want to sell it. [*Shaking it out.*] Doesn't anyone want to buy it?

PISHTCHIK [*wonderingly*]: Fancy that!

CHARLOTTA: *Ein, zwei, drei!*

[*Quickly picks up rug she has dropped; behind the rug stands* ANYA; *she makes a curtsey, runs to her mother, embraces her and runs back into the larger drawing room amidst general enthusiasm.*]

LYUBOV [*applauds*]: Bravo! Bravo!

CHARLOTTA: Now again; *Ein, zwei, drei!*

[*Lifts up the rug; behind the rug stands* VARYA, *bowing.*]

PISHTCHIK [*wonderingly*]: Fancy that now!

CHARLOTTA: That's the end. [*Throws the rug at* PISHTCHIK, *makes a curtsey, runs into the larger drawing room.*]

PISHTCHIK [*hurries after her*]: Mischievous creature! Fancy! [*Goes out.*]

LYUBOV: And still Leonid doesn't come. I can't understand what he's doing in the town so long! Why, everything must be over by now. The estate is sold, or the sale has not taken place. Why keep us so long in suspense?

VARYA [*trying to console her*]: Uncle's bought it. I feel sure of that.

TROFIMOV [*ironically*]: Oh, yes!

VARYA: Great-aunt sent him an authorization to buy it in her name, and transfer the debt. She's doing it for Anya's sake, and I'm sure God will be merciful. Uncle will buy it.

LYUBOV: My aunt in Yaroslavl sent fifteen thousand to buy the estate in her name, she doesn't trust us—but that's not enough even to pay the arrears. [*Hides her face in her hands.*] My fate is being sealed today, my fate. . . .

TROFIMOV [*teasing* VARYA]: Madame Lopahin.

VARYA [*angrily*]: Perpetual student! Twice already you've been sent down from the University.

LYUBOV: Why are you angry, Varya? He's teasing you about Lopahin. Well, what of that? Marry Lopahin if you like, he's a good man, and interesting; if you don't want to, don't! Nobody compels you, darling.

VARYA: I must tell you plainly, mamma, I look at the matter seriously; he's a good man, I like him.

LYUBOV: Well, marry him. I can't see what you're waiting for.

VARYA: Mamma. I can't make him an offer myself. For the last two years, everyone's been talking to me about him. Everyone talks; but he says nothing or else makes a joke. I see what it means. He's growing rich, he's absorbed in business, he has no thoughts for me. If I had money, were it ever so little, if I had only a hundred rubles, I'd throw everything up and go far away. I would go into a nunnery.

TROFIMOV: What bliss!

VARYA [*to* TROFIMOV]: A student ought to have sense! [*In a soft tone with tears.*] How ugly you've grown, Petya! How old you look! [*To* LYUBOV ANDREYEVNA, *no longer crying.*] But I can't do without work, mamma; I must have something to do every minute.

[*Enter* YASHA.]

YASHA [*hardly restraining his laughter*]: Epihodov has broken a billiard cue! [*Goes out.*]

VARYA: What is Epihodov doing here? Who gave him leave to play billiards? I can't make these people out. [*Goes out.*]

LYUBOV: Don't tease her, Petya. You see she has grief enough without that.

TROFIMOV: She is so very officious, meddling in what's not her business. All the summer she's given Anya and me no peace. She's afraid of a love affair between us. What's it to do with her? Besides, I have given no grounds for it. Such triviality is not in my line. We are above love!

LYUBOV: And I suppose I am beneath love. [*Very uneasily.*] Why is it Leonid's not here? If only I could know whether the estate is sold or not! It seems such an incredible calamity that I really don't know what to think. I am distracted.... I shall scream in a minute ... I shall do something stupid. Save me, Petya, tell me something, talk to me!

TROFIMOV: What does it matter whether the estate is sold today or not? That's all done with long ago. There's no turning back, the path is overgrown. Don't worry yourself, dear Lyubov Andreyevna. You mustn't deceive yourself; for once in your life you must face the truth!

LYUBOV: What truth? You see where the truth lies, but I seem to have lost my sight, I see nothing. You settle every great problem so boldly, but tell me, my dear boy, isn't it because you're young—because you haven't yet understood one of your problems through suffering? You look forward boldly, and isn't it that you don't see and don't expect anything dreadful because life is still hidden from your young eyes? You're bolder, more honest, deeper than we are, but think, be just a little magnanimous, have pity on me. I was born here, you know, my father and mother lived here, my grandfather lived here, I love this house. I can't conceive of life without the cherry orchard, and if it really must be sold, then sell me with the orchard. [*Embraces* TROFIMOV, *kisses him on the forehead.*] My boy was drowned here. [*Weeps.*] Pity me, my dear kind fellow.

TROFIMOV: You know I feel for you with all my heart.

LYUBOV: But that should have been said differently, so differently. [*Takes out her handkerchief, telegram falls on the floor.*] My heart is so heavy today. It's so noisy here, my soul is quivering at every sound, I'm shuddering all over, but I can't go away; I'm afraid to be quiet and alone. Don't be hard on me, Petya . . . I love you as though you were one of ourselves. I would gladly let you marry Anya— I swear I would—only, my dear boy, you must take your degree, you do nothing—you're simply tossed by fate from place to place. That's so strange. It is, isn't it? And you must do something with your beard to make it grow somehow. [*Laughs.*] You look so funny!

TROFIMOV [*picks up the telegram*]: I've no wish to be a beauty.

LYUBOV: That's a telegram from Paris. I get one every day. One yesterday and one today. That savage creature is ill again, he's in trouble again. He begs forgiveness, beseeches me to go, and really I ought to go to Paris to see him. You look shocked, Petya. What am I to do, my dear boy, what am I to do? He is ill, he is alone and unhappy, and who'll look after him, who'll keep him from doing the wrong thing, who'll give him his medicine at the right time? And why hide it or be silent? I love him, that's clear. I love him! I love him! He's a millstone about my neck, I'm going to the bottom with him, but I love that stone and can't live without it. [*Presses* TROFIMOV's *hand.*] Don't think ill of me, Petya, don't tell me anything, don't tell me. . . .

TROFIMOV [*through his tears*]: For God's sake forgive my frankness: why, he robbed you!

LYUBOV: No! No! No! You mustn't speak like that. [*Covers her ears.*]

TROFIMOV: He is a wretch! You're the only person that doesn't know it! He's a worthless creature! A despicable wretch!

LYUBOV [*getting angry, but speaking with restraint*]: You're twenty-six or twenty-seven years old, but you're still a schoolboy.

TROFIMOV: Possibly.

LYUBOV: You should be a man at your age! You should understand what love means! And you ought to be in love yourself. You ought to fall in love! [*Angrily.*] Yes, yes, and it's not purity in you, you're simply a prude, a comic fool, a freak.

TROFIMOV [*in horror*]: The things she's saying!

LYUBOV: I am above love! You're not above love, but simply as our Firs here says, "You are a good-for-nothing." At your age not to have a mistress!

TROFIMOV [*in horror*]: This is awful! The things she is saying! [*Goes rapidly into the larger drawing room clutching his head.*] This is awful! I can't stand it! I'm going. [*Goes off, but at once returns.*] All is over between us! [*Goes off into the anteroom.*]

LYUBOV [*shouts after him*]: Petya! Wait a minute! You funny creature! I was joking! Petya!

[*There is a sound of somebody running quickly downstairs and suddenly falling with a crash.* ANYA *and* VARYA *scream, but there is a sound of laughter at once.*]

LYUBOV: What has happened?

[ANYA *runs in.*]

ANYA [*laughing*]: Petya's fallen downstairs! [*Runs out.*]

LYUBOV: What a queer fellow that Petya is!

[*The* STATION MASTER *stands in the middle of the larger room and reads* The Magdalene, *by Alexey Tolstoy. They listen to him, but before he has recited many lines strains of a waltz are heard from the anteroom and the reading is broken off. All dance.* TROFIMOV, ANYA, VARYA *and* LYUBOV ANDREYEVNA *come in from the anteroom.*]

LYUBOV: Come, Petya—come, pure heart! I beg your pardon. Let's have a dance!

[*Dances with* PETYA. ANYA *and* VARYA *dance.* FIRS *comes in, puts his stick down near the side door.* YASHA *also comes into the drawing room and looks on at the dancing.*]

YASHA: What is it, old man?

FIRS: I don't feel well. In old days we used to have generals, barons and admirals dancing at our balls, and now we send for the post-office clerk and the station master and even they're not overanxious to come. I am getting feeble. The old master, the grandfather, used to give sealing-wax for all complaints. I have been taking sealing-wax for twenty years or more. Perhaps that's what's kept me alive.

YASHA: You bore me, old man! [*Yawns.*] It's time you were done with.

FIRS: Ach, you're a good-for-nothing! [*Mutters.*]

[TROFIMOV *and* LYUBOV ANDREYEVNA *dance in larger room and then on to the stage.*]

LYUBOV: *Merci.* I'll sit down a little. [*Sits down.*] I'm tired.

[*Enter* ANYA.]

ANYA [*excitedly*]: There's a man in the kitchen has been saying that the cherry orchard's been sold today.

LYUBOV: Sold to whom?

ANYA: He didn't say to whom. He's gone away.

[*She dances with* TROFIMOV, *and they go off into the larger room.*]

YASHA: There was an old man gossiping there, a stranger.

FIRS: Leonid Andreyevitch isn't here yet, he hasn't come back. He has his light overcoat on, *demi-saison,* he'll catch cold for sure. *Ach!* Foolish young things!

LYUBOV: I feel as though I should die. Go, Yasha, find out to whom it has been sold.

YASHA: But he went away long ago, the old chap. [*Laughs.*]

LYUBOV [*with slight vexation*]: What are you laughing at? What are you pleased at?

YASHA: Epihodov is so funny. He's a silly fellow, two and twenty misfortunes.

LYUBOV: Firs, if the estate is sold, where will you go?

FIRS: Where you bid me, there I'll go.

LYUBOV: Why do you look like that? Are you ill? You ought to be in bed.

FIRS: Yes. [*Ironically*.] Me go to bed and who's to wait here? Who's to see to things without me? I'm the only one in all the house.

YASHA [*to* LYUBOV ANDREYEVNA]: Lyubov Andreyevna, permit me to make a request of you; if you go back to Paris again, be so kind as to take me with you. It's positively impossible for me to stay here. [*Looking about him; in an undertone*.] There's no need to say it, you see for yourself—an uncivilized country, the people have no morals, and then the dullness! The food in the kitchen's abominable, and then Firs runs after one muttering all sorts of unsuitable words. Take me with you, please do!

[*Enter* PISHTCHIK.]

PISHTCHIK: Allow me to ask you for a waltz, my dear lady. [LYUBOV ANDREYEVNA *goes with him*.] Enchanting lady, I really must borrow of you just 180 rubles, [*dances*] only 180 rubles.

[*They pass into the larger room. In the larger drawing room, a figure in a gray top hat and in checked trousers is gesticulating and jumping about. Shouts of* "Bravo, Charlotta Ivanovna."]

DUNYASHA [*she has stopped to powder herself*]: My young lady tells me to dance. There are plenty of gentlemen, and too few ladies, but dancing makes me giddy and makes my heart beat. Firs, the post-office clerk said something to me just now that quite took my breath away.

[*Music becomes more subdued.*]

FIRS: What did he say to you?

DUNYASHA: He said I was like a flower.

YASHA [*yawns*]: What ignorance! [*Goes out.*]

DUNYASHA: Like a flower. I am a girl of such delicate feelings, I am awfully fond of soft speeches.

FIRS: Your head's being turned.

[*Enter* EPIHODOV.]

EPIHODOV: You have no desire to see me, Dunyasha. I might be an insect. [*Sighs.*] Ah! life!

DUNYASHA: What is it you want?

EPIHODOV: Undoubtedly you may be right. [*Sighs.*] But, of course, if one looks at it from that point of view, if I may so express myself, you have, excuse my plain speaking, reduced me to a complete state of mind. I know my destiny. Every day some misfortune befalls me and I have long ago grown accustomed to it, so that I look upon my fate with a smile. You gave me your word, and though I—

DUNYASHA: Let us have a talk later, I entreat you, but now leave me in peace, for I am lost in reverie. [*Plays with her fan.*]

EPIHODOV: I have a misfortune every day, and if I may venture to express myself, I merely smile at it, I even laugh.

[VARYA *enters from the larger drawing room.*]

VARYA: You still have not gone, Epihodov. What a disrespectful creature you are, really! [*To* DUNYASHA.] Go along, Dunyasha! [*To* EPIHODOV.] First you play billiards and break the cue, then you go wandering about the drawing room like a visitor!

EPIHODOV: You really cannot, if I may so express myself, call me to account like this.

VARYA: I'm not calling you to account, I'm speaking to you. You do nothing but wander from place to place and don't do your work. We keep you as a counting-house clerk, but what use you are I can't say.

EPIHODOV [*offended*]: Whether I work or whether I walk, whether I eat or whether I play billiards, is a matter to be judged by persons of understanding and my elders.

VARYA: You dare to tell me that! [*Firing up.*] You dare! You mean to say I've no understanding. Begone from here! This minute!

EPIHODOV [*intimidated*]: I beg you to express yourself with delicacy.

VARYA [*beside herself with anger*]: This moment! get out! away! [*He goes toward the door, she following him.*] Two and twenty misfortunes! Take yourself off! Don't let me set eyes on you! [EPIHODOV *has gone out, behind the door his voice,* "I shall lodge a complaint against you."] What!

You're coming back? [*Snatches up the stick* FIRS *has put down near the door.*] Come! Come! Come! I'll show you! What! you're coming? Then take that! [*She swings the stick, at the very moment that* LOPAHIN *comes in.*]

LOPAHIN: Very much obliged to you!

VARYA [*angrily and ironically*]: I beg your pardon!

LOPAHIN: Not at all! I humbly thank you for your kind reception!

VARYA: No need of thanks for it. [*Moves away, then looks round and asks softly.*] I haven't hurt you?

LOPAHIN: Oh, no! Not at all! There's an immense bump coming up, though!

VOICES FROM LARGER ROOM: Lopahin has come! Yermolay Alexeyevitch!

PISHTCHIK: What do I see and hear? [*Kisses* LOPAHIN.] There's a whiff of cognac about you, my dear soul, and we're making merry here too!

[*Enter* LYUBOV ANDREYEVNA.]

LYUBOV: Is it you, Yermolay Alexeyevitch? Why have you been so long? Where's Leonid?

LOPAHIN: Leonid Andreyevitch arrived with me. He is coming.

LYUBOV [*in agitation*]: Well! Well! Was there a sale? Speak!

LOPAHIN [*embarrassed, afraid of betraying his joy*]: The sale was over at four o'clock. We missed our train—had to wait till half-past nine. [*Sighing heavily.*] Ugh! I feel a little giddy.

[*Enter* GAEV. *In his right hand he has purchases, with his left hand he is wiping away his tears.*]

LYUBOV: Well, Leonid? What news? [*Impatiently, with tears.*] Make haste, for God's sake!

GAEV [*makes her no answer, simply waves his hand. To* FIRS, *weeping*]: Here, take them; there's anchovies, Kertch herrings. I have eaten nothing all day. What I have been through! [*Door into the billiard room is open. There is heard a knocking of balls and the voice of* YASHA *saying*

"Eighty-seven." GAEV'S *expression changes, he leaves off weeping.*] I am fearfully tired. Firs, come and help me change my things. [*Goes to his own room across the larger drawing room.*]

PISHTCHIK: How about the sale? Tell us, do!

LYUBOV: Is the cherry orchard sold?

LOPAHIN: It is sold.

LYUBOV: Who has bought it?

LOPAHIN: I have bought it.

[*A pause.* LYUBOV *is crushed; she would fall down if she were not standing near a chair and table.* VARYA *takes keys from her waistband, flings them on the floor in middle of drawing room and goes out.*]

LOPAHIN: I have bought it! Wait a bit, ladies and gentlemen, pray. My head's a bit muddled, I can't speak. [*Laughs.*] We came to the auction. Deriganov was there already. Leonid Andreyevitch only had 15,000 and Deriganov bid 30,000, besides the arrears, straight off. I saw how the land lay. I bid against him. I bid 40,000, he bid 45,000, I said 55, and so he went on, adding 5 thousands and I adding 10. Well ... So it ended. I bid 90, and it was knocked down to me. Now the cherry orchard's mine! Mine! [*Chuckles.*] My God, the cherry orchard's mine! Tell me that I'm drunk, that I'm out of my mind, that it's all a dream. [*Stamps with his feet.*] Don't laugh at me! If my father and my grandfather could rise from their graves and see all that has happened! How their Yermolay, ignorant, beaten Yermolay, who used to run about barefoot in winter, how that very Yermolay has bought the finest estate in the world! I have bought the estate where my father and grandfather were slaves, where they weren't even admitted into the kitchen. I am asleep, I am dreaming! It is all fancy, it is the work of your imagination plunged in the darkness of ignorance. [*Picks up keys, smiling fondly.*] She threw away the keys; she means to show she's not the housewife now. [*Jingles the keys.*] Well, no matter. [*The orchestra is heard tuning up.*] Hey, musicians! Play! I want to hear you. Come, all of you, and look how Yermolay Lopahin will take the ax to the cherry orchard, how the trees will fall to the ground! We will build houses on it and our grandsons and great-grandsons will see a new life springing up there. Music! Play up!

[*Music begins to play.* LYUBOV ANDREYEVNA *has sunk into a chair and is weeping bitterly.*]

LOPAHIN [*reproachfully*]: Why, why didn't you listen to me? My poor friend! Dear lady, there's no turning back now. [*With tears.*] Oh, if all this could be over, oh, if our miserable disjointed life could somehow soon be changed!

PISHTCHIK [*takes him by the arm, in an undertone*]: She's weeping, let us go and leave her alone. Come. [*Takes him by the arm and leads him into the larger drawing room.*]

LOPAHIN: What's that? Musicians, play up! All must be as I wish it. [*With irony.*] Here comes the new master, the owner of the cherry orchard! [*Accidentally tips over a little table, almost upsetting the candelabra.*] I can pay for everything!

[*Goes out with* PISHTCHIK. *No one remains on the stage or in the larger drawing room except* LYUBOV, *who sits huddled up, weeping bitterly. The music plays softly.* ANYA *and* TROFIMOV *come in quickly.* ANYA *goes up to her mother and falls on her knees before her.* TROFIMOV *stands at the entrance to the larger drawing room.*]

ANYA: Mamma! Mamma, you're crying, dear, kind, good mamma! My precious! I love you! I bless you! The cherry orchard is sold, it is gone, that's true, that's true! But don't weep, mamma! Life is still before you, you have still your good, pure heart! Let us go, let us go, darling, away from here! We will make a new garden, more splendid than this one; you will see it, you will understand. And joy, quiet, deep joy, will sink into your soul like the sun at evening! And you will smile, mamma! Come, darling, let us go!

CURTAIN

act 4

Scene: Same as in First Act. There are neither curtains on the windows nor pictures on the walls: only a little furniture remains piled up in a corner as if for sale. There is a sense of desolation; near the outer door and in the background of the scene are packed trunks, traveling bags, etc. On the left the door is open, and from here the voices of VARYA *and* ANYA *are audible.* LOPAHIN *is standing waiting.* YASHA *is holding a tray with glasses full of champagne. In front of the stage* EPIHODOV *is tying up a box. In the background behind the scene a hum of talk from the peasants who have come to say good-by. The voice of* GAEV: *"Thanks, brothers, thanks!"*

YASHA: The peasants have come to say good-by. In my opinion, Yermolay Alexeyevitch, the peasants are good-natured, but they don't know much about things.

[*The hum of talk dies away. Enter across front of stage.* LYUBOV ANDREYEVNA *and* GAEV. *She is not weeping, but is pale; her face is quivering—she cannot speak.*]

GAEV: You gave them your purse, Lyuba. That won't do —that won't do!

LYUBOV: I couldn't help it! I couldn't help it!

[*Both go out.*]

LOPAHIN [*in the doorway, calls after them*]: You will take a glass at parting? Please do. I didn't think to bring any from the town, and at the station I could only get one bottle. Please take a glass. [*A pause.*] What? You don't care for any? [*Comes away from the door.*] If I'd known, I wouldn't have bought it. Well, and I'm not going to drink it. [YASHA *carefully sets the tray down on a chair.*] You have a glass, Yasha, anyway.

YASHA: Good luck to the travelers, and luck to those that stay behind! [*Drinks.*] This champagne isn't the real thing, I can assure you.

LOPAHIN: It cost eight rubles the bottle. [*A pause.*] It's devilish cold here.

YASHA: They haven't heated the stove today—it's all the same since we're going. [*Laughs.*]

LOPAHIN: What are you laughing for?

YASHA: For pleasure.

LOPAHIN: Though it's October, it's as still and sunny as though it were summer. It's just right for building! [*Looks at his watch; says in doorway.*] Take note, ladies and gentlemen, the train goes in forty-seven minutes; so you ought to start for the station in twenty minutes. You must hurry up!

[TROFIMOV *comes in from out of doors wearing a greatcoat.*]

TROFIMOV: I think it must be time to start, the horses are ready. The devil only knows what's become of my goloshes; they're lost. [*In the doorway.*] Anya! My goloshes aren't here. I can't find them.

LOPAHIN: And I'm getting off to Harkov. I am going in the same train with you. I'm spending all the winter at Harkov. I've been wasting all my time gossiping with you and fretting with no work to do. I can't get on without work. I don't know what to do with my hands, they flap about so queerly, as if they didn't belong to me.

TROFIMOV: Well, we're just going away, and you will take up your profitable labors again.

LOPAHIN: Do take a glass.

TROFIMOV: No, thanks.

LOPAHIN: Then you're going to Moscow now?

TROFIMOV: Yes. I shall see them as far as the town, and tomorrow I shall go on to Moscow.

LOPAHIN: Yes, I daresay, the professors aren't giving any lectures, they're waiting for your arrival.

TROFIMOV: That's not your business.

LOPAHIN: How many years have you been at the University?

TROFIMOV: Do think of something newer than that—that's stale and flat. [*Hunts for goloshes.*] You know we shall most likely never see each other again, so let me give you one piece of advice at parting: don't wave your arms about —get out of the habit. And another thing, building villas, reckoning up that the summer visitors will in time become independent farmers—reckoning like that, that's not the thing to do either. After all, I am fond of you: you have fine delicate fingers like an artist, you've a fine delicate soul.

LOPAHIN [*embraces him.*] Good-by, my dear fellow. Thanks for everything. Let me give you money for the journey, if you need it.

TROFIMOV: What for? I don't need it.

LOPAHIN: Why, you haven't got a half-penny.

TROFIMOV: Yes, I have, thank you. I got some money for a translation. Here it is in my pocket, [*anxiously*] but where can my goloshes be!

VARYA [*from the next room*]: Take the nasty things! [*Flings a pair of goloshes on to the stage.*]

TROFIMOV: Why are you so cross, Varya? h'm! . . . but those aren't my goloshes.

LOPAHIN: I sowed three thousand acres with poppies in the spring, and now I have cleared forty thousand profit. And when my poppies were in flower, wasn't it a picture! So here, as I say, I made forty thousand, and I'm offering you a loan because I can afford to. Why turn up your nose? I am a peasant—I speak bluntly.

TROFIMOV: Your father was a peasant, mine was a chemist—and that proves absolutely nothing whatever. [LOPAHIN *takes out his pocket-book.*] Stop that—stop that. If you were to offer me two hundred thousand I wouldn't take it. I am an independent man, and everything that all of you, rich and poor alike, prize so highly and hold so dear, hasn't the slightest power over me—it's like so much fluff fluttering in the air. I can get on without you. I can pass by you. I am strong and proud. Humanity is advancing toward the highest truth, the highest happiness which is possible on earth, and I am in the front ranks.

LOPAHIN: Will you get there?

TROFIMOV: I shall get there. [*A pause.*] I shall get there, or I shall show others the way to get there.

[*In the distance is heard the strike of an ax on a tree.*]

LOPAHIN: Good-by, my dear fellow; it's time to be off. We turn up our noses at one another, but life is passing all the while. When I am working hard without resting, then my mind is more at ease, and it seems to me as though I too know what I exist for; but how many people are in Russia, my dear boy, who exist, one doesn't know what for. Well, it doesn't matter. That's not what keeps things spinning. They tell me Leonid Andreyevitch has taken a situation. He is going to be a clerk at the bank—6,000 rubles a year. Only, of course, he won't stick to it—he's too lazy.

ANYA [*in the doorway*]: Mamma begs you not to let them chop down the orchard until she's gone.

TROFIMOV: Yes, really, you might have the tact. [*Walks out across the front of the stage.*]

LOPAHIN: I'll see to it! I'll see to it! Stupid fellows! [*Goes out after him.*]

ANYA: Has Firs been taken to the hospital?

YASHA: I told them this morning. No doubt they have taken him.

ANYA [*to EPIHODOV, who passes across the drawing room*]: Semyon Pantaleyevitch, inquire, please, if Firs has been taken to the hospital.

YASHA [*in a tone of offense*]: I told Yegor this morning— why ask a dozen times?

EPIHODOV: Firs is advanced in years. It's my conclusive opinion no treatment would do him good; it's time he was gathered to his fathers. And I can only envy him. [*Puts a trunk down on a cardboard hat-box and crushes it.*] There, now, of course—I knew it would be so.

YASHA [*jeeringly*]: Two and twenty misfortunes!

VARYA [*through the door*]: Has Firs been taken to the hospital?

ANYA: Yes.

VARYA: Why wasn't the note for the doctor taken too?

ANYA: Oh, then, we must send it after them. [*Goes out.*]

VARYA [*from the adjoining room*]: Where's Yasha? Tell him his mother's come to say good-by to him.

YASHA [*waves his hand*]: They put me out of all patience! [DUNYASHA *has all this time been busy about the luggage. Now, when* YASHA *is left alone, she goes up to him.*]

DUNYASHA: You might just give me one look, Yasha. You're going away. You're leaving me. [*Weeps and throws herself on his neck.*]

YASHA: What are you crying for? [*Drinks the champagne.*] In six days I shall be in Paris again. Tomorrow we shall get into the express train and roll away in a flash. I can scarcely believe it! *Vive la France!* It doesn't suit me here—it's not the life for me; there's no doing anything. I have seen enough of the ignorance here. I have had enough of it. [*Drinks champagne.*] What are you crying for? Behave yourself properly, and then you won't cry.

DUNYASHA [*powders her face, looking in a pocket-mirror*]: Do send me a letter from Paris. You know how I loved you, Yasha—how I loved you! I am a tender creature, Yasha.

YASHA: Here, they are coming!

[*Busies himself about the trunks, humming softly. Enter* LYUBOV ANDREYEVNA, GAEV, ANYA *and* CHARLOTTA IVANOVNA.]

GAEV: We ought to be off. There's not much time now. [*Looking at* YASHA.] What a smell of herrings!

LYUBOV: In ten minutes we must get into the carriage. [*Casts a look about the room.*] Farewell, dear house, dear old home of our fathers! Winter will pass and spring will come, and then you will be no more; they will tear you down! How much those walls have seen! [*Kisses her daughter passionately.*] My treasure, how bright you look! Your eyes are sparkling like diamonds! Are you glad? Very glad?

ANYA: Very glad! A new life is beginning, mamma!

GAEV: Yes, really, everything is all right now. Before the cherry orchard was sold, we were all worried and wretched, but afterward, when once the question was settled conclusively, irrevocably, we all felt calm and even cheerful. I am a bank clerk now—I am a financier—cannon off the red. And you, Lyuba, after all, you are looking better; there's no question of that.

LYUBOV: Yes. My nerves are better, that's true. [*Her hat and coat are handed to her.*] I'm sleeping well. Carry out my things, Yasha. It's time. [*To* ANYA.] My darling, we shall soon see each other again. I am going to Paris. I can live there on the money your Yaroslavl auntie sent us to buy the estate with—hurrah for auntie!—but that money won't last long.

ANYA: You'll come back soon, mamma, won't you? I'll be working up for my examination in the high school, and when I have passed that, I shall set to work and be a help to you. We will read all sorts of things together, mamma, won't we? [*Kisses her mother's hands.*] We will read in the autumn evenings. We'll read lots of books, and a new wonderful world will open out before us. [*Dreamily.*] Mamma, come soon.

LYUBOV: I shall come, my precious treasure.

[*Embraces her. Enter* LOPAHIN. CHARLOTTA *softly hums a song.*]

GAEV: Charlotta's happy; she's singing!

CHARLOTTA [*picks up a bundle like a swaddled baby*]: By, by, my baby. [*A baby is heard crying:* "Ooah! ooah!"] Hush, hush, my pretty boy! ["Ooah! ooah!"] Poor little thing! [*Throws the bundle back.*] You must please find me a situation. I can't go on like this.

LOPAHIN: We'll find you one, Charlotta Ivanovna. Don't worry yourself.

GAEV: Everyone's leaving us. Varya's going away. We have become of no use all at once.

CHARLOTTA: There's nowhere for me to be in the town. I must go away. [*Hums.*] What care I . . .

[*Enter* PISHTCHIK.]

LOPAHIN: The freak of nature.

PISHTCHIK [*gasping*]: Oh . . . Let me get my breath. . . . I'm worn out . . . my most honored . . . Give me some water.

GAEV: Want some money, I suppose? Your humble servant! I'll go out of the way of temptation. [*Goes out.*]

PISHTCHIK: It's a long while since I have been to see you . . . dearest lady. [*To* LOPAHIN.] You are here . . . glad to see you . . . a man of immense intellect . . . take . . . here. [*Gives to* LOPAHIN.] 400 rubles. That leaves me owing 840.

LOPAHIN [*shrugging his shoulders in amazement*]: It's like a dream. Where did you get it?

PISHTCHIK: Wait a bit . . . I'm hot . . . a most extraordinary occurrence! Some Englishmen came along and found in my land some sort of white clay. [*To* LYUBOV ANDREYEVNA.] And 400 for you . . . most lovely . . . wonderful. [*Gives money.*] The rest later. [*Sips water.*] A young man in the train was telling me just now that a great philosopher advises jumping off a house-top. "Jump!" says he; "the whole gist of the problem lies in that." [*Wonderingly.*] Fancy that, now! Water, please!

LOPAHIN: What Englishmen?

PISHTCHIK: I have made over to them the rights to dig the clay for twenty-four years . . . and now, excuse me . . . I can't stay . . . I must be trotting on. I'm going to Znoikovo . . . to Kardamanovo. . . . I'm in debt all round. [*Sips.*] . . . To your very good health! . . . I'll come in on Thursday.

LYUBOV: We are just off to the town, and tomorrow I start for abroad.

PISHTCHIK: What! [*In agitation.*] Why to the town? Oh, I see the furniture . . . the boxes. No matter . . . [*Through his tears.*] . . . no matter . . . men of enormous intellect . . . these Englishmen. . . . Never mind . . . be happy. God will succor you . . . no matter . . . everything in this world must have an end. [*Kisses* LYUBOV ANDREYEVNA's *hand.*] If the

rumor reaches you that my end has come, think of this ...
old horse, and say: "There once was such a man in the
world ... Semyonov-Pishtchik ... the Kingdom of Heaven
be his!" ... most extraordinary weather ... yes. [*Goes out
in violent agitation, but at once returns and says in the doorway.*] Dashenka wishes to be remembered to you. [*Goes
out.*]

LYUBOV:Now we can start. I leave with two cares in my
heart. The first is leaving Firs ill. [*Looking at her watch.*]
We have still five minutes.

ANYA: Mamma, Firs has been taken to the hospital.
Yasha sent him off this morning.

LYUBOV: My other anxiety is Varya. She is used to getting
up early and working; and now, without work, she's like a
fish out of water. She is thin and pale, and she's crying,
poor dear! [*A pause.*] You are well aware, Yermolay Alexeyevitch, I dreamed of marrying her to you, and everything
seemed to show that you would get married. [*Whispers to
ANYA and motions to CHARLOTTA and both go out.*] She loves
you—she suits you. And I don't know—I don't know why
it is you seem, as it were, to avoid each other. I can't understand it!

LOPAHIN: I don't understand it myself, I confess. It's
queer somehow, altogether. If there's still time, I'm ready
now at once. Let's settle it straight off, and go ahead; but
without you, I feel I shan't make her an offer.

LYUBOV: That's excellent. Why, a single moment's all
that's necessary. I'll call her at once.

LOPAHIN: And there's champagne all ready too. [*Looking into the glasses.*] Empty! Someone's emptied them already. [YASHA *coughs.*] I call that greedy.

LYUBOV [*eagerly*]: Capital! We will go out. Yasha, *allez!*
I'll call her in. [*At the door.*] Varya, leave all that; come
here. Come along! [*Goes out with* YASHA.]

LOPAHIN [*looking at his watch*]: Yes.

[*A pause. Behind the door, smothered laughter and
whispering, and, at last, enter* VARYA.]

VARYA [*looking a long while over the things*]: It is strange, I can't find it anywhere.

LOPAHIN: What are you looking for?

VARYA: I packed it myself, and I can't remember.

[*A pause.*]

LOPAHIN: Where are you going now, Varvara Mihaïlova?

VARYA: I? To the Ragulins. I have arranged to go to them to look after the house—as a housekeeper.

LOPAHIN: That's in Yashnovo? It'll be seventy miles away. [*A pause.*] So this is the end of life in this house!

VARYA [*looking among the things*]: Where is it? Perhaps I put it in the trunk. Yes, life in this house is over—there will be no more of it.

LOPAHIN: And I'm just off to Harkov—by this next train. I've a lot of business there. I'm leaving Epihodov here, and I've taken him on.

VARYA: Really!

LOPAHIN: This time last year we had snow already, if you remember; but now it's so fine and sunny. Though it's cold, to be sure—three degrees of frost.

VARYA: I haven't looked. [*A pause.*] And besides, our thermometer's broken.

[*A pause. Voice at the door from the yard:* "Yermolay Alexeyevitch!"]

LOPAHIN [*as though he had long been expecting this summons*]: This minute!

[LOPAHIN *goes out quickly.* VARYA *sitting on the floor and laying her head on a bag full of clothes, sobs quietly. The door opens,* LYUBOV ANDREYEVNA *comes in cautiously.*]

LYUBOV: Well? [*A pause.*] We must be going.

VARYA [*has wiped her eyes and is no longer crying*]: Yes, mamma, it's time to start. I shall have time to get to the Ragulins today, if only you're not late for the train.

LYUBOV [*in the doorway*]: Anya, put your things on.

[*Enter* ANYA, *then* GAEV *and* CHARLOTTA IVANOVNA. GAEV *has on a warm coat with a hood. Servants and cabmen come in.* EPIHODOV *bustles about the luggage.*]

LYUBOV: Now we can start on our travels.

ANYA [*joyfully*]: On our travels!

GAEV: My friends—my dear, my precious friends! Leaving this house forever, can I be silent? Can I refrain from giving utterance at leave-taking to those emotions which now flood all my being?

ANYA [*supplicatingly*]: Uncle!

VARYA: Uncle, you mustn't!

GAEV [*dejectedly*]: Cannon and into the pocket... I'll be quiet...

[*Enter* TROFIMOV *and afterward* LOPAHIN.]

TROFIMOV: Well, ladies and gentlemen, we must start.

LOPAHIN: Epihodov, my coat!

LYUBOV: I'll stay just one minute. It seems as though I have never seen before what the walls, what the ceilings in this house were like, and now I look at them with greediness, with such tender love.

GAEV: I remember when I was six years old sitting in that window on Trinity Day watching my father going to church.

LYUBOV: Have all the things been taken?

LOPAHIN: I think all. [*Putting on overcoat, to* EPIHODOV.] You, Epihodov, mind you see everything is right.

EPIHODOV [*in a husky voice*]: Don't you trouble, Yermolay Alexeyevitch.

LOPAHIN: Why, what's wrong with your voice?

EPIHODOV: I've just had a drink of water, and I choked over something.

YASHA [*contemptuously*]: The ignorance!

LYUBOV: We are going—and not a soul will be left here.

LOPAHIN: Not till the spring.

VARYA [*pulls a parasol out of a bundle, as though about to hit someone with it.* LOPAHIN *makes a gesture as though alarmed*]: What is it? I didn't mean anything.

TROFIMOV: Ladies and gentlemen, let us get into the carriage. It's time. The train will be in directly.

VARYA: Petya, here they are, your goloshes, by that box. [*With tears.*] And what dirty old things they are!

TROFIMOV [*putting on his goloshes*]: Let us go, friends!

GAEV [*greatly agitated, afraid of weeping*]: The train—the station! Double balk, ah!

LYUBOV: Let us go!

LOPAHIN: Are we all here? [*Locks the side door on left.*] The things are all here. We must lock up. Let us go!

ANYA: Good-by, home! Good-by to the old life!

TROFIMOV: Welcome to the new life!

[TROFIMOV *goes out with* ANYA. VARYA *looks round the room and goes out slowly.* YASHA *and* CHARLOTTA IVANOVNA, *with her dog, go out.*]

LOPAHIN: Till the spring, then! Come, friends, till we meet! [*Goes out.*]

[LYUBOV ANDREYEVNA *and* GAEV *remain alone. As though they had been waiting for this, they throw themselves on each other's necks, and break into subdued smothered sobbing, afraid of being overheard.*]

GAEV [*in despair*]: Sister, my sister!

LYUBOV: Oh, my orchard!—my sweet, beautiful orchard! My life, my youth, my happiness, good-by! good-by!

VOICE OF ANYA [*calling gaily*]: Mamma!

VOICE OF TROFIMOV [*gaily, excitedly*]: Aa—oo!

LYUBOV: One last look at the walls, at the windows. My dear mother loved to walk about this room.

GAEV: Sister, sister!

VOICE OF ANYA: Mamma!

VOICE OF TROFIMOV: Aa—oo!

LYUBOV: We are coming.

[*They go out. The stage is empty. There is the sound of the doors being locked up, then of the carriages driving away. There is silence. In the stillness there is the dull stroke of an ax in a tree, clanging with a mournful lonely sound. Footsteps are heard.* FIRS *appears in the doorway on the right. He is dressed as always—in a pea-jacket and white waistcoat, with slippers on his feet. He is ill.*]

FIRS [*goes up to the doors, and tries the handles*]: Locked! They have gone ... [*Sits down on sofa.*] They have forgotten me.... Never mind ... I'll sit here a bit.... I'll be bound Leonid Andreyevitch hasn't put his fur coat on and has gone off in his thin overcoat. [*Sighs anxiously.*] I didn't see after him. . . . These young people . . . [*Mutters something that can't be distinguished.*] Life has slipped by as though I hadn't lived. [*Lies down.*] I'll lie down a bit. . . . There's no strength in you, nothing left you—all gone! Ech! I'm good for nothing.

> [*Lies motionless. A sound is heard that seems to come from the sky, like a breaking harp-string, dying away mournfully. All is still again, and there is heard nothing but the strokes of the ax far away in the orchard.*]

CURTAIN

The Lower
Depths

MAXIM GORKY

Translated by Jenny Covan

CHARACTERS

MIKHAIL IVANOFF KOSTILYOFF,
keeper of a night lodging

VASSILISA KARPOVNA, *his wife*

NATASHA, *her sister*

MIEDVIEDIEFF,
her uncle, a policeman

VASKA PEPEL, *a young thief*

ANDREI MITRITCH KLESHTCH, *a locksmith*

ANNA, *his wife*

NASTYA, *a street-walker*

KVASHNYA, *a vendor of meat-pies*

BUBNOFF, *a cap-maker*

THE BARON

SATINE

THE ACTOR

LUKA, *a pilgrim*

ALYOSHKA, *a shoemaker*

KRIVOY ZOB
THE TARTAR ⎱ *Porters*

NIGHT LODGERS, TRAMPS
AND OTHERS

*The action takes place in a Night Lodging
and in "The Waste," an area in its rear.*

act 1

A cellar resembling a cave. The ceiling, which merges into stone walls, is low and grimy, and the plaster and paint are peeling off. There is a window, high up on the right wall, from which comes the light. The right corner, which constitutes PEPEL'S *room, is partioned off by thin boards. Close to the corner of this room is* BUBNOFF'S *wooden bunk. In the left corner stands a large Russian stove. In the stone wall, left, is a door leading to the kitchen where live* KVASHNYA, THE BARON, *and* NASTYA. *Against the wall, between the stove and the door, is a large bed covered with dirty chintz. Bunks line the walls. In the foreground, by the left wall, is a block of wood with a vise and a small anvil fastened to it, and another smaller block of wood somewhat further toward the back.* KLESHTCH *is seated on the smaller block, trying keys into old locks. At his feet are two large bundles of various keys, wired together, also a battered tin samovar, a hammer, and pincers. In the center are a large table, two benches, and a stool, all of which are of dirty, unpainted wood. Behind the table* KVASHNYA *is busying herself with the samovar.* THE BARON *sits chewing a piece of black bread, and* NASTYA *occupies the stool, leans her elbows on the table, and reads a tattered book. In the bed, behind curtains,* ANNA *lies coughing.* BUBNOFF *is seated on his bunk, attempting to shape a pair of old trousers with the help of an ancient hat shape which he holds between his knees, Scattered about him are pieces of buckram, oilcloth, and rags.* SATINE, *just awakened, lies in his bunk, grunting. On top of the stove,* THE ACTOR, *invisible to the audience, tosses about and coughs.*

It is an early spring morning.

THE BARON: And then?

KVASHNYA: No, my dear, said I, keep away from me with such proposals. I've been through it all, you see—and not for a hundred baked lobsters would I marry again!

BUBNOFF [*to* SATINE]: What are you grunting about?

[SATINE *keeps on grunting.*]

KVASHNYA: Why should I, said I, a free woman, my own mistress, enter my name into somebody else's passport and sell myself into slavery—no! Why—I wouldn't marry a man even if he were an American prince!

KLESHTCH: You lie!

KVASHNYA: Wha-at?

KLESHTCH: You lie! You're going to marry Abramka. . . .

THE BARON [*snatching the book out of* NASTYA'S *hand and reading the title*]: "Fatal Love". . . [*Laughs.*]

NASTYA [*stretching out her hand*]: Give it back—give it back! Stop fooling!

[THE BARON *looks at her and waves the book in the air.*]

KVASHNYA [*to* KLESHTCH]: You crimson goat, you—calling me a liar! How dare you be so rude to me?

THE BARON [*hitting* NASTYA *on the head with the book*]: Nastya, you little fool!

NASTYA [*reaching for the book*]: Give it back!

KLESHTCH: Oh—what a great lady . . . but you'll marry Abramka just the same—that's all you're waiting for . . .

KVASHNYA: Sure! Anything else? You nearly beat your wife to death!

KLESHTCH: Shut up, you old bitch! It's none of your business!

KVASHNYA: Ho-ho! can't stand the truth, can you?

THE BARON: They're off again! Nastya, where are you?

NASTYA [*without lifting her head*]: Hey—go away!

ANNA [*putting her head through the curtains*]: The day has started. For God's sake, don't row!

KLESHTCH: Whining again!

ANNA: Every blessed day . . . let me die in peace, can't you?

BUBNOFF: Noise won't keep you from dying.

KVASHNYA [*walking up to* ANNA]: Little mother, how did you ever manage to live with this wretch?

ANNA: Leave me alone—get away from me. . . .

KVASHNYA: Well, well! You poor soul . . . how's the pain in the chest—any better?

THE BARON: Kvashnya! Time to go to market. . . .

KVASHNYA: We'll go presently. [*To* ANNA.] Like some hot dumplings?

ANNA: No, thanks. Why should I eat?

KVASHNYA: You must eat. Hot food—good for you! I'll leave you some in a cup. Eat them when you feel like it. Come on, sir! [*To* KLESHTCH.] You evil spirit! [*Goes into kitchen.*]

ANNA [*coughing*]: Lord, Lord . . .

THE BARON [*painfully pushing forward* NASTYA'S *head*]: Throw it away—little fool!

NASTYA [*muttering*]: Leave me alone— I don't bother you . . .

[THE BARON *follows* KVASHNYA, *whistling*.]

SATINE [*sitting up in his bunk*]: Who beat me up yesterday?

BUBNOFF: Does it make any difference who?

SATINE: Suppose they did—but why did they?

BUBNOFF: Were you playing cards?

SATINE: Yes!

BUBNOFF: That's why they beat you.

SATINE: Scoundrels!

THE ACTOR [*raising his head from the top of the stove*]: One of these days they'll beat you to death!

SATINE: You're a jackass!

THE ACTOR: Why?

SATINE: Because a man can die only once!

THE ACTOR [*after a silence*]: I don't understand—

KLESHTCH: Say! You crawl from that stove—and start cleaning house! Don't play the delicate primrose!

THE ACTOR: None of your business!

KLESHTCH: Wait till Vassilisa comes—she'll show you whose business it is!

THE ACTOR: To hell with Vassilisa! Today is the Baron's turn to clean. . . . Baron!

[THE BARON *comes from the kitchen*.]

THE BARON: I've no time to clean . . . I'm going to market with Kvashnya.

THE ACTOR: That doesn't concern me. Go to the gallows if you like. It's your turn to sweep the floor just the same— I'm not going to do other people's work . . .

THE BARON: Go to blazes! Nastya will do it. Hey there— fatal love! Wake up! [*Takes the book away from* NASTYA.]

NASTYA [*getting up*]: What do you want? Give it back to me! You scoundrel! And that's a nobleman for you!

THE BARON [*returning the book to her*]: Nastya! Sweep the floor for me—will you?

NASTYA [*goes to kitchen*]: Not so's you'll notice it!

KVASHNYA [*to* THE BARON *through kitchen door*]: Come on—you! They don't need you! Actor! You were asked to do it, and now you go ahead and attend to it—it won't kill you . . .

THE ACTOR: It's always I . . . I don't understand why. . . .

[THE BARON *comes from the kitchen, across his shoulders a wooden beam from which hang earthen pots covered with rags.*]

THE BARON: Heavier than ever!

SATINE: It paid you to be born a Baron, eh?

KVASHNYA [*to* ACTOR]: See to it that you sweep up! [*Crosses to outer door, letting* THE BARON *pass ahead.*]

THE ACTOR [*climbing down from the stove*]: It's bad for me to inhale dust. [*With pride.*] My organism is poisoned with alcohol. [*Sits down on a bunk, meditating.*]

SATINE: Organism—organon. . . .

ANNA: Andrei Mitrich. . . .

KLESHTCH: What now?

ANNA: Kvashnya left me some dumplings over there— you eat them.

KLESHTCH [*coming over to her*]: And you—don't you want any?

ANNA: No. Why should I eat? You're a workman—you need it.

KLESHTCH: Frightened, are you? Don't be! You'll get all right!

ANNA: Go and eat! It's hard on me. . . . I suppose very soon . . .

KLESHTCH [*walking away*]: Never mind—maybe you'll get well—you can never tell! [*Goes into kitchen.*]

THE ACTOR [*loud, as if he had suddenly awakened*]: Yesterday the doctor in the hospital said to me: "Your organism," he said, "is entirely poisoned with alcohol. . . ."

SATINE [*smiling*]: Organon . . .

THE ACTOR [*stubbornly*]: Not organon—organism!

SATINE: Sibylline. . . .

THE ACTOR [*shaking his fist at him*]: Nonsense! I'm telling you seriously . . . if the organism is poisoned . . . that means it's bad for me to sweep the floor—to inhale the dust . . .

SATINE: Macrobistic . . . hah!

BUBNOFF: What are you muttering?

SATINE: Words—and here's another one for you—transcendentalistic. . . .

BUBNOFF: What does it mean?

SATINE: Don't know—I forgot. . . .

BUBNOFF: Then why did you say it?

SATINE: Just so! I'm bored, brother, with human words—all our words. Bored! I've heard each one of them a thousand times surely.

THE ACTOR: In Hamlet they say: "Words, words, words!" It's a good play. I played the grave-digger in it once. . . .

[KLESHTCH *comes from the kitchen.*]

KLESHTCH: Will you start playing with the broom?

THE ACTOR: None of your business. [*Striking his chest.*] Ophelia! O—remember me in thy prayers!

[*Back stage is heard a dull murmur, cries, and a police whistle.* KLESHTCH *sits down to work, filing screechily.*]

SATINE: I love unintelligible, obsolete words. When I was a youngster—and worked as a telegraph operator—I read heaps of books. . . .

BUBNOFF: Were you really a telegrapher?

SATINE: I was. There are some excellent books—and lots of curious words. . . . Once I was an educated man, do you know?

BUBNOFF: I've heard it a hundred times. Well, so you were! That isn't very important! Me—well—once I was a furrier. I had my own shop—what with dyeing the fur all day long, my arms were yellow up to the elbows, brother. I thought I'd never be able ever to get clean again—that I'd go to my grave, all yellow! But look at my hands now— they're plain dirty—that's what!

SATINE: Well, and what then?

BUBNOFF: That's all!

SATINE: What are you trying to prove?

BUBNOFF: Oh, well—just matching thoughts—no matter how much dye you get on yourself, it all comes off in the end—yes, yes—

SATINE: Oh—my bones ache!

THE ACTOR [*sits, nursing his knees*]: Education is all rot. Talent is the thing. I knew an actor—who read his parts by heart, syllable by syllable—but he played heroes in a way that . . . why—the whole theater would rock with ecstasy!

SATINE: Bubnoff, give me five kopecks.

BUBNOFF: I only have two—

THE ACTOR: I say—talent, that's what you need to play heroes. And talent is nothing but faith in yourself, in your own powers—

SATINE: Give me five kopecks and I'll have faith that you're a hero, a crocodile, or a police inspector— Kleshtch, give me five kopecks.

KLESHTCH: Go to hell! All of you!

SATINE: What are you cursing for? I know you haven't a kopeck in the world!

ANNA: Andrei Mitrich—I'm suffocating—I can't breathe—

KLESHTCH: What shall I do?

BUBNOFF: Open the door into the hall.

KLESHTCH: All right. You're sitting on the bunk, I on the floor. You change places with me, and I'll let you open the door. I have a cold as it is.

BUBNOFF [*unconcernedly*]: I don't care if you open the door—it's your wife who's asking—

KLESHTCH [*morosely*]: I don't care who's asking—

SATINE: My head buzzes—ah—why do people have to hit each other over the heads?

BUBNOFF: They don't only hit you over the head, but over the rest of the body as well. [*Rises.*] I must go and buy some thread—our bosses are late today—seems as if they've croaked.

[*Exit.* ANNA *coughs;* SATINE *is lying down motionless, his hands folded behind his head.*]

THE ACTOR [*looks about him morosely, then goes to* ANNA]: Feeling bad, eh?

ANNA: I'm choking—

THE ACTOR: If you wish, I'll take you into the hallway. Get up, then, come! [*He helps her to rise, wraps some sort of a rag about her shoulders, and supports her toward the hall.*] It isn't easy. I'm sick myself—poisoned with alcohol. . . .

[KOSTILYOFF *appears in the doorway.*]

KOSTILYOFF: Going for a stroll? What a nice couple— the gallant cavalier and the lady fair!

THE ACTOR: Step aside, you—don't you see that we're invalids?

KOSTILYOFF: Pass on, please! [*Hums a religious tune, glances about him suspiciously, and bends his head to the left as if listening to what is happening in* PEPEL'S *room.* KLESHTCH *is jangling his keys and scraping away with his file, and looks askance at the other.*] Filing?

KLESHTCH: What?

KOSTILYOFF: I say, are you filing? [*Pause.*] What did I want to ask? [*Quick and low.*] Hasn't my wife been here?

KLESHTCH: I didn't see her.

KOSTILYOFF [*carefully moving toward* PEPEL'S *room*]: You take up a whole lot of room for your two rubles a month. The bed—and your bench—yes—you take up five rubles' worth of space, so help me God! I'll have to put another half ruble to your rent—

KLESHTCH: You'll put a noose around my neck and choke me ... you'll croak soon enough, and still all you think of is half rubles—

KOSTILYOFF: Why should I choke you? What would be the use? God be with you—live and prosper! But I'll have to raise you half a ruble—I'll buy oil for the ikon lamp, and my offering will atone for my sins, and for yours as well. You don't think much of your sins—not much! Oh, Andrushka, you're a wicked man! Your wife is dying because of your wickedness—no one loves you, no one respects you—your work is squeaky, jarring on everyone.

KLESHTCH [*shouts*]: What do you come here for—just to annoy me?

[SATINE *grunts loudly.*]

KOSTILYOFF [*with a start*]: God, what a noise!

[THE ACTOR *enters.*]

THE ACTOR: I've put her down in the hall and wrapped her up.

KOSTILYOFF: You're a kindly fellow. That's good. Some day you'll be rewarded for it.

THE ACTOR: When?

KOSTILYOFF: In the Beyond, little brother—there all our deeds will be reckoned up.

THE ACTOR: Suppose you reward me right now?

KOSTILYOFF: How can I do that?

THE ACTOR: Wipe out half my debt.

KOSTILYOFF: He-ho! You're always jesting, darling—always poking fun ... can kindliness of heart be repaid with gold? Kindliness—it's above all other qualities. But your debt to me—remains a debt. And so you'll have to pay me back. You ought to be kind to me, an old man, without seeking for reward!

THE ACTOR: You're a swindler, old man!

[*Goes into kitchen.* KLESHTCH *rises and goes into the hall.*]

KOSTILYOFF [*to* SATINE]: See that squeaker—? He ran away—he doesn't like me!

SATINE: Does anybody like you besides the Devil?

KOSTILYOFF [*laughing*]: Oh—you're so quarrelsome! But I like you all—I understand you all, my unfortunate downtrodden, useless brethren . . . [*Suddenly, rapidly.*] Is Vaska home?

SATINE: See for yourself—

KOSTILYOFF [*goes to the door and knocks*]: Vaska!

[THE ACTOR *appears at the kitchen door, chewing something.*]

PEPEL: Who is it?

KOSTILYOFF: It's I—I, Vaska!

PEPEL: What do you want?

KOSTILYOFF [*stepping aside*]: Open!

SATINE [*without looking at* KOSTILYOFF]: He'll open—and she's there—

[THE ACTOR *makes a grimace.*]

KOSTILYOFF [*in a low, anxious tone*]: Eh? Who's there? What?

SATINE: Speaking to me?

KOSTILYOFF: What did you say?

SATINE: Oh—nothing—I was just talking to myself.

KOSTILYOFF: Take care, brother. Don't carry your joking too far! [*Knocks loudly at door.*] Vassily!

PEPEL [*opening door*]: Well? What are you disturbing me for?

KOSTILYOFF [*peering into room*]: I—you see—

PEPEL: Did you bring the money?

KOSTILYOFF: I've something to tell you—

PEPEL: Did you bring the money?

KOSTILYOFF: What money? Wait—

PEPEL: Why—the seven rubles for the watch—well?

KOSTILYOFF: What watch, Vaska? Oh, you—

PEPEL: Look here. Yesterday, before witnesses, I sold you a watch for ten rubles, you gave me three—now let me have the other seven. What are you blinking for? You hang around here—you disturb people—and don't seem to know yourself what you're after.

KOSTILYOFF: Sh-sh! Don't be angry, Vaska. The watch —it is—

SATINE: Stolen!

KOSTELYOFF [sternly]: I do not accept stolen goods— how can you imagine—

PEPEL [taking him by the shoulder]: What did you disturb me for? What do you want?

KOSTILYOFF: I don't want—anything. I'll go—if you're in such a state—

PEPEL: Be off, and bring the money!

KOSTILYOFF: What ruffians! I—I— [Exit.]

THE ACTOR: What a farce!

SATINE: That's fine—I like it.

PEPEL: What did he come here for?

SATINE [laughing]: Don't you understand? He's looking for his wife. Why don't you beat him up once and for all, Vaska?

PEPEL: Why should I let such trash interfere with my life?

SATINE: Show some brains! And then you can marry Vassilisa—and become our boss—

PEPEL: Heavenly bliss! And you'd smash up my household and, because I'm a soft-hearted fool, you'll drink up everything I possess. [Sits on a bunk.] Old devil—woke me up—I was having such a pleasant dream. I dreamed I was fishing—and I caught an enormous trout—such a trout as you only see in dreams! I was playing him—and I was so afraid the line would snap. I had just got out the gaff—and I thought to myself—in a moment—

SATINE: It wasn't a trout, it was Vassilisa—

THE ACTOR: He caught Vassilisa a long time ago.

PEPEL [*angrily*]: You can all go to the devil—and Vassilisa with you—

[KLESHTCH *comes from the hall.*]

KLESHTCH: Devilishly cold!

THE ACTOR: Why didn't you bring Anna back? She'll freeze, out there—

KLESHTCH: Natasha took her into the kitchen—

THE ACTOR: The old man will kick her out—

KLESHTCH [*sitting down to his work*]: Well—Natasha will bring her in here—

SATINE: Vassily—give me five kopecks!

THE ACTOR [*to* SATINE]: Oh, you—always five kopecks—Vassya—give us twenty kopecks—

PEPEL: I'd better give it to them now before they ask for a ruble. Here you are!

SATINE: Gibraltar! There are no kindlier people in the world than thieves!

KLESHTCH [*morosely*]: They earn their money easily—they don't work—

SATINE: Many earn it easily, but not many part with it so easily. Work? Make work pleasant—and maybe I'll work too. Yes—maybe. When work's a pleasure, life's, too. When it's toil, then life is a drudge. [*To* THE ACTOR.] You, Sardanapalus! Come on!

THE ACTOR: Let's go, Nebuchadnezzar! I'll get as drunk as forty thousand topers!

[*They leave.*]

PEPEL [*yawning*]: Well, how's your wife?

KLESHTCH: It seems as if soon—

[*Pause.*]

PEPEL: Now I look at you—seems to me all that filing and scraping of yours is useless.

KLESHTCH: Well—what else can I do?

PEPEL: Nothing.

KLESHTCH: How can I live?

PEPEL: People manage, somehow.

KLESHTCH: Them? Call them people? Muck and dregs—

that's what they are! I'm a workman—I'm ashamed even
to look at them. I've slaved since I was a child. . . . D'you
think I shan't be able to tear myself away from here? I'll
crawl out of here, even if I have to leave my skin behind—
but crawl out I will! Just wait . . . my wife'll die . . . I've
lived here six months, and it seems like six years.

PEPEL: Nobody here's any worse off than you . . . say
what you like . . .

KLESHTCH: No worse is right. They've neither honor nor
conscience.

PEPEL [*indifferently*]: What good does it do—honor or
conscience? Can you get them on their feet instead of on
their uppers—through honor and conscience? Honor and
conscience are needed only by those who have power and
energy. . . .

BUBNOFF [*coming back*]: Oh—I'm frozen.

PEPEL: Bubnoff! Got a conscience?

BUBNOFF: What? A conscience?

PEPEL: Exactly!

BUBNOFF: What do I need a conscience for? I'm not rich.

PEPEL: Just what I said: honor and conscience are for
the rich—right! And Kleshtch is upbraiding us because
we haven't any!

BUBNOFF: Why—did he want to borrow some of it?

PEPEL: No—he has plenty of his own. . . .

BUBNOFF: Oh—are you selling it? You won't sell much
around here. But if you had some old boxes, I'd buy them
—on credit. . . .

PEPEL [*didactically*]: You're a jackass, Andrushka! On
the subject of conscience you ought to hear Satine—or the
Baron . . .

KLESHTCH: I've nothing to talk to them about!

PEPEL: They have more brains than you—even if they're
drunkards . . .

BUBNOFF: He who can be drunk and wise at the same
time is doubly blessed . . .

PEPEL: Satine says every man expects his neighbor to

have a conscience, but—you see—it isn't to anyone's advantage to have one—that's a fact.

[NATASHA *enters, followed by* LUKA *who carries a stick in his hand, a bundle on his back, a kettle and a teapot slung from his belt.*]

LUKA: How are you, honest folks?

PEPEL [*twisting his mustache*]: Aha—Natasha!

BUBNOFF [*to* LUKA]: I was honest—up to spring before last.

NATASHA: Here's a new lodger . . .

LUKA: Oh, it's all the same to me. Crooks—I don't mind them, either. For my part there's no bad flea—they're all black—and they all jump— . . . Well, dearie, show me where I can stow myself.

NATASHA [*pointing to kitchen door*]: Go in there, granddad.

LUKA: Thanks, girlie. One place is like another—as long as an old fellow keeps warm, he keeps happy. . . .

PEPEL: What an amusing old codger you brought in, Natasha!

NATASHA: A hanged sight more interesting than you! . . . Andrei, your wife's in the kitchen with us—come and fetch her after a while. . . .

KLESHTCH: All right—I will. . . .

NATASHA: And be a little more kind to her—you know she won't last much longer.

KLESHTCH: I know. . . .

NATASHA: Knowing won't do any good—it's terrible—dying—don't you understand?

PEPEL: Well—look at me—I'm not afraid. . . .

NATASHA: Oh—you're a wonder, aren't you?

BUBNOFF [*whistling*]: Oh—this thread's rotten. . . .

PEPEL: Honestly, I'm not afraid! I'm ready to die right now. Knife me to the heart—and I'll die without making a sound . . . even gladly—from such a pure hand. . . .

NATASHA [*going out*]: Spin that yarn for someone else!

BUBNOFF: Oh—that thread is rotten—rotten—

NATASHA [*at hallway door*]: Don't forget your wife, Andrei!

KLESHTCH: All right.

PEPEL: She's a wonderful girl!

BUBNOFF: She's all right.

PEPEL: What makes her so curt with me? Anyway—
she'll come to no good here . . .

BUBNOFF: Through you—sure!

PEPEL: Why through me? I feel sorry for her. . . .

BUBNOFF: As the wolf for the lamb!

PEPEL: You lie! I feel very sorry for her . . . very . . .
very sorry! She has a tough life here—I can see that. . . .

KLESHTCH: Just wait till Vassilisa catches you talking to
her!

BUBNOFF: Vassilisa? She won't give up so easily what belongs to her—she's a cruel woman!

PEPEL [*stretching himself on the bunk*]: You two proph-
ets can go to hell!

KLESHTCH: Just wait—you'll see!

LUKA [*singing in the kitchen*]: "In the dark of the night
the way is black . . ."

KLESHTCH: Another one who yelps!

PEPEL: It's dreary! Why do I feel so dreary? You live—
and everything seems all right. But suddenly a cold chill
goes through you—and then everything gets dreary. . . .

BUBNOFF: Dreary? Hm-hm—

PEPEL: Yes—yes—

LUKA [*sings*]: "The way is black . . ."

PEPEL: Old fellow! Hey there!

LUKA [*looking from kitchen door*]: You call me?

PEPEL: Yes. Don't sing!

LUKA [*coming in*]: You don't like it?

PEPEL: When people sing well I like it—

LUKA: In other words—I don't sing well?

PEPEL: Evidently!

LUKA: Well, well—and I thought I sang well. That's always the way: a man imagines there's one thing he can do

well, and suddenly he finds out that other people don't think
so. . . .

PEPEL [laughs]: That's right . . .

BUBNOFF: First you say you feel dreary—and then you
laugh!

PEPEL: None of your business, raven!

LUKA: Who do they say feels dreary?

PEPEL: I do.

[THE BARON enters.]

LUKA: Well, well—out there in the kitchen there's a girl
reading and crying! That's so! Her eyes are wet with tears
. . . I say to her: "What's the matter, darling?" And she
says: "It's so sad!" "What's so sad?" say I. "The book!"
says she.—And that's how people spend their time. Just because they're bored. . . .

THE BARON: She's a fool!

PEPEL: Have you had tea, Baron?

THE BARON: Yes. Go on!

PEPEL: Well—want me to open a bottle?

THE BARON: Of course. Go on!

PEPEL: Drop on all fours, and bark like a dog!

THE BARON: Fool! What's the matter with you? Are you
drunk?

PEPEL: Go on—bark a little! It'll amuse me. You're an
aristocrat. You didn't even consider us human formerly,
did you?

THE BARON: Go on!

PEPEL: Well—and now I am making you bark like a
dog—and you will bark, won't you?

THE BARON: All right. I will. You jackass! What pleasure
can you derive from it, since I myself know that I have
sunk almost lower than you. You should have made me
drop on all fours in the days when I was still above you.

BUBNOFF: That's right. . . .

LUKA: I say so, too!

BUBNOFF: What's over, is over. Remain only trivialities.
We know no class distinctions here. We've shed all pride and

self-respect. Blood and bone—man—just plain man—that's what we are!

LUKA: In other words, we're all equal . . . and you, friend, were you really a Baron?

THE BARON: Who are you? A ghost?

LUKA [*laughing*]: I've seen counts and princes in my day —this is the first time I meet a baron—and one who's decaying—at that!

PEPEL [*laughing*]: Baron, I blush for you!

THE BARON: It's time you knew better, Vassily. . . .

LUKA: Hey-hey—I look at you, brothers—the life you're leading. . . .

BUBNOFF: Such a life! As soon as the sun rises, our voices rise, too—in quarrels!

THE BARON: We've all seen better days—yes! I used to wake up in the morning and drink my coffee in bed—coffee—with cream! Yes—

LUKA: And yet we're all human beings. Pretend all you want to, put on all the airs you wish, but man you were born, and man you must die. And as I watch I see that the wiser people get, the busier they get—and though from bad to worse, they still strive to improve—stubbornly—

THE BARON: Who are you, old fellow? Where do you come from?

LUKA: I?

THE BARON: Are you a tramp?

LUKA: We're all of us tramps—why—I've heard said that the very earth we walk on is nothing but a tramp in the universe.

THE BARON [*severely*]: Perhaps. But have you a passport?

LUKA [*after a short pause*]: And what are you—a police inspector?

PEPEL [*delighted*]: You scored, old fellow! Well, Barosha, you got it this time!

BUBNOFF: Yes—our little aristocrat got his!

THE BARON [*embarrassed*]: What's the matter? I was only joking, old man. Why, brother, I haven't a passport, either.

BUBNOFF: You lie!

THE BARON: Oh—well—I have some sort of papers—but they have no value—

LUKA: They're papers just the same—and no papers are any good—

PEPEL: Baron—come on to the saloon with me—

THE BARON: I'm ready. Good-by, old man—you old scamp—

LUKA: Maybe I am one, brother—

PEPEL [*near doorway*]: Come on—come on!

[*Leaves,* BARON *following him quickly.*]

LUKA: Was he really once a Baron?

BUBNOFF: Who knows? A gentleman—? Yes. That much he's even now. Occasionally it sticks out. He never got rid of the habit.

LUKA: Nobility is like small-pox. A man may get over it—but it leaves marks. . . .

BUBNOFF: He's all right all the same—occasionally he kicks—as he did about your passport . . .

[ALYOSHKA *comes in, slightly drunk, with a concertina in his hand, whistling.*]

ALYOSHKA: Hey there, lodgers!

BUBNOFF: What are you yelling for?

ALYOSHKA: Excuse me—I beg your pardon! I'm a well-bred man—

BUBNOFF: On a spree again?

ALYOSHKA: Right you are! A moment ago Medyakin, the precinct captain, threw me out of the police station and said: "Look here—I don't want as much as a smell of you to stay in the streets—d'you hear?" I'm a man of principles, and the boss croaks at me—and what's a boss anyway —pah!—it's all bosh—the boss is a drunkard. I don't make any demands on life. I want nothing—that's all. Offer me one ruble, offer me twenty—it doesn't affect me. [NASTYA *comes from the kitchen.*] Offer me a million—I won't take it! And to think that I, respectable man, should be ordered about by a pal of mine—and he a drunkard! I won't have it—I won't!

[NASTYA *stands in the doorway, shaking her head at* ALYOSHKA.]

LUKA [*good-naturedly*]: Well, boy, you're a bit confused—

BUBNOFF: Aren't men fools!

ALYOSHKA [*stretches out on the floor*]: Here, eat me up alive—and I don't want anything. I'm a desperate man. Show me one better! Why am I worse than others? There! Medyakin said: "If you show yourself on the streets I smash your face!" And yet I shall go out—I'll go—and stretch out in the middle of the street—let them choke me—I don't want a thing!

NASTYA: Poor fellow—only a boy—and he's already putting on such airs—

ALYOSHKA [*kneeling before her*]: Lady! Mademoiselle! *Parlez français—? Prix courrant?* I'm on a spree—

NASTYA [*in a loud whisper*]: Vassilisa!

VASSILISA [*opens door quickly; to* ALYOSHKA]: You here again?

ALYOSHKA: How do you do—? Come in—you're welcome—

VASSILISA: I told you, young puppy, that not a shadow of you should stick around here—and you're back—eh?

ALYOSHKA: Vassilisa Karpovna . . . shall I tune up a funeral march for you?

VASSILISA [*seizing him by the shoulders*]: Get out!

ALYOSHKA [*moving toward the door*]: Wait—you can't put me out this way! I learned this funeral march a little while ago! It's refreshing music . . . wait—you can't put me out like that!

VASSILISA: I'll show whether I can or not. I'll rouse the whole street against you—you foul-mouthed creature— you're too young to bark about me—

ALYOSHKA [*running out*]: All right—I'll go—

VASSILISA: Look out—I'll get you yet!

ALYOSHKA [*opens the door and shouts*]: Vassilisa Karpovna—I'm not afraid of you—

[*Hides.* LUKA *laughs.*]

VASSILISA: Who are you?

LUKA: A passer-by—a traveler . . .

VASSILISA: Stopping for the night or going to stay here?

LUKA: I'll see.

VASSILISA: Have you a passport?

LUKA: Yes.

VASSILISA: Give it to me.

LUKA: I'll bring it over to your house—

VASSILISA: Call yourself a traveler? If you'd say a tramp —that would be nearer the truth—

LUKA [*sighing*]: You're not very kindly, mother!

[VASSILISA *goes to door that leads to* PEPEL'S *room.* AL-YOSHKA *pokes his head through the kitchen door.*]

ALYOSHKA: Has she left?

VASSILISA [*turning around*]: Are you still here?

[ALYOSHKA *disappears, whistling.* NASTYA *and* LUKA *laugh.*]

BUBNOFF [*to* VASSILISA]: He isn't here—

VASSILISA: Who?

BUBNOFF: Vaska.

VASSILISA: Did I ask you about him?

BUBNOFF: I noticed you were looking around—

VASSILISA: I am looking to see if things are in order, you see? Why aren't the floors swept yet? How often did I give orders to keep the house clean?

BUBNOFF: It's the actor's turn to sweep—

VASSILISA: Never mind whose turn it is! If the health inspector comes and fines me, I'll throw out the lot of you—

BUBNOFF [*calmly*]: Then how are you going to earn your living?

VASSILISA: I don't want a speck of dirt! [*Goes to kitchen; to* NASTYA.] What are you hanging round here for? Why's your face all swollen up? Why are you standing there like a dummy? Go on—sweep the floor! Did you see Natalia? Was she here?

NASTYA: I don't know—I haven't seen her . . .

VASSILISA: Bubnoff! Was my sister here?

BUBNOFF: She brought him along.

VASSILISA: That one—was he home?

BUBNOFF: Vassily? Yes—Natalia was here talking to Kleshtch—

VASSILISA: I'm not asking you whom she talked to. Dirt everywhere—filth—oh, you swine! Mop it all up—do you hear? [*Exit rapidly.*]

BUBNOFF: What a savage beast she is!

LUKA: She's a lady that means business!

NASTYA: You grow to be an animal, leading such a life—any human being tied to such a husband as hers. . . .

BUBNOFF: Well—that tie isn't worrying her any—

LUKA: Does she always have these fits?

BUBNOFF: Always. You see, she came to find her lover—but he isn't home—

LUKA: I guess she was hurt. Oh-ho! Everybody is trying to be boss—and is threatening everybody else with all kinds of punishment—and still there's no order in life . . . and no cleanliness—

BUBNOFF: All the world likes order—but some people's brains aren't fit for it. All the same—the room should be swept—Nastya—you ought to get busy!

NASTYA: Oh, certainly? Anything else? Think I'm your servant? [*Silence.*] I'm going to get drunk tonight—dead-drunk!

BUBNOFF: Fine business!

LUKA: Why do you want to get drunk, girlie? A while ago you were crying—and now you say you'll get drunk—

NASTYA [*defiantly*]: I'll drink—then I cry again—that's all there's to it!

BUBNOFF: That's nothing!

LUKA: But for what reason—tell me. Every pimple has a cause! [NASTYA *remains silent, shaking her head.*] Oh—you men—what's to become of you? All right—I'll sweep the place. Where's your broom?

BUBNOFF: Behind the door—in the hall— [LUKA *goes into the hall.*] Nastinka!

NASTYA: Yes?

BUBNOFF: Why did Vassilisa jump on Alyoshka?

NASTYA: He told her that Vaska was tired of her and was going to get rid of her—and that he's going to make up to Natasha— I'll go away from here—I'll find another lodging-house—

BUBNOFF: Why? Where?

NASTYA: I'm sick of this—I'm not wanted here!

BUBNOFF [*calmly*]: You're not wanted anywhere—and, anyway, all people on earth are superfluous—

[NASTYA *shakes her head. Rises and slowly, quietly, leaves the cellar.* MIEDVIEDIEFF *comes in.* LUKA, *with the broom, follows him.*]

MIEDVIEDIEFF: I don't think I know you—

LUKA: How about the others—d'you know them all?

MIEDVIEDIEFF: I must know everybody in my precinct. But I don't know you.

LUKA: That's because, uncle, the whole world can't stow itself away in your precinct—some of it was bound to remain outside. . . . [*Goes into kitchen.*]

MIEDVIEDIEFF [*crosses to* BUBNOFF]: It's true—my precinct is rather small—yet it's worse than any of the very largest. Just now, before getting off duty, I had to bring Alyoshka, the shoemaker, to the station house. Just imagine —there he was, stretched right in the middle of the street, playing his concertina and yelping: "I want nothing, nothing!" Horses going past all the time—and with all the traffic going on, he could easily have been run over—and so on! He's a wild youngster—so I just collared him—he likes to make mischief—

BUBNOFF: Coming to play checkers tonight?

MIEDVIEDIEFF: Yes—I'll come—how's Vaska?

BUBNOFF: Same as ever—

MIEDVIEDIEFF: Meaning—he's getting along—?

BUBNOFF: Why shouldn't he? He's able to get along all right.

MIEDVIEDIEFF [*doubtfully*]: Why shouldn't he? [LUKA *goes into hallway, carrying a pail.*] M—yes—there's a lot of talk about Vaska. Haven't you heard?

BUBNOFF: I hear all sorts of gossip . . .

MIEDVIEDIEFF: There seems to have been some sort of talk concerning Vassilisa. Haven't you heard about it?

BUBNOFF: What?

MIEDVIEDIEFF: Oh—why—generally speaking. Perhaps you know—and lie. Everybody knows— [*Severely.*] You mustn't lie, brother!

BUBNOFF: Why should I lie?

MIEDVIEDIEFF: That's right. Dogs! They say that Vaska and Vassilisa . . . but what's that to me? I'm not her father. I'm her uncle. Why should they ridicule me? [KVASHNYA *comes in.*] What are people coming to? They laugh at everything. Aha—you here?

KVASHNYA: Well—my love-sick garrison—? Bubnoff! He came up to me again on the marketplace and started pestering me about marrying him. . . .

BUBNOFF: Go to it! Why not? He has money and he's still a husky fellow.

MIEDVIEDIEFF: Me—? I should say so!

KVASHNYA: You ruffian! Don't you dare touch my sore spot! I've gone through it once already, darling. Marriage to a woman is just like jumping through a hole in the ice in winter. You do it once, and you remember it the rest of your life. . . .

MIEDVIEDIEFF: Wait! There are different breeds of husbands. . . .

KVASHNYA: But there's only one of me! When my beloved husband kicked the bucket, I spent the whole day all by my lonely—just bursting with joy. I sat and simply couldn't believe it was true. . . .

MIEDVIEDIEFF: If your husband beat you without cause, you should have complained to the police.

KVASHNYA: I complained to God for eight years—and He didn't help.

MIEDVIEDIEFF: Nowadays the law forbids to beat your wife . . . all is very strict these days—there's law and order everywhere. You can't beat up people without due cause. If you beat them to maintain discipline—all right. . . .

LUKA [*comes in with* ANNA]: Well—we finally managed to get here after all. Oh, you! Why do you, weak as you are, walk about alone? Where's your bunk?

ANNA [*pointing*]: Thank you, granddad.

KVASHNYA: There—she's married—look at her!

LUKA: The little woman is in very bad shape . . . she was creeping along the hallway, clinging to the wall and moaning—why do you leave her by herself?

KVASHNYA: Oh, pure carelessness on our part, little father—forgive us! Her maid, it appears, went out for a walk. . . .

LUKA: Go on—poke fun at me . . . but, all the same, how can you neglect a human being like that? No matter who or what, every human life has its worth. . . .

MIEDVIEDIEFF: There should be supervision! Suppose she died suddenly—? That would cause a lot of bother . . . we must look after her!

LUKA: True, sergeant!

MIEDVIEDIEFF: Well—yes—though I'm not a sergeant—ah—yet!

LUKA: No! But you carry yourself most martially!
   [*Noise of shuffling feet is heard in the hallway. Muffled cries.*]

MIEDVIEDIEFF: What now—a row?

BUBNOFF: Sounds like it?

KVASHNYA: I'll go and see . . .

MIEDVIEDIEFF: I'll go, too. It is my duty! Why separate people when they fight? They'll stop sooner or later of their own accord. One gets tired of fighting. Why not let them fight all they want to—freely? They wouldn't fight half as often—if they'd remember former beatings. . . .

BUBNOFF [*climbing down from his bunk*]: Why don't you speak to your superiors about it?

KOSTILYOFF [*throws open the door and shouts*]: Abram! come quick—Vassilisa is killing Natasha—come quick.
   [KVASHNYA, MIEDVIEDIEFF, *and* BUBNOFF *rush into hallway;* LUKA *looks after them, shaking his head*].

ANNA: Oh, God—poor little Natasha . . .

LUKA: Who's fighting out there?

ANNA: Our landladies—they're sisters . . .

LUKA [crossing to ANNA]: Why?

ANNA: Oh—for no reason—except that they're both fat and healthy . . .

LUKA: What's your name?

ANNA: Anna . . . I look at you . . . you're like my father— my dear father . . . you're as gentle as he was—and as soft. . . .

LUKA: Soft! Yes! They pounded me till I got soft! [Laughs tremulously.]

CURTAIN

act 2

Same as Act 1—Night.

On the bunks near the stove, SATINE, THE BARON, KRIVOY ZOB, *and* THE TARTAR *play cards.* KLESHTCH *and* THE ACTOR *watch them.* BUBNOFF, *on his bunk, is playing checkers with* MIEDVIEDIEFF. LUKA *sits on a stool by* ANNA'S *bedside. The place is lit by two lamps, one on the wall near the card players, the other is on* BUBNOFF'S *bunk.*

THE TARTAR: I'll play one more game—then I'll stop. . . .

BUBNOFF: Zob! Sing! [He sings.]
        "The sun rises and sets . . ."

ZOB [joining in]:
        "But my prison is dark, dark . . ."

THE TARTAR [to SATINE]: Shuffle the cards—and shuffle them well. We know your kind—

ZOB and BUBNOFF [together]:
        "Day and night the wardens
        Watch beneath my window . . ."

ANNA: Blows—insults—I've had nothing but that all my life long . . .

LUKA: Don't worry, little mother!

MIEDVIEDIEFF: Look where you're moving!

BUBNOFF: Oh, yes—that's right . . .

THE TARTAR [*threatening* SATINE *with his fist*]: You're trying to palm a card? I've seen you—you scoundrel . . .

ZOB: Stop it, Hassan! They'll skin us anyway . . . come on, Bubnoff!

ANNA: I can't remember a single day when I didn't go hungry . . . I've been afraid, waking, eating, and sleeping . . . all my life I've trembled—afraid I wouldn't get another bite . . . all my life I've been in rags—all through my wretched life—and why . . . ?

LUKA: Yes, yes, child—you're tired—never you mind!

THE ACTOR [*to* ZOB]: Play the Jack—the Jack, devil take you!

THE BARON: And we play the King!

KLESHTCH: They always win.

SATINE: Such is our habit.

MIEDVIEDIEFF: I have the Queen!

BUBNOFF: And so have I!

ANNA: I'm dying. . . .

KLESHTCH: Look, look! Prince, throw up the game—throw it up, I tell you!

THE ACTOR: Can't he play without your assistance?

THE BARON: Look out, Andrushka, or I'll beat the life out of you!

THE TARTAR: Deal once more—the pitcher went after water—and got broke—and so did I!

[KLESHTCH *shakes his head and crosses to* BUBNOFF.]

ANNA: I keep on thinking—is it possible that I'll suffer in the other world as I did in this—is it possible? There, too?

LUKA: Nothing of the sort! Don't you disturb yourself! You'll rest there . . . be patient. We all suffer, dear, each in our own way. . . . [*Rises and goes quickly into kitchen.*]

BUBNOFF [*sings*]:

"Watch as long as you please . . ."

ZOB:

"I shan't run away . . ."

BOTH [*together*]:

"I long to be free, free—
Alas! I cannot break my chains. . . ."

THE TARTAR [*yells*]: That card was up his sleeve!

THE BARON [*embarrassed*]: Do you want me to shove it up your nose?

THE ACTOR [*emphatically*]: Prince! You're mistaken—nobody—ever . . .

THE TARTAR: I saw it! You cheat! I won't play!

SATINE [*gathering up the cards*]: Leave us alone, Hassan . . . you knew right along that we're cheats—why did you play with us?

THE BARON: He lost forty kopecks and he yelps as if he had lost a fortune! And a Prince at that!

THE TARTAR [*excitedly*]: Then play honest!

SATINE: What for?

THE TARTAR: What do you mean "what for"?

SATINE: Exactly. What for?

THE TARTAR: Don't you know?

SATINE: I don't. Do you?

[THE TARTAR *spits out, furiously; the others laugh at him.*]

ZOB [*good-naturedly*]: You're a funny fellow, Hassan! Try to understand this! If they should begin to live honestly, they'd die of starvation inside of three days.

THE TARTAR: That's none of my business. You must live honestly!

ZOB: They did you brown! Come and let's have tea. . . . [*Sings.*]

"O my chains, my heavy chains . . ."

BUBNOFF [*sings*]:

"You're my steely, clanking wardens . . ."

ZOB: Come, Hassanka! [*Leaves the room, singing.*]

"I cannot tear you, cannot break you . . ."

[THE TARTAR *shakes his fist threateningly at* THE BARON, *and follows the other out of the room.*]

SATINE [*to* BARON, *laughing*]: Well, Your Imperial Highness, you've again sat down magnificently in a mud puddle! You've learned a lot—but you're an ignoramus when it comes to palming a card.

THE BARON [*spreading his hands*]: The Devil knows how it happened. . . .

THE ACTOR: You're not gifted—you've no faith in yourself—and without that you can never accomplish anything. . . .

MIEDVIEDIEFF: I've one Queen—and you've two—oh, well . . .

BUBNOFF: One's enough if she has brains—play!

KLESHTCH: You lost, Abram Ivanovitch?

MIEDVIEDIEFF: None of your business—see? Shut up!

SATINE: I've won fifty-three kopecks.

THE ACTOR: Give me three of them . . . though, what'll I do with them?

LUKA [*coming from kitchen*]: Well—the Tartar was fleeced all right, eh? Going to have some vodka?

THE BARON: Come with us.

SATINE: I wonder what you'll be like when you're drunk.

LUKA: Same as when I'm sober.

THE ACTOR: Come on, old man—I'll recite verses for you . . .

LUKA: What?

THE ACTOR: Verses. Don't you understand?

LUKA: Verses? And what do I want with verses?

THE ACTOR: Sometimes they're funny—sometimes sad.

SATINE: Well, poet, are you coming? [*Exit with* THE BARON.]

THE ACTOR: I'm coming. I'll join you. For instance, old man, here's a bit of verse—I forget how it begins—I forget . . . [*Brushes his hand across his forehead.*]

BUBNOFF: There! Your Queen is lost—go on, play!

MIEDVIEDIEFF: I made the wrong move.

THE ACTOR: Formerly, before my organism was poisoned with alcohol, old man, I had a good memory. But now it's all over with me, brother. I used to declaim these verses with tremendous success—thunders of applause...you have no idea what applause means ... it goes to your head like vodka! I'd step out on the stage—stand this way— [*Strikes a pose.*] —I'd stand there and ... [*Pause.*] I can't remember a word—I can't remember! My favorite verses—isn't it ghastly, old man?

LUKA: Yes—is there anything worse than forgetting what you loved? Your very soul is in the thing you love!

THE ACTOR: I've drunk my soul away, old man—brother, I'm lost ... and why? Because I had no faith ... I'm done with. . . .

LUKA: Well—then—cure yourself! Nowadays they have a cure for drunkards. They treat you free of charge, brother. There's a hospital for drunkards—where they're treated for nothing. They've owned up, you see, that even a drunkard is a human being, and they're only too glad to help him get well. Well—then—go to it!

THE ACTOR [*thoughtfully*]: Where? Where is it?

LUKA: Oh—in some town or other ... what do they call it—? I'll tell you the name presently—only, in the meanwhile, get ready. Don't drink so much! Take yourself in hand—and bear up! And then, when you're cured, you'll begin life all over again. Sounds good, brother, doesn't it, to begin all over again? Well—make up your mind!

THE ACTOR [*smiling*]: All over again—from the very beginning—that's fine ... yes ... all over again. . . . [*Laughs.*] Well—then—I can, can't I?

LUKA: Why not? A human being can do anything—if he only makes up his mind.

THE ACTOR [*suddenly, as if coming out of a trance*]: You're a queer bird! See you anon! [*Whistles.*] Old man— *au revoir!* [*Exit.*]

ANNA: Granddad!

LUKA: Yes, little mother?

ANNA: Talk to me.

LUKA [*close to her.*] Come on—let's chat. . . .

[KLESHTCH, *glancing around, silently walks over to his wife, looks at her, and makes queer gestures with his hands, as though he wanted to say something.*]

LUKA: What is it, brother?

KLESHTCH [*quietly*]: Nothing . . . [*Crosses slowly to hall-way door, stands on the threshold for a few seconds, and exit.*]

LUKA [*looking after him*]: Hard on your man, isn't it?

ANNA: He doesn't concern me much . . .

LUKA: Did he beat you?

ANNA: Worse than that—it's he who's killed me—

BUBNOFF: My wife used to have a lover—the scoundrel —how clever he was at checkers!

MIEDVIEDIEFF: Hh-hm—

ANNA: Granddad! Talk to me, darling—I feel so sick. . . .

LUKA: Never mind—it's always like this before you die, little dove—never mind, dear! Just have faith! Once you're dead, you'll have peace—always. There's nothing to be afraid of—nothing. Quiet! Peace! Lie quietly! Death wipes out everything. Death is kindly. You die—and you rest— that's what they say. It is true, dear! Because—where can we find rest on this earth?

[PEPEL *enters. He is slightly drunk, disheveled, and sullen. Sits down on bunk near door, and remains silent and motionless.*]

ANNA: And how is it—there? More suffering?

LUKA: Nothing of the kind! No suffering! Trust me! Rest —nothing else! They'll lead you into God's presence, and they'll say: "Dear God! Behold! Here is Anna, Thy serv-ant!"

MIEDVIEDIEFF [*sternly*]: How do you know what they'll say up there? Oh, you . . .

[PEPEL, *on hearing* MIEDVIEDIEFF'S *voice, raises his head and listens.*]

LUKA: Apparently I do know, Mr. Sergeant!

MIEDVIEDIEFF [*conciliatory*]: Yes—it's your own affair
—though I'm not exactly a sergeant—yet—

BUBNOFF: I jump two!

MIEDVIEDIEFF: Damn—play!

LUKA: And the Lord will look at you gently and tenderly
and He'll say: "I know this Anna!" Then He'll say: "Take
Anna into Paradise. Let her have peace. I know. Her life
on earth was hard. She is very weary. Let Anna rest in
peace!"

ANNA [*choking*]: Grandfather—if it were only so—if
there were only rest and peace . . .

LUKA: There won't be anything else! Trust me! Die in
joy and not in grief. Death is to us like a mother to small
children. . . .

ANNA: But—perhaps—perhaps I get well . . . ?

LUKA [*laughing*]: Why—? Just to suffer more?

ANNA: But—just to live a little longer . . . just a little
longer! Since there'll be no suffering hereafter, I could bear
it a little longer down here. . . .

LUKA: There'll be nothing in the hereafter . . . but only . . .

PEPEL [*rising*]: Maybe yes—maybe no!

ANNA [*frightened*]: Oh—God!

LUKA: Hey—Adonis!

MIEDVIEDIEFF: Who's that yelping?

PEPEL [*crossing over to him*]: I! What of it?

MIEDVIEDIEFF: You yelp needlessly—that's what! People
ought to have some dignity!

PEPEL: Block-head! And that's an uncle for you—ho-ho!

LUKA [*to* PEPEL, *in an undertone*]: Look here—don't
shout—this woman's dying—her lips are already gray—
don't disturb her!

PEPEL: I've respect for you, granddad. You're all right,
you are! You lie well, and you spin pleasant yarns. Go on
lying, brother—there's little fun in this world. . . .

BUBNOFF: Is the woman really dying?

LUKA: You think I'm joking?

BUBNOFF: That means she'll stop coughing. Her cough
was very disturbing. I jump two!

MIEDVIEDIEFF: I'd like to murder you!

PEPEL: Abramka!

MIEDVIEDIEFF: I'm not Abramka to you!

PEPEL: Abrashka! Is Natasha ill?

MIEDVIEDIEFF: None of your business!

PEPEL: Come—tell me! Did Vassilisa beat her up very badly?

MIEDVIEDIEFF: That's none of your business, either! It's a family affair! Who are you anyway?

PEPEL: Whoever I am, you'll never see Natashka again if I choose!

MIEDVIEDIEFF [*throwing up the game*]: What's that? Who are you alluding to? My niece by any chance? You thief!

PEPEL: A thief whom you were never able to catch!

MIEDVIEDIEFF: Wait—I'll catch you yet—you'll see— sooner than you think!

PEPEL: If you catch me, God help your whole nest! Do you think I'll keep quiet before the examining magistrate? Every wolf howls! They'll ask me: "Who made you steal and showed you where?" "Mishka Kostilyoff and his wife!" "Who was your fence?" "Mishka Kostilyoff and his wife!"

MIEDVIEDIEFF: You lie! No one will believe you!

PEPEL: They'll believe me all right—because it's the truth! And I'll drag you into it, too. Ha! I'll ruin the lot of you—devils—just watch!

MIEDVIEDIEFF [*confused*]: You lie! You lie! And what harm did I do to you, you mad dog?

PEPEL: And what good did you ever do me?

LUKA: That's right!

MIEDVIEDIEFF [*to* LUKA]: Well—what are you croaking about? Is it any of your business? This is a family matter!

BUBNOFF [*to* LUKA]: Leave them alone! What do we care if they twist each other's tails?

LUKA [*peacefully*]: I meant no harm. All I said was that if a man isn't good to you, then he's acting wrong. . . .

MIEDVIEDIEFF [*uncomprehending*]: Now then—we all of us here know each other—but you—who are you? [*Frowns and exit.*]

LUKA: The cavalier is peeved! Oh-ho, brothers, I see your affairs are a bit tangled up!

PEPEL: He'll run to complain about us to Vassilisa. . . .

BUBNOFF: You're a fool, Vassily. You're very bold these days, aren't you? Watch out! It's all right to be bold when you go gathering mushrooms, but what good is it here? They'll break your neck before you know it!

PEPEL: Well—not as fast as all that! You don't catch us Yaroslavl boys napping! If it's going to be war, we'll fight. . . .

LUKA: Look here, boy, you really ought to go away from here—

PEPEL: Where? Please tell me!

LUKA: Go to Siberia!

PEPEL: If I go to Siberia, it'll be at the Tsar's expense!

LUKA: Listen! You go just the same! You can make your own way there. They need your kind out there. . . .

PEPEL: My way is clear. My father spent all his life in prison, and I inherited the trait. Even when I was a small child, they called me thief—thief's son.

LUKA: But Siberia is a fine country—a land of gold. Anyone who has health and strength and brains can live there like a cucumber in a hot-house.

PEPEL: Old man, why do you always tell lies?

LUKA: What?

PEPEL: Are you deaf? I ask—why do you always lie?

LUKA: What do I lie about?

PEPEL: About everything. According to you, life's wonderful everywhere—but you lie . . . why?

LUKA: Try to believe me. Go and see for yourself. And some day you'll thank me for it. What are you hanging round here for? And, besides, why is truth so important to you? Just think! Truth may spell death to you!

PEPEL: It's all one to me! If that—let it be that!

LUKA: Oh—what a madman! Why should you kill yourself?

BUBNOFF: What are you two jawing about, anyway? I don't understand. What kind of truth do you want, Vaska?

And what for? You know the truth about yourself—and so does everybody else. . . .

PEPEL: Just a moment! Don't crow! Let him tell me! Listen, old man! Is there a God?

[LUKA *smiles silently.*]

BUBNOFF: People just drift along—like shavings on a stream. When a house is built—the shavings are thrown away!

PEPEL: Well? Is there a God? Tell me.

LUKA [*in a low voice*]: If you have faith, there is; if you haven't, there isn't . . . whatever you believe in, exists. . . .

[PEPEL *looks at* LUKA *in staring surprise.*]

BUBNOFF: I'm going to have tea—come on over to the restaurant!

LUKA [*to* PEPEL]: What are you staring at?

PEPEL: Oh—just because! Wait now—you mean to say . . .

BUBNOFF: Well—I'm off.

[*Goes to door and runs into* VASSILISA.]

PEPEL: So—you . . .

VASSILISA [*to* BUBNOFF]: Is Natasha home?

BUBNOFF: No. [*Exit.*]

PEPEL: Oh—you've come—?

VASSILISA [*crossing to* ANNA]: Is she alive yet?

LUKA: Don't disturb her!

VASSILISA: What are you loafing around here for?

LUKA: I'll go—if you want me to. . . .

VASSILISA [*turning toward* PEPEL'S *room*]: Vassily! I've some business with you . . .

[LUKA *goes to hallway door, opens it, and shuts it loudly, then warily climbs into a bunk, and from there to the top of the stove.*]

VASSILISA [*calling from* PEPEL'S *room*] Vaska—come here!

PEPEL: I won't come—I don't want to. . . .

VASSILISA: Why? What are you angry about?

PEPEL: I'm sick of the whole thing. . . .

VASSILISA: Sick of me, too?

PEPEL: Yes! Of you, too! [VASSILISA *draws her shawl about her, pressing her hands over her breast. Crosses to* ANNA, *looks carefully through the bed curtains, and returns to* PEPEL.] Well—out with it!

VASSILISA: What do you want me to say? I can't force you to be loving, and I'm not the sort to beg for kindness. Thank you for telling me the truth.

PEPEL: What truth?

VASSILISA: That you're sick of me—or isn't it the truth? [PEPEL *looks at her silently. She turns to him.*] What are you staring at? Don't you recognize me?

PEPEL [*sighing*]: You're beautiful, Vassilisa! [*She puts her arm about his neck, but he shakes it off.*] But I never gave my heart to you. . . . I've lived with you and all that—But I never really liked you. . . .

VASSILISA [*quietly*]: That so? Well—?

PEPEL: What is there to talk about? Nothing. Go away from me!

VASSILISA: Taken a fancy to someone else?

PEPEL: None of your business! Suppose I have—I wouldn't ask you to be my matchmaker!

VASSILISA [*significantly*]: That's too bad . . . perhaps I might arrange a match. . . .

PEPEL [*suspiciously*]: Who with?

VASSILISA: You know—why do you pretend? Vassily—let me be frank. [*With lower voice.*] I won't deny it—you've offended me . . . it was like a bolt from the blue . . . you said you loved me—and then all of a sudden . . .

PEPEL: It wasn't sudden at all. It's been a long time since I . . . woman, you've no soul! A woman must have a soul . . . we men are beasts—we must be taught—and you, what have you taught me—?

VASSILISA: Never mind the past! I know—no man owns his own heart—you don't love me any longer . . . well and good, it can't be helped!

PEPEL: So that's over. We part peaceably, without a row as it should be!

VASSILISA: Just a moment! All the same, when I lived with you, I hoped you'd help me out of this swamp—I thought you'd free me from my husband and my uncle—from all this life—and perhaps, Vassya, it wasn't you whom I loved—but my hope—do you understand? I waited for you to drag me out of this mire. . . .

PEPEL: You aren't a nail—and I'm not a pair of pincers! I thought you had brains—you are so clever—so crafty. . . .

VASSILISA [*leaning closely toward him*]: Vassya—Let's help each other!

PEPEL: How?

VASSILISA [*low and forcibly*]: My sister—I know you've fallen for her. . . .

PEPEL: And that's why you beat her up, like the beast you are! Look out, Vassilisa! Don't you touch her!

VASSILISA: Wait. Don't get excited. We can do everything quietly and pleasantly. You want to marry her. I'll give you money . . . three hundred rubles—even more than . . .

PEPEL [*moving away from her*]: Stop! What do you mean?

VASSILISA: Rid me of my husband! Take that noose from around my neck. . . .

PEPEL [*whistling softly*]: So that's the way the land lies! You certainly planned it cleverly . . . in other words, the grave for the husband, the gallows for the lover, and as for yourself . . .

VASSILISA: Vassya! Why the gallows? It doesn't have to be yourself—but one of your pals! And supposing it were yourself—who'd know? Natalia—just think—and you'll have money—you go away somewhere . . . you free me forever—and it'll be very good for my sister to be away from me—the sight of her enrages me. . . . I get furious with her on account of you, and I can't control myself. I tortured the girl—I beat her up—beat her up so that I myself cried with pity for her—but I'll beat her—and I'll go on beating her!

PEPEL: Beast! Bragging about your beastliness?

VASSILISA: I'm not bragging—I speak the truth. Think now, Vassya. You've been to prison twice because of my husband—through his greed. He clings to me like a bedbug—he's been sucking the life out of me for the last four years—and what sort of a husband is he to me? He's forever abusing Natasha—calls her a beggar—he's just poison, plain poison, to everyone. . . .

PEPEL: You spin your yarn cleverly. . . .

VASSILISA: Everything I say is true. Only a fool could be as blind as you. . . .

[KOSTILYOFF *enters stealthily and comes forward noisily.*]

PEPEL [*to* VASSILISA]: Oh—go away!

VASSILISA: Think it over! [*Sees her husband.*] What? You? Following me?

[PEPEL *leaps up and stares at* KOSTILYOFF *savagely.*]

KOSTILYOFF: It's I, I! So the two of you were here alone —you were—ah—conversing? [*Suddenly stamps his feet and screams.*] Vassilisa—you bitch! You beggar! You damned hag! [*Frightened by his own screams which are met by silence and indifference on the part of the others.*] Forgive me, O Lord . . . Vassilisa—again you've led me into the path of sin. . . . I've been looking for you everywhere. It's time to go to bed. You forgot to fill the lamps— oh, you . . . beggar! Swine!

[*Shakes his trembling fist at her, while* VASSILISA *slowly goes to door, glancing at* PEPEL *over her shoulder.*]

PEPEL [*to* KOSTILYOFF]: Go away—clear out of here—

KOSTILYOFF [*yelling*]: What? I? The Boss? I get out? You thief!

PEPEL [*sullenly*]: Go away, Mishka!

KOSTILYOFF: Don't you dare—I—I'll show you.

[PEPEL *seizes him by the collar and shakes him. From the stove comes loud noises and yawns.* PEPEL *releases* KOSTILYOFF *who runs into the hallway, screaming.*]

PEPEL [*jumping on a bunk*]: Who is it? Who's on the stove?

LUKA [*raising his head*]: Eh?

PEPEL: You?

LUKA [*undisturbed*]: I—I myself—oh, dear Jesus!

PEPEL [*shuts hallway door, looks for the wooden closing bar, but can't find it*]: The devil! Come down, old man!

LUKA: I'm climbing down—all right. . . .

PEPEL [*roughly*]: What did you climb on that stove for?

LUKA: Where was I to go?

PEPEL: Why—didn't you go out into the hall?

LUKA: The hall's too cold for an old fellow like myself, brother.

PEPEL: You overheard?

LUKA: Yes—I did. How could I help it? Am I deaf? Well, my boy, happiness is coming your way. Real, good fortune I call it!

PEPEL [*suspiciously*]: What good fortune—?

LUKA: In so far as I was lying on the stove . . .

PEPEL: Why did you make all that noise?

LUKA: Because I was getting warm . . . it was your good luck . . . I thought if only the boy wouldn't make a mistake and choke the old man . . .

PEPEL: Yes—I might have done it . . . how terrible. . . .

LUKA: Small wonder! It isn't difficult to make a mistake of that sort.

PEPEL [*smiling*]: What's the matter? Did you make the same sort of mistake once upon a time?

LUKA: Boy, listen to me. Send that woman out of your life. Don't let her near you! Her husband—she'll get rid of him herself—and in a shrewder way than you could—yes! Don't you listen to that devil! Look at me! I am bald-headed —know why? Because of all these women. . . . Perhaps I knew more women than I had hair on the top of my head— but this Vassilisa—she's worse than the plague. . . .

PEPEL: I don't understand . . . I don't know whether to thank you—or—well . . .

LUKA: Don't say a word! You won't improve on what I said. Listen: take the one you like by the arm, and march out of here—get out of here—clean out . . .

PEPEL [*sadly*]: I can't understand people. Who is kind and who isn't? It's all a mystery to me. . . .

LUKA: What's there to understand? There's all breeds of men . . . they all live as their hearts tell them . . . good today, bad tomorrow! But if you really care for that girl . . . take her away from here and that's all there is to it. Otherwise go away alone . . . you're young—you're in no hurry for a wife. . . .

PEPEL [*taking him by the shoulder*]: Tell me! Why do you say all this?

LUKA: Wait. Let me go. I want a look at Anna . . . she was coughing so terribly . . . [*Goes to* ANNA'S *bed, pulls the curtains, looks, touches her.* PEPEL, *thoughtfully and distraught, follows him with his eyes.*] Merciful Jesus Christ! Take into Thy keeping the soul of this woman Anna, newcomer amongst the blessed!

PEPEL [*softly*]: Is she dead? [*Without approaching, he stretches himself and looks at the bed.*]

LUKA [*gently*]: Her sufferings are over! Where's her husband?

PEPEL: In the saloon, most likely . . . .

LUKA: Well—he'll have to be told . . . .

PEPEL [*shuddering*]: I don't like corpses!

LUKA [*going to door*]: Why should you like them? It's the living who demand our love—the living. . . .

PEPEL: I'm coming with you. . . .

LUKA: Are you afraid?

PEPEL: I don't like it. . . .

[*They go out quickly. The stage is empty and silent for a few moments. Behind the door is heard a dull, staccato, incomprehensible noise. Then* THE ACTOR *enters.*]

THE ACTOR [*stands at the open door, supporting himself against the jamb, and shouts*]: Hey, old man—where are you—? I just remembered—listen . . . [*Takes two staggering steps forward and, striking a pose, recites.*]

"Good people! If the world cannot find
    A path to holy truth,

> Glory be to the madman who will enfold
> all humanity
> In a golden dream . . ."

[NATASHA *appears in the doorway behind* THE ACTOR]
Old man! [*Recites*]:

> "If tomorrow the sun were to forget
> To light our earth,
> Tomorrow then some madman's thought
> Would bathe the world in sunshine. . . ."

NATASHA [*laughing*]: Scarecrow! You're drunk!

THE ACTOR [*turns to her*]: Oh—it's you? Where's the old man, the dear old man? Not a soul here, seems to me . . . Natasha, farewell—right—farewell!

NATASHA [*entering*]: Don't wish me farewell, before you've wished me how-d'you-do!

THE ACTOR [*barring her way*]: I am going. Spring will come—and I'll be here no longer—

NATASHA: Wait a moment! Where do you propose going?

THE ACTOR: In search of a town—to be cured—And you, Ophelia, must go away! Take the veil! Just imagine—there's a hospital to cure—ah—organisms for drunkards—a wonderful hospital—built of marble—with marble floors . . . light—clean—food—and all gratis! And a marble floor— yes! I'll find it—I'll get cured—and then I shall start life anew. . . . I'm on my way to regeneration, as King Lear said. Natasha, my stage name is . . . Svertchkoff—Zavoloushski . . . do you realize how painful it is to lose one's name? Even dogs have their names . . . [NATASHA *carefully passes* THE ACTOR, *stops at* ANNA's *bed and looks.*] To be nameless —is not to exist!

NATASHA: Look, my dear—why—she's dead. . . .

THE ACTOR [*shakes his head*]: Impossible . . .

NATASHA [*stepping back*]: So help me God—look . . .

BUBNOFF [*appearing in doorway*]: What is there to look at?

NATASHA: Anna—she's dead!

BUBNOFF: That means—she's stopped coughing! [*Goes to* ANNA'S *bed, looks, and returns to his bunk*.] We must tell Kleshtch—it's his business to know. . . .

THE ACTOR: I'll go—I'll say to him—she lost her name— [*Exit*.]

NATASHA [*in center of room*]: I, too—some day—I'll be found in the cellar—dead. . . .

BUBNOFF [*spreading out some rags on his bunk*]: What's that? What are you muttering?

NATASHA: Nothing much . . .

BUBNOFF: Waiting for Vaska, eh? Take care—Vassilisa'll break your head!

NATASHA: Isn't it the same who breaks it? I'd much rather he'd do it!

BUBNOFF [*lying down*]: Well—that's your own affair. . . .

NATASHA: It's best for her to be dead—yet it's a pity . . . oh, Lord—why do we live?

BUBNOFF: It's so with all . . . we're born, live, and die— and I'll die, too—and so'll you—what's there to be gloomy about?

   [*Enter* LUKA, THE TARTAR, ZOB, *and* KLESHTCH. *The latter comes after the others, slowly, shrunk up*.]

NATASHA: Sh-sh! Anna!

ZOB: We've heard—God rest her soul. . . .

THE TARTAR [*to* KLESHTCH]: We must take her out of here. Out into the hall! This is no place for corpses—but for the living . . .

KLESHTCH [*quietly*]: We'll take her out—
   [*Everybody goes to the bed,* KLESHTCH *looks at his wife over the others' shoulders*.]

ZOB [*to* THE TARTAR]: You think she'll smell? I don't think she will—she dried up while she was still alive. . . .

NATASHA: God! If they'd only a little pity . . . if only someone would say a kindly word—oh, you . . .

LUKA: Don't be hurt, girl—never mind! Why and how should we pity the dead? Come, dear! We don't pity the living—we can't even pity our own selves—how can we?

BUBNOFF [*yawning*]: And, besides, when you're dead, no

word will help you—when you're still alive, even sick, it may. . . .

THE TARTAR [*stepping aside*]: The police must be notified. . . .

ZOB: The police—must be done! Kleshtch! Did you notify the police?

KLESHTCH: No—she's got to be buried—and all I have is forty kopecks—

ZOB: Well—you'll have to borrow then—otherwise we'll take up a collection . . . one'll give five kopecks, others as much as they can. But the police must be notified at once— or they'll think you killed her or God knows what not. . . . [*Crosses to* THE TARTAR'S *bunk and prepares to lie down by his side.*]

NATASHA [*going to* BUBNOFF'S *bunk*]: Now—I'll dream of her . . . I always dream of the dead. . . . I'm afraid to go out into the hall by myself—it's dark there. . . .

LUKA [*following her*]: You better fear the living—I'm telling you. . . .

NATASHA: Take me across the hall, grandfather.

LUKA: Come on—come on—I'll take you across—
[*They go away. Pause.*]

ZOB [*to* THE TARTAR]: Oh-ho! Spring will soon be here, little brother, and it'll be quite warm. In the villages the peasants are already making ready their plows and harrows, preparing to till . . . and we . . . Hassan? Snoring already? Damned Mohammedan!

BUBNOFF: Tartars love sleep!

KLESHTCH [*in center of room, staring in front of him*]: What am I to do now?

ZOB: Lie down and sleep—that's all. . . .

KLESHTCH [*softly*]: But—she . . . how about . . .
[*No one answers him.* SATINE *and* THE ACTOR *enter.*]

THE ACTOR [*yelling*]: Old man! Come here, my trusted Duke of Kent!

SATINE: Miklookha-Maklai is coming—ho-ho!

THE ACTOR: It has been decided upon! Old man, where's the town—where are you?

SATINE: Fata Morgana, the old man bilked you from top to bottom! There's nothing—no towns—no people—nothing at all!

THE ACTOR: You lie!

THE TARTAR [*jumping up*]: Where's the boss? I'm going to the boss. If I can't sleep, I won't pay! Corpses—drunkards . . .

[*Exit quickly.* SATINE *looks after him and whistles.*]

BUBNOFF [*in a sleepy voice*]: Go to bed, boys—be quiet . . . night is for sleep. . . .

THE ACTOR: Yes—so—there's a corpse here. . . . "Our net fished up a corpse. . . ." Verses by Béranger. . . .

SATINE [*screams*]: The dead can't hear . . . the dead do not feel—Scream!—Roar! . . . the deaf don't hear!

[*In the doorway appears* LUKA.]

CURTAIN

act 3

"The Waste," a yard strewn with rubbish and overgrown with weeds. Back, a high brick wall which shuts out the sight of the sky. Near it are elder-bushes. Right, the dark, wooden wall of some sort of house, barn or stable. Left, the gray tumbledown wall of KOSTILYOFF'S *night asylum. It is built at an angle so that the farther corner reaches almost to the center of the yard. Between it and the wall runs a narrow passage. In the gray, plastered wall are two windows, one on a level with the ground, the other about six feet higher up and closer to the brick wall. Near the latter wall is a big sledge turned upside down and a beam about twelve feet long. Right of the wall is a heap of old planks. Evening.*

*The sun is setting, throwing a crimson light on the brick
wall. Early spring, the snow having only recently melted.
The elder-bushes are not yet in bud.*

NATASHA *and* NASTYA *are sitting side by side on the beam.*
LUKA *and* THE BARON *are on the sledge.* KLESHTCH *is
stretched on the pile of planks to the right.* BUBNOFF'S *face
is at the ground floor window.*

NASTYA [*with closed eyes, nodding her head in rhythm to
the tale she is telling in a sing-song voice*]: So then at night
he came into the garden. I had been waiting for him quite
a while. I trembled with fear and grief—he trembled, too
... he was as white as chalk—and he had the pistol in his
hand. ...

NATASHA [*chewing sun-flower seeds*]: Oh—are these
students really such desperate fellows? ...

NASTYA: And he says to me in a dreadful voice: "My precious darling ..."

BUBNOFF: Ho-ho! Precious—

THE BARON: Shut up! If you don't like it, you can lump it!
But don't interrupt her. ... Go on ...

NASTYA: "My one and only love," he says, "my parents,"
he says, "refuse to give their consent to our wedding—and
threaten to disown me because of my love for you. Therefore," he says, "I must take my life." And his pistol was
huge—and loaded with ten bullets ... "Farewell," he says,
"beloved comrade! I have made up my mind for good and
all ... I can't live without you ..." and I replied: "My un-
forgettable friend—my Raoul. ..."

BUBNOFF [*surprised*]: What? What? Krawl—did you call
him—?

THE BARON: Nastka! But last time his name was Gaston. ...

NASTYA [*jumping up*]: Shut up, you bastards! Ah—you
lousy mongrels! You think for a moment that you can understand love—true love? My love was real honest-to-God
love! [*To* THE BARON.] You good-for-nothing! ... educated,
you call yourself—drinking coffee in bed, did you?

LUKA: Now, now! Wait, people! Don't interfere! Show a little respect to your neighbors . . . it isn't the word that matters, but what's in back of the word. That's what matters! Go on, girl! It's all right!

BUBNOFF: Go on, crow! See if you can make your feathers white!

THE BARON: Well—continue!

NATASHA: Pay no attention to them . . . what are they? They're just jealous . . . they've nothing to tell about themselves . . .

NASTYA [sits down again]: I'm going to say no more! If they don't believe me they'll laugh. [Stops suddenly, is silent for a few seconds, then, shutting her eyes, continues in a loud and intense voice, swaying her hands as if to the rhythm of far music.] And then I replied to him: "Joy of my life! My bright moon! And I, too, I can't live without you—because I love you madly, so madly—and I shall keep on loving you as long as my heart beats in my bosom. But—" I say—"don't take your young life! Think how necessary it is to your dear parents whose only happiness you are. Leave me! Better that I should perish from longing for you, my life! I alone! I—ah—as such, such! Better that I should die —it doesn't matter . . . I am of no use to the world—and I have nothing, nothing at all—" [Covers her face with her hand and weeps gently.]

NATASHA [in a low voice]: Don't cry—don't!

[LUKA, smiling, strokes NASTYA's head.]

BUBNOFF [laughs]: Ah—you limb of Satan!

THE BARON [also laughs]: Hey, old man? Do you think it's true? It's all from that book, Fatal Love . . . it's all nonsense! Let her alone!

NATASHA: And what's it to you? Shut up—or God'll punish you!

NASTYA [bitterly]: God damn your soul! You worthless pig! Soul—bah!—you haven't got one!

LUKA [takes NASTYA's hand]: Come, dear! It's nothing! Don't be angry—I know—I believe you! You're right, not they! If you believe you had a real love affair, then you did —yes! And as for him—don't be angry with a fellow-lodger ... maybe he's really jealous, and that's why he's laughing. Maybe he never had any real love—maybe not—come on—let's go!

NASTYA [*pressing her hand against her breast*]: Grandfather! So help me God—it happened! It happened! He was a student, a Frenchman—Gastotcha was his name—he had a little black beard—and patent leathers—may God strike me dead if I'm lying! And he loved me so— My God, how he loved me!

LUKA: Yes, yes, it's all right. I believe you! Patent leathers, you said? Well, well, well—and you loved him, did you? [*Disappears with her around the corner.*]

THE BARON: God—isn't she a fool, though? She's goodhearted—but such a fool—it's past belief!

BUBNOFF: And why are people so fond of lying—just as if they were up before the judge—really!

NATASHA: I guess lying is more fun than speaking the truth—I, too . . .

THE BARON: What—you, too? Go on!

NATASHA: Oh—I imagine things—invent them—and I wait—

THE BARON: For what?

NATASHA [*smiling confusedly*]: Oh—I think that perhaps —well—tomorrow somebody will really appear—someone —oh—out of the ordinary—or something'll happen—also out of the ordinary. . . . I've been waiting for it—oh—always . . . But, really, what is there to wait for?

[*Pause.*]

THE BARON [*with a slight smile*]: Nothing—I expect nothing! What is past, is past! Through! Over with! And then what?

NATASHA: And then—well—tomorrow I imagine suddenly that I'll die—and I get frightened . . . in summer it's all right to dream of death—then there are thunder storms— one might get struck by lightning. . . .

THE BARON: You've a hard life . . . your sister's a wicked-tempered devil!

NATASHA: Tell me—does anybody live happily? It's hard for all of us—I can see that. . . .

KLESHTCH [*who until this moment has sat motionless and indifferent, jumps up suddenly*]: For all? You lie! Not for all! If it were so—all right! Then it wouldn't hurt—yes!

BUBNOFF: What in hell's bit you? Just listen to him yelping!

[KLESHTCH *lies down again and grunts.*]

THE BARON: Well—I'd better go and make my peace with Nastinka—if I don't, she won't treat me to vodka. . . .

BUBNOFF: Hm—people love to lie . . . with Nastka—I can see the reason why. She's used to painting that mutt of hers —and now she wants to paint her soul as well . . . put rouge on her soul, eh? But the others—why do they? Take Luka for instance—he lies a lot . . . and what does he get out of it? He's an old fellow, too—why does he do it?

THE BARON [*smiling and walking away*]: All people have drab-colored souls—and they like to brighten them up a bit. . . .

LUKA [*appearing from round the corner*]: You, sir, why do you tease the girl? Leave her alone—let her cry if it amuses her . . . she weeps for her own pleasure—what harm is it to you?

THE BARON: Nonsense, old man! She's a nuisance. Raoul today, Gaston tomorrow—always the same old yarn, though! Still—I'll go and make up with her. [*Leaves.*]

LUKA: That's right—go—and be nice to her. Being nice to people never does them any harm. . . .

NATASHA: You're so good, little father—why are you so good?

LUKA: Good, did you say? Well—call it that! [*Behind the brick wall is heard soft singing and the sounds of a concertina.*] Someone has to be kind, girl—someone must pity people! Christ pitied everybody—and he said to us: "Go and do likewise!" I tell you—if you pity a man when he most needs it, good comes of it. Why—I used to be a watchman on the estate of an engineer near Tomsk—all right—the house was right in the middle of a forest—lonely place— winter came—and I remained all by myself. Well—one night I heard a noise—

NATASHA: Thieves?

LUKA: Exactly! Thieves creeping in! I took my gun—I went out. I looked and saw two of them opening a window —and so busy that they didn't even see me. I yell: "Hey there—get out of here!" And they turn on me with their axes—I warn them to stand back, or I'd shoot—and as I speak, I keep on covering them with my gun, first the one, then the other—they go down on their knees, as if to im- plore me for mercy. And by that time I was furious—be- cause of those axes, you see—and so I say to them: "I was chasing you, you scoundrels—and you didn't go. Now you go and break off some stout branches!"—and they did so —and I say: "Now—one of you lie down and let the other one flog him!" So they obey me and flog each other—and then they begin to implore me again. "Grandfather," they say, "for God's sake give us some bread! We're hungry!" There's thieves for you, my dear! [*Laughs.*] And with an ax, too! Yes—honest peasants, both of them! And I say to them, "You should have asked for bread straight away!" And they say: "We got tired of asking—you beg and beg— and nobody gives you a crumb—it hurts!" So they stayed with me all that winter—one of them, Stepan, would take my gun and go shooting in the forest—and the other, Yakoff, was ill most of the time—he coughed a lot . . . and so the three of us together looked after the house . . . then spring came . . . "Good-by, grandfather," they said—and they went away—back home to Russia. . . .

NATASHA: Were they escaped convicts?

LUKA: That's just what they were—escaped convicts— from a Siberian prison camp . . . honest peasants! If I hadn't felt sorry for them—they might have killed me—or maybe worse—and then there would have been trial and prison and afterward Siberia—what's the sense of it? Prison teaches no good—and Siberia doesn't either—but another human being can . . . yes, a human being can teach another one kindness—very simply!

[*Pause.*]

BUBNOFF: Hm—yes—I, for instance, don't know how to lie . . . why—as far as I'm concerned, I believe in coming out with the whole truth and putting it on thick . . . why fuss about it?

KLESHTCH [*again jumps up as if his clothes were on fire, and screams*]: What truth? Where is there truth? [*Tearing at his ragged clothes.*] Here's truth for you! No work! No strength! That's the only truth! Shelter—there's no shelter! You die—that's the truth! Hell! What do I want with the truth? Let me breathe! Why should I be blamed? What do I want with truth? To live—Christ Almighty!—they won't let you live—and that's another truth!

BUBNOFF: He's mad!

LUKA: Dear Lord . . . listen to me, brother—

KLESHTCH [*trembling with excitement*]: They say: there's truth! You, old man, try to console everyone . . . I tell you —I hate everyone! And there's your truth—God curse it— understand? I tell you—God curse it! [*Rushes away round the corner, turning as he goes.*]

LUKA: Ah—how excited he got! Where did he run off to?

NATASHA: He's off his head. . . .

BUBNOFF: God—didn't he say a whole lot, though? As if he was playing drama—he gets those fits often . . . he isn't used to life yet. . . .

PEPEL [*comes slowly round the corner*]: Peace on all this honest gathering! Well, Luka, you wily old fellow—still telling them stories?

LUKA: You should have heard how that fellow carried on!

PEPEL: Kleshtch—wasn't it? What's wrong with him? He was running like one possessed!

LUKA: You'd do the same if your own heart were breaking!

PEPEL [*sitting down*]: I don't like him ... he's got such a nasty, bad temper—and so proud! [*Imitating* KLESHTCH.] "I'm a workman!" And he thinks everyone's beneath him. Go on working if you feel like it—nothing to be so damned haughty about! If work is the standard—a horse can give us points—pulls like hell and says nothing! Natasha—are your folks at home?

NATASHA: They went to the cemetery—then to night service. ...

PEPEL: So that's why you're free for once—quite a novelty.

LUKA [*to* BUBNOFF, *thoughtfully*]: There—you say— truth! Truth doesn't always heal a wounded soul. For instance, I knew of a man who believed in a land of righteousness. ...

BUBNOFF: In what?

LUKA: In a land of righteousness. He said: "Somewhere on this earth there must be a righteous land— and wonderful people live there—good people! They respect each other, help each other, and everything is peaceful and good!" And so that man—who was always searching for this land of righteousness—he was poor and lived miserably—and when things got to be so bad with him that it seemed there was nothing else for him to do except lie down and die— even then he never lost heart—but he'd just smile and say; "Never mind! I can stand it! A little while longer—and I'll have done with this life—and I'll go in search of the righteous land."—it was his one happiness—the thought of that land. ...

PEPEL: Well? Did he go there?

BUBNOFF: Where? Ho-ho!

LUKA: And then to this place—in Siberia, by the way— there came a convict—a learned man with books and maps —yes, a learned man who knew all sorts of things—and the other man said to him: "Do me a favor—show me where is the land of righteousness and how I can get there." At once the learned man opened his books, spread out his maps, and looked and looked and he said—no—he couldn't find this land anywhere ... everything was correct—all the lands on earth were marked—but not this land of righteousness ...

PEPEL [*in a low voice*]: Well? Wasn't there a trace of it?

[BUBNOFF *roars with laughter.*]

NATASHA: Wait ... well, little father?

LUKA: The man wouldn't believe it. ... "It must exist," he said, "look carefully. Otherwise," he says, "your books and maps are of no use if there's no land of righteousness." The learned man was offended. "My plans," he said, "are correct. But there exists no land of righteousness anywhere." Well, then the other man got angry. He'd lived and lived and suffered and suffered, and had believed all the time in the existence of this land—and now, according to the plans, it didn't exist at all. He felt robbed! And he said to the learned man: "Ah—you scum of the earth! You're not a learned man at all—but just a damned cheat!"—and he gave him a good wallop in the eye—then another one ... [*After a moment's silence.*] And then he went home and hanged himself!

[*All are silent.* LUKA, *smiling, looks at* PEPEL *and* NA-*tasha.*]

PEPEL [*low-voiced*]: To hell with this story—it isn't very cheerful. ...

NATASHA: He couldn't stand the disappointment. ...

BUBNOFF [*sullen*]: Ah—it's nothing but a fairy tale. ...

PEPEL: Well—there is the righteous land for you—doesn't exist, it seems. ...

NATASHA: I'm sorry for that man ...

BUBNOFF: All a story—ho-ho!—land of righteousness—what an idea! [*Exit through window.*]

LUKA [*pointing to window*]: He's laughing! [*Pause.*] Well, children, God be with you! I'll leave you soon. ...

PEPEL: Where are you going to?

LUKA: To the Ukraine—I heard they discovered a new religion there—I want to see—yes! People are always seeking—they always want something better—God grant them patience!

PEPEL: You think they'll find it?

LUKA: The people? They will find it! He who seeks, will find! He who desires strongly, will find!

NATASHA: If only they could find something better—invent something better. . . .

LUKA: They're trying to! But we must help them, girl—we must respect them. . . .

NATASHA: How can I help them? I am helpless myself!

PEPEL [*determined*]: Again—listen—I'll speak to you again, Natasha—here—before him—he knows everything . . . run away with me?

NATASHA: Where? From one prison to another?

PEPEL: I told you—I'm through with being a thief, so help me God! I'll quit! If I say so, I'll do it! I can read and write— I'll work— He's been telling me to go to Siberia on my own hook—let's go there together, what do you say? Do you think I'm not disgusted with my life? Oh—Natasha—I know . . . I see . . . I console myself with the thought that there are lots of people who are honored and respected—and who are bigger thieves than I! But what good is that to me? It isn't that I repent . . . I've no conscience . . . but I do feel one thing: One must live differently. One must live a better life . . . one must be able to respect one's own self. . . .

LUKA: That's right, friend! May God help you! It's true! A man must respect himself!

PEPEL: I've been a thief from childhood on. Everybody always called me "Vaska—the thief—the son of a thief!" Oh—very well then—I am a thief— . . . just imagine—now, perhaps, I'm a thief out of spite—perhaps I'm a thief because no one ever called me anything different. . . . Well, Natasha—?

NATASHA [*sadly*]: Somehow I don't believe in words—and I'm restless today—my heart is heavy . . . as if I were expecting something . . . it's a pity, Vassily, that you talked to me today. . . .

PEPEL: When should I? It isn't the first time I speak to you. . . .

NATASHA: And why should I go with you? I don't love you so very much—sometimes I like you—and other times the mere sight of you makes me sick . . . it seems—no—I don't really love you . . . when one really loves, one sees no fault. . . . But I do see. . . .

PEPEL: Never mind—you'll love me after a while! I'll make you care for me . . . if you'll just say yes! For over a year I've watched you . . . you're a decent girl . . . you're kind—you're reliable—I'm very much in love with you. . . .

[VASSILISA, *in her best dress, appears at window and listens.*]

NATASHA: Yes—you love me—but how about my sister? . . .

PEPEL [*confused*]: Well, what of her? There are plenty like her . . .

LUKA: You'll be all right, girl! If there's no bread, you have to eat weeds . . .

PEPEL [*gloomily*]: Please—feel a little sorry for me! My life isn't all roses—it's a hell of a life . . . little happiness in it . . . I feel as if a swamp were sucking me under . . . and whatever I try to catch and hold on to, is rotten . . . it breaks. . . . Your sister—oh—I thought she was different . . . if she weren't so greedy after money . . . I'd have done anything for her sake, if she were only all mine . . . but she must have someone else . . . and she has to have money—and freedom . . . because she doesn't like the straight and narrow . . . she can't help me. But you're like a young fir-tree . . . you bend, but you don't break. . . .

LUKA: Yes—go with him, girl, go! He's a good lad—he's all right! Only tell him every now and then that he's a good lad so that he won't forget it—and he'll believe you. Just you keep on telling him "Vasya, you're a good man—don't you forget it!" Just think, dear, where else could you go except with him? Your sister is a savage beast . . . and as for her husband, there's little to say of him? He's rotten beyond words . . . and all this life here, where will it get you? But this lad is strong. . . .

NATASHA: Nowhere to go—I know—I thought of it. The only thing is—I've no faith in anybody—and there's no place for me to turn to. . . .

PEPEL: Yes, there is! But I won't let you go that way—I'd rather cut your throat!

NATASHA [*smiling*]: There—I'm not his wife yet—and he talks already of killing me!

PEPEL [*puts his arms around her*]: Come, Natasha! Say yes!

NATASHA [*holding him close*]: But I'll tell you one thing, Vassily—I swear it before God . . . the first time you strike me or hurt me any other way, I'll have no pity on myself . . . I'll either hang myself . . . or . . .

PEPEL: May my hand wither if ever I touch you!

LUKA: Don't doubt him, dear! He needs you more than you need him!

VASSILISA [*from the window*]: So now they're engaged! Love and advice!

NATASHA: They've come back—oh, God—they saw—oh, Vassily . . .

PEPEL: Why are you frightened? Nobody'll dare touch you now!

VASSILISA: Don't be afraid, Natalia! He won't beat you . . . he don't know how to love or how to beat . . . I know!

LUKA [*in a low voice*]: Rotten old hag—like a snake in the grass. . . .

VASSILISA: He dares only with the word!

KOSTILYOFF [*enters*]: Natashka! What are you doing here, you parasite? Gossiping? Kicking about your family? And the samovar not ready? And the table not cleared?

NATASHA [*going out*]: I thought you were going to church . . . ?

KOSTILYOFF: None of your business what we intended doing! Mind your own affairs—and do what you're told!

PEPEL: Shut up, you! She's no longer your servant! Don't go, Natalia—don't do a thing!

NATASHA: Stop ordering me about—you're commencing too soon! [*Leaves.*]

PEPEL [*to* KOSTILYOFF]: That's enough. You've used her long enough—now she's mine!

KOSTILYOFF: Yours? When did you buy her—and for how much?

[VASSILISA *roars with laughter.*]

LUKA: Go away, Vassya!

PEPEL: Don't laugh, you fools—or first thing you know I'll make you cry!

VASSILISA: Oh, how terrible! Oh—how you frighten me!

LUKA: Vassily—go away! Don't you see—she's goading you on . . . ridiculing you, don't you understand? . . .

PEPEL: Yes . . . You lie, lie! You won't get what you want!

VASSILISA: Nor will I get what I don't want, Vassya!

PEPEL [*shaking his fist at her*]: We'll see. . . . [*Exit.*]

VASSILISA [*disappears through window*]: I'll arrange some wedding for you . . .

KOSTILYOFF [*crossing to* LUKA]: Well, old man, how's everything?

LUKA: All right!

KOSTILYOFF: You're going away, they say—?

LUKA: Soon.

KOSTILYOFF: Where to?

LUKA: I'll follow my nose. . . .

KOSTILYOFF: Tramping, eh? Don't like stopping in one place all the time, do you?

LUKA: Even water won't pass beneath a stone that's sunk too firmly in the ground, they say. . . .

KOSTILYOFF: That's true for a stone. But man must settle in one place. Men can't live like cockroaches, crawling about wherever they want. . . . A man must stick to one place—and not wander about aimlessly. . . .

LUKA: But suppose his home is wherever he hangs his hat?

KOSTILYOFF: Why, then—he's a vagabond—useless . . . a human being must be of some sort of use—he must work. . . .

LUKA: That's what you think, eh?

KOSTILYOFF: Yes—sure . . . just look! What's a vagabond? A strange fellow . . . unlike all others. If he's a real pilgrim then he's some good in the world . . . perhaps he discovered a new truth. Well—but not every truth is worth while. Let him keep it to himself and shut up about it! Or else—let him speak in a way which no one can understand . . . don't let him interfere . . . don't let him stir up people without cause! It's none of his business how other people live! Let him follow his own righteous path . . . in the woods—or in a monastery—away from everybody! He mustn't interfere— nor condemn other people—but pray—pray for all of us— for all the world's sins—for mine—for yours—for every-body's. To pray—that's why he forsakes the world's turmoil! That's so! [*Pause.*] But you—what sort of pilgrim are you—? An honest person must have a passport . . . all honest people have passports . . . yes! . . .

LUKA: In this world there are people—and also just plain men. . . .

KOSTILYOFF: Don't coin wise sayings! Don't give me riddles! I'm as clever as you . . . what's the difference— people and men?

LUKA: What riddle is there? I say—there's sterile and there's fertile ground . . . whatever you sow in it, grows . . . that's all. . . .

KOSTILYOFF: What do you mean?

LUKA: Take yourself for instance . . . if the Lord God himself said to you: "Mikhailo, be a man!"—it would be useless—nothing would come of it—you're doomed to re-main just as you are. . . .

KOSTILYOFF: Oh—but do you realize that my wife's uncle is a policeman, and that if I . . .

VASSILISA [*coming in*]: Mikhail Ivanitch—come and have your tea . . .

KOSTILYOFF [*to* LUKA]: You listen! Get out! You leave this place—hear?

VASSILISA: Yes—get out, old man! Your tongue's too

long! And—who knows—you may be an escaped convict. . . .

KOSTILYOFF: If I ever see sign of you again after today—well—I've warned you!

LUKA: You'll call your uncle, eh? Go on—call him! Tell him you've caught an escaped convict—and maybe uncle'll get a reward—perhaps all of three kopecks. . . .

BUBNOFF [*in the window*]: What are you bargaining about? Three kopecks—for what?

LUKA: They're threatening to sell me. . . .

VASSILISA [*to her husband*]: Come. . . .

BUBNOFF: For three kopecks? Well—look out, old man—they may even do it for one!

KOSTILYOFF [*to* BUBNOFF]: You have a habit of jumping up like a jack-in-the-box!

VASSILISA: The world is full of shady people and crooks—

LUKA: Hope you'll enjoy your tea!

VASSILISA [*turning*]: Shut up! You rotten toadstool! [*Leaves with her husband.*]

LUKA: I'm off tonight.

BUBNOFF: That's right. Don't outstay your welcome!

LUKA: True enough.

BUBNOFF: I know. Perhaps I've escaped the gallows by getting away in time . . .

LUKA: Well?

BUBNOFF: That's true. It was this way. My wife took up with my boss. He was great at his trade—could dye a dog's skin so that it looked like a raccoon's—could change cat's skin into kangaroo—muskrats, all sorts of things. Well—my wife took up with him—and they were so mad about each other that I got afraid they might poison me or something like that—so I commenced beating up my wife—and the boss beat me . . . we fought savagely! Once he tore off half my whiskers—and broke one of my ribs . . . well, then I, too, got enraged. . . . I cracked my wife over the head with an iron yard-measure—well—and altogether it was like an honest-to-God war! And then I saw that nothing really could come of it . . . they were planning to get the best of me! So I started planning—how to kill my wife—I thought of it a whole lot ... but I thought better of it just in time ... and got away. ...

LUKA: That was best! Let them go on changing dogs into raccoons!

BUBNOFF: Only—the shop was in my wife's name ... and so I did myself out of it, you see? Although, to tell the truth, I would have drunk it away ... I'm a hard drinker, you know ...

LUKA: A hard drinker—oh ...

BUBNOFF: The worst you ever met! Once I start drinking, I drink, everything in sight, I'll spend every bit of money I have—everything except my bones and my skin ... what's more, I'm lazy ... it's terrible how I hate work!

[*Enter* SATINE *and* THE ACTOR, *quarreling.*]

SATINE: Nonsense! You'll go nowhere—it's all a damned lie! Old man, what did you stuff him with all those fairy tales for?

THE ACTOR: You lie! Grandfather! Tell him that he lies!—I am going away. I worked today—I swept the streets ... and I didn't have a drop of vodka. What do you think of that? Here they are—two fifteen-kopeck pieces—and I'm sober!

SATINE: Why—that's absurd! Give it to me—I'll either drink it up—or lose it at cards. ...

THE ACTOR: Get out—this is for my journey ...

LUKA [*to* SATINE]: And you—why are you trying to lead him astray?

SATINE: Tell me, soothsayer, beloved by the gods, what's my future going to be? I've gone to pieces, brother—but everything isn't lost yet, grandfather ... there are sharks in this world who got more brains than I!

LUKA: You're cheerful, Constantine—and very agreeable!

BUBNOFF: Actor, come over here!

[THE ACTOR *crosses to window, sits down on the sill before* BUBNOFF, *and speaks in a low voice with him.*]

SATINE: You know, brother, I used to be a clever young-

ster. It's nice to think of it. I was a devil of a fellow . . .
danced splendidly, played on the stage, loved to amuse
people . . . it was awfully gay. . . .

LUKA: How did you get to be what you are?

SATINE: You're inquisitive, old man! You want to know
everything? What for?

LUKA: I want to understand the ways of men—I look at
you, and I don't understand. You're a bold lad, Constantine,
and you're no fool . . . yet, all of a sudden . . .

SATINE: It's prison, grandfather—I spent four years and
seven months in prison . . . afterward—where could I go?

LUKA: Aha! What were you there for?

SATINE: On account of a scoundrel—whom I killed in a
fit of rage . . . and despair . . . and in prison I learned to
play cards. . . .

LUKA: You killed—because of a woman?

SATINE: Because of my own sister. . . . But look here—
leave me alone! I don't care for these cross-examinations
—and all this happened a long time ago. It's already nine
years since my sister's death. . . . Brother, she was a wonderful girl. . . .

LUKA: You take life easily! And only a while ago that
locksmith was here—and how he did yell!

SATINE: Kleshtch?

LUKA: Yes—"There's no work," he shouted, "there isn't
anything. . . ."

SATINE: He'll get used to it. What could I do?

LUKA [softly]: Look—here he comes!

[KLESHTCH walks in slowly, his head bowed low.]

SATINE: Hey, widower! Why are you so down in the
mouth? What are you thinking?

KLESHTCH: I'm thinking—what'll I do? I've no food—
nothing—the funeral ate up all. . . .

SATINE: I'll give you a bit of advice . . . do nothing! Just
be a burden to the world at large!

KLESHTCH: Go on—talk—I'd be ashamed of myself. . . .

SATINE: Why—people aren't ashamed to let you live
worse than a dog. Just think . . . you stop work—so do I—

so do hundreds, thousands of others—everybody—understand?—everybody'll quit working...nobody'll do a damned thing—and then what'll happen?

KLESHTCH: They'll all starve to death....

LUKA [to SATINE]: If those are your notions, you ought to join the order of Béguines—you know—there's some such organization...

SATINE: I know—grandfather—and they're no fools....

[NATASHA is heard screaming behind KOSTILYOFF'S window: "What for? Stop! What have I done?"]

LUKA [worried]: Natasha! That was she crying—oh, God...

[From KOSTILYOFF'S room is heard noise, shuffling, breaking of crockery, and KOSTILYOFF'S shrill cry: "Ah! Heretic! Bitch!"]

VASSILISA: Wait, wait—I'll teach her—there, there!

NATASHA: They're beating me—killing me...

SATINE [shouts through the window]: Hey—you there—

LUKA [trembling]: Where's Vassily—? Call Vaska—oh, God—listen, brothers...

THE ACTOR [running out]: I'll find him at once!

BUBNOFF: They beat her a lot these days....

SATINE: Come on, old man—we'll be witnesses....

LUKA [following SATINE]: Oh—witnesses—what for? Vassily—he should be called at once!

NATASHA: Sister—sister dear! Va-a-a...

BUBNOFF: They've gagged her—I'll go and see....

[The noise in KOSTILYOFF'S room dies down gradually as if they had gone into the hallway. The old man's cry: "Stop!" is heard. A door is slammed noisily, and the latter sound cuts off all the other noises sharply. Quiet on the stage. Twilight.]

KLESHTCH [seated on the sledge, indifferently, rubbing his hands; mutters at first indistinguishably, then]: What then? One must live. [Louder.] Must have shelter—well? There's no shelter, no roof—nothing...there's only man—man alone—no hope...no help...

[Exit slowly, his head bent. A few moments of ominous

silence, then somewhere in the hallway a mass of sounds, which grows in volume and comes nearer. Individual voices are heard.]

VASSILISA: I'm her sister—let go ...

KOSTILYOFF: What right have you ... ?

VASSILISA: Jail-bird!

SATINE: Call Vaska—quickly! Zob—hit him!

[*A police whistle.* THE TARTAR *runs in, his right hand in a sling.*]

THE TARTAR: There's a new law for you—kill only in daytime!

[*Enter* ZOB, *followed by* MIEDVIEDIEFF.]

ZOB: I handed him a good one!

MIEDVIEDIEFF: You—how dare you fight?

THE TARTAR: What about yourself? What's your duty?

MIEDVIEDIEFF [*running after*]: Stop—give back my whistle!

KOSTILYOFF [*runs in*]: Abram! Stop him! Hold him! He's a murderer—he ...

[*Enter* KVASHNYA *and* NASTYA *supporting* NATASHA *who is disheveled.* SATINE *backs away, pushing away* VASSILISA *who is trying to attack her sister, while, near her,* ALYOSHKA *jumps up and down like a madman, whistles into her ear, shrieking, roaring. Also other ragged men and women.*]

SATINE [*to* VASSILISA]: Well—you damned bitch!

VASSILISA: Let go, you jail-bird! I'll tear you to pieces—if I have to pay for it with my own life!

KVASHNYA [*leading* NATASHA *aside*]: You—Karpovna—that's enough—stand back—aren't you ashamed? Or are you crazy?

MIEDVIEDIEFF [*seizes* SATINE]: Aha—caught at last!

SATINE: Zob—beat them up! Vaska—Vaska ...

[*They all, in a chaotic mass, struggle near the brick wall. They lead* NATASHA *to the right, and set her on a pile of wood.* PEPEL *rushes in from the hallway and, silently, with powerful movements, pushes the crowd aside.*]

PEPEL: Natalia, where are you . . . you . . .

KOSTILYOFF [*disappearing behind a corner*]: Abram! Seize Vaska! Comrades—help us get him! The thief! The robber!

PEPEL: You—you old bastard!

[*Aiming a terrific blow at* KOSTILYOFF. KOSTILYOFF *falls so that only the upper part of his body is seen.* PEPEL *rushes to* NATASHA.]

VASSILISA: Beat Vaska! Brothers! Beat the thief!

MIEDVIEDIEFF [*yells to* SATINE]: Keep out of this—it's a family affair . . . they're relatives—and who are you? . . .

PEPEL [*to* NATASHA]: What did she do to you? She used a knife?

KVASHNYA: God—what beasts! They've scalded the child's feet with boiling water!

NASTYA: They overturned the samovar. . . .

THE TARTAR: Maybe an accident—you must make sure— you can't exactly tell . . .

NATASHA [*half fainting*]: Vassily—take me away—

VASSILISA: Good people! Come! Look! He's dead! Murdered!

[*All crowd into the hallway near* KOSTILYOFF. BUB- NOFF *leaves the crowd and crosses to* PEPEL.]

BUBNOFF [*in a low voice, to* PEPEL]: Vaska—the old man is done for!

PEPEL [*looks at him, as though he does not understand*]: Go—for help—she must be taken to the hospital. . . . I'll settle with them. . . .

BUBNOFF: I say—the old man—somebody's killed him. . . .

[*The noise on the stage dies out like a fire under water. Distinct, whispered exclamations:* "Not really?" "Well —let's go away, brothers!" "The devil!" "Hold on now!" "Let's get away before the police comes!" *The crowd disappears.* BUBNOFF, THE TARTAR, NASTYA, *and* KVASHNYA, *rush up to* KOSTILYOFF'S *body.*]

VASSILISA [*rises and cries out triumphantly*]: Killed—

my husband's killed! Vaska killed him! I saw him! Brothers, I saw him! Well—Vaska—the police!

PEPEL [*moves away from* NATASHA]: Let me alone. [*Looks at* KOSTILYOFF; *to* VASSILISA.] Well—are you glad? [*Touches the corpse with his foot.*] The old bastard is dead! Your wish has been granted! Why not do the same to you?

[*Throws himself at her.* SATINE *and* ZOB *quickly overpower him, and* VASSILISA *disappears in the passage.*]

SATINE: Come to your senses!

ZOB: Hold on! Not so fast!

VASSILISA [*appearing*]: Well, Vaska, dear friend? You can't escape your fate. . . . police—Abram—whistle!

MIEDVIEDIEFF: Those devils tore my whistle off!

ALYOSHKA: Here it is!

[*Whistles,* MIEDVIEDIEFF *runs after him.*]

SATINE [*leading* PEPEL *to* NATASHA]: Don't be afraid, Vaska! Killed in a row! That's nonsense—only manslaughter —you won't have to serve a long term. . . .

VASSILISA: Hold Vaska—he killed him—I saw it!

SATINE: I, too, gave the old man a couple of blows—he was easily fixed . . . you call me as witness, Vaska!

PEPEL: I don't need to defend myself . . . I want to drag Vassilisa into this mess—and I'll do it—she was the one who wanted it . . . she was the one who urged me to kill him—she goaded me on. . . .

NATASHA [*sudden and loud*]: Oh—I understand—so that's it, Vassily? Good people! They're both guilty—my sister and he—they're both guilty! They had it all planned! So, Vassily, that's why you spoke to me a while ago—so that she should overhear everything—? Good people! She's his mistress—you know it—everybody knows it—they're both guilty! She—she urged him to kill her husband—he was in their way—and so was I! And now they've maimed me. . . .

PEPEL: Natalia! What's the matter with you? What are you saying?

SATINE: Oh—hell!

VASSILISA: You lie. She lies. He—Vaska killed him. . . .

NATASHA: They're both guilty! God damn you both!

SATINE: What a mix-up! Hold on, Vassily—or they'll ruin you between them!

ZOB: I can't understand it—oh—what a mess!

PEPEL: Natalia! It can't be true! Surely you don't believe that I—with her—

SATINE: So help me God, Natasha! Just think . . .

VASSILISA [*in the passage*]: They've killed my husband— Your Excellency! Vaska Pepel, the thief, killed him, Captain! I saw it—everybody saw it. . . .

NATASHA [*tossing about in agony; her mind wandering*]: Good people—my sister and Vaska killed him! The police —listen—this sister of mine—here—she urged, coaxed her lover—there he stands—the scoundrel! They both killed him! Put them in jail! Bring them before the judge! Take me along, too! To prison! Christ Almighty—take me to prison, too!

CURTAIN

act 4

Same as Act 1. But PEPEL'S *room is no longer there, and the partition has been removed. Furthermore, there is no anvil at the place where* KLESHTCH *used to sit and work. In the corner, where* PEPEL'S *room used to be,* THE TARTAR *lies stretched out, rather restless, and groaning from time to time.* KLESHTCH *sits at one end of the table, repairing a concertina and now and then testing the stops. At the other end of the table sit* SATINE, THE BARON, *and* NASTYA. *In*

*front of them stand a bottle of vodka, three bottles of beer,
and a large loaf of black bread.* THE ACTOR *lies on top of
the stove, shifting about and coughing. It is night. The
stage is lit by a lamp in the middle of the table. Outside
the wind howls.*

KLESHTCH: Yes ... he disappeared during the confusion and noise. ...

THE BARON: He vanished under the very eyes of the police—just like a puff of smoke. ...

SATINE: That's how sinners flee from the company of the righteous!

NASTYA: He was a dear old soul! But you—you aren't men—you're just—oh—like rust on iron!

THE BARON [*drinks*]: Here's to you, my lady!

SATINE: He was an inquisitive old fellow—yes! Nastenka here fell in love with him. ...

NASTYA: Yes! I did! I did! Madly! It's true! He saw everything—understood everything. ...

SATINE [*laughing*]: Yes, generally speaking, I would say that he was—oh—like mush to those who can't chew. ...

THE BARON [*laughing*]: Right! Like plaster on a boil!

KLESHTCH: He was merciful—you people don't know what pity means. ...

SATINE: What good can I do you by pitying you?

KLESHTCH: You needn't have pity—but you needn't harm or offend your fellow-beings, either!

THE TARTAR [*sits up on his bunk, nursing his wounded hand carefully*]: He was a fine old man. The law of life was the law of his heart ... and he who obeys this law, is good, while he who disregards it, perishes. ...

THE BARON: What law, Prince?

THE TARTAR: There are a number—different ones—you know. ...

THE BARON: Proceed!

THE TARTAR: Do not do harm unto others—such is the law!

SATINE: Oh—you mean the Penal Code, criminal and correctional, eh?

THE BARON: And also the Code of Penalties inflicted by Justices of the Peace!

THE TARTAR: No. I mean the Koran. It is the supreme law—and your own soul ought to be the Koran—yes!

KLESHTCH [testing his concertina]: It wheezes like all hell! But the Prince speaks the truth—one must live abiding by the law—by the teachings of the Gospels. . . .

SATINE: Well—go ahead and do it!

THE BARON: Just try it!

THE TARTAR: The Prophet Mohammed gave to us the law. He said: "Here is the law! Do as it is written therein!" Later on a time will arrive when the Koran will have outlived its purpose—and time will bring forth its own laws—every generation will create its own. . . .

SATINE: To be sure! Time passed on—and gave us the Criminal Code . . . It's a strong law, brother—it won't wear off so very soon!

NASTYA [banging her glass on the table]: Why—why do I stay here—with you? I'll go away somewhere—to the ends of the world!

THE BARON: Without any shoes, my lady?

NASTYA: I'll go—naked, if must be—creeping on all fours!

THE BARON: That'll be rather picturesque, my lady—on all fours!

NASTYA: Yes—and I'll crawl if I have to—anything at all—as long as I don't have to see your faces any longer—oh, I'm so sick of it all—the life—the people—everything!

SATINE: When you go, please take the actor along—he's preparing to go to the very same place—he has learned that within a half mile's distance of the end of the world there's a hospital for diseased organons. . . .

THE ACTOR [raising his head over the top of the stove]: A hospital for organisms—you fool!

SATINE: For organons—poisoned with vodka!

THE ACTOR: Yes! He will go! He will indeed! You'll see!

THE BARON: Who is he, sir?

THE ACTOR: I!

THE BARON: Thanks, servant of the goddess—what's her name—? The goddess of drama—tragedy—whatever is her name—?

THE ACTOR: The muse, idiot! Not the goddess—the muse!

SATINE: Lachesis—Hera—Aphrodite—Atropos—oh! To hell with them all! You see—Baron—it was the old man who stuffed the actor's head full with this rot. . . .

THE BARON: That old man's a fool. . . .

THE ACTOR: Ignoramuses! Beasts! Melpomene—that's her name! Heartless brutes! Bastards! You'll see! He'll go! "On with the orgy, dismal spirits"—poem—ah—by Béranger! Yes—he'll find some spot where there's no—no . . .

THE BARON: Where there's nothing, sir?

THE ACTOR: Right! Nothing! "This hole shall be my grave—I am dying—ill and exhausted. . . ." Why do you exist? Why?

THE BARON: You! God or genius or orgy—or whatever you are—don't roar so loud!

THE ACTOR: You lie! I'll roar all I want to!

NASTYA [*lifting her head from the table and throwing up her hands*]: Go on! Yell! Let them listen to you!

THE BARON: Where is the sense, my lady?

SATINE: Leave them alone, Baron! To hell with the lot! Let them yell—let them knock their damned heads off if they feel like it! There's a method in their madness! Don't you go and interfere with people as that old fellow did! Yes—it's he—the damned old fool—he bewitched the whole gang of us!

KLESHTCH: He persuaded them to go away—but failed to show them the road. . . .

THE BARON: That old man was a humbug!

NASTYA: Liar! You're a humbug yourself!

THE BARON: Shut up, my lady!

KLESHTCH: The old man didn't like truth very much—as

a matter of fact he strongly resented it—and wasn't he right, though? Just look—where is there any truth? And yet, without it, you can't breathe! For instance, our Tartar Prince over there, crushed his hand at his work—and now he'll have to have his arm amputated—and there's the truth for you!

SATINE [*striking the table with his clenched fist*]: Shut up! You sons of bitches! Fools! Not another word about that old fellow! [*To* THE BARON.] You, Baron, are the worst of the lot! You don't understand a thing, and you lie like the devil! The old man's no humbug! What's the truth? Man! Man—that's the truth! He understood man—you don't! You're all as dumb as stones! I understand the old man— yes! He lied—but lied out of sheer pity for you. . . . God damn you! Lots of people lie out of pity for their fellow- beings! I know! I've read about it! They lie—oh—beauti- fully, inspiringly, stirringly! Some lies bring comfort, and others bring peace—a lie alone can justify the burden which crushed a workman's hand and condemns those who are starving! I know what lying means! The weakling and the one who is a parasite through his very weakness—they both need lies—lies are their support, their shield, their armor! But the man who is strong, who is his own master, who is free and does not have to suck his neighbors' blood —he needs no lies! To lie—it's the creed of slaves and mas- ters of slaves! Truth is the religion of the free man!

THE BARON: Bravo! Well spoken! Hear, hear! I agree! You speak like an honest man!

SATINE: And why can't a crook at times speak the truth —since honest people at times speak like crooks? Yes—I've forgotten a lot—but I still know a thing or two! The old man? Oh—he's wise! He affected me as acid affects a dirty old silver coin! Let's drink to his health! Fill the glasses. . . . [NASTYA *fills a glass with beer and hands it to* SATINE, *who laughs.*] The old man lives within himself . . . he looks upon all the world from his own angle. Once I asked him: "Grand- dad, why do people live?" [*Tries to imitate* LUKA'S *voice and gestures.*] And he replied: "Why, my dear fellow, people live in the hope of something better! For example—let's say there are carpenters in this world, and all sorts of trash ... people ... and they give birth to a carpenter the like of which has never been seen upon the face of the earth ... he's way above everybody else, and has no equal among carpenters! The brilliancy of his personality was reflected on all his trade, on all the other carpenters, so that they advanced twenty years in one day! This applies to all other trades—blacksmiths and shoemakers and other workmen—and all the peasants—and even the aristocrats live in the hopes of a higher life! Each individual thinks that he's living for his own self, but in reality he lives in the hope of something better. A hundred years—sometimes longer—do we expect, live for the finer, higher life ..." [NASTYA *stares intently into* SATINE'S *face.* KLESHTCH *stops working and listens.* THE BARON *bows his head very low, drumming softly on the table with his fingers.* THE ACTOR, *peering down from the stove, tries to climb noiselessly into the bunk.*] "Everyone, brothers, everyone lives in the hope of something better. That's why we must respect each and every human being! How do we know who he is, why he was born, and what he is capable of accomplishing? Perhaps his coming into the world will prove to be our good fortune. ... Especially must we respect little children! Children—need freedom! Don't interfere with their lives! Respect children!"

[*Pause.*]

THE BARON [*thoughtfully*]: Hm—yes—something better? —That reminds me of my family ... an old family dating back to the time of Catherine ... all noblemen, soldiers, originally French—they served their country and gradually rose higher and higher. In the days of Nicholas the First my grandfather, Gustave DeBille, held a high post—riches—hundreds of serfs ... horses—cooks—

NASTYA: You liar! It isn't true!

THE BARON [*jumping up*]: What? Well—go on—

NASTYA: It isn't true.

THE BARON [*screams*]: A house in Moscow! A house in Petersburg! Carriages! Carriages with coats of arms!

> [KLESHTCH *takes his concertina and goes to one side, watching the scene with interest*.]

NASTYA: You lie!

THE BARON: Shut up!—I say—dozens of footmen . . .

NASTYA [*delighted*]: You lie!

THE BARON: I'll kill you!

NASTYA [*ready to run away*]: There were no carriages!

SATINE: Stop, Nastenka! Don't infuriate him!

THE BARON: Wait—you bitch! My grandfather . . .

NASTYA: There was no grandfather! There was nothing!

> [SATINE *roars with laughter*.]

THE BARON [*worn out with rage, sits down on bench*]: Satine! Tell that slut—what—? You, too, are laughing? You don't believe me either? [*Cries out in despair, pounding the table with his fists*.] It's true—damn the whole lot of you!

NASTYA [*triumphantly*]: So—you're crying? Understand now what a human being feels like when nobody believes him?

KLESHTCH [*returning to the table*]: I thought there'd be a fight. . . .

THE TARTAR: Oh—people are fools! It's too bad. . . .

THE BARON: I shall not permit anyone to ridicule me! I have proofs—documents—damn you!

SATINE: Forget it! Forget about your grandfather's carriages! You can't drive anywhere in a carriage of the past!

THE BARON: How dare she—just the same—?

NASTYA: Just imagine! How dare I—?

SATINE: You see—she does dare! How is she any worse than you are? Although, surely, in her past there wasn't even a father and mother, let alone carriages and a grandfather. . . .

THE BARON [*quieting down*]: Devil take you—you do know how to argue dispassionately—and I, it seems—I've no will-power. . . .

SATINE: Acquire some—it's useful.... [*Pause.*] Nastya! are you going to the hospital?

NASTYA: What for?

SATINE: To see Natashka.

NASTYA: Oh—just woke up, did you? She's been out of the hospital for some time—and they can't find a trace of her....

SATINE: Oh—that woman's a goner!

KLESHTCH: It's interesting to see whether Vaska will get the best of Vassilisa, or the other way around—?

NASTYA: Vassilisa will win out! She's shrewd! And Vaska will go to the gallows!

SATINE: For manslaughter? No—only to jail....

NASTYA: Too bad—the gallows would have been better ... that's where all of you should be sent ... swept off into a hole—like filth....

SATINE [*astonished*]: What's the matter? Are you crazy?

THE BARON: Oh—give her a wallop—that'll teach her to be less impertinent....

NASTYA: Just you try to touch me!

THE BARON: I shall!

SATINE: Stop! Don't insult her! I can't get the thought of the old man out of my head! [*Roars with laughter.*] Don't offend your fellow-beings! Suppose I were offended once in such a way that I'd remember it for the rest of my life? What then? Should I forgive? No, no!

THE BARON [*to* NASTYA]: You must understand that I'm not your sort ... you—ah—you piece of dirt!

NASTYA: You bastard! Why—you live off me like a worm off an apple!

[*The men laugh amusedly.*]

KLESHTCH: Fool! An apple—?

THE BARON: You can't be angry with her—she's just an ass—

NASTYA: You laugh! Liars? Don't strike you as funny, eh?

THE ACTOR [*morosely*]: Give them a good beating!

NASTYA: If I only could! [*Takes a cup from the table*

and throws it on the floor.] That's what I'd like to do to you all!

THE TARTAR: Why break dishes—eh—silly girl?

THE BARON [*rising*]: That'll do! I'll teach her manners in half a second!

NASTYA [*running toward the door*]: Go to hell!

SATINE [*calling after her*]: Hey! That's enough! Whom are you trying to frighten? What's all the row about, anyway?

NASTYA: Dogs! I hope you'll croak! Dogs! [*Runs out.*]

THE ACTOR [*morosely*]: Amen!

THE TARTAR: Allah! Mad women, these Russians! They're bold, wilful; Tartar women aren't like that! They know the law and abide by it. . . .

KLESHTCH: She ought to be given a sound hiding!

THE BARON: The slut!

KLESHTCH [*testing his concertina*]: It's ready! But its owner isn't here yet—that young fellow is burning his life away. . . .

SATINE: Care for a drink—now?

KLESHTCH: Thanks . . . it's time to go to bed. . . .

SATINE: Getting used to us?

KLESHTCH [*drinks, then goes to his bunk*]: It's all right . . . there are people everywhere—at first you don't notice it . . . but after a while you don't mind. . . .

[THE TARTAR *spreads some rags over his bunk, then kneels on them and prays.*]

THE BARON [*to* SATINE, *pointing at* THE TARTAR]: Look!

SATINE: Stop! He's a good fellow! Leave him alone! [*Roars with laughter.*] I feel kindly today—the devil alone knows the reason why. . . .

THE BARON: You always feel kindly when you're drunk —you're even wiser at such times. . . .

SATINE: When I'm drunk? Yes—then I like everything— right— He prays? That's fine! A man may believe or not— that's his own affair—a man is free—he pays for everything himself—belief or unbelief—love—wisdom . . . a man pays for everything—and that's just why he's free! Man is—truth! And what is man? It's neither you nor I nor they—oh, no—it's you and they and I and the old man—and Napoleon—Mohammed—all in one! [*Outlines vaguely in the air the contour of a human being.*] Do you understand? It's tremendous! It contains the beginning and the end of everything—everything is in man—and everything exists for him! Man alone exists—everything else is the creation of his hands and his brain! Man! It is glorious! It sounds—oh—so big! Man must be respected—not degraded with pity—but respected, respected! Let us drink to man, Baron! [*Rises.*] It is good to feel that you are a man! I'm a convict, a murderer, a crook—granted!— When I'm out on the street people stare at me as if I were a scoundrel—they draw away from me—they look after me and often they say: "You dog! You humbug! Work!" Work? And what for? to fill my belly? [*Roars with laughter.*] I've always despised people who worry too much about their bellies. It isn't right, Baron! It isn't! Man is loftier than that! Man stands above hunger!

THE BARON: You—reason things out. . . . Well and good —it brings you a certain amount of consolation. . . . Personally I'm incapable of it . . . I don't know how. [*Glances around him and then, softly, guardedly.*] Brother—I am afraid—at times. Do you understand? Afraid!—Because— what next?

SATINE: Rot! What's a man to be afraid of?

THE BARON [*pacing up and down*]: You know—as far back as I can remember, there's been a sort of fog in my brain. I was never able to understand anything. Somehow I feel embarrassed—it seems to me that all my life I've done nothing but change clothes—and why? I don't understand! I studied—I wore the uniform of the Institute for the Sons of the Nobility . . . but what have I learned? I don't remember! I married—I wore a frock-coat—then a dressing-gown . . . but I chose a disagreeable wife . . . and why? I don't understand. I squandered everything that I possessed—I wore some sort of a gray jacket and brick-colored trousers—but how did I happen to ruin myself? I haven't the slightest idea. . . . I had a position in the Department of State. . . . I wore a uniform and a cap with insignia of rank. . . . I embezzled government funds . . . so they dressed me in a convict's garb—and later on I got into these clothes here—and it all happened as in a dream —it's funny. . . .

SATINE: Not very! It's rather—silly!

THE BARON: Yes—silly! I think so, too. Still—wasn't I born for some sort of purpose?

SATINE [laughing]:Probably—a man is born to conceive a better man. [Shaking his head.]—It's all right!

THE BARON: That she-devil Nastka! Where did she run to? I'll go and see—after all, she . . .

[Exit; pause.]

THE ACTOR: Tartar! [Pause.] Prince! [THE TARTAR looks round.] Say a prayer for me. . . .

THE TARTAR: What?

THE ACTOR [softly]: Pray—for me!

THE TARTAR [after a silence]: Pray for your own self!

THE ACTOR [quickly crawls off the stove and goes to the table, pours out a drink with shaking hands, drinks, then almost runs to passage]: All over!

SATINE: Hey proud Sicambrian! Where are you going? [SATINE whistles. MIEDVIEDIEFF enters, dressed in a woman's flannel shirtwaist; followed by BUBNOFF. Both are slightly drunk. BUBNOFF carries a bunch of pretzels in one hand, a couple of smoked fish in the other, a bottle of vodka under one arm, another bottle in his coat pocket.]

MIEDVIEDIEFF: A camel is something like a donkey— only it has no ears. . . .

BUBNOFF: Shut up! You're a variety of donkey yourself!

MIEDVIEDIEFF: A camel has no ears at all, at all—it hears through its nostrils. . . .

BUBNOFF [to SATINE]: Friend! I've looked for you in all

the saloons and all the cabarets! Take this bottle—my hands are full. . . .

SATINE: Put the pretzels on the table—then you'll have one hand free—

BUBNOFF: Right! Hey—you donkey—look! Isn't he a clever fellow?

MIEDVIEDIEFF: All crooks are clever—I know! They couldn't do a thing without brains. An honest man is all right even if he's an idiot . . . but a crook must have brains. But, speaking about camels, you're wrong . . . you can ride them—they have no horns . . . and no teeth either. . . .

BUBNOFF: Where's everybody? Why is there no one here? Come on out . . . I treat! Who's in the corner?

SATINE: How soon will you drink up everything you have? Scarecrow!

BUBNOFF: Very soon! I've very little this time. Zob—where's Zob?

KLESHTCH [crossing to table]: He isn't here. . . .

BUBNOFF: Waughrr! Bull-dog! Br-zz-zz—Turkey-cock! Don't bark and don't growl! Drink—make merry—and don't be sullen!—I treat everybody—Brother, I love to treat —if I were rich, I'd run a free saloon! So help me God, I would! With an orchestra and a lot of singers! Come, everyone! Drink and eat—listen to the music—and rest in peace! Beggars—come, all you beggars—and enter my saloon free of charge! Satine—you can have my capital—just like that!

SATINE: You better give me all you have straight away!

BUBNOFF: All my capital? Right now? Well—here's a ruble—here's twenty kopecks—five kopecks—sun-flower seeds—and that's all!

SATINE: That's splendid! It'll be safer with me—I'll gamble with it. . . .

MIEDVIEDIEFF: I'm a witness—the money was given you for safe-keeping. How much is it?

BUBNOFF: You? You're a camel—we don't need witnesses. . . .

ALYOSHKA [*comes in barefoot*]: Brothers, I got my feet wet!

BUBNOFF: Go on and get your throat wet—and nothing'll happen—you're a fine fellow—you sing and you play— that's all right! But it's too bad you drink—drink, little brother, is harmful, very harmful. . . .

ALYOSHKA: I judge by you! Only when you're drunk do you resemble a human being. . . . Kleshtch! Is my con-certina fixed? [*Sings and dances.*]

"If my mug were not so attractive,
My sweetheart wouldn't love me at all . . ."

Boys, I'm frozen—it's cold. . . .

MIEDVIEDIEFF: Hm—and may I ask who's this sweet-heart?

BUBNOFF: Shut up! From now on, brother, you are neither a policeman nor an uncle!

ALYOSHKA: Just auntie's husband!

BUBNOFF: One of your nieces is in jail—the other one's dying. . . .

MIEDVIEDIEFF [*proudly*]: You lie! She's not dying—she disappeared—without trace. . . .

[SATINE *roars*.]

BUBNOFF: All the same, brothers—a man without nieces isn't an uncle!

ALYOSHKA: Your Excellency! Listen to the drummer of the retired billygoats' brigade! [*Sings.*]

"My sweetheart has money,
I haven't a cent.
But I'm a cheerful,
Merry lad!"

Oh—isn't it cold!

[*Enter* ZOB. *From now until the final curtain men and women drift in, undress, and stretch out on the bunks, grumbling.*]

ZOB: Bubnoff! Why did you run off?

BUBNOFF: Come here—sit down—brother, let's sing my favorite ditty, eh?

THE TARTAR: Night was made for sleep! Sing your songs in the daytime!

SATINE: Well—never mind, Prince—come here!

THE TARTAR: What do you mean—never mind? There's going to be a noise—there always is when people sing!

BUBNOFF [crossing to THE TARTAR]: Count—ah—I mean Prince—how's your hand? Did they cut it off?

THE TARTAR: What for? We'll wait and see—perhaps it won't be necessary . . . a hand isn't made of iron—it won't take long to cut it off. . . .

ZOB: It's your own affair, Hassanka! You'll be good for nothing without your hand. We're judged by our hands and backs—without the pride of your hand, you're no longer a human being. Tobacco-carting—that's your business! Come on—have a drink of vodka—and stop worrying!

KVASHNYA [comes in]: Ah, my beloved fellow-lodgers! It's horrible outside—snow and slush . . . is my policeman here?

MIEDVIEDIEFF: Right here!

KVASHNYA: Wearing my blouse again? And drunk, eh? What's the idea?

MIEDVIEDIEFF: In celebration of Bubnoff's birthday . . . besides, it's cold. . . .

KVASHNYA: Better look out—stop fooling about and go to sleep!

MIEDVIEDIEFF [goes to kitchen]: Sleep? I can—I want to —it's time— [Exit.]

SATINE: What's the matter? Why are you so strict with him?

KVASHNYA: You can't be otherwise, friend. You have to be strict with his sort. I took him as a partner. I thought he'd be of some benefit to me—because he's a military man —and you're a rough lot . . . and I am a woman—and now he's turned drunkard—that won't do at all!

SATINE: You picked a good one for partner!

KVASHNYA: Couldn't get a better one. You wouldn't want to live with me . . . you think you're too fine! And even if you did it wouldn't last more than a week ... you'd gamble me and all I own away at cards!

SATINE [*roars with laughter*]: That's true, landlady—I'd gamble. . . .

KVASHNYA: Yes, yes. Alyoshka!

ALYOSHKA: Here he is—I, myself!

KVASHNYA: What do you mean by gossiping about me?

ALYOSHKA: I? Speak out everything—whatever my conscience tells me. There, I say, is a wonderful woman! Splendid meat, fat, bones—over four hundred pounds! But brains—? Not an ounce!

KVASHNYA: You're a liar! I've a lot of brains! What do you mean by saying I beat my policeman?

ALYOSHKA: I thought you did—when you pulled him by the hair!

KVASHNYA [*laughs*]: You fool! You aren't blind, are you? Why wash dirty linen in public? And—it hurts his feelings—that's why he took to drink. . . .

ALYOSHKA: It's true, evidently, that even a chicken likes vodka. . . .

[SATINE *and* KLESHTCH *roar with laughter.*]

KVASHNYA: Go on—show your teeth! What sort of a man are you anyway, Alyoshka?

ALYOSHKA: Oh—I am first-rate! Master of all trades! I follow my nose!

BUBNOFF [*near* THE TARTAR'S *bunk*]: Come on! At all events—we won't let you sleep! We'll sing all night. Zob!

ZOB: Sing—? All right . . .

ALYOSHKA: And I'll play. . . .

SATINE: We'll listen!

THE TARTAR [*smiling*]: Well—Bubnoff—you devil—bring the vodka—we'll drink—we'll have a hell of a good time! The end will come soon enough—and then we'll be dead!

BUBNOFF: Fill his glass, Satine! Zob—sit down! Ah—brothers—what does a man need after all? There, for instance, I've had a drink—and I'm happy! Zob! Start my favorite song! I'll sing—and then I'll cry. . . .

ZOB [*begins to sing*]:
     "The sun rises and sets . . ."
BUBNOFF [*joining in*]:
     "But my prison is all dark . . ."
THE BARON [*on the threshold; yells*]: Hey—you—come—
come here! Out in the waste—in the yard . . . over there . . .
The actor—he's hanged himself. . . .

> [*Silence. All stare at* THE BARON. *Behind him appears*
> NASTYA, *and slowly, her eyes wide with horror, she
> walks to the table.*]

SATINE [*in a matter-of-fact voice*]: Damned fool—he
ruined the song . . . !

CURTAIN

He Who Gets

Slapped

LEONID ANDREYEV

Adapted by Judith Guthrie

CHARACTERS

CONSUELA, *a bareback circus rider, known as "The Bareback Tango Queen"*

COUNT MANCINI, *Consuela's father*

HE, *a clown in* BRIQUET'S *circus*

BRIQUET, *the manager of the circus*

ZINAIDA, *a lion tamer,* BRIQUET'S *unmarried wife*

ALFRED BEZANO, *a jockey and bareback rider*

A GENTLEMAN

BARON REGNARD

JIM JACKSON, *the chief clown*

TILLY
POLLY } *Musical clowns*

THOMAS, ANGELICA *and other artistes of* BRIQUET'S *circus*

The action takes place in a circus in a provincial city in France.

act 1

A very large, rather dirty room, with whitewashed walls. The room is used for many purposes. It is the office of PAPA BRIQUET, *manager of the circus; here he keeps his little desk. It is the cloakroom of some of the actors. It is also the room where the cast gathers between calls, during rehearsals or performances. Again it is a checkroom for used circus property, such as broken gilt armchairs, scenery for pantomimes and other wares of the circus household. The walls are covered with circus announcements and glaring posters.*

The time is morning. In the circus hall a rehearsal is going on, and preparations are being made for the evening performance. As the curtain goes up, the cracking whip and the shouts of the riding-master are heard from the ring. TILLY *and* POLLY *are rehearsing. Enter* COUNT MANCINI. *They go on rehearsing and ignore him.*

MANCINI: Good morning. [*No answer.*] Good morning to you, rogues and vagabonds. [*No answer.*] Count Mancini does you the honor of wishing you a good morning.

TILLY *and* POLLY [*without stopping work*]: Good morning.

MANCINI: Where is Consuela? [*No answer.*] I said where is my daughter? [*No answer.*] I said where is my daughter, the Countess Consuela?

TILLY *and* POLLY: Busy.

MANCINI: Where is your little manager person, where is Papa Briquet?

TILLY *and* POLLY: Busy.

MANCINI: What *are* you doing?

TILLY *and* POLLY: Busy.

MANCINI: I wonder if you could oblige me . . . I said I wonder if you could oblige . . . little temporary financial . . . so stupid . . . absurd, really . . . left one's check book in a— never mind. Could you be so kind . . . little favor.

TILLY *and* POLLY [*emptying pockets and showing lining*]: All gone. All empty.

[*They dance him out of focus. Enter* BRIQUET.]

BRIQUET: *Bonjour, mes enfants.*

TILLY *and* POLLY: Good morning, Papa Briquet.

POLLY [*confidentially*]: That Mancini's about.

[BRIQUET *hastily puts away cash box.*]

BRIQUET: So early?

POLLY: Yes.

BRIQUET: What does he want?

POLLY: The usual. Don't lend him anything, Papa. He's no more a count than I am. Tilly's in bad form today.

BRIQUET: Why?

POLLY: Says he's not well. Says his throat's sore.

BRIQUET: Shall I look at it?

POLLY: Yes, please, papa.

[BRIQUET *calls* TILLY *over. While* BRIQUET *is looking at his throat* MANCINI *reappears.*]

BRIQUET: Little wider please. Oh, it's nothing. Paint it with iodine.

POLLY: I told him it was nothing. Come on.

MANCINI: Hm! . . . *Doctor* Briquet! . . . Better be care-ful—you're not qualified.

BRIQUET: They only want a little looking after. They're all so fussy about their healths—almost as nervous as the animals.

MANCINI: His throat's just burnt with drink. That's all. Those two get sozzled. Every night. Sozzled. Absinthe. Well, I *mean!* It's their *morals* that want "looking after."

BRIQUET: Oh, shut up, Mancini! I'm tired of you.

MANCINI: *Count* Mancini *à votre service!* Oh, look, I wonder if you could oblige me . . . a little temporary financial . . . Left one's check book—well, somewhere . . . absurd of course . . . little favor.

BRIQUET: No. *And* I won't have you "touching" my artistes.

MANCINI: "Touching"—*quel phrase!* The indignity!

BRIQUET: Tired of you, poking your nose into everything. You worry the artistes. One day they'll turn on you and I shan't stop them.

MANCINI: As a man of entirely different society—*l'alta societa*—I can't be expected to treat your artistes as equals . . . now you . . . I do you the honor of speaking to you quite informally.

BRIQUET [*slightly threatening*]: Well . . . well . . . really!

MANCINI: Never mind . . . it's all a joke. Still if your artistes did turn nasty . . . ever seen this, Briquet? [*Draws stiletto.*] Useful little thing. Oh, by the way I found such a girl out by the gas works yesterday. Oh, well, I know you don't approve . . . but *chacun à son gout* . . . and anyhow what about you and Zinaida . . . does everybody know you're not married? I say, lend me a hundred francs.

BRIQUET: Not a sou.

MANCINI: Then I'll take Consuela away and that'll be that.

BRIQUET: You threaten that every day.

MANCINI: And so would you if you were as hard up as I am, as shamefully hard up. Listen, you know as well as I do that I've got to keep up the prestige of my name . . . somehow . . . and all because of the misfortunes of my ancestors I have to make my daughter, Consuela, the Countess Veronica, an equestrienne . . . an equestrienne. . . . just for bread and butter.

BRIQUET: You spend too much on women . . . you'll end up in prison.

MANCINI: Prison! Of course not. Why, I've got to live up to my name, haven't I? The Mancinis are known all over Italy for their love of women. Is it my fault that I have to pay such terrible prices for what my ancestors had for nothing? What do you know about family tradition? You're no better than a—well, we won't say what. Now, I don't drink and I stopped playing cards after that ... well, case. No need to laugh. Now if I give up women what will be left of Mancini? Only a coat of arms! So ... in the name of family tradition ... lend me a hundred francs.

BRIQUET: No, I've told you I won't.

MANCINI: You know I let Consuela keep half her salary ... perhaps you think I don't love my child ... my only little daughter! All I have left to keep alive the memory of her sainted mother! How can you be so hard. [*Pretends to cry into dirty lace hanky.*]

BRIQUET: What you mean is she's silly enough to give you half her salary. No, no, Mancini, I've had enough of you.

[*Enter* ZINAIDA, *the lion tamer; burningly beautiful. Her quiet gestures at first glance give an impression of languor. She is* BRIQUET'S *unmarried wife.*]

ZINAIDA: Good morning.

MANCINI [*kissing her hand*]: Madame Zinaida! This barbarian ... this boor ... may pierce me with his dagger but I cannot control this outburst of my love! Madame ... Count Mancini has the honor of soliciting one look from those lustrous eyes.

ZINAIDA [*to* BRIQUET]: Money?

BRIQUET: Yes.

ZINAIDA: Don't give him any.

[*She sits down wearily on a torn sofa, shuts her eyes.* MANCINI *gets up and wipes his knees.*]

MANCINI: Duchess! Don't be so hard-hearted! I am no lion, no tiger, no savage beast for you to tame ... I am a poor modest domestic puss who begs, gnum, gnum ... [*eating noises*] for a saucer, a little saucer of milk.

ZINAIDA [*without opening her eyes*]: Jackson says you've got a teacher for Consuela—whatever for?

MANCINI: The solicitude of a father, Duchess, the never-ceasing care of a loving father. The terrible misfortunes of our family, when I was a child, have left their mark on her education. Friends! The daughter of Count Mancini, the Countess Veronica, known to thousands as Consuela, is scarcely literate . . . is that to be? . . . And you, Briquet, you ask me why I need money!

ZINAIDA: Swindler!

BRIQUET: What's she being taught?

MANCINI: Everything. A student has been giving her lessons, but I had to get rid of him yesterday. He fell in love with her, the cheek of it! He miaowed outside her door like a cat. Everything, Briquet, everything that you don't know . . . literature, history, astronomy, ornithology, philosophy, orthography, mythology . . . I don't wish my daughter . . .

[*Enter* TWO YOUNG GIRLS, *in practice dress. They are tired and sit down in the corner.*]

ZINAIDA: Swindler!

BRIQUET: You are a fool, Mancini. [*In a didactic tone.*] What is the point? What does she need with book-learning? While she's here she needn't know anything about that kind of life . . . ordinary life . . . audience life. What's geography? . . . I would be twice as happy if I didn't know any geography. If I were the government I would forbid artists to read books. Let them read the posters. That's enough. [*During* BRIQUET'S *speech the* TWO CLOWNS *and another* ACTOR *enter. They sit wearily.*] Consuela is a fine artist— now; but as soon as you teach her . . . mythology . . . and she begins to read, she'll be good for nothing, she'll get moody, morbid, it'll make her miserable, and she'll go and poison herself. . . . Oh, I know these books. . . . All they teach is immoralities and how to kill yourself.

1ST GIRL: I love the serials that come out in mags.

BRIQUET: More fool you. *And* you'll take a wrong turning. Believe me, my friends, we ought to forget entirely what happens in books. . . . How can we understand what happens in books. . . .

MANCINI: Briquet, you are an obscurantist! An enemy of enlightenment.

BRIQUET: And you are a fool. You're one of the public, and what has it taught you? If you'd been born in a circus

like me, you'd know something. Education is nonsense.
Ask Zinaida—she's done all that book-learning . . . she
knows everything they teach . . . geology, mythology, I don't
know what ology. . . . Has it made her any happier? Has
it made her any happier? Tell them, my darling.

ZINAIDA: Oh, leave me out of this, Louis.

MANCINI [angry]: Oh, go to blazes . . . and when I listen
to your asinine philosophy I want to fleece you for more
than a hundred francs . . . two hundred . . . a thousand! My
God, what a manager . . . a stingy old skinflint . . . that's
what you are. . . . Listen, my honorable vagabonds . . . he
pays you starvation wages. I'll make you give Consuela a
raise. Tell me, who is it who brings in full houses every
night? You? A couple of musical donkeys? Tigers? Lions?
Who cares for those starveling cats?

ZINAIDA: Please leave my tigers alone.

MANCINI: I beg your pardon, Zinaida, on my word of
honor I didn't mean to hurt your feelings . . . I'm captivated
by your bravery . . . your grace . . . you are a heroine. . . . I
kiss your tiny hands. But what do they understand about
heroism? [Tango offstage played softly. He continues with
enthusiasm.] Listen! Tell me, Messieurs, mesdames, who but
Consuela and Bezano bring them in? That Tango on horseback . . . it is divine! God! . . . its magic would seduce even
His Holiness the Pope.

POLLY: Yes, it's a wonderful trick! And whose idea was
it? Bezano's?

MANCINI: Idea! Idea! The boy Bezano's in love, like a
cat. That's the idea! But what's an idea without a woman.
You wouldn't get far with just an idea, would you, Papa
Briquet? You can't do without Consuela.

BRIQUET: We've got a contract with Consuela.

MANCINI: Such a mercenary mind.

ZINAIDA: Oh, give him the money and let him go!

MANCINI: Ten! Never! Fifteen! Don't be stingy, Papa . . .
for the sake of family tradition—twenty. I swear on my
word of honor I can't do with less. [BRIQUET hands him
twenty francs. Nonchalantly.] Merci . . . thank you.

ZINAIDA: Borrow from the Baron.

MANCINI: Baron Regnard?

ZINAIDA: Yes.

MANCINI: My friend the banker?

ZINAIDA: If he is a banker.

MANCINI: Such a sordid suggestion from such beautiful lips! One doesn't go to a man like the Baron for a little, squalid, paltry, petty, piffling sum like this. You don't understand, beautiful lady; the Baron is a person who thinks in terms of millions—no! Billions. Billions.

ZINAIDA: You're up to something. And he's up to something. Men like that don't come hanging round here for nothing, any more than you do.

MANCINI: Love of art, my dear.

ZINAIDA: You're an out and out old swindler.

MANCINI: And *you're* an out and out old busker.

[*Enter an* ARTISTE—*apparently an athlete.*]

ATHLETE: Papa Briquet, there's a gentleman from another world to see you.

ACTRESS: Another world? A ghost?

ATHLETE: Ever seen a ghost drunk?

BRIQUET: If he's drunk I'm out. Thomas, does he want to see me or the Count?

ATHLETE: You. He's not drunk, Papa. P'rhaps he is a ghost.

MANCINI: Is he a gentleman? Eh? A person like me?

ATHLETE: Yes; I'll go and fetch him.

[*Exit. The whip cracks in the ring. The Tango sounds very low and distant—then comes nearer—louder. Silence.*]

BRIQUET [*touching* ZINAIDA'S *arm*]: Tired?

ZINAIDA [*drawing back a little*]: No.

POLLY: Your big brown lion is nervous today, Madame Zinaida.

ZINAIDA: Sultan! You've been teasing him.

POLLY: I played a tune from *Traviata* to him and he howled. That would make a good turn, wouldn't it, Papa? It's an idea?

[*Enter* HE, *brought in by crowd.* HE *is middle-aged and plain, but his strange face has a lively expression. He is formally dressed in an expensive overcoat with a fur collar.*]

HE [*bowing and smiling*]: Excuse me ... Are you the manager?

BRIQUET: Yes. How do you do? Sit down. Polly, a chair.

HE: Oh, please don't bother— [*Looks round.*] Your company? Delighted to ...

MANCINI [*preening himself*]: Count Mancini.

BRIQUET: And tell me your name?

HE: I haven't got one yet. You usually make up your own names, don't you? I haven't thought of one ... yet. Perhaps you'll help me. I *have* thought of something but I'm afraid it may sound a little ... out of key ... bookish.

BRIQUET: Bookish?

HE: Yes. Too highbrow. [*They all look surprised.*] These two gentlemen are clowns? I am so proud to meet them. [*Shakes hands with the* CLOWNS, *who make silly faces.*]

BRIQUET: Look here ... what do you want me to do for you?

HE: Oh, no, I want to do something for you, Papa Briquet.

BRIQUET: Papa! But you aren't like ... you don't look like ...

HE [*reassuringly*]: I could become "like." ... Shall I imitate these gentlemen?

BRIQUET [*involuntarily*]: Are you drunk, sir?

HE: No, I don't drink ... it's just my personality.

BRIQUET: Where did you work before, my boy? Are you a *jongleur*?

HE: No, I'm afraid not, but I'm glad, Papa Briquet, that you think of me as one of you.

MANCINI: But you look ... *distingué* ... quite the gentleman.

HE [*evasively*]: Good of you to say so.

BRIQUET: Well ... what d'you want? My company is full up. What do you want?

HE [*pause*]: I want to be a clown.

[*Some of the* ACTORS *smile*.]

BRIQUET: You're asking rather a lot. What can you do?

HE: Nothing. I can't do a thing! That's funny in itself, isn't it?

BRIQUET: Not to me.

HE [*rather helpless, but looking round smiling*]: We must invent something.

BRIQUET: Something . . . bookish?

[*The clown* JACKSON *enters slowly without being noticed by the others. He stands behind* HE.]

HE: Yes . . . a nice little speech, for instance, on some religious theme . . . some little debate among the clowns.

BRIQUET: Debate! What the hell! This is a circus, not a college.

HE [*sadly*]: Oh, I'm sorry . . . something else . . . something funny about the creation of the world and its rulers.

BRIQUET: Wonderful . . . and get my license suspended?

JACKSON [*coming forward*]: Don't you like the rulers of the world? I don't either. Shake hands.

BRIQUET: Our chief clown. The famous Jackson.

HE: This is a great honor . . . your genius has given me such great pleasure. . . .

JACKSON: Very nice of you to say so.

BRIQUET: He wants to be a clown. What about him, Jim?

[JACKSON *signs to* HE *to take off his coat. He turns him round and examines him critically*.]

JACKSON: Clown? Hm . . . let's look at you. Take off your hat . . . turn round . . . smile . . . go on, more. Broader . . . hm . . . One could do something with that face. [*Sadly*.] I suppose you can't even turn a somersault?

HE [*sighing*]: No.

JACKSON: How old are you?

HE: Thirty-nine. Is that too old to begin?

[JACKSON *whistles*.]

BRIQUET [*after a pause*]: But I've told you, you know, we don't need you, we're full up. We'll let you know.

ZINAIDA [*aside*]: Louis, take him on.

BRIQUET: What on earth shall I do with him? He's drunk.

HE: Thank you, Madame. Aren't you Madame Zinaida, the lion tamer? Whose wonderful courage and beauty . . .

ZINAIDA: Yes, but I don't like flattery.

HE: But this isn't flattery.

MANCINI [*to* ZINAIDA]: You're evidently not used to high society, my dear. This gentleman expresses himself with sincerity, beautifully phrased . . . and it is bad manners to . . . well . . . as for me . . . I—

[*Enter* CONSUELA *and* BEZANO *in circus costume.*]

CONSUELA: Oh, are you here, Daddy?

MANCINI: Yes, my child. Are you tired, pet? [*Kisses her.*] May I introduce my daughter, sir . . . the Countess Veronica . . . known on the stage as Consuela, the Bareback Tango Queen. Have you ever seen her?

HE: Yes, she's beautiful.

MANCINI: Of course! Everyone acknowledges it! And how do you like her name? Consuela . . . I took it from a novel by George Sand. It means "consolation."

HE: Quite a reader.

MANCINI: Oh, that's nothing. In spite of your strange wish I can see, sir, that you are a person of one's own class . . . I must explain that only the terrible misfortune of our ancient clan . . . *sic transit, gloria mundi,* sir . . .

CONSUELA: Shut up, Daddy. Where's my handkerchief, Alfred?

BEZANO: Here you are.

CONSUELA [*showing it to* HE]: Real Venetian lace . . . d'you like it?

HE [*bowing*]: Beautiful! Papa Briquet—the more I see the more I want to stay! On the one hand—a Count, on the other . . . [*Makes a face.*]

JACKSON: That's not bad . . . listen . . . rack your brains . . . think of something. Everybody here thinks out his own line of business.

HE [*hand to head, thinking, pause*]: Think . . . Think . . . Eureka!

POLLY: That means "got it" . . . well?

HE: I'll be He Who Gets Slapped . . . the Funny Man Who Gets Knocked About. [*All laugh.*] You see . . . I've made you laugh . . . and that's not easy.

[*All now serious,* POLLY *sighs.*]

TILLY: No, it's not easy. Did you laugh, Polly?

POLLY: Like hell. Did you?

TILLY: Yes, I laughed. [*Imitating an instrument, he sings a little tune.*]

JACKSON: "He Who Gets Slapped." Not bad.

HE: I rather like it myself. It suits my personality . . . and, friends—I've found a name. How's this—"HE"?

JACKSON [*thinking*]: "HE." Not bad.

CONSUELA [*in a singing voice*]: "HE" is so funny! "HE" like a dog!

[JACKSON *smacks* HE, *who exclaims. General laughter covers his exclamation.*]

JACKSON: "He Who Gets Slapped!"

POLLY [*in baby talk*]: He says he wants some more!

[HE *smiles, rubbing his face.*]

HE: So unexpected! How funny! You didn't hurt me a bit . . . but my face burns!

[*Again there is loud laughter. The* CLOWNS *bleat and cackle and bark.* MANCINI *assumes a bored air and looks at his watch. The* TWO GIRLS *go out.*]

JACKSON: Engage him, Papa Briquet . . . new blood.

MANCINI [*looking at watch*]: Mind you, my dear sir, Papa Briquet is a perfect old miser—if you think you'll get good money here you've come to the wrong shop. A slap . . . a blow . . . a cuff . . . what are they worth? Three a penny! Go back to the *beau monde,* you'll make more there. Why! For a slap—just a tap as one might say—my friend the Marquis Justi got damages to the tune of fifty thou—

BRIQUET: Don't interfere, Mancini. Will you look after him, Jackson?

JACKSON: I don't mind.

POLLY: D'you like music? Beethoven on broomsticks? Mozart on bottles?

HE: I'll be everlastingly grateful if you'll teach me. A clown! A funny man! The dream of my childhood! When all my friends at school were thrilled by Plutarch's heroes and the wonders of science ... I dreamed of clowns, Beethoven on broomsticks, Mozart on bottles—I have been looking for this all my life! Oh, but listen ... I must have a costume.

JACKSON: Oh, dear! You don't know much. [*Putting finger on his forehead.*] You don't think of a costume just like that. I've got a rising sun just here on my costume. [*Strikes his posterior.*] I took two years to think it out.

HE: Yes, I must think too.

[JACKSON *and* HE *move away talking.*]

MANCINI: And I must go. Consuela my child, get dressed. [*To* HE.] We're lunching with Baron Regnard, a friend of mine, the banker.

CONSUELA: But, Daddy, I can't go. Alfred says I must work.

MANCINI: Work! Indeed! And do you call this equitation work? Mere antics, *pour faire passer le temps.* Antics! This is serious ... *money.*

CONSUELA: Oh, Daddy!

MANCINI: Just think of the position you put one in! One promises the Baron ... the Baron expects one ... It's impossible. Oh, I'm getting quite hot.

CONSUELA: But why does the silly old Baron matter?

MANCINI: *Ciel!* Do you hear that, O Heaven!

BEZANO: She must rehearse. [*To* CONSUELA.] If you are rested we'll start.

MANCINI: Rehearse! I *mean!* Young man, you must be mad! *Mad!* I allow you—in the cause of art, solely in the cause of *art*—to develop my daughter's physique, and you ...

CONSUELA: Oh, never mind, Daddy, run along and don't be silly. Of course we must work. Go and have lunch with your Baron. Oh, and Daddy, you forgot your clean handkerchief again. I washed it for you yesterday.

MANCINI [*ashamed, blushing*]: Absurd! My linen is washed by the laundress while you play with your dolls ... you don't know what you're saying ... these people might think, heaven knows what. Ridiculous. I'm going.

CONSUELA: Shall I write him a little note?

MANCINI [*angrily*]: Little note! Your little notes would make a horse laugh! Good-by.

[*He goes out, toying angrily with his cane. The* CLOWNS *follow him respectfully, playing a funeral march. The* ARTISTES *have gone.*]

CONSUELA [*laughing*]: Oh, and I love writing! Do I really write badly? Did you like my note, Alfred? Or did it make you laugh?

BEZANO [*blushing*]: No. I didn't laugh. Come on, Consuela.

[*They go out, meeting* ZINAIDA *entering.* CONSUELA *goes off.*]

ZINAIDA: Are you going back to work, Bezano?

BEZANO [*politely*]: Yes. There's still a lot of work to be done on the new tango. How are your lions, Madame Zinaida? I expect they're feeling this weather.

CONSUELA [*calling him from the ring*]: Alfred!

ZINAIDA: You're being called. You'd better go. [*Exit* BEZANO. *To* BRIQUET.] Finished?

BRIQUET: Mm.

JACKSON: Then so long till the show. Go on thinking about a costume, HE, and I'll think too. Be here at ten tomorrow and I'll work with you. Don't be late or I'll catch you an extra clip on the mug.

HE: I'll be here. [*Looks after* JACKSON, *who goes out.*] What a kind man! All the people around you are so kind, Papa Briquet. I suppose that good-looking young fellow is in love with Consuela, isn't he? [*Laughs.*]

ZINAIDA: Not your business, Nosy Parker. How much does he want, Papa?

BRIQUET: Just a minute. Listen, HE. I don't want to make a contract with you.

HE: Just as you like ... don't let's talk about money ... we can trust one another ... let's wait and see what I'm worth to you and then ...

BRIQUET [*pleased*]: Now that's very decent of you. Really, Zinaida, the man doesn't know anything.

ZINAIDA: All right ... better take his particulars though. Where's the book?

BRIQUET: Here. [*To* HE.] We have to keep a register of all our artistes you know ... It's police regulations ... then if we have trouble or a suicide or that ...

[*Tango and calls heard from the ring.*]

ZINAIDA: What's your name?

HE [*smiling*]: He Who Gets Slapped! That's what I chose. Or don't you like it?

BRIQUET: Oh, yes, we like it, but we must have your real name. Haven't you got a passport?

HE [*confused*]: A passport? No ... oh, well, yes ... I mean I have ... but I had no idea the rules here were so strict. What do you want it for?

[ZINAIDA *and* BRIQUET *look at one another.* ZINAIDA *pushes book aside.*]

ZINAIDA: Then we can't engage you. We can't get on the wrong side of the police just for you.

BRIQUET: Oh, by the way ... you don't know, she's my wife. She's quite right, you know ... you might get kicked by a horse ... have an accident or something ... never know. I don't care myself ... but the authorities think different. If anything happens, well, that's that, and I don't want to know any more ... but they want to know ... oh, well, I suppose it's necessary ... I don't know. ... Got a card?

HE: Well, yes, I have ... but you do understand I don't want my name known?

BRIQUET: Some little? ... er ... ?

HE: Something like that. Look here, can't we imagine that I've got no name? That I've lost it? Like an umbrella? Or that someone's taken it by mistake? When a stray dog walks in, you don't ask him his name, you just give him another ... that's all I am, HE the Dog. [*Laughs.*]

ZINAIDA: Why don't you just tell us your name ... no one else need know.

HE: Honestly?

ZINAIDA: Honestly.

HE: All right.

[*Hands* ZINAIDA *his card. She looks at it and hands it to* BRIQUET, *both look at* HE.]

BRIQUET: Well, if this is true, sir ...

HE: Oh, for heaven's sake—this doesn't exist any more ... this is something that was lost ages ago ... it's just a lost umbrella ... forget it ... I've forgotten it. I'm the funny man who gets knocked about. That's all.

[*Pause.*]

BRIQUET: Listen ... forgive me, sir ... but I ask you ... *are* you drunk? I'm sorry to have to ask it, but you look a bit ...

HE: No. But please don't call me sir.

ZINAIDA: It's his business after all. [*Hides card.*] I knew there was something funny about you. You've seen that Bezano is in love with our equestrienne and you see that I love my Briquet?

HE [*also smiling*]: Oh yes. You adore him.

ZINAIDA: I adore him. Now take him, Briquet, and show him the ring and the stables. I must finish these.

HE: The circus ... the spangles ... the ring, where I shall get knocked about.... Come on, Briquet, let's go ... until I feel the actual sawdust under my feet, I shan't believe it.

BRIQUET: All right. [*Kisses* ZINAIDA.] Come on!

ZINAIDA: Half a mo'! HE, you're a clever man ... perhaps you can explain ...

HE: What?

ZINAIDA: Well—I've got a man who looks after the cages ... just an ordinary, low type sort of man ... we don't really know anything about him ... he only cleans the cages. He goes in and out without so much as looking at the lions ... perfectly at home. Why d'you suppose that is? Nobody knows him ... everybody knows me and everybody's terrified of my doing it, but . . . and he's quite stupid . . . you'll probably come across him—but don't *you* think of going into the cages, my Sultan wouldn't half bash you about.

BRIQUET [*displeased*]: Oh, don't go on about that, Zinaida.

ZINAIDA [*laughing*]: Oh, all right. Well . . . you go on, oh, and Louis, send Bezano in. I want a word with him.

[HE *and* BRIQUET *exit.* ZINAIDA *looks again at the card then hides it. She walks quickly up and down the room, she stops and listens to the Tango, which ends abruptly. She stands motionless, staring at the dark door through which* BEZANO *comes.*]

BEZANO: D'you want me, Madame Zinaida, because I haven't much time.

[ZINAIDA *looks at him silently.* BEZANO *flushes with anger and frowns. He turns to go.*]

ZINAIDA: Bezano! [BEZANO *stops.*] Bezano! People keep telling me you're in love with Consuela. Are you?

BEZANO: We work together.

ZINAIDA [*pause*]: Alfred, tell me the truth. Are you in love with her?

BEZANO [*looks straight into* ZINAIDA'S *eyes. Proudly*]: I'm not in love with anybody. How could I be in love with Consuela? She's here today, and gone tomorrow. Her father might take her away. Anyhow, who am I? A jockey? My father was a cobbler in Milan. Consuela! . . . I can't even talk about it any more than my horses can. How could I love Consuela?

ZINAIDA: Do you love me?

BEZANO: No. I told you that before.

ZINAIDA: Not even a little bit?

[*Pause.*]

BEZANO: I'm afraid of you.

ZINAIDA [*represses a cry, controls herself and shuts her eyes*]: Am I very frightening?

BEZANO: You're very beautiful—like a queen, sort of. Almost as beautiful as Consuela. But I don't like your eyes.

Your eyes order me to love you. And I don't like being ordered about. I'm afraid of you.

ZINAIDA: I'm not ordering you, Bezano. I'm begging.

BEZANO: Then why don't you look at me? I know why.
You know yourself that your eyes can't beg. Lion tamer.

ZINAIDA: Sultan loves me.

BEZANO: Then why is he so sad?

ZINAIDA: Yesterday he licked my hand like a dog.

BEZANO: And today he would have torn you to pieces.
He stares and stares out of his cage as though you were
the only one he saw. He's afraid of you and he hates you.
D'you want me to lick your hand like a dog?

ZINAIDA: No. [*Passionately.*] I want to kiss your hand.

BEZANO [*severely*]: I'm ashamed when you say things like
that.

ZINAIDA [*controlling herself*]: No one should be so cruel
to anyone as you are to me. Alfred! I love you. No, I'm
not ordering you. Look at me! I love you. [*Pause.* BEZANO
starts to go.] Alfred . . .

BEZANO: Don't say it again ever. I don't like it. I shall
have to pack up. When you say "love" it sounds like cracking a whip. It's disgusting. You know it is.

   [*He turns brusquely and goes out as* HE *comes in.*]

HE: Oh, I'm sorry . . . I . . . er . . . beg your pardon.

ZINAIDA: Nosy Parkering again . . . d'you really want a
smack.

HE: No. I just forgot my hat. I didn't hear anything.

ZINAIDA: I don't care if you did or not.

HE: May I take my hat?

ZINAIDA: Yes, if it's yours. HE—could you love me?

HE [*laughs*]: I? Love? Now look at me, Zinaida. . . . Have
I got a face of a lover?

ZINAIDA: One *could* love a face like that.

HE: That's because I'm happy . . . because I've lost my
umbrella . . . because I'm drunk . . . because I'm not drunk.
. . . Oh, I feel light-headed like a young girl at her first ball.
. . . Oh, it's so lovely here. Hit me . . . beat me . . . knock
me about . . . I want to begin my part. Perhaps it'll do

something to my heart ... perhaps I shall feel love ... love!
[*As if listening to his own heart with pretended terror.*]
D'you know? I can feel it!

[*In the circus the Tango is played again.*]

ZINAIDA [*listening too*]: Love for me?

HE: No. I don't know yet. Love for everybody. Listen!
They're dancing. ... Consuela is very beautiful! The boy's
very beautiful, too. He looks like a Greek god. ... like a
statue. Love!

[*Pause.*]

ZINAIDA: HE?

HE: What are your orders, Queen?

ZINAIDA: HE—how can I make my lions love me?

CURTAIN

act 2

*Same scene. During the show. Music and laughter are
audible offstage.*

CONSUELA *and the* BARON *occupy the stage.* CONSUELA *is
dressed for the performance, with a shawl round her shoulders. The* BARON *stands in front of her, a tall stout man in
evening dress, a rose in his buttonhole. Grasping the ground
with feet well apart, he gazes at her heavily with spiderlike
eyes.*

BARON: Is it true that your father has introduced you to
Marquis Justi? A very rich man?

CONSUELA: No, he's joking. I've heard him talk about
the Marquis, but I've never met him.

BARON: And do you know that your father is a charlatan?

CONSUELA: Oh, you mustn't say that. . . . Daddy's such a dear.

BARON: Did you like the jewels?

CONSUELA: Oh, yes, they were lovely! I was very sorry when Daddy said I must send them back. He said it wouldn't be at all the thing to keep them. I cried.

BARON: Your father is a beggar and a charlatan.

CONSUELA: I don't think you ought to say such nasty things about him. He's . . .

BARON: Let me kiss your hand. [*He takes her hand.*]

CONSUELA: No, no, it isn't done! When one says how do you do or good-by, yes. Not at any other time.

BARON: Everyone is in love with you. That's why you and your father think so much of yourselves. Who is this new clown called HE? I don't like him. There's something odd about him. Is he in love with you? I've caught him looking at you as . . .

CONSUELA: Of course not. He makes me die laughing. D'you know he got fifty-two slaps last night . . . we counted. Fifty-two! Daddy said, "Think if they'd been gold louis!"

BARON: And Bezano, Consuela—d'you like him?

CONSUELA: Oh, yes, very much. He's so handsome! HE says Bezano and me make the most beautiful couple in the whole world. He calls him Adam and me Eve. Adam and Eve, he calls us. But that's not nice actually, is it? But HE does go a bit far, doesn't he . . . actually?

BARON: D'you have much conversation with HE?

CONSUELA: Oh, quite a lot really. But I don't understand him really. It's like as though he drank.

BARON: Consuela . . . that's Spanish . . . consolation. Your father's an ass. Consuela, I love you.

CONSUELA: Oh . . . well . . . you must talk that over with Daddy.

BARON: Your father's a rogue. He ought to be handed over to the police. *I* can't marry *you*.

CONSUELA: Daddy says you can.

BARON: No, I can't. And suppose I shoot myself? Consuela, you silly girl, I love you unbearably. I'm mad, I suppose. I ought to be behind bars. Why do I love you, Consuela?

CONSUELA: You'd better marry me, you know.

BARON: I've had a hundred beautiful women, but I simply didn't notice them. You're the first one I've ever really loved. I can't see any other girl but you. Does God make men fall in love? Or is it the Devil? In my case, obviously the Devil. Let me kiss your hand.

CONSUELA: No.

[*Pause.*]

BARON: What are you thinking about now, Consuela? I suppose you *do* think?

CONSUELA: [*sighing*]: I don't know why, I just feel so sorry for Bezano. He's so kind when he teaches me; and his little room is *so* tiny.

BARON: Have you *been* to his room?

CONSUELA: No, HE told me about it. [*Smiling.*] Listen! Hear that noise? HE getting knocked about. Poor thing! . . . it doesn't hurt, though, it isn't like real. The intermission's due soon.

[*The* BARON *throws away his cigar and falls on his knees in front of her.*]

BARON: Consuela!

CONSUELA: Please don't! . . . Do get up . . . . Please, let go my hand . . .

BARON: Consuela!

CONSUELA: Please get up! It's disgusting. You're so fat!

[*It is intermission. Applause and voices offstage.* BARON *gets up.* CLOWNS *and* ACTORS *rush in; there is much chatter, noise and movement, and congratulations for* HE.]

POLLY: A hundred slaps! Well done, HE! Good for you!

JACKSON: Not bad. Not bad at all! You've made quite a hit.

TILLY: He was the Professor tonight, and we were the Boys. Here goes!

[*Gives him a clown's slap. Laughter and noise, greetings to the* BARON, *which he barely acknowledges.*

Enter MANCINI.]

MANCINI: *Succès fou!* ... Ah, Baron, how are we? *Succès fou!* How the public does love to see the other chap getting knocked about. That's what they want! A whipping boy—a scapegoat, eh? [*Aside.*] Your knees are dusty, Baron; brush them, [*Aloud.*] Mmm ... dust everywhere. ... Circus life! Consuela, my dear child, how are you?

[*General chatter; drinks are brought in.*]

CONSUELA [*searching and calling*]: Bezano! Alfred!

HE: Recognize me, Baron?

BARON: Yes, I do.

HE: Oh?

BARON: You're the clown, HE.

HE: Right. He Who Gets Slapped. Forgive me asking, Baron, but you got your jewels back all right?

[*The* BARON *is very surprised.*]

HE: I was asked to return them to you, so naturally I ...

JACKSON [*bringing* HE *a drink*]: Have a wet, you've earned it. Believe me, ladies and gents, this young man will go far. I'm an old clown ... I know my stuff ... I know what people like ... but today, my boy, you outshone even me. A cloud has covered my sun. They're sick of back-chat ... tired of talky-talk. It's knockabout they want ... slapstick, slapstick every time. They long for someone to get knocked about ... they yearn for someone to get knocked about ... they dream about it when they get home. Chin chin, HE. He took as many slaps as ... oh ... made his century.

TILLY: Bet you he didn't.

POLLY: Bet you he did.

TILLY: I'll count next time.

A VOICE: The front rows weren't laughing.

JACKSON: Of course not. They're too near. They were laughing all right up in the gods. The gods are the right distance away. Skoal, HE!

HE: Skoal! But Jackson, look here, you cut me ... you didn't let me finish my speech, you butted in just as I was getting going.

JACKSON: Putting your foot in it, old boy. Politics—all

right—manners—all right—but religion—never touch it. Take it from me, my boy, I just shut you up in time— didn't I, Papa Briquet?

BRIQUET: *Mais certainement* ... of course. Where do you think you are, HE? This isn't a college.

TILLY [*defending* HE]: But still ... to cut in on a person's gag ... I mean ...

BRIQUET [*piously*]: The point is, a person has no business to say the kind of things that need shutting up unless they happen to be dru ... I'll have a drink.

VOICES: Drink for the boss!

BRIQUET: Not pleased with you tonight, HE. Trying to be clever at the expense of the audience. They don't like it. It's not what they pay for. [*Drinks.*] Bottoms up! No—what they want is a good clean slap—biff! bang! crash! They like that, it's nice. It makes them laugh, and then they'll love you. But that clever-clever stuff of yours—well, it's not nice, it's nasty.

HE: They laughed.

BRIQUET: On the wrong side of their faces.

JACKSON: Just what I tell him. Bit more of that, and you'll get them ugly.

[*Enter* BEZANO.]

BEZANO: Oh, *there* you are, Consuela—I've been looking for you. Come on!

[BEZANO *and* CONSUELA *go out, followed by the* BARON.]

HE: But listen ... times have changed ... audiences have changed ...

JACKSON: Here, what's the idea—teaching me my business?

HE: Oh, no, Jackson—don't be angry. After all, it's a sort of game, isn't it?—the most wonderful sort of game—glorious! One goes on—into the ring—there's music—there are the people— Lord, what a house! And there's me, in my make-up, feeling fine. It's like a dream. You can hide behind all this—[*indicating costume and mask*] and you can act—free to do anything, free to say anything ... like being

drunk. Oh, surely you understand? [*To* JACKSON.] Tonight,
I was a philosopher, a great man ... I walked like this—
[*Imitating.*] I told them how wise I was, how great—super-
latively great—how God lives in me, how high I stood
above the earth, how glory shone about my head and then
—and then—and then you slapped me in the face, Jim, and
there was an enormous laugh, so I said to you, "What are
they laughing at?" and you gave me another, and then
after you'd hit me a dozen times, I suddenly said, "I do believe the Vice-Chancellor wants me at the College!" [JACK-
SON *boxes his ears. Laughter. Holding face.*] Here! Why did
you do that?

JACKSON: Because you asked for it. Trying it on us. Save
that stuff for the customers.

[*A bell rings. The performers start to leave, chattering.*]

BRIQUET: Come on, boys ... Act two, please! Act two
beginners, please ...

MANCINI: You're not on in this, are you?

HE: No. This is my wait.

MANCINI: Want a word with you.

BRIQUET [*offstage*]: Beginners, act two ... all on, please....
[*Everyone except* HE *and* MANCINI *have gone. Loud
music from the direction of the ring.*]

MANCINI: HE, you've got something my ancestors never
had.

HE: Oh?

MANCINI: Yes. Money. Let's have another on you. [*Orders drinks from an ancient* WAITER *who is clearing up
glasses and debris left by the crowd.*]

HE: You look depressed, Mancini. [*Stretches—tired.*]
Oh dear—I'm tired—a bit old for getting knocked about—
a hundred slaps at my age! Yes, you look down in the
mouth. How are things going with that girl of yours—out
by the gasworks?

MANCINI: Terrible . . . difficult . . . complications . . .
parents!

HE: Prison?

MANCINI: Prison! HE, I'm joking, but there's tragedy in

my heart. You understand me, but even you can't explain this passion . . . it'll be the end of me. Why can't I like the things that are allowed? Even at the moment of my ecstasy I'm conscious of the law . . . the policeman's always waiting to tap me on the shoulder. Oh, dear!

HE: Can't you settle things somehow?

MANCINI: Can't I get money somehow?

HE: What about the Baron?

MANCINI: Oh, that! Just biding his time, the old blood-sucker. He'll get what he wants too. One of these days you'll see me give him Consuela for ten thousand francs—or five.

HE: Cheap!

MANCINI: Did I say it wasn't? You know those jewels—well, when I sent them back—damn honesty!—I didn't even tinker with the diamonds.

HE: Why not?

MANCINI: Don't tell me he wouldn't weigh them.

HE: He won't marry her.

MANCINI: Oh, yes, he will. I know him. There've been heaps of women before, but this is the first time he's ever been in love. Devil take him with those big cars! Have you seen that car?

HE: Yes. Let the jockey have Consuela.

MANCINI: Bezano? [Laughs.] Nonsense! Oh, I know, it's all that stuff about Adam and Eve. But—please—no. Clever, of course, mais pas convenable.

HE: Or let me have her.

MANCINI: Are you a millionaire? I'll thank you not to try to be funny. They say the prisons in this country are fright-ful—frightful, and no discrimination of any kind made be-tween people of one's own class—decent people—and just riff-raff. Are you laughing at me?

HE: No.

MANCINI [angry]: One can't tell—made up like that.

HE: He won't marry her. It's obvious. What is Consuela? She's completely uneducated. She talks like a char. You'd take her for a char—except on horseback, of course. Don't you think she's very silly? [Nonchalantly.]

MANCINI: No. And you are. What does a woman want to be *educated* for? You amaze me! Consuela is an unpolished jewel. And only a donkey could fail to notice her sparkle. [*Confidentially.*] D'you know what happened? I *tried* to polish her.

HE: I know ... you got a tutor. Well?

MANCINI [*nodding his head*]: Alarming! Went too fast. Had to sack him. Another month, and she would have kicked *me* out. Those old diamond merchants in Amsterdam are clever. They keep their precious stones unpolished and fool the thieves. My father taught me that.

HE: The sleep of the diamond. So it *is* only sleeping. You know a thing or two, Mancini.

MANCINI: The women of Italy! ... Do you know what blood it is that flows in their veins? The blood of Hannibal ... of a Medici ... of a Borgia ... of a dirty Lombardy peasant ... of a Moor. In her all forms are possible, as in our marble. Strike here—out springs a washerwoman! Strike there—a sloppy street girl with a screeching voice! Strike there—but gently, gently—for there rises a queen. A goddess—the Venus of the capitol, who sings like a Stradivarius to draw tears from the eyes. An Italian woman is ...

HE: And what'll the Baron make of her?

MANCINI: A baroness. But there is a fly in the ointment.

HE: Oh?

MANCINI: Yes. What will become of *me?* A year after the wedding—within a year, a little year, I shan't be allowed into their kitchen. Think of it! I! Count Mancini— and she no more than the simplest, vulgarest, little ... oh!

HE: *What?* You aren't her father?

MANCINI: Damme, I'm not myself today. Heavens! Not her father? Can't you see the likeness—the eyes, the mouth— [*Suddenly sighing.*] Oh, my dear sir, how unhappy I am! Here am I—a nobleman—almost beaten in my struggle to uphold the honor of my name; and there—out in the audience—sits that old beast, that old elephant, that old spider, staring, staring at Consuela.... But he must, he shall marry her. *Nous verrons.* All my life I have been preparing for this battle. . . .

HE: And when do you think . . . [*Stops and listens. Pause and silence from the ring.*] Funny silence! Very quiet out there!

MANCINI [*indifferently*]: Is it? It may be quiet out there, but here [*touching his own head*] here there is a storm, a whirlwind. Shall I tell you a funny thing—a freak of nature? For three centuries the Counts Mancini have had no children.

HE: Then how were you born?

MANCINI: Ssh! That is the secret of our sainted mothers. We are too fastidious to trouble ourselves with a matter that a peasant can manage better. [CIRCUS BOUNCER *enters.*] Yes? The manager's on the stage.

BOUNCER [*giving letter*]: I've been sent round from the front with this. It's from the Baron Regnard.

MANCINI: Is he waiting for an answer?

BOUNCER: No; he's gone.

MANCINI [*nervously opening note*]: Oh, my God! My God!

HE [*to* BOUNCER, *who is on his way out*]: Where have they got to in the show?

BOUNCER: Madame Zinaida and her lions. [*Exit* BOUNCER.]

HE: What on earth's the matter with you?

MANCINI: What? What? [*Dances about gaily.*] That's what!

HE: Oh, come on—tell me!

MANCINI: Give me ten francs, quick—it's in the bag. Listen, HE, if by the end of the month I've not got a car of my own—bigger than the Baron's—*you* can slap my face!

[*Enter* BRIQUET.]

HE: What's the matter, Papa? What is it?

BRIQUET: I can't bear it! . . . I can't!

HE: What is it? Are you ill?

BRIQUET: I can't watch it! Why does she do it? Oh, she must give up this act! She's mad! Oh, I couldn't watch it.

HE, those lions'll tear her to pieces.

MANCINI: Pull yourself together, Briquet! She does it every night. Don't be a baby. Ought to be ashamed of yourself.

BRIQUET: No. This time she's mad. And what's the matter with the audience? Not a sound—still as death! I couldn't stand it. Listen! What's that?

[*All listen. Silence.*]

MANCINI: I'll go and see.

BRIQUET [*yelling*]: No! Don't! You're not to ... Oh, God, what· a profession! You mustn't look at her. You mustn't look at those awful, awful lions! It's wicked to look at things like that. I ran away. HE, they'll tear her to pieces.

HE: That's all right. You keep quiet, Papa Briquet, and you'll be all right in a minute. What a fuss to make! You'll be all right—have a drink. Mancini, get him a drink.

BRIQUET: No, I don't want one. [*Pause.*] If only it would end! Never in all my born days ...

[*Thunderous applause. The men on stage relax.*]

MANCINI: There you are, you see. It's all right.

BRIQUET [*Laughing and crying*]: I'll never let her do it again ... never ... never ... not if I live to be a—

HE: Ssh! Here she is.

[*Enter* ZINAIDA, *distraught—like a mad Victory. All behave as if afraid of her.* TILLY *and* POLLY *follow, later* CONSUELA *and* BEZANO.]

BRIQUET: You've gone mad! You're a madwoman!

ZINAIDA: No. No ... I'm not mad. Were you watching? Well?

TILLY: Pull yourself together, Zinaida.

ZINAIDA: Were you watching too?

BRIQUET [*to* ZINAIDA]: Come home ... time you came home ... [*To the others.*] You can all carry on here. [*To* ZINAIDA.] Come home, Zinaida.

POLLY: You can't go, Papa, you've got to lock up.

ZINAIDA [*laughing happily*]: Oh, Bezano, Bezano ... Alfred! Did you see? My lions *do* love me?

[BEZANO *does not answer and exits.* ZINAIDA *wilts and grows pale.* BRIQUET *bends low over her.*]

BRIQUET: Fetch a chair, someone! [*Someone fetches a chair, someone calls for brandy.*] What is the matter, Zinaida, my darling?

MANCINI [*running about*]: She must be kept quiet! Clear out—all of you . . . clear out! I'll arrange everything, Papa Briquet . . . leave everything to me. Her shawl—where's her shawl? She's cold.

TILLY [*baby talk*]: Would you like some pretty music?

MANCINI [*giving brandy*]: Drink . . . Duchess . . . drink. [ZINAIDA *drinks it all up as though it were water.* CONSUELA *falls on her knees in front of* ZINAIDA.]

CONSUELA: Oh, my darling . . . you are cold . . . your poor dear little hands . . . oh, my darling . . .

ZINAIDA [*pushing her away gently*]: Home . . . I'll soon be all right . . . it's nothing really . . . I'm very . . . Home . . . You stay here, Briquet . . . you must. I'm all right.

CONSUELA: Have my scarf. Are you cold?

ZINAIDA: No.

BRIQUET: Oh, Zinaida! Why do you do it? Why do you want those awful lions to love you? It's all that terrible reading and that . . . things we aren't meant to know. [*To* HE.] Do you understand, HE? . . . You read books too— you try to explain to her, she might listen to you. Tell her wild beasts can't love human beings . . . they don't . . . they can't—can they? Except in olden times . . . magic . . . gods and goddesses and that. You talk to her.

HE [*kindly*]: Well, I think they can only love their own kind. [*Gently.*] And I must say I think the same thing applies to us.

BRIQUET: Yes, yes. of course . . . stands to reason. Law of nature. Anything else would be . . . well . . . not natural, wouldn't it, HE?

HE: Yes, I think you're right, Briquet.

BRIQUET [*kindly*]: There, you see, you dear silly woman . . . we all agree.

MANCINI: Oh, *Mon Dieu*, Briquet . . . forcing your illiterate point of view on a cultivated woman!

ZINAIDA [*faint smile*]: I'm all right now.

BRIQUET: My darling!

ZINAIDA: Don't fuss, Louis, I'm going home.

BRIQUET: Can you manage alone?

MANCINI: Churl! And shall Count Mancini desert a woman in distress? I, Count Mancini, shall escort her home. Set your boorish heart at rest. I shall escort her. Thomas!— a conveyance! Madam's cloak, someone! Out of the way, Briquet! You are as clumsy as a hippopotamus! There, there, gently does it! [*To* CONSUELA.] I shall return for you, my child.

> [*All leave but* HE *and* CONSUELA. *Laughter and shrieks from the ring.* CONSUELA *unconsciously strikes an affected pose.*]

HE: Consuela!

CONSUELA: What? . . . *dear* HE . . .

HE: Where did you learn to look like that? You look like a statue . . . you look like Psyche . . .

CONSUELA: I don't know— [*sighs*] It's a sad night tonight, isn't it, HE?

HE: Mm.

CONSUELA: Are you sorry for Zinaida?

HE: What did she do?

CONSUELA: Oh, I didn't watch. I shut my eyes all the time. Alfred says she is a cruel woman, but she isn't. She has ever such nice eyes and tiny hands . . . but they're always cold, like as though she was dead, actually. What does she do it all for? Alfred says it's all right when she's just brave and doesn't get sort of excited, but that when she's sort of excited it's kind of disgusting. Is that true, HE?

HE: She's in love with Alfred.

CONSUELA [*surprised*]: Bezano? My Alfred? Does she love the same way as other people?

HE: Yes—but a bit more, perhaps.

CONSUELA: Alfred? No, that's nonsense. [*Pause.*] That's a beautiful costume, HE—did you think it out yourself?

HE: Jackson helped me.

CONSUELA: Jackson is so kind. All clowns are kind.

HE: I'm not. I'm horrid.

CONSUELA [*laughs*]: Oh, no! You're not! You're the kindest of them all. Oh dear! Alfred and me are on soon. Will you watch me?

HE: Of course. I always do. How beautiful you are, Consuela.

CONSUELA: Like Eve?

HE: Yes. If the Baron asks you to marry him, will you say yes?

CONSUELA: Of course! That's all Daddy and I are waiting for. Daddy said yesterday he thinks the Baron's as good as in the bag. I don't love him, of course, but I'll be his loyal and faithful wife. Daddy wants to teach me to play the piano.

HE: His loyal and faithful wife. Did you make that up yourself?

CONSUELA: Of course . . . why ever not? Poor thing . . . he loves me ever so much. HE, darling—

HE: Mm?

CONSUELA: HE, what *is* love? Everybody goes on talking about love. Even Zinaida. Fancy Zinaida being in love! Poor Madame! *Hasn't* this been a sad evening?

HE: Mm?

CONSUELA: Did you paint that expression on your face yourself? [HE *nods*.] I don't know how you do it, all of you . . . I tried a make up like that once, but I only made ever such a mess. I wonder why women can't be clowns? You *are* quiet, HE. D'you feel sad too?

HE: No, I feel happy tonight. Give me your hand, Consuela—I want to read it.

CONSUELA: Oh, can you? You clever thing! But don't you just make up a lot of stuff like the gypsies. . . . D'you see good luck in it? [*They both bend over her hand.*]

HE: Yes, there is good luck in it, but . . . Hullo! This is funny! Ah, Consuela! What have we here? [*Acting.*] I tremble! I do not dare foretell! . . .

CONSUELA: Oh, don't be so silly!

HE: . . . foretell the fateful signs . . .

CONSUELA: What do the stars say?

HE: This is what the stars say . . . but their voices are faint and far away, and their light is pale like the ghosts of young girls. They've cast their spell on you, Consuela, beautiful Consuela, and you stand at the threshold of eternity.

CONSUELA: I don't understand. Does it mean I shall live a long time?

HE: Yes . . . look how far this line goes. Consuela, you will live forever.

CONSUELA: There, you see, you *are* lying—you're no better than a gypsy!

HE: But it's written here—look, silly—here is eternal life. Love and glory. Listen to Jupiter! He says, "Goddess, thou must not marry anyone born of mankind"—and Consuela, if you marry the Baron—you'll be lost . . . and you'll die.

CONSUELA: Will he gobble me up?

HE: No, but you'll die before he's had time to gobble you up.

CONSUELA: And what's going to happen to Daddy? Isn't there anything about him? [*She laughs and softly sings the waltz which is being played offstage.*]

HE: Don't mock the stars, Consuela. Their spell is powerful and dark. Your fate is decreed. Even Alfred whom you love in your heart of hearts cannot save you. He is a god too —a lost god. He is locked in a deep sleep. He is a lost god who can never find his way to happiness again. Forget Bezano.

CONSUELA: I don't understand a word . . . there aren't gods really, are there? My tutor told me about them, but he said it was all myths or something. . . . Fancy my Alfred being a god! [*She laughs.*]

HE: Forget him. Consuela, I am the only one who can save you.

CONSUELA [*laughs*]: Oh, HE!

HE: Look, there's my name written on your hand.

CONSUELA: Is He Who Gets Slapped written down too?

HE: Yes. The stars know everything. But look . . . this is about me too. Consuela, welcome me . . . I am an old god in disguise. I have come down to earth to love you, just to love you, silly little Consuela.

CONSUELA: What a funny god! [*Laughing and singing.*]

HE: No, don't laugh. The gods don't like it. The gods get sad and die when they're not believed in. Oh, Consuela, my love, my joy, welcome this god! Listen! One day—a man found that his soul was sublime, and he went mad. He trembled with an anguish not of this earth and he realized the immense loneliness of the divine soul.

CONSUELA: I don't even know what language you're talking.

HE: The language that will awaken the sleeping jewel. Consuela, welcome your god who was pitched from the height like a stone . . . who came to earth to live—to act— to be everlastingly drunk with happiness. Hail, Goddess! [*Kisses her hand.*]

CONSUELA: Oh, don't . . . let go my hand. Do stop reading my hand.

HE: Sleep. And when you wake, remember. Remember the time when you rose from the sea. The blue sea and the foam. Remember the sky and the quiet breeze from the east and the murmur of spray at your marble feet.

CONSUELA [*with her eyes shut*]: I seem to remember . . . go on.

HE: Don't you see the waves breaking? Don't you remember how the mermaids sang their songs, their happy songs? The mermaids shining blue in the blue waters. Can't you hear the sun singing? Singing like a golden harp? Can't you see the hand of God spreading light and love over the world? Can't you see the mountains in their blue cloud of incense singing their praise? Remember, Consuela . . . remember the mountains . . . remember the sea . . . [*Pause, commanding her.*] Remember, Consuela.

CONSUELA [*opening her eyes*]: Oh, HE, I was feeling so happy and now I've forgotten it all. No, not quite all . . . go on . . . tell me again . . . it sort of hurts. I can hear sort of talking ... no sort of singing, saying "Consuela" ... Go on, HE. [*Pause. The tempestuous gallop heard from the ring. Pause.*] Oh, HE—that's Alfred galloping! That's his tune!

HE [*furiously*]: Forget Alfred! I love you, Consuela. You are the inspiration of my heart ... I love you! [CONSUELA *hits him.*] What—!

CONSUELA [*angry*]: You've forgotten who you are ... You're He Who Gets Slapped ... a god who gets slapped ... perhaps they slapped you out of heaven.

HE: Stop! I haven't finished acting.

CONSUELA: Oh, then you were acting! You did it so well you quite took me in.

HE [*sadly*]: I'm the funny man who gets slapped in the face.

CONSUELA: You're not cross with me for hitting you? I didn't want to—not really—but you were so ridiculous ... but now you're all right again. You're very clever—or are you drunk?

HE: Hit me again.

CONSUELA: No.

HE: I can't act unless you do.

CONSUELA [*touches him gently*]: There!

HE: Don't you know that you're a queen and I'm a jester? And don't you know that all queens have fools, and that their fools always love them and always get beaten for it?

CONSUELA: Do they?

HE: Of course. Beauty has a fool. So has Wisdom—her court is full of fools, and the sound of whipping never stops all through the night. But no fool was ever given so sweet a slap as you've just given me. He Who Gets Slapped has no rival ... [*Someone appears at the door.* HE *notices, and acts more exaggeratedly. Crying aloud.*] Have pity on me! I am only a poor jester!

[*Enter a* BAREBACK RIDER, *and a* GENTLEMAN *from the audience. The* GENTLEMAN *is very* comme il faut, *dressed in black, and carries his hat.*]

CONSUELA [*embarrassed*]: That's enough, HE ... people are listening!

HE [*getting up*]: Who dares to enter the palace of my queen?

[*He stops suddenly.* CONSUELA, *laughing, jumps up and runs away after a quick glance at the* GENTLEMAN.]

CONSUELA: You've made me feel better. I'm not so sad. Good-by! I'll write you a little note! [*Exit* CONSUELA.]

BAREBACK RIDER [*laughing*]: This is a knockabout man, sir ... oh, he is a one! HE, this gentleman wants to see you.

HE: At your service, sir.

[*Exit* RIDER, *smiling. The men approach one another.*]

GENTLEMAN: So here you are.

HE: Yes, here I am.

GENTLEMAN: I can hardly recognize you, my dear ... [*About to say his name.*]

HE [*fiercely cutting in*]: HE. That's my name. I haven't any other name. He Who Gets Slapped. And while you're here, don't you forget it.

GENTLEMAN [*expressing surprise at* HE'S *manner*]: Your manner has certainly changed!

HE: It's how we all behave here. Take it or leave it.

GENTLEMAN [*humbly*]: Have you forgiven me?

HE [*after pause*]: Have you brought my wife here, too?

GENTLEMAN: Oh, no, I'm alone.

HE: Have you parted already?

GENTLEMAN: No. We have a son. After you disappeared so suddenly, leaving that insulting letter ...

HE [*mocking*]: Insulting? Can you still feel insulted? What brought you here? Were you looking for me, or is it just chance?

GENTLEMAN: I've been searching for you—for six months —all over the place—and tonight, just by chance, I happened to come to the circus. We must talk it over ... don't you think perhaps ... we must.

[*Pause.*]

HE: *Der Doppelgänger*—the specter that can't be laid. [*Pause.*] Talk things over! Very well. Leave your address at the stage door, and I'll let you know when I can see you. Now you must go. [*Proudly*.] I'm busy.

> [*The* GENTLEMAN *bows and goes out.* HE *does not return the bow but stands with outstretched hand in the pose of a great man who shows a boring visitor to the door.*]

CURTAIN

act 3

Same scene. Morning, before rehearsal. HE *is walking thoughtfully up and down the room. He wears a bright checked coat and a loud tie. His hat is on the back of his head and his face is clean-shaven like an actor's. The* GENTLEMAN *enters.* HE *does not see him.*

GENTLEMAN: Good morning.

HE [*turning round absent-mindedly*]: Oh it's you.

GENTLEMAN: Am I early? I don't seem to be expected. . . am I disturbing you? . . . You made this appointment yourself so . . .

HE: Let's get down to business.

GENTLEMAN [*looking round with distress*]: I would have thought you would have asked me somewhere else . . . your home . . .

HE: This is my home.

GENTLEMAN: But we shall be disturbed.

HE: All the more reason for getting it over. Well?

GENTLEMAN [*after a pause*]: May I sit down?

HE: Of course . . . mind! That one's broken.

> [*The* GENTLEMAN, *afraid, pushes the chair away and looks helplessly round. Everything seems to him*

dangerous and strange. He chooses an apparently solid little gilt divan, sits down and takes off his hat and gloves. HE *watches him indifferently.*]

GENTLEMAN: You look even *more* extraordinary dressed like that. Yesterday it was a dream ... but today ...

HE: I told you my name, my name is HE.

GENTLEMAN: Must you be offensive?

HE: Yes. Well?

GENTLEMAN [*looking round*]: I hardly know ... everything here is so ... these glaring lights ... all those animals, I saw them when I was looking for you ... this smell ... this junk ... and you! A clown! You in a circus ... it's scarcely credible. Yet, when all our friends said you were dead, I was the only one that didn't agree, something told me you were alive. ... Still in these surroundings it *is* scarcely credible.

HE: You said you had a son. Is he like me?

GENTLEMAN: Like you?

HE: Yes. Women often have children by a new husband who look like the old one. Has that happened to you? [*Laughs.*] And your book is a great success I hear?

GENTLEMAN: I don't know what you mean.

HE [*ironically*]: Don't you? Never mind. Why did you try to find me?

GENTLEMAN: My conscience...

HE: Surely you haven't a conscience. Or did you think you hadn't taken quite everything I had? I've nothing left now ... except my clown's get-up ... not quite your style. Get out.

GENTLEMAN: You can't forgive me, that your wife ...

HE: To hell with my wife.

GENTLEMAN: Really! [*Sound of whip cracking and puppy crying.*] What's that?

HE: A dog being taught new tricks. [GENTLEMAN *winces.*] Yes, the process of learning is sometimes painful.

GENTLEMAN: It's so difficult for me ... it's so difficult to talk here ... in these surroundings. If you cared so little for your wife, who loved you and thought you a saint, why did you take such a drastic step? Running away and hiding here? [*Hypocritically.*] I know it's not entirely deserved. I suppose you want to take your revenge by embarrassing us with your degradation. But why are you jealous of my success? You were always so indifferent to applause . . . or was your indifference just an act? And when I, a more successful rival . . .

HE [*laughs*]: Rival? . . . you!

GENTLEMAN: But my book!

HE: Are you still talking to *me* about your *book*? [*Pause.*]

GENTLEMAN: I'm so unhappy.

HE: Why?

GENTLEMAN: Please, will you forgive me? I am incurably . . . irrevocably unhappy.

HE: Why? . . . Your book is an immense success . . . you are famous . . . every dirty rag of a newspaper is full of you and your notions. And who knows me? Who can cope with my highfalutin philosophies? You take my ideas and make them popular by making them vulgar. And then, as Jackson says, you knock them cold. I feel as though I was walking down a long corridor lined with distorting mirrors . . . all reflecting an image of myself. You are a distorted image of me, your ideas are a distortion of mine. Your son —he's like me, isn't he? My image distorted. How ugly my son must be if he's like me. Why are you unhappy? You haven't been found out yet . . . but how can you be found out? You're always within the law. . . . The only reason you're tormenting yourself about my wife is that you're not legally married to her. . . . Marry her, I'm dead. Or isn't my wife enough? D'you want my ideas? D'you want my fame? Keep them! I bequeath them to you, my lawful heir. . . . I am dead . . . and dying I forgave you.

[*Makes a stupidly pious face and then bursts out laughing. The* GENTLEMAN *raises his head and bending forward looks straight into* HE'S *eyes.*]

GENTLEMAN: What about my pride?

HE: Pride! . . . don't come so near me . . . And to think

that once I was really fond of you and thought a lot of you . . . my shadow!

GENTLEMAN: I am your shadow.

HE [*mocking him*]: Oh, you're wonderful! Listen . . . tell me . . . truthfully . . . do you hate me?

GENTLEMAN: Yes. With all the hatred there is in the world. Sit down.

HE: Are those your orders?

GENTLEMAN: Yes. Thank you. I hate you. I am respected and famous. I have a wife and son. [*Laughs bitterly.*] But my wife loves you. Your genius is our favorite topic. We talk about you even in bed. We love you even in bed. [HE *grimaces.*] It is for me to wince. Yes, my son will be like you. . . . When I want to rest from my ordinary work and go to my desk to my own books and my own pen, I find you there. . . . I can never get away from you. Even at night, when I'm left to my own thoughts . . . in my wretched brain I'm haunted by your image.

HE [*speaking slowly*]: This is rich. The robber turns out to be the victim. The robber weeps and wails because he can't enjoy the fruits of the crime. You are not my shadow —I'll tell you what you are—you are the mob. You live on my ideas and you hate me. My breath is stifling you . . . you're choking with hatred and you try to smother your pride, but you follow in my footsteps, but in the wrong direction . . . yes, this is rich. [*Walking about, smiling.*] Tell me, would it be easier for you if I were to die?

GENTLEMAN: Yes. But you don't look like a man who . . .

HE: Yes . . . death . . . of course . . .

GENTLEMAN: Do sit down.

HE: All right. Well?

GENTLEMAN: Of course I daren't ask you to die, but you won't ever come back, will you? Don't laugh. [*He approaches* HE *and tries to take his hands, with abasement.*] *Won't* you forgive me?

HE [*recoiling*]: Don't touch me . . . get out.

[*Enter* TILLY *and* POLLY, *playing as in the first act. For a long time they do not see the two men.*]

HE: Tilly! Hullo!

TILLY: Oh! Good morning, HE. We're rehearsing... March of the Ants. Polly's got no ear....

HE: For the benefit?

POLLY: Yes. I bet you've got something new up your sleeve?... you are a dark horse... Consuela told us you were rehearsing something. She's going soon.

HE: Really?

TILLY: Zinaida told us. She wouldn't get a benefit otherwise, would she? She's a good girl.

POLLY: Don't walk like an elephant, you're an ant. [*They exit playing.*]

GENTLEMAN: Are these your new colleagues? Very extraordinary.

HE: Nothing here is ordinary.

GENTLEMAN [*indicating* HE'S *attire*]: You used to be so well turned out, and look at you!

HE [*looking at himself*]: Why, it's pretty! There's the rehearsal beginning.... You must go now... you're in the way.

GENTLEMAN: But you haven't answered my question.

[*Slow strains of the Tango heard offstage.*]

HE [*listening to music*]: What question?

GENTLEMAN [*who does not hear music*]: Please tell me ... will you ever come back?

HE: [*listening to music*]: Never. Never. Never.

GENTLEMAN [*getting up*]: Thank you. I'm going.

HE: Never. Never. Never. Yes, go and don't come back, you have your uses *there* ... but *not here.*

GENTLEMAN: But supposing something happens to you ... you're quite a strong man, but in these surroundings ... accidents might happen... how shall I find out? Do they know your name here?

HE: No. But you *will* find out ... anything else?

GENTLEMAN: Can I be sure? Are you speaking the truth?

HE: Yes, yes. Never.

[*They walk to the door, the* GENTLEMAN *stops.*]

GENTLEMAN: May I come to the circus sometimes?

HE: Of course. You're the public ... but don't ask for free seats. Why do you want to come? Are you fond of the circus?

GENTLEMAN: I want to watch you. Perhaps I shall understand. I know you well enough to think you must be here for a reason ... but what? [*Looks short-sightedly at* HE. HE *grimaces and thumbs his nose.*] What?!! [*Offended.*] What's that?

HE: My reason ... Good-by, Marquis, my regards to your esteemed consort and charming son.

[*During this* MANCINI *has entered.*]

MANCINI: You revel in your part, HE! Whenever I turn up you're acting away.... a glutton for work!

HE [*introducing*]: The Marquis of Chateau Nowhere— Count Mancini.

MANCINI [*preening*]: Delighted! D'you know this eccentric, Marquis? [*Touching* HE *patronizingly with his cane.*] Hasn't he got an attractive little phiz?

GENTLEMAN [*embarrassed*]: Yes, I have had the pleasure. [*Going.*] Delighted to have ...

MANCINI: Delighted ...

HE [*showing him out*]: Take care, Marquis ... it's dark in the passage ... there are some steps ... unfortunately it's not possible for me to see you out.

GENTLEMAN [*quietly*]: Won't you shake hands? We shan't ever meet again.

HE: There's no need ... I hope to meet you—in the Kingdom of Heaven. ... You'll be there, won't you?

GENTLEMAN [*disdainfully*]: How you have changed. ... You *are* a clown!

HE: I am He Who Gets Slapped. Good-by, Marquis.

GENTLEMAN: Good-by. [*Looking* HE *in the eyes. Very quietly.*] Are you mad?

HE [*just as quietly, his eyes wide open*]: I'm afraid you were never so right in your life. I am mad. [*He shows him out, with a big, affected gesture, a sweep of his hand and arm from his head to the floor. Laughs.*] Marquis, au revoir! [*The* GENTLEMAN *goes out.* HE *comes skipping back and takes a pose.*] Mancini! Let us dance the Tango! Mancini! I adore you.

MANCINI [*sitting back comfortably and playing with his cane*]: You forget yourself! You are a dark horse, old boy, but I always guessed you were a person of one's own class ... you're so easy to talk to. Is this Marquis the genuine article?

HE: Absolutely hallmarked, like you.

MANCINI: A pleasant face! But at first I took him for an undertaker. Oh, HE! When shall I say farewell to these dirty walls and Papa Briquet and these silly posters and these common jockeys?

HE: Soon now.

MANCINI: Oh, HE! I wilt in this milieu ... I'm turning into a horse myself ... you know what high society means ... one is adequately dressed ... one goes to receptions ... one indulges in witty exchanges ... one plays occasional baccarat—without cheating! [*Laughs.*]

HE [*joining in*]: And in the evening one slinks out to the suburbs where one is considered a man of honorable intentions.

MANCINI: And picks someone up? [*Laughs.*] I'll wear a black silk mask and footmen shall follow me to guard me from hoi polloi ... look, HE! Look at my stiletto! D'you think it ever had blood on it?

HE [*acting sham fright*]: Oh!

MANCINI: Ass!

HE: What about that girl out by the gas works?

MANCINI: The parents are completely satisfied ... but completely. They bless my name. [*Laughs.*] Apropos ... what make of car d'you think the best? Money no object! [*Enter* BRIQUET. *They shake hands.*] Ah! Papa Briquet.

BRIQUET: Well, Mancini, you've got your farewell benefit for Consuela at last. But only because Zinaida ...

MANCINI: It's done you a good turn too ... the Baron's bought up all the grand circle—every reservable seat. What more do you want?

BRIQUET: I've got very fond of Consuela ... very sorry

to part with her. Don't know why she's leaving . . . she's got honest work . . . good friends . . . the atmosphere . . . what more does she want?

MANCINI: She doesn't. But I do. [*Laughs.*] I asked you to give her a raise, Stingy! And now, Director, will you change me a thousand-franc note?

BRIQUET [*sighing*]: All right. Give it me.

MANCINI [*nonchalantly*]: Tomorrow . . . I left it at home. [*All laugh.*] We're going to motor out to the Baron's villa today—they say it's *tout à fait* the thing.

HE: What for?

MANCINI: Oh, the whim of a billionaire! He wants to show Consuela his hothouse roses and he wants to show me his cellar. He's calling for us here. [*Enter* CONSUELA *almost crying.*] What's the matter, my little Consuela?

CONSUELA: Oh, Daddy! It's Alfred! He mustn't . . . he's no business to shout at me . . . he nearly hit me with the whip . . .

MANCINI [*blazing*]: Briquet! I call on you as Director . . . what are these? Stable manners? . . . To strike my daughter with a horse whip? Some jockey! I am outraged!

CONSUELA: Oh, Daddy, don't create . . . !

BRIQUET: I'll speak to him.

CONSUELA: Oh, please don't . . . Alfred didn't mean to . . . it was silly of me to tell you . . . he's sorry himself.

BRIQUET: I'll have a word with him all the same.

CONSUELA: Oh, don't go at him, he didn't mean it.

MANCINI: He must be *forced* to apologize . . . the brute!

CONSUELA: But he *has* apologized! How silly you are . . . I couldn't do the act. I was nervy . . . it's all nothing. Oh, HE dear, good morning. *How* that tie suits you. [BRIQUET *starts going.*] Where are you going, Briquet? To Alfred?

BRIQUET: No, home. Zinaida sent you her love . . . she's still resting. [*Exits.*]

CONSUELA: Zinaida's so sweet. Daddy, why is everybody so kind to me now? Because I'm going away? Have you heard the march Tilly and Polly are going to play? For the benefit? It's ever so novelty!

MANCINI: Yes. We're getting a wonderful benefit.

CONSUELA: Yes. Aren't we? Daddy, I'm so hungry . . . let's have some sandwiches.

HE: I'll fetch some, my Princess. [*Exits.*]

CONSUELA: Oh, do please! [*Calling after him.*] Not cheese! I hate it.

[MANCINI *and* CONSUELA *left alone,* MANCINI *scrutinizing his daughter with a searching eye.*]

MANCINI: You look . . . peculiar, my child . . . I don't know whether it's an improvement or not . . . have you been crying?

CONSUELA: Well, a tiny bit . . . I'm so hungry.

MANCINI: Didn't you have any breakfast?

CONSUELA: No, that's why I'm so hungry . . . you forgot to leave me any money.

MANCINI: Oh, *mon Dieu!* How forgetful . . . but we shall get a very good dinner today, so don't eat many sandwiches. Yes, I like it . . . you must cry often . . . it washes off that naïveté . . . you look more . . . *feminine.*

CONSUELA: Am I very naïve, Daddy?

MANCINI: Very. Too much so. All very well in some types. But not you. Besides, the Baron . . .

CONSUELA: Nonsense! I'm not all that naïve. But you know Alfred was so horrid to me . . . even you would have cried. God knows . . .

MANCINI: Tut! Tut! Never say "God knows" . . . it isn't done.

CONSUELA: Well, I only say it to you. [*Circus noises and music heard offstage.*] Oh, listen, Daddy! That's Alfred's new number . . . That's the new trick. Jackson says he's bound to break his neck . . . poor thing!

MANCINI [*indifferently*]: Or his legs . . . or his spine . . . they all break something in the end. [*Laughs.*] Brittle toys!

CONSUELA [*listening to the music*]: Oh, how I shall miss it all! Daddy, the Baron promised to make a ring for me to gallop in whenever I want. D'you think he's just showing off?

MANCINI: No, he's not showing off. And don't say that about a Baron.

CONSUELA: Doesn't matter. Oh, it must be lovely to be rich! You could do anything.

MANCINI [*enthusiastically*]: Everything. Oh ... our fate will be decided today, my child. It's touch and go with the Baron.

CONSUELA [*indifferently*]: Is it?

MANCINI: Touch and go! I'm almost certain he'll propose today. [*Laughs.*] Hothouse roses! And among the roses a spider's web to catch our dear little fly!

CONSUELA [*indifferently*]: Horrid old spider! Daddy? Oughtn't I to let him kiss my hand?

MANCINI: Of course not! You don't know, pet, what these men are like!

CONSUELA: Alfred never kisses my hand.

MANCINI: Alfred? Alfred is a young puppy ... he mustn't dare. One can't be too careful with men like the Baron ... nice men ... today he would kiss your little finger ... tomorrow your wrist and the day after ... oh, I don't know what.

CONSUELA: Really, Daddy! ... I mean! ...

MANCINI: Oh, I know ...

CONSUELA: I don't want to hear nasty talk. I shan't half give the Baron a slap ... a better one than HE gets, if he only as much as tries.

MANCINI [*deprecatingly*]: All men are like that.

CONSUELA: They aren't. Alfred isn't. Where's HE and the sandwiches?

MANCINI: The bar won't be open at this hour, he's gone round to that little Greek place. Consuela, I must warn you ... a father's duty ... don't trust HE. Something about him ... snake in the grass ... snake in the grass ... [*Makes a gesture, twirling his fingers close to his forehead.*]

CONSUELA: Oh, you say that about everyone. I know HE. HE's such a kind man and ever so fond of me.

MANCINI [*darkly*]: Something behind it.

CONSUELA: Oh, Daddy! I'm sick of your advice.

[*Enter* HE, *puffing, with sandwiches.*]

HE: Here, Consuela!

CONSUELA: Oh, lovely fresh ones! . . . You *are* puffy! . . . oh, thanks ever so. [*Eats.*] HE, d'you love me?

HE: Yes, my Princess. I'm your jester.

CONSUELA [*eating*]: And when I go, will you find a new princess?

HE [*making a ceremonious bow*]: I shall follow you, my peerless one, I shall carry the white train of your dress and use it to wipe away my tears. [*Pretends to cry.*]

MANCINI [*laughing*]: Idiot! But what a pity those beautiful old days are gone . . . when in the courts of Mancini dozens of motley jesters received their kicks and halfpence. And now . . . the last of the Mancinis, to see a jester, must go to the circus! And is he my jester? No . . . he is anybody's who can pay. Democracy is stifling us! Democracy needs jesters! Just think of it, dear sir . . . the cheek! . . . Well, when I'm rich I'll employ you. That's that.

CONSUELA: Oh, yes, Daddy, do!

HE: And when the Count is tired of me and kicks me with his noble foot, then I'll come to my Princess and . . .

CONSUELA [*laughing*]: . . . get another kick! [*Stops eating.*] There! I'm done . . . hanky, Daddy . . . sticky fingers. you've got another. Oh dear, work again . . . what a life!

MANCINI [*anxiously*]: Don't forget.

CONSUELA: No, I won't forget.

MANCINI [*looking at watch*]: Yes . . . time . . . he wants me to call for him when you are ready . . . make your toilette before I come back. [*Laughing and bowing.*] *Signori, miei complimenti.*

[*Exit, playing with cane.* CONSUELA *sits on divan and covers herself with her shawl.*]

CONSUELA: HE, come and talk to me. You know, when you've got your make-up on you're very handsome, but you look nice now too. [*Pats sofa.*]

HE: Consuela, are you going to marry the Baron?

CONSUELA [*indifferently*]: I believe so. The Baron is touch and go. Here's half . . . you eat it. [*Gives him sandwich.*]

HE: Thanks. [*Eats.*] Do you remember my prophecy?

CONSUELA: Which one? How funnily you swallow! Like it?

HE: Mm. That if you marry the Baron...

CONSUELA: Oh, *that!* But that was only joking!

HE: Who knows... sometimes a joke is true. The stars never prophesy in vain. If it's difficult for humans to talk ... think how difficult it is for a star.

CONSUELA [*laughing*]: Yes, indeed.

HE: So, my dear, if I were you I should think twice. Suppose you should die. Consuela... don't marry the Baron.

CONSUELA [*thinking*]: What is death?

HE: No one knows—like love—no one knows. But your dear little eyes will be closed and you won't be here. The music will play alone and mad Bezano will gallop alone and Tilly and Polly will play their tunes without you... Tilly Polly. Tilly Polly... tilly tilly polly polly... [*Hums.*]

CONSUELA: Don't, HE darling. I'm sad enough as it is. [*Pause.*]

HE: Have you been crying?

CONSUELA: Yes.

HE: Why?

CONSUELA: Alfred upset me a bit. Nothing really. [*With her hand to her heart.*] I feel something here. HE, I must be ill.

HE: You're not ill. It's the spell of the stars. Consuela, it's your fate.

CONSUELA: Rubbish. Why should the stars bother with me? Tell me a fairy story about the blue sea and the beautiful gods. Are *they* all dead?

HE: They're alive, but they're sleeping.

CONSUELA: In the woods? Or in the mountains? Could I ever meet one? Just think, supposing I met a god and he took a look at me. I'd run away. [*Laughs.*] When I had no breakfast this morning I got so bored and I thought... think if a god appeared with some food and as I thought it I heard someone calling "Consuela." [*Crossly.*] Don't laugh.

HE: I didn't laugh.

CONSUELA: It's true. But he didn't come, he only called and went away. It's sad, isn't it? Oh, why did you remind me ... I'd forgotten ... the sea ... [*closing her eyes*] ... and there was something else ...

HE: Remember, Consuela.

CONSUELA: No. [*Opening her eyes.*] I've forgotten. Seen my benefit poster? It's Daddy's idea. The Baron likes it.

HE [*slowly*]: Consuela, my Princess, don't go to the Baron today.

CONSUELA: Why? [*Pause.*]

HE [*lowering his head slowly*]: I don't wish it.

CONSUELA: What cheek!

HE [*bowing his head still lower*]: I don't wish you to marry the Baron ... I shan't allow it ... I *implore you.*

CONSUELA [*angry laugh*]: Oh! Then who *can* I marry, *if* you please? You're out of your mind ... "I shan't allow it" ... well! Who d'you think you are? You're a funny man, they could kick you out any minute. I'm tired of you ... your silly old stories are all right, but when you start interfering ... then you deserve a slap ... is that why you do it?

HE: Forgive me, Consuela.

CONSUELA: You like it when they slap you and laugh at you ... I shan't forgive you. I know. [*Imitates* MANCINI'*s gesture.*] "Something in it" ... ever so nice for a bit and then ... "obey me"! ... well ... I'm not that sort of girl. You can just go on carrying my train, that's all you're good for. See?

HE: I see everything, my Princess, and I see how low your jester's lying at your feet. Away down there his little bells are jingling ... he kneels and prays ... he was impertinent and lost his tiny reason. Forgive him!

CONSUELA [*laughing*]: Oh, all right ... I forgive you. *Now* can I marry the Baron?

HE: No ... but what does a princess care for the opinion of a doting slave?

CONSUELA: D'you know why you're forgiven? ... not because of all that talk, but because of the sandwiches. Poor old HE! You'll be at my feet again and I'll whistle and . . .

HE: And I'll come to heel!

[*Enter* BEZANO, *confused.*]

BEZANO: Oh!

CONSUELA: Is it time to rehearse again?

BEZANO: Yes, shall we start, Consuela?

CONSUELA: You aren't cross any more?

BEZANO: Don't be offended because I shouted at you . . . you know when you are teaching . . .

CONSUELA: Goodness! Of course I know . . . you're much too good to have to teach a silly like me.

BEZANO: Come on then.

[BEZANO *and* CONSUELA *start to go.*]

HE: Here! Wait a minute, both of you . . . stand side by side . . .

[*They stand side by side, ill at ease,* BEZANO *blushing.*]

BEZANO [*grumpily*]: What's the game, HE?

CONSUELA [*laughing*]: Like Adam and Eve? You *are* an idiot! I'm going to change my shoes, Alfred. [*Starts to exit.*]

HE [*calling after her*]: How about your father and the Baron? They're coming for you any minute.

CONSUELA [*going*]: Oh, let them . . . doesn't matter.

[*Exit.* BEZANO *starts to follow.*]

HE: Don't go, Bezano.

BEZANO: Well, what d'you want? I've not got much time.

HE: Bezano, d'you love Consuela?

[*Pause.*]

BEZANO: That's not your business. You want to know too much. I don't know you. You're not one of us. How do I know I can trust you?

HE: D'you know the Baron? Listen . . . it's difficult to say this . . . she loves you. Save her from that old spider. Can't you see the web he's weaving round her? Get out of the vicious circle. Stop galloping blindly round and round. Take her away . . . kidnap her . . . kill her . . . take her to heaven . . . take her to hell . . . but don't let her marry the Baron. That sort of man profanes love. And if you're afraid to kill Consuela—kill the Baron.

BEZANO [*with a smile*]: And who'll kill all the other men?

HE: She loves you.

BEZANO: Did she tell *you* that?

HE: What human pride! And you're a god! Don't you want to believe me? D'you mind my not being one of you? Look at me ... I'm not lying, am I? Oh, I know I'm ugly, I make idiotic faces and they laugh at me, but can't you see I'm a god? Behind all this—a god like you. [BEZANO *laughs.*] What are you laughing at?

BEZANO: You were talking like you did that night when you said the Vice-Chancellor sent for you from the college.

HE [*sees that* BEZANO *cannot understand, so with an effort he returns to his "acting vein"*]: So I am ... "And I do believe the Vice-Chancellor wants me at the college."

BEZANO [*angry*]: Now look here, you can get yourself knocked about if you like, but don't let me in for it. [*Starts going.*]

HE: Bezano!

BEZANO: And never talk to me about Consuela. And never tell me I'm a god. I don't like it.

[*Goes out angrily.* HE *walks about with a tortured expression and then stops and throws back his head in noiseless laughter. The* BARON *and* MANCINI *find him in this position when they enter.*]

MANCINI [*laughing*]: What spirit! Laughing and alone! Shut up ... you'll break something.

HE [*bowing exaggeratedly*]: How do you do, Baron. Greetings, Count. You must forgive me ... the funny man was amused at his own joke ... busman's holiday, Baron!

MANCINI: You've got your head screwed on ... shall I ask Papa Briquet to give you a benefit?

HE [*more exaggerated bow*]: If you will be so kind, Count.

MANCINI: Oh, now you're overacting. Think of the slap you'll get at your benefit, when on ordinary nights they strike you like a gong! A strange profession, Baron.

BARON: Very strange. Where's the Countess?

MANCINI: She shall be fetched ... the dear child ... heart

and soul in her work. They call these antics *work,* Baron.

BARON: I can wait. [*Sits down with his silk hat on his head.*]

MANCINI: No need, I will hurry her up. [*To* HE.] Entertain the Baron! [*To* BARON.] He will not bore you, Baron.

[*Exit.* HE *strides about the stage, smiling and glancing from time to time at the* BARON. *The* BARON *sits with his legs spread apart and his chin on the top of his cane. The silk hat on his head. He is silent.*]

HE: Shall I entertain you, Baron?

BARON: No, I don't like clowns.

HE: And I don't like barons. [*Pause.* HE *puts on his bowler, takes a chair with a large gesture, puts it down heavily in front of the* BARON *and looks him in the eyes. Pause.*] Chatty, aren't you?

BARON: No.

HE [*tapping floor with foot*]: Can you wait a long time?

BARON: A long time.

HE: Until you get it?

BARON: Until I get it. Can you?

HE: Yes, I can.

[*Both look at each other silently, their heads close together. From the ring one hears the strains of the Tango.*]

CURTAIN

act 4

The farewell performance: BRIQUET *is having his shoes shined by one of the artistes;* JACKSON *is blowing up colored balloons; two* JOCKEYS *are dressing and making-up.*

JACKSON: Farewell performance! [*Spits.*]

BRIQUET: We're sold out, you know.

JACKSON: If you call it sold out.

BRIQUET: The Baron's bought up every reservable seat—every reservable seat. And paid good money—it's not just paper, you know.

JACKSON: It's all one. Barons in the stalls and Egyptian mummies in the circle. I know their sort—not a laugh out of them— I get bellyache from fright.

BRIQUET: Oh, well; so do I. So does everyone—all the artistes, all the animals. The animals seem to know something's up.

JACKSON: I hope HE gives them a bit of their own back.

SECOND JOCKEY: Have you seen the Baron's roses, Papa?

BRIQUET: Yes.

SECOND JOCKEY: Have you, Jackson?

JACKSON: Yes.

BRIQUET: Shut up. No one's talking to you. Get on. You'll be late.

FIRST JOCKEY: They must have cost thousands.

SECOND JOCKEY: The Baron's got his own hothouses—they won't cost him a penny.

FIRST JOCKEY: But there's a whole truck full. You can smell them a mile off. The whole ring's to be covered.

SECOND JOCKEY: Oh? Only the ring? What else?

FIRST JOCKEY: It's taken thousands of roses and rosebuds to cover the ring. It's like a carpet. A carpet—if you please—

SECOND JOCKEY: I must say it's an idea. The Tango on a blood-red carpet of blood-red roses in the middle of winter. Nice.

BOOT-CLEANING ARTISTE [*sentimentally*]: A beautiful car-- pet of beautiful roses for a beautiful young lady on a beautiful . . .

BRIQUET: Shut up! [BEZANO's *music heard offstage*.] That's Bezano on.

FIRST JOCKEY: Consuela will gallop on roses. What about Bezano?

SECOND JOCKEY: Bezano will gallop on thorns.

JACKSON: One of these days that young man will break his neck. He tries to fly—like a god. It's not nice watching him. It's not like honest work.

BRIQUET: To tell you the truth, it's not been like honest work since these Barons started coming about. What do they want—coming about? It gets my goat. . . . If I were the government, d'you know what I'd do? I'd set up iron bars between those sort of people and us.

JACKSON: And who'd be in the cage—them or us?

BRIQUET: Us, of course. We're the decent people—we're the animals.

JACKSON: Poor little Consuela.

BRIQUET: Yes, I wish she wasn't leaving.

JACKSON: I'm very sorry for poor little Consuela.

FIRST JOCKEY: So am I.

SECOND JOCKEY: So am I.

BRIQUET: It's her lookout. It's her funeral. [*Pause. Enter* THIRD JOCKEY, *breathless and running. The pace of the whole scene now quickens*.] Where the hell have you been? You'll be late. Hurry up.

THIRD JOCKEY: Looking through the peep-hole.

FIRST JOCKEY [*low*]: Hope Madame didn't catch you at it.

THIRD JOCKEY: To see the house. You should see . . .

give me my boots, quick... have you seen the Baron's roses?

ALL [*shouting*]: Yes.

THIRD JOCKEY: They smell like...

JACKSON: Get on and don't talk.

THIRD JOCKEY: You should see the audience—it's a real gala. And hear them. You can hear the hum.... It's a wonderful night, Papa, isn't it?

BRIQUET: Sold out—not an empty seat. Nearly your call, boys. [*Dismissing boot-cleaner.*] Thanks, Marco.

THIRD JOCKEY: Give me my coat. And I saw Madame Zinaida....

BRIQUET: Oh? Where?

THIRD JOCKEY: Down by the cages.

BRIQUET [*displeased*]: Oh. What was she doing?

THIRD JOCKEY: Looking at the lions. And I saw HE— looking all worked up.

JACKSON: It's all this damned gala.

THIRD JOCKEY: Madame doesn't half look blazing. She was taking the mike out of old...

[*Other* JOCKEYS *nudge him as* ZINAIDA *appears.* HE *comes with her.*]

ZINAIDA: What the devil are you boys hanging about for? You ought to be standing by.

FIRST AND SECOND JOCKEYS: Yes, Madame... we're ready... just going, Madame.

THIRD JOCKEY: It's a wonderful gala, Madame, it's one up for Papa Briquet. You don't often get Barons and people like...

ZINAIDA [*shouting*]: Shut up! Shut up and get down to the ring!

BRIQUET [*soft*]: You'd better go. *Tais-toi, maman.*

[*The boys have gone.*]

ZINAIDA [*striding about*]: My God, what a night! *What* a night!

[*Enter* ARTISTE *in a panic.*]

ARTISTE: Papa, papa, can you come a minute....

BRIQUET: What is it?

ARTISTE: It's that Madam O'Malley Romanoff.

BRIQUET: What about her?

ARTISTE: She won't go on.

BRIQUET: Drunk again?

ARTISTE: Hysterics.

BRIQUET: Well, I don't care. [*Turns away.*]

ARTISTE: But when she sets up all the animals . . .

BRIQUET [*whizzing round*]: The *animals!* My God! [*Goes out like a bullet from a gun, followed by* ARTISTE.]

JACKSON: Gala performance! [*Exit* JACKSON.]

ZINAIDA: HE, what were you doing so near my lions? You gave me a fright.

HE: Oh, my queen, I only wanted to hear what they were saying about the benefit . . . they're walking round and round in their cages growling.

ZINAIDA: All this excitement makes them restless. For heaven's sake, HE, stop pacing round and round. I'm thankful Consuela's going. Have you heard about the Baron's roses?

HE: I've heard of nothing else. Bridal bouquets!

ZINAIDA [*Pushing bouquet aside*]: More here too! . . . Roses, roses all the bloody way. Yes, it's a good thing she's going . . . she's out of place here and she disturbs our work . . . she's too pretty to be in a company like this and too . . . accessible.

HE: But her marriage is perfectly legal.

ZINAIDA: As if I care.

HE: Spiders need new blood sometimes. Think, Zinaida, what attractive little spiders they'll have . . . with faces like their mother and stomachs like their father. . . . What could be better for any circus?

ZINAIDA: Rather sarcastic aren't we, tonight?

HE: I was having a good laugh.

ZINAIDA: Were you?

HE: Yes. [*Pause.*] How's Bezano feeling about tonight?

ZINAIDA: I haven't spoken to him. D'you know what I think, my dear? I think *you're* out of place here too.

[*Pause.*]

HE [*surprised*]: What d'you mean by that?

ZINAIDA: Just what I said. As a matter of fact Consuela's got a rotten bargain . . . what'll she make of the Baron in spite of all that money? Did you guess that Consuela's not Mancini's daughter?

HE [*startled*]: Does she know she isn't?

ZINAIDA: No, why should she? She's a little nobody he picked up in Corsica and he's using her for business instead of pleasure. But he adopted her legally.

HE [*ironically*]: Nice to have everything legal, isn't it?

ZINAIDA: Yes, you are sarcastic tonight! . . . I've changed my mind, HE, you'd better stay with us after all.

HE: Won't I be out of place?

ZINAIDA: Not when she's gone. You haven't been here long enough yet to know how lovely it really is! How good for body and soul! Oh, I know how you feel. . . . I used to be the same, for ages I longed for security . . . I wanted to cage myself up . . . to chain myself to something.

HE: To Bezano?

ZINAIDA: Not only Bezano . . . anything to feel safe. I was dreadful about Sultan . . . worse than Bezano . . . I was terribly in love with Sultan. Oh, but it's all nonsense this longing for security. But it's sort of painful . . . getting rid of it. Like getting rid of old employees who pinch things. Leave Consuela alone . . . let her go her own way.

HE: Cars and jewels?

ZINAIDA: Well, of course. If the Baron doesn't buy her, someone will . . . everything pretty gets bought up. I know how it'll be . . . she'll be a raging beauty for the first ten years, people will look round at her in the street, then she'll begin to rouge a little round the eyes and smile a bit too much and then . . .

HE: She'll take her chauffeur or her butler as her lover? You're a good guesser, Zinaida.

ZINAIDA: Aren't I right? Listen, it's no business of mine, but I'm sorry for you, it's no good struggling against fate. I like you, only don't mind what I'm going to say—you're ugly, you're not young any more and you're poor and . . .

HE: And my place is in the sawdust, looking up at the raging beauties. [*Laughs.*] Suppose that's not what I want?

ZINAIDA: What does it matter—what you "want"? I'm sorry for you but you're a strong man and there's only one thing to do—forget her.

HE: And you call that being strong? That comes funnily from you, Zinaida, when you want to be loved by a lion! When you're ready to risk your life for a moment's illusion of power . . . illusion of love, if you like . . . and you tell me to forget!

[*Enter* BRIQUET *and* MANCINI. *The latter is in exaggerated evening dress.*]

ZINAIDA [*whispering to* HE]: So you *will* stay with us after all?

HE [*quietly*]: Yes.

MANCINI: And how are we, my dear lady? You are radiant, my dear lady. I vow you are magnificent! Your lion would be an ass [*laughs*] if he did not kiss your hand, as I do. [*Kisses her hand. Seriously.*] My friends! My daughter Consuela—the Countess,—and the Baron have expressed their wish to bid farewell to the whole company.

HE: Hhm. The Baron?

MANCINI: Of course, Auguste, as well. They want to meet here during the intermission, so, I ask you to assemble here and fetch the others, the more presentable ones, that is—but please, not too noisy . . . not too crowded. HE, will you be so kind, my dear sir, as to run to the bar. Tell them to bring drinks . . . champagne . . . glasses . . .

HE: At your service, Count.

MANCINI [*to* HE]: Wait a moment! You're in a new costume . . . black! Rather funereal for a funny man.

HE: I'm not a funny man. Only a poor sinner . . . Doing penance. [*Exit, bowing like a clown.*]

MANCINI: Clever chap . . . but no good!

BRIQUET: It's for the new finale in honor of Consuela. . . .

MANCINI: Oh . . . by the way . . . what do you think of my new suit, Zinaida? Your taste is infallible! [*Spreads out his lace tie and lace cuffs.*]

ZINAIDA: Perfect. Quite the gentleman.

MANCINI: D'you think it's a tiny bit too far-fetched? Who wears silks and satins now? This drab democracy will dress us all in sackcloth ... or whatever it's called. [*Sighing.*] Auguste tells me this jabot's not quite the thing. I'm afraid he's right. I've got a bit circusy. [HE *returns. Two waiters follow him carrying champagne and glasses. They prepare everything on the table.*] Merci! ... But please ... no popping corks! No chinking glasses! Nothing rowdy. All must be refined—discreet. Oh! the bill? Send that to Baron Regnard.

[ZINAIDA *takes a bottle of cognac from the table and moves away with it.*]

BRIQUET [*trying to take bottle from her*]: Mama, Mama, Mama, *please*, not tonight.

ZINAIDA: Oh, Louis! Leave me alone.

BRIQUET: But Mamouchka ...

ZINAIDA: Leave me alone. [*She settles in a corner to get drunk. Meanwhile the company has begun to assemble.*]

ANGELICA: Is this where they're going to have the ... Oo! champagne!

BRIQUET: I'll trouble you to behave yourself and who asked you to come anyway?

ANGELICA: I met the Count in the passage, he told me to come.

BRIQUET [*angrily*]: Oh all right, if he said so, but there's nothing to carry on about ... don't have too much, Angelica, or you'll come to grief. How is she shaping in the new routine, Thomas?

THOMAS: O.K.

ANGELICA [*aside*]: How cross Papa Briquet is tonight!

[*Enter* TILLY, POLLY *and* HE *and other actors all in their costumes.*]

TILLY [*longing for it*]: D'you really want champagne?

POLLY [*longing for it*]: I don't want it a bit, do you, Tilly?

TILLY: And I awfully don't want it. HE, d'you know how the Count walks?

[*Imitates* MANCINI. *Laughter.*]

POLLY: Oh, let me be the Baron ... take my arm ... Oh take care, ass, you trod on my best family tree!

ANGELICA: The act's nearly over ... Consuela's doing her waltz now. [*All listen to waltz being played offstage.* TILLY *and* POLLY *are singing it softly.*] For the last time! [*Sees bouquet.*] Oh, are those her flowers?

[*They all listen ... suddenly there is a crash of applause, shouting, screaming. Much movement ... the actors pour champagne. More come in talking and laughing. When they notice the Director and champagne they are shy.*]

VOICES: They're coming ... what a night ... no wonder with all the circle ... think when they see the Tango ... don't be jealous ...

BRIQUET: Silence! Quiet, don't push! [*Aside to* ZINAIDA.] Cheer up, Zinaida ... high society!

[*Enter* CONSUELA *on the* BARON'S *arm. The* BARON *is stiff and correct.* MANCINI *is serious and happy.* CONSUELA *is happy. Behind them come actors and actresses and riders. The* BARON *has a blood-red rose in his buttonhole. All applaud and cry* "Bravo! Bravo!"]

CONSUELA: Oh, my friends ... oh, my dears ... Daddy, I can't ...

[*Throws herself into* MANCINI'S *arms and hides her face.* MANCINI *smiles over her head at the* BARON. *The* BARON *smiles slightly but remains earnest and immobile. A new burst of applause.*]

BRIQUET: That'll do ... children ... that'll do ...

MANCINI: Well, well calm yourself, child. How they all love you. [*Steps forward.*] Ladies and gentlemen ... the Baron Regnard has done me the honor of asking for the hand of my daughter in marriage ... my daughter, the Countess Veronica, who you know as Consuela. Please fill your glasses!

CONSUELA: No. Tonight I'm Consuela ... I always will be Consuela. [*Falls on* ZINAIDA'S *neck.*] Darling Madame.

[*Fresh applause.*]

BRIQUET: Sh! Silence! Fill your glasses! What are you

all standing about for?... As you've come, you may as
well drink!

TILLY [*baby talk and trembling*]: They're very shy...
you take your glass first, and then we all will.

[*They take their glasses.* CONSUELA *is near the* BARON
*holding the sleeve of his dress coat with her left hand,
in her right she has her champagne which spills over.*]

BARON: You're spilling your wine, Consuela!

CONSUELA: Oh, never mind. I'm shy. Are you shy,
Daddy?

MANCINI: Silly child!

[*Awkward silence.*]

ALL: Speech! Speech!

BRIQUET [*attempting flowery speech*]: Countess! As manager of the circus... who was so happy... to have...
as manager... [*kissing her.*] Oh, Consuela... [*Shaking
his head sadly.*] It's all that awful, awful book reading!

[*Weeps and kisses her. Laughter and applause. The*
CLOWNS *cluck, bark, bleat and express their emotions
in many other ways. The* BARON *is motionless, isolated.
People clink glasses with him in a hurry and move
aside. With* CONSUELA *they clink willingly and cheer-
fully. She kisses the women.*]

JACKSON: Pray silence for a speech! Consuela, I put out
my sun. After you've gone it will be night... You've been
a good girl and a steady worker. We've all loved you...
and now... all we'll have left of you will be your little
tune.

[*All hum the Tango.*]

CONSUELA: Oh, Alfred, there you are.... I've been looking for you!

BEZANO: Congratulations, Baroness!

CONSUELA: Oh, Alfred... I'm Consuela...

BEZANO: Yes, in the ring, but now you're going to be a
baroness.

[*He passes by only slightly clinking* CONSUELA'S *glass.*
CONSUELA *still holds it.* MANCINI *smiles at the* BARON.
The BARON *is still motionless.*]

BRIQUET: Shut up, Alfred ... you're upsetting her ... she's a good girl.

CONSUELA: No, I'm all right—

ANGELICA: You must call her Consuela if you're going to do the Tango with her tonight.

TILLY: May I congratulate you, Consuela? May I drink your health? Polly's already dead of grief and I shall die soon—I've no stomach for fat.

[*Laughter. The* BARON *shows displeasure. General movement.*]

MANCINI: *Assez!* Enough! *Taisez-vous!* Friends ... the intermission is over!

CONSUELA [*disappointed*]: Oh, and this is so lovely!

BRIQUET: Oh, we can have a minute or two more ... Thomas, tell them to hold up the intermission ... the band can play something.... [*Raising his glass, speaking spontaneously.*] Consuela ... be happy ... like you were with us ... [*Sincerely.*] We will always remember you and love you ... I can't say any more....

[*Applause, compliments.* CONSUELA *is almost crying.*]

MANCINI: Don't be so upset, my child ... it's going too far ... restrain yourself. I had no idea you'd take this little comedy to heart. Auguste ... look at this little heart!

BARON: There, there.

CONSUELA: I'm all right, really ... [*Tango heard off-stage, exclamations.*] Oh, listen, Daddy!

BRIQUET: Your tune! It's for you!

CONSUELA: Isn't that sweet of them? My Tango! Who'll dance my Tango with me? [*Looks for* BEZANO, *who turns away sadly.*]

BARON: Very well ... I can't dance ... but I can hold tight.... [*Takes* CONSUELA'S *arm and stands in the center of a circle which is formed.*] Dance, Consuela ... [*He stands, pulling* CONSUELA *to him suggestively.*]

MANCINI [*applauding*]: Bravo! ... Bravo!

ZINAIDA: Disgusting!

CONSUELA: No, I can't dance like that ... let go!

[*She goes to* ZINAIDA *and embraces her as if hiding*

herself. The music goes on playing. The BARON *moves
quietly to the side. There is a hostile silence among
the company.*]

MANCINI [*alone*]: Bravo! Bravo! Perfect! Perfect!

JACKSON: Not quite perfect, Count. [TILLY *and* POLLY
imitate the BARON *and* CONSUELA *without moving from
their places.*]

TILLY [*squeaking in a girl's voice*]: Let me go!

POLLY: No . . . I won't . . . go on . . . dance!

[*The music stops abruptly. General too loud laughter.
The* CLOWNS *bark and roar. Papa* BRIQUET *gesticu-
lates to re-establish silence. The* BARON *apparently as
indifferent as before.*]

MANCINI: Really, these vagabonds forget themselves! It
reeks of the stable! What can one do, Auguste?

BARON: Don't get excited, Count.

HE [*approaching* BARON, *holding his glass*]: May I be allowed to propose a toast?

BARON: Certainly.

HE: Let us drink to your dance.

[*Sniggering laughter from crowd.*]

BARON: I don't dance.

HE: Then how's this? . . . let us drink to those who can
wait until they get it.

BARON: I don't drink toasts I cannot understand.

[*Woman's voice calls out* "Bravo, HE." *Sniggering
laughter again.* JACKSON *takes* HE *by the arm.*]

JACKSON: Leave him alone, HE . . . the Baron's not in the
mood for jokes.

HE: But I want to drink with the Baron . . . what else
can one say? Baron! . . . let's drink to the slip 'twixt cup
and lip!

[*Spills his wine. The* BARON *turns his back on him indifferently. The music plays in the ring. The bell rings.*]

BRIQUET [*relieved*]: All on . . . m'sieurs, dames . . . to the
ring. . . . All on for the finale.

[*The crowd becomes smaller, laughter and voices.*]

MANCINI [*excitedly whispering to* BARON]: Auguste . . .

Auguste ... don't take any notice ... it's ...

BRIQUET [*aside to* ZINAIDA]: Thank heavens that's over. [*Sighs with relief, he must blame someone and turns angrily on* ZINAIDA.] Well, Maman, you always enjoy a scene ... but this time ... really ... it was ...

ZINAIDA: Oh, Louis, shut up.

[HE *approaches* CONSUELA.]

HE: I was only waiting my turn, Princess ... there was such a crowd round you.

CONSUELA: Was there? I'm alone now. Come and tell me, HE, what you said when they all laughed? I couldn't hear ... what was it all about?

HE: I was being funny.

CONSUELA: Oh, please don't get him worked up! He's so horrid when he's cross. Did you see how he squeezed my arm? I nearly cried.... [*With tears in her eyes.*] He hurt me.

HE: Don't marry him ... it's not too late.

CONSUELA: Don't go on about it. It *is* too late.

HE: Shall I take you away?

CONSUELA: Where to? [*Laughs.*] How could you? [HE *starts to speak. Gently.*] Don't say any more. Oh, you do look ... D'you love me too? Oh HE, *don't* love me ... please don't ... *why* do they all love me?

HE: You're so beautiful.

CONSUELA: No, no ... I'm not ... they mustn't love me. I was still a tiny bit happy but when they said all those nice things about my going away as if I was dying— I thought I should cry.... Don't let's talk.... Let's drink to my happiness! What are you doing?

HE [*throwing down her glass*]: I'm throwing away the glass you drank out of before. I shall give you a new one ... for another toast ... to drink with me this time ...

MANCINI [*coming to* CONSUELA]: It's getting awkward, Veronica! Auguste is too patient, waiting for you while you stay here gossiping with this clown ... stupid secrets ... Everybody's looking at you ... it's getting quite noticeable! You must break yourself of these habits.

CONSUELA [*loudly*]: Leave me alone, Daddy, I'll do as I please. Do leave me alone.

BARON: Don't bother her, Count. Consuela! Talk to anyone you like as much as you like. Cigar, Count?

[MANCINI *and* BARON *move away*.]

HE [*giving glass to* CONSUELA]: Here you are! To your happiness and to your freedom!

CONSUELA [*taking glass*]: Where's yours? We must clink glasses.

HE: Leave me half yours.

CONSUELA: Must I drink such a lot? HE, darling, I shall get drunk. . . . I've still got the finale.

HE: You won't get drunk. [*Lovingly*.] Have you forgotten that I'm an old god in disguise? [*As to a child*.] Drink. . . . I've charmed the wine . . . it's got magic in it.

CONSUELA [*hesitating and looking at him*]: You *have* got kind eyes! You look so . . .

HE: Because I love you. Look in my eyes and drink . . . give yourself up to the magic . . . sleep . . . and wake . . . and remember. Remember your own country . . . your own sea . . . your own sky.

CONSUELA [*putting glass to her lips*]: Shall I see it? Is that true?

HE: Yes, awake, Goddess, and remember the time when you rose from the sea . . . remember the sky and the quiet breeze from the east and the murmur of foam at your marble feet.

CONSUELA [*drinks. Pause*]: There! [*Passes him the glass. He drinks*.] What's the matter? Are you laughing or crying?

HE: I'm laughing *and* crying.

MANCINI [*pushing* HE *away*]: Now come on. Countess, I've had enough. I can't put up with it even if Auguste can. Come along. [*To* HE.] Be off with you, sir!

CONSUELA: I'm tired.

MANCINI: Not too tired for gossip, not too tired for drink, not too tired for clowns. Briquet, isn't it time for this child's number?

CONSUELA: I'm tired, Daddy.

ZINAIDA: Look here, Count, don't be hard on the girl. . . .
Get some black coffee . . . can't you see she's not well?

BARON: What's the matter, Consuela?

CONSUELA: Nothing . . . just . . .

ZINAIDA: Let her rest . . . she's been on her feet all day
. . . all this excitement . . . sit down, ducky, and rest.
[*Wraps her up.*]

CONSUELA: But there's still the finale. [*Shuts her eyes.*]
Are the roses ready?

ZINAIDA: Yes, ducky, they are. . . . [*As to a child.*] You'll
have such a wonderful carpet . . . you'll just fly over it!

POLLY: Would you like some pretty music? Shall we play
you a pretty little tune?

CONSUELA: Oh, yes, do.

[*She smiles and shuts her eyes. The* CLOWNS *sing a
soft little song . . . "Tilly-Polly, Tilly-Polly" . . . general silence.* HE *sits in the corner with his face turned
away.* JACKSON *watches him out of the corner of his
eye and drinks lazily. The* BARON *in his usual pose,
wide and heavily spread legs, stares at* CONSUELA. *She
gives a sudden cry.*]

ZINAIDA: What's the matter? [*Really alarmed for the first
time.*]

MANCINI: My child! Are you ill! Keep quite quiet.

BARON: She's overexcited.

CONSUELA: . . . it hurts . . . here. [*Hand to heart.*] Daddy?
I'm frightened . . . what is it? . . . I can't stand up . . . [*Falls
on divan, her eyes wide open.*]

MANCINI [*running about, fussing*]: Fetch a doctor . . .
God! This is appalling. . . . Auguste . . . Baron, it has never
happened before . . . nerves! nerves! nothing but nerves!

BRIQUET: Fetch a doctor!

[*Somebody goes off.*]

JACKSON [*suddenly very frightened*]: HE? What's wrong
with you? HE?

HE: This is death, my little Princess. I've killed you.
You're dying.

[*All are in terrible agitation. The* BARON *is motionless*

and sees only CONSUELA.]

MANCINI [*hissing*]: It's a lie! Villain! You damned clown
....you've poisoned her ... fetch a doctor!

HE: A doctor can't help. You're dying, my little love.
Consuela! Consuela!

[BEZANO *rushes in calling*, "Where's Consuela! We're
on next! That's our ..." *He sees* CONSUELA.]

CONSUELA [*in a far-away voice*]: Is it true, HE? Don't
frighten me. I'm so frightened. Is *this* death? I don't want
... HE, my darling HE, say it's all a joke ... my darling,
precious HE.

HE [*pushing the* BARON *away, he stands in his place, in
front of* CONSUELA]: Yes it *is* a joke. Can't you hear me
laughing? Everybody's laughing, silly. Don't laugh, Jackson, she's tired. She wants to go to sleep ... how can you
laugh, Jackson? Sleep, my darling, sleep ... sleep, my
little heart ... sleep, my dear love!

CONSUELA: All the pain's gone. Why did you pretend?
You frightened me. You said I would live forever, didn't
you?

HE [*lifting his arms as if trying with all his strength to
lift her soul higher*]: Yes, Consuela. Forever. Sleep ... rest
... how lovely it is now! How bright it is!

CONSUELA: Yes, *isn't it*. All those lights, is that the ring?

HE: No, it's the sea and the sun. Such wonderful sunshine! You are the spray ... flying to the sun! You're so
light ... you haven't any body ... fly higher, my love!
Higher!

[*She dies.* HE *moves away.*]

BRIQUET [*to* ZINAIDA. *Slowly*]: Is she asleep, Mama?

ZINAIDA [*letting fall the dead hand*]: I'm afraid not, Louis,
she's dead.

[*The* CLOWNS *and* BRIQUET *weep.* MANCINI *is over-
whelmed. The* BARON *and* HE *are motionless.*]

·JACKSON [*draws out a large bright handkerchief and
cries*]: What have you done, HE? ... Why did you come
here?

[*Music heard from the ring.*]

BRIQUET [*fussing*]: Stop the music! They're mad . . . what a tragedy.

[*Someone runs off.* ZINAIDA *strokes the top of* BEZANO'S *head. When he notices her he takes her hand and presses it to his eyes. The* BARON *tears the rose from his buttonhole.*]

ZINAIDA [*still stroking* BEZANO'S *head*]: Louis, call the police.

MANCINI [*waking from stupor*]: The police . . . yes, call the police! I am the Count Mancini . . . Count Mancini . . . it's murder! . . . you'll hang for it . . . you damned fool . . . you murderer! You thief! I'll kill you myself!

BRIQUET [*trying to shut up* MANCINI]: I *will* fetch the police . . . keep quiet, I *am* going . . . pull yourself together.

BARON [*yelling*]: I am a witness, I saw . . . I am a witness . . . I saw him put the poison into . . . I . . . [*Exit.*]

JACKSON [*wringing his hands*]: Poison . . . so it is true . . . Oh, HE, now you've asked for it, you've asked for it this time.

ZINAIDA [*to* JACKSON]: Leave his soul in peace, Jim. After all he *loved* her . . . happy Consuela!

[THOMAS *runs in frightened, pointing to his head.*]

THOMAS: Quick! The Baron . . . He's dead . . . he's shot himself!

BRIQUET [*throwing his arms up*]: God! The Baron! What a terrible thing for the box office!

MANCINI [*incoherent*]: The Baron! . . . No . . . but why . . . the Baron's . . . do something . . .

BRIQUET: Be quiet, Mancini. Who'd have thought it? . . . such an important gentleman . . .

HE [*with difficulty*]: The Baron? [*Laughs.*] Then the Baron went off, pop!

JACKSON [*shocked*]: Sh! That's a shocking thing to say . . . a man's just killed himself and you go on fooling . . . [*With alarm.*] What's the matter, HE?

HE [*standing up, using all his strength, speaking powerfully*]: Killed himself? So you really loved her, Baron. You loved my Consuela. And you wanted to get there first.

No . . . I'm coming, Consuela, don't listen to him, I'm coming, I'm coming.

> [*He catches at his throat and falls. People run to him. General agitation.*]

CURTAIN

FOUR GREAT RUSSIAN
SHORT NOVELS

A rich sampling of the short novel at its best, in the hands of four immortal Russian writers

TURGENEV: First Love

DOSTOYEVSKY: The Gambler

TOLSTOY: Master and Man

CHEKHOV: The Duel

A Laurel Edition   *50c*